PEACE AND MILK, DROUGHT AND WAR

Peace and Milk, Drought and War

Somali Culture, Society and Politics

Essays in Honour of I.M. Lewis

Edited by
Markus V. Hoehne and Virginia Luling

HURST & COMPANY, LONDON

First published in the United Kingdom in 2010 by
C. Hurst & Co. (Publishers) Ltd.,
41 Great Russell Street, London, WC1B 3PL

Printed in India

A Cataloguing-in-Publication data record for this book is available from the British Library.

ISBN: 978-1-84904-044-0 *clothbound*
978-1-84904-045-7 *paperback*

www.hurstpub.co.uk

The title of the book has been inspired by a Somali proverb:
nabad iyo caano, colaad iyo abaar

CONTENTS

LIST OF ABBREVIATIONS

AFIS	Amministrazione Fiduciaria Italiana della Somalia
BMA	British Military Administration
CT	Consiglio Territoriale
DSO	Distinguished Service Order
GDP	Gross Domestic Product
HDM	Hizbia Digil Mirifle
HDMS (also XDMS)	Hizbia Digil Mirifle Somalia
ICRC	International Committee of the Red Cross
IDP	Internally displaced person
ISA	Inter-Riverine Studies Association
MP	Member of Parliament
NCO	Non-Commissioned Officer
NGO	Non-Governmental Organisation
NSS	National Security Service
NUF	National United Front
OAU	Organisation of African Unity
PLO	Palestine Liberation Organisation
SAIS	Società Agricola Italo-Somala
SAMO	Somali African Muki Organisation
SDU	Somali Democratic Union
SNF	Somali National Front
SNL	Somali National League
SNM	Somali National Movement
SPM	Somali Patriotic Movement
SRC	Somali Revolutionary Council
SRSP	Somali Revolutionary Socialist Party
SSDF	Somali Salvation Democratic Front
SYL	Somali Youth League

TFG	Transitional Federal Government
TFI	Transitional Federal Institutions
UIC	Union of Islamic Courts
UN	United Nations
UNESCO	United Nations Educational, Scientific and Cultural Organisation
UNOSOM	United Nations Operation in Somalia
USC	United Somali Congress
USP	United Somali Party
USSR	Union of Soviet Socialist Republics
WSLF	Western Somali Liberation Front

ACKNOWLEDGMENTS

Bringing two dozen scholars from all over the world together to work on a common project is not an easy task. Besides endurance, persistence and a high tolerance of frustrations, it needs strong institutional support. This support was provided by the Max Planck Institute (MPI) for Social Anthropology in Halle/Saale, Germany, where Markus was based throughout the time of the gestation process of this *Festschrift*. We wish to thank Prof. Günther Schlee, the managing director of the Institute, who provided all the necessary support. In particular, the invitation of Virginia to the Institute in August 2009 greatly aided the effective cooperation of the co-editors, sitting, 'suffering' and laughing together in one place, and discussing the progress of the manuscript. Günther Schlee also helped to upgrade the quality of the book through critical comments on the whole manuscript. Katharina Lindt and Kristin Teichman, two student assistants at the MPI in Halle, tirelessly worked on the compilation of I.M. Lewis' truly impressive list of publications. Both deserve the greatest thanks. Additionally Katharina produced the list of abbreviations.

Martin Orwin not only contributed a co-authored chapter to the *Festschrift*, but was also kind enough to critically review and comment on several language-related chapters and thus helped to improve the overall quality of the reviewed texts. Philipp Reichmuth from the Institute for Islamic Studies at Martin Luther University of Halle-Wittenberg kindly helped with the correct Arabic-English transliteration of several quotations from the Qur'an.

We owe particular thanks to Ann Lewis, Sheila Andrzejewski and Anita Adam for allowing us to draw on their memories in the introduction.

Michael Dwyer and Daisy Leitch of Hurst publishers accompanied the project professionally and, where necessary, showed the flexibility to overcome deadlocks when conceptualising the book.

Finally, Markus particularly wishes to express his gratitude to his wife, Rano Turaeva-Hoehne, for her patience during many hours of overtime, and hopes that his children Feruza and Ali one day may enjoy reading this book.

Markus Hoehne, Virginia Luling
Halle/Saale, London, December 2009.

NOTE ON LANGUAGE AND SPELLING

We strove to 'standardise' the Somali spelling used by the different authors in this volume. However, contemporary Somali orthography is not completely fixed and one finds a considerable variation of spellings of, for example, personal and place names in Somali newspapers, homepages, and books. Additionally, some texts in the volume include names of Somali and Arab personalities, and it was not always possible to sort these out in order to spell them 'correctly' (either in Somali or in an anglicised transliteration of Arabic). To add to the complexity, some Somali authors themselves prefer to use anglicised versions of their names. Thus, complete standardisation was impossible. Somali words are generally given in the Somali alphabet, as found in dictionaries and most published works and newspapers. However there is in practise considerable variation in the way this is used; we have used what seem to be the most usual spellings. For readers unfamiliar with Somali orthography, most of the letters are pronounced much as they would expect. Double letters indicate long vowels, as in Darood and Majeerteen. 'r' is as in Italian, or Scottish English; 'g' is always hard. Some of the sounds however are more troublesome. 'c' stands for the 'voiced pharyngeal fricative' known as 'ayn in Arabic, a sound made at the far back of the throat, which to most speakers of European languages is not only unpronounceable but inaudible. Thus Cali (Ali), Jaamac, Laacaanood. 'x' stands for the 'voiceless pharyngeal fricative', a heavy 'h'-like sound made in the same part of the throat as 'c', e.g. in xeer. 'q' is the 'voiced uvular plosive' made at the back of the throat like a French 'r'. 'dh' is a plosive similar to 'd' but made with the tongue at the back of the palate. (A fuller account of standard Somali pronunciation can be found in Orwin 1995, and a rather more technical one in Saeed 1987.)

The 'Maay' language has a different spelling system (see Mukhtar in this volume) but it is not yet in widespread use and it was not practical to use it here.

References

Orwin, M. 1995. *Colloquial Somali*. London/New York: Routledge.

Saeed, J.I. 1987. *Somali Reference Grammar*. Wheaton Maryland, Dunwoody Press.

I.M. Lewis

1

INTRODUCTION

LEWIS AND THE REMAINING CHALLENGES IN SOMALI STUDIES

Markus V. Hoehne and *Virginia Luling*

Introduction

I.M. Lewis can well be called the founding father of Somali Studies, and to approach his *oeuvre* leads directly to a general engagement with Somali culture, politics and society.[1] Such an engagement, as the contributions to this volume illustrate, shows that, despite all the analyses produced by area specialists, Somali affairs continue to challenge any premature conclusions.

We first present the academic/biographical background of Ioan Myrddin Lewis. This is part of the *Festschrift* tradition (as is the list of publications of the honoured scholar at the end of the volume). It also provides the background for situating Lewis' work and introducing a major controversy in which he and others have been involved, about transformation and continuity in Somali society. The themes of the book, which are briefly outlined at the end of this introduction, in many ways continue and reflect the ongoing debates. They also show where (younger) researchers are required to break new ground, without lightly dismissing the positions of older generations.

Lewis' career

Few anthropologists have been as identified with a particular people as Professor I.M. Lewis with the Somali. Throughout a long and distinguished career he has not only written classic works on their society and history, but known most of their leading political figures, and repeatedly pleaded their cause in his publications and broadcasts. Yet his association with them and with social anthropology came about by a double accident.

Born in 1930, as the son of a Welsh father and a Scottish mother, after his father's death he grew up in Glasgow with his mother's family. He was a student of chemistry at the University of Glasgow, when he happened to see some advertisements offering 'conversion studentships' for people trained in the natural sciences to move into the human sciences and 'thought they looked interesting' (Geshekter 2001: 53). He applied, successfully, and studied at the Department of Social Anthropology at Oxford, then presided over by Professor Evans-Pritchard, whose work on the segmentary lineage system of the Nuer of Sudan was so influential. His supervisor there, the distinguished Czech anthropologist Franz Steiner, happened to be working on the International African Institute's ethnographic survey of the peoples of the Horn of Africa, but had only got as far as compiling the bibliography; he suggested that Lewis should take on the project as his thesis for the BLitt degree (equivalent to an MA). Lewis completed the work—a summary of the then available written materials (in English, Italian, French and German) on the Somali, Afar and Saho, which was published in 1955. Intrigued by these people whom he had met only in print, he determined that the Somali would be the subject of his field research. Meanwhile he had met various Somalis in London, notably Muuse Galaal, who was working with B.W. ('Goosh') Andrzejewski on the Somali language. It was Andrzejewski who gave Lewis his first lessons in Somali, as Sheila Andrzejewski recently remembered (Wardheer News 2009). Lewis succeeded in obtaining a grant from the Colonial Development and Welfare Fund; meanwhile he had married, and he and his wife Ann travelled out to British Somaliland (by ship) in 1955.

Like most young anthropologists at that time, Lewis had been trained to distrust the colonial establishment. As he recalled, and as anyone who remembers the British anthropological world of the period knows, '[m]ost of my contemporaries who were doing anthropology were probably leftist in political orientation, and certainly very anti–colonial' (Geshekter 2001: 57). He was therefore disconcerted to find that he had been officially listed as the lowest member of the Somaliland Protectorate Administration, fearing that officialdom would obstruct his research, or try to dictate his results. However he found no interference, and indeed had access to files and information. 'The Protectorate authorities never once asked me what I thought I was up to, nor advised me to keep out of politics' (Lewis 1994: 12).

It was a challenging time in all the Somali lands. The British protectorate was understood to be preparing for independence—though not as early as in fact happened (see Drysdale in this volume)—and many in the administration were very committed to the country and its people. There were of course almost no Europeans there apart from those in government employment, by contrast with Italian Somalia with its settler population. Ann Lewis (Interview, London, March 2009) recalls: 'I think it was a sort of golden era. People were really well-informed; there was a culture that one ought to be well-informed [...] Somaliland was just a lovely place to be—a wonderful climate [...] so there was a sort of critical mass of people who just felt they were in a wonderful place, at a very interesting time, and everything was filled with potential.' Among those people was John Drysdale, who had been engaged with Somalis since the early 1940s (see his contribution here).

At the same time, with memories still alive of the war of Maxamed Cabdille Xassan, and anger over the recent handover of the Haud grazing lands to Ethiopia (Fitzgibbon 1982; Drysdale in this volume), the administration was anxious to avoid trouble and wary of 'upsetting the Somali'. Lewis as he travelled through the country encountered distrust and hostility before he was accepted. But there was something in him which responded to the tough, aggressive people. 'His heart was with the Somali nomads, no doubt about it,' says Ann Lewis, 'and the difficulties and the abrasiveness, he just liked' (Interview, London, March 2009).

One young sheikh in particular seemed fiercely hostile, wrapping his cloth around his mouth when near to Lewis to avoid contamination. Many years later Lewis met him again in Mogadishu. The Sheikh explained that by listening to Lewis' interviews he had come to understand the nature of social anthropological research, and had decided he could do the same thing himself—even better, since he was a native-speaker. This was Aw Jaamac Cumar Ciise, the writer on the history and poetry of Maxamed Cabdille Xassan and the Dervish movement (see e.g. Aw Jaamac 1976 and 1999). One of the things Lewis says he remembers with the greatest pleasure is having been the means of launching this outstanding scholar (Geshekter 2001: 62, Ann Lewis, Interview).[2]

Lewis strongly supported the Somali nationalist cause. He attended meetings of the Somali Youth League (SYL), the main pro-independence party, and indeed addressed them. Visiting the south, then under the Italian Trusteeship Administration, he also observed meetings of the federalist Hizbia Digil-Mirifle Somali (HDMS).[3]

Two major works came out of his initial field research, *The Somali Lineage System and the Total Genealogy* and *A Pastoral Democracy*. The latter was written while Lewis was teaching in 1957–60 at the then University College of Rhodesia and Nyasaland, where he was one of the founding members. But Rhodesia was a country moving in the opposite direction from Somaliland; the lively intellectual life of the university contrasted with the increasing racism and repressiveness of the surrounding society. Returning to Britain, Lewis taught at Glasgow University (1960), then in London, first at University College (1963) and then at the London School of Economics (from 1969). There he became Professor of Anthropology, and spent the reminder of his career. In a life of constant teaching and writing, which included the editorship of the *Journal of the Royal Anthropological Institute* (previously called *Man*) and a variety of visiting professorships, he frequently revisited Somalia, both north and south, up to the 1990s when his health prevented him from travelling. His ties with the country continue and the Lewises' London home is constantly open to Somali friends. Typical of his commitment to the Somali is his work for the Africa Educational Trust, of which he remains a trustee; not so well known but of equal importance are his many reports and testimonies as an 'expert witness' for Somali asylum seekers in the British courts.

Lewis' influence and legacy

Lewis certainly is the most prolific and influential writer on Somali affairs so far. He has put Somalis on the map of the social sciences, described the foundations of their society and politics, and outlined their (mostly 20th century) history. He has struggled with the complexities of post-colonial Somalia, from the irredentist policies of the time of independence, through regime change, natural disasters, the refugee crisis after the Ogaden war, to guerrilla war, state collapse, intervention and the ongoing civil war. For him, his field research in Somalia was not merely the foundation of his career, though it was that, but the beginning of a permanent relationship in which he always felt that he had to give something back—if only by providing accurate analyses of Somali affairs (Geshekter 2001: 81).

Tradition versus transformation. Lewis' analyses established a paradigm, which emphasizes agnation or patrilineal descent as the basic social institution and enduring principle of socio-political organisation among the Somali, and identified 'clan-family', 'clan', sub-clan' and 'lineage' as the main segments of their society. This society predominantly consisted of independent-minded pastoralists and agro-pastoralists who hardly accepted any superior authority but God, and only came together in order to facilitate herding and farming, or to mobilise for raiding or defence. Communal decisions were taken at public gatherings (sing. *shir*) at which all males (theoretically) had the same right to speak. In Lewis' perspecvtive, Somali society was essentially egalitarian and acephalous.

This established the context of much research into Somali culture, society and politics. It applied particularly to the pastoral-nomadic segments of society which dominate in the northern Somali peninsula, where Lewis did most of his original field research. The south, however, was characterised by additional dynamics emanating from co-residence in villages and towns, cooperation in farming, adoption of newcomers into the community, and intensive external influences through caravan and sea trade. Social and political hierarchies and bonds beyond agnation were more prevalent here (Lewis 1961: 90–126; Lewis 1969; Cassanelli 1982; Menkhaus 1999; Luling 2002; Helander 2003). Nonetheless, in many later publications, Lewis maintained that the principles of kinship constituted the overarching logic of Somali cultural nationalism and generally informed traditional as well as modern (nation-state) politics.

Lewis himself insisted on the flexibility within the segmentary lineage system based on patrilineal descent (*tol*) and contract (*xeer*). He maintained that lineages, which in theory would be located at the same level of segmentation, were in reality often quite different in strength. Weak lineages could use affinal ties and/or contractual agreements to increase their manpower and fighting potential (Lewis 1961: 151–9). In some cases contract bound people without any agnatic base (ibid.: 193). He also pointed out that the lineage system lends itself to manipulation and instrumentalisation (Lewis 1994: 233–4). Thus, even if agnation was basic, Somalis did not function like robots, and their social system was far from static.

It took three decades before this 'clan-paradigm' was challenged by a new generation of Western educated Somali and non-Somali researchers.[4] Their focus was on political, social and economic changes over the second half of the 20th century, and they emphasised the transformation of Somali society from 'clan based' to 'class based'. In this perspective, the introduction of the state apparatus in the colonial period, and the manipulations of post-colonial regimes that could rely on external support in the context of Cold War rivalries, had undermined the foundations of Somali society. Once the traditional system had been stripped of its 'checks and balances' in the form of Islam, *xeer*, and cross-cutting ties, clan became isolated and, in the form of clanism, a largely destructive force in contemporary identity politics (Abdi I. Samatar 1992; Ahmed I. Samatar 1994: 109–146; Kapteijns 1995). Catherine Besteman meanwhile argued that inequalities and racial sentiments—or class and race—informed post-colonial politics and the patterns of violence, leading to an acrimonious debate with Lewis and Helander.

What this discussion teaches us is certainly that Somali studies were and still are confronted by two problems. The first one is rather banal. It can be called the 'career problem' and is the problem of how to contribute something to Somali studies which Lewis has not already touched upon. The second problem, which is much more serious, is related to the correct interpretation of the Somali tragedy of civil war and state collapse. One has to bear in mind that for most researchers (Somali and non-Somali) this involves making sense of their families' and close friends' lot. Helander (1998: 490) reminded us that the 'professional responsibility we have in seeking to represent accurately and to analyze the Somali tragedy must go beyond the rhetorical gains of refuting the understanding developed by previous generations of researchers.' This is in accordance with Lewis' desire to provide accurate analyses of Somali affairs as a way of 'paying his debt' to the Somalis (Geshekter 2001: 68). The personal feelings involved, which certainly also played a role in Besteman's writings, made the debate between her, Helander and Lewis so bitter. None of them could admit defeat—for academic, but also for 'moral' reasons.

In our perspective, however, the truth lies—as usual—in between. There have been transformations. The introduction of a central state, institutionalising permanent positions of power, left an imprint on the egalitarian spirit of Somalis. It arguably introduced a 'new tradition' of autocracy and dictatorship that certainly contributed to the ruin of Somalia, and still constitutes a risk to the newly built Somali states in Somaliland and Puntland, as well as to the endeavours of the transitional government(s) in the south. Statehood also fuelled new dynamics of fusion and fission.[5] Additionally, urbanisation, environmental changes, and of course external interference introduced new 'wildcards' in the Somali 'game'. On the other hand, continuities can be observed with regard to the strategies of most post-colonial politicians to divide and rule, and the mobilisation of followers and fighters before and after 1991 (Schlee 2002). In the worst moments of the civil war, descent and ethnic belonging helped to make a clear distinction between 'us' and 'them'. This referred to pastoral-nomadic groups as well as to other (ethnic) minority groups (Menkhaus in this volume).[6] Pastoral-nomadic traditions related to *tol* and *xeer* also provided the basis for the peace processes in the north (Farah and Lewis 1993), and supported the social and political reconstruction in Somaliland and Puntland.

The differences between the situation in northern and southern Somalia, however, point to the fact that indeed, neither of the two opposed approaches discussed above 'fits it all'. The traditionalist argument that Somalis were 'doing what they have always done—only with greater access to more lethal weapons' (Lewis 1998: 101) does not in fact explain why it is so hard to find some basic consensus among the groups fighting in the south, similar to what has been achieved in the north. Certainly, colonial politics impacted differently on southern and northern Somali society (see Prunier in this volume). Moreover, power and resources were and still are concentrated in the south, which is one factor that keeps the civil war going. Therefore, in addition to the social differences which have been in place for centuries along the Benadir coast and in the inter-riverine area, some dynamics beyond the segmentary lineage system seem at be at work here. Empirically founded analyses of contemporary southern Somali society are rare, owing to the risks involved with research.[7] Still, the transformationist emphasis on class and race certainly overstates economic differences in Somali society and fails to understand war and peace in northern Somalia (Somaliland and Puntland), where the segmentary model still has explanatory power (Hoehne 2002: 103–14, 130–1).

The time factor, or: how a researcher gets 'overtaken' by his field. Besides the interpretative battles between different 'age sets' of scholars, the sheer fact of dramatic and unforeseen political changes in Somalia itself shook Somali studies. Established positions had to be rethought in the light of the events since 1991.[8] It was only logical that Lewis and his work that had been so central to 20th century Somali studies was scrutinised for what he and others following his line of analysis had got wrong. How could the pastoral democracy, which was characterised by force and feud, but also by basic respect towards (for example) religious leaders, elders, women and children, and by elaborate strategies of conflict settlement and consensus-based decision making, crumble so completely?

This reinterpretation of the Somali society and its history was of course a legitimate endeavour. Yet, unluckily, it was frequently done without carefully studying the existing sources and literature. Frequently, Lewis was summarily accused of being a 'colonial anthropologist' and/or a 'primordialist' whose aim was to divide Somalis through his clan thesis.[9] Illustrative of this position is the outrage that the publication of Lewis' most recent book *Understanding Somalia and Somaliland* caused among some Somali intellectuals who perceived the title as indicating Lewis' aim to divide and rule Somalis in colonial fashion. This, however, was a crude misinterpretation of Lewis 'academic personality'. First, he himself testified in a somewhat (self-)ironic way about what he called his time as a 'government anthropologist' and clearly outlined how he was, on the one hand, a marginal figure in the Protectorate and perceived with suspicion by the administrators (this is a situation most social anthropologists, even today, may know from their time in the field). Lewis also mentioned that, on the other hand, he was quite happy to be left on his own without much interference by Protectorate officials (Lewis 1977). Second, Lewis (and this may be more difficult to understand for his younger critics), like many other social anthropologists in the mid-20th century, had the aspiration to free 'tribal' societies from the stigma of primitivism. In Lewis' view 'this first-hand testimony, delivered with appropriate scholarly documentation, helped restore to the so-called "primitive" his full humanity and dignity' (Lewis 1992: 35). Certainly, things may look differently from a late 20th, early 21st century perspective. Yet, historical sources (which those first-hand testimonies constitute by now) have to be interpreted in their contexts, not just abused for cheap contemporary polemics.

Furthermore, one has only to read Lewis' (1983) introduction and the contributions in *Nationalism and Self Determination in the Horn of Africa* to understand that Lewis was not in the business of dividing Somalis (or Oromos, or other so called ethnic groups), but to the contrary, explained their struggle for independence and unity, against the powers in the region, the Organisation of African Unity (OAU), and the international community. There, he confirmed that 'Somali cultural nationalism is a centuries old phenomenon and not something which has been recently drummed up to give credence to political aims' (ibid.: 9). The introduction outlined the problems stemming from Britain's 'illegal' treaties with Ethiopia, and the double standards employed by the OAU with regard to the right to self-determination of peoples (ibid. 13, 17). These statements fly in the face of those accusing Lewis of having a 'colonial' agenda. His present very open support for the newly established Republic of Somaliland (which structurally is very different from the former British Protectorate of Somaliland) derives rather from disappointment and shock at what had become of the united Somalia. He only expressed what many Somalis think in view of the current situation of the south when he called Somaliland and, to some extent, Puntland exemplary and a lesson in what Somalis can achieve if they put their minds to it constructively' (Geshekter 2001: 71).

Finally, Lewis was among the first observers who directly pointed to the shortcomings of the revolutionary Somali government under Siyad Barre only three years after the coup d'état in 1969:

> The Supreme Revolutionary Council's obsessive preoccupation with treachery and betrayal, and its growing reliance on harsh and repressive sanctions, inevitably suggests that its leaders no longer enjoy the public confidence which they claimed when they seized power in 1969. The strident, almost hysterical tone of the Leader's repeated denunciation of 'tribalism', which he seeks to link to colonialism and sinister 'neo-colonial plots', is a measure of the frustration and desperation which those who seek to achieve dramatic changes in the socio-economic conditions of the country must feel when they consider the glaring discrepancy between their aims and what has actually been achieved. (Lewis 1972: 406)

Lewis concluded his 1972 essay on the politics of the 1969 Somali coup with an almost prophetic assessment of the political situation in the region: '[I]t will not have escaped the attention of shrewd Somali nationalists that if further political uncertainties favour an expansion of Russian involvement in Ethiopia, a serious conflict of interest may develop.' This was written two years before Haile Selassie's fall and five years before the beginning of the Ogaden war that was decided by the shift of Moscow away from Somalia and towards Ethiopia. Somalia's defeat in 1978 marked the beginning of the end of the Somali state, as many analysts argue *ex–post*.

The themes of the present volume

The contributions to this volume pursue the above outlined issues from various angles. Drysdale's very personal memories of the Second World War and the period between that war and independence provide a glimpse of the 'mood of the time', as seen by one directly involved, and conclude provocatively by proposing some lessons that could be learned from past mistakes. It sheds a sidelight on Prunier's historical analysis of British and Italian colonial policies and their impact on the later developments in Somalia. Prunier's distinction of modes of colonial rule should encourage further investigations into the colonial history of the Somali, based on a firm grip of the original sources, and equipped with the will to go beyond the anachronistic gaze of those who already know what they wish to find before they start investigating. This concerns not only the (re-)interpretation of Italian colonialism, but also, as a careful reading of Timocadde's poetry presented by Boobe suggests, the question of how Somalis in the northwest perceived the British and their 'light' indirect rule. This is of considerable contemporary relevance against the background of the ongoing endeavours of Somaliland's politicians to present the British as their 'eternal' friends in order to gain support for their claim to independence (Hoehne 2006: 402–4).

The articles in section III (on clan politics, economy and change) in many regards contribute to the above outlined discussion of the relevance of the clan paradigm and the interpretation of Somali society and history. Cassanelli looks at the 'total genealogy' of the Somalis, which famously links all these genealogies into one, and which Lewis analysed. He suggests an origin in Islamic reform in the late 19th century. Ciabarri offers a fresh look at dynamics of trade and politics in today's Somaliland, inspired by the earlier debate on this topic, which basically can be situated along the continuum between continuities and transformations. Marcel Djama argues that Somali pastoral dynamics are controlled not only by ecology but also by a number of factors external to the pastoral world itself. Menkhaus' paper highlights the persistent inequalities in southern Somali society and the relevance of race as a social category. He shows how outside observers have imposed their own categories on the divisions which already existed in Somali society.[10]

Section IV (Islam) engages with another aspect of transformation in Somali society instigated by political Islam. Hussein Adam provides an overview of the formation of Islamism in the Somali peninsula and, most importantly with regard to the present, the potential of political Islam to wreck or contribute to peace and reconciliation. Abdurahman Baadiyow adds his analysis of a particular moment in Somali political history. He identifies the conflicts around the new Family Law introduced in 1975 as one source of contemporary political Islam, and shows how the misguided reformatory seal of the revolutionary government produced results opposite to those intended.

Tiilikainen's and Adam's papers in section V (Spirit Possession) follow the topic of religion (in the wider sense, including possession cults as one expression of religiosity) and gender in their papers on spirits and *saar* among Somalis. Tiilikainen, in particular, shows that this 'occult field' is currently contested between traditional and reform-oriented Somali Moslems. Adam's account of a *saar gamuuri* session she observed in 1988 is on the one hand a contribution to the so far underdeveloped gender studies within Somali studies; on the other it continues Lewis' earlier work on the complex economic, political and other factors which influence the development of religious movements.

Section VI focuses on poetry and its immense significance in Somali life. Johnson's paper, pointing out how poems, while keeping the same words, can change their meaning in different contexts, underlines the political relevance of Somali poetry. It is capable of moving people to the point where they take action. This emotional force depends on the words and their rhythms; hence the importance of work like that of Orwin and Gaarriye on metrics, which bears the same relation to poetry as musical analysis does to the experience of music. Boobe Yusuf Duale introduces Cabdullahi Suldaan Timocadde's life and poetry. His verses, illustrating Johnson's point, exhibit an astonishing analytical depth of the perennial Somali problems with clanism, (ab-)use of political power, and dependence on external powers. Long ago

Timocadde protested bitterly against the enclosures of grazing lands, which today provide a major obstacle to pastoralism particularly in Somaliland, as mentioned by Ciabarri. Said Samatar's account of literary death in Somalia continues the political theme, contrasting the (perceived) glorious poetic past with the disappointing present and seeing this as the result of political breakdown.[11]

In section VII (Cultural Variations) the papers by Mukhtar and Luling can be read as a contribution to the discussions on homogeneity versus heterogeneity in Somali society, which have far more than only academic relevance. Mukhtar describes how the establishment under the Siyad Barre government of a single national language and script contributed to marginalising the agro-pastoral Digil and Mirifle or Reewiin (Raxanweyn), including their distinctive poetic tradition. Luling describes a social group, the Gibil Cad (light skinned) lineages of the Shabeelle valley, whose existence has so far escaped academic attention. Both texts can be seen as part of 'enlightenment' in Somali studies. A Bravanese refugee observed that '[t]he fact that Somalia is home to peoples of diverse ethnicity speaking different languages still comes as a surprise to many' (Banafunzi 1996: 332). More than a decade later, this statement has not lost any of its relevance.

Section VIII on language provides a contribution to the analysis of Somali grammar from one of its best known exponents, Annarita Puglielli, while Hoehne, Muuse and Axmed contribute a chapter on Somali (nick)names which testifies to the richness and beauty of Somali social and cultural traditions while also shedding light on cultural change in Somali society.

In conclusion, Healy's paper, echoing earlier themes, argues that the 'nomadic' social organisation of many Somalis adapts remarkably successfully to life in the diaspora, and Geshekter sums up Lewis' contribution both as anthropologist and historian.

This volume is presented as a *Festschrift* and thus, as an academic gift to Ioan Myrddin Lewis himself, and to all those engaging in contemporary Somali studies.

Notes

1. Lewis has made important contributions outside Somali studies, concerning general anthropology and the anthropology of religion, shamanism, and possession cults. For the sake of consistency of content, these are not dis-

cussed in this book (unless they are related to Somali spirit possession, as in the chapters by Tiilikainen and Adam).

2. In May 2009, Hoehne met Aw Jaamac in Hargeysa, where he came for a visit and presented his most recent book on Somali poetry and culture, which had just been published in Djibouti. Aw Jaamac warmly remembered Lewis.
3. In the Somali spelling after 1972, the party's name changed to Xisbia Digil-Mirifle Somali (XDMS).
4. Abdi I. Samatar (1992) roughly summarised these critics under the term 'transformationists', in contrast to the 'traditionalists' among whom he counted Lewis.
5. Heyer (1997) interpreted the state in the Somali context as a meta-segment. As long as enough resources were provided or 'state interests' could be convincingly evoked, Somalis united at the state level; yet, when the state lost its economic and political power, the centrifugal forces increased and conflicts over the remaining resources/spoils escalated.
6. Militant Islamists repeatedly tried to overcome clan divisions and unite under the banner of religion, with mixed success.
7. The only well-founded sociological and ethnographic studies on aspects of contemporary southern Somalia are those of Roland Marchal (1993 and 1996), and, in parts, Luling (2002).
8. A Somali commentator, Hassan Ahmed (n.d.), for instance, provided the following list of truly horrific problems which Somalis had to face over the last century and particularly since the state collapse (*wakhtiga burburka*): colonialism (*gumeysi*), religious fighting (*dagaalo diineed*), civil war (*dagaal sokeeye*), hunger and many massacres (*gaajo iyo xasuuq farabadan*), breakdown of the family (*burbur qoys*), dispersal of the nation (*ummad kala ood oodan*), the mutual killing of closest relatives (*laba wada dhalata oo is disha*), businessmen rusty with blood (*ganacsato dhiig miridh ah*), a huge number of refugees (*qaxooti fara badan*), the arrogance of clan (*isla weyni qabiil*) and clanism fuelled by money (*qabyaalad lacag lagu tabco*). Such a list would have not come to mind before the descent into civil war in the late 1980s.
9. It is worth noting that the term 'primordial' is often wrongly used in the academic literature. According to Geertz (1963: 109), who popularised the term, it referred to what *actors* assume as 'givens' in a particular context, e.g. kinship, religious belief, language, particular social practices. It was originally *not* used to brand researchers.
10. Genealogical identities and clan divisions are also reified by political concepts such as the '4.5' formula employed in Somali peace and reconciliation conferences since the late 1990s in order to 'represent' Somali 'clans' (Schlee, personal communication 31.08.2009; Schlee 2008: 114–48; Menkhaus in this volume).
11. It is, however, doubtful if this distinction holds true in the light of the continued poetic traditions of poets such as Hadraawi and Gaarriye, and

many young talents presenting their verses in poetic competitions organised in schools and universities in Somaliland, Puntland and the south, or on the internet.

References

Aw Jaamac Cumar Ciise 1976. *Taariikhdii Darawiishta iyo Sayid Maxamed Cabdille Xasan*, Mogadishu: National Printing Press.

——— 1999. *Diiwaanka Gabayadii Sayid Muxammad Cabdulle Xasan (1856–1921)*. Oslo: Darwiish Publishing House.

Banafunzi, Bana 1996. 'The Education of the Bravanese Community: Key Issues of Culture and Identity,' *Educational studies*, 22 (3), 331–42.

Cassanelli, Lee V. 1982. *The Shaping of Somali Society*. Philadelphia University Press.

Farah, Ahmed Yusuf with I.M. Lewis 1993. *Somalia: the Roots of Reconciliation: Peace-making Endeavours of Contemporary Lineage Leaders: a Survey of Grassroots Peace Conferences in 'Somaliland'*. London: ActionAid.

Fitzgibbon, Louis 1982. *The Betrayal of the Somalis*. London: Rex Collings.

Geertz, Clifford 1963. 'The Integrative Revolution: Primordial Sentiments and Civil Politics in the New States.' In C. Geertz (ed.) *Old Societies and New States: The Quest for Modernity in Asia and Africa*. New York: The Free Press of Glencoe, pp. 105–57.

Geshekter, Charles 2001. 'Interview with Professor Ioan Lewis at his Home in London.' *Bildhaan*, 1, 53–86.

Hassan Ahmed n.d. *Qaabka tariikh ay kutimid, dowlada madaxweyne Cabdullahi Yusuf (1891–2004)*. Online at: http://www.qaranimo.com/qaabka_taarikh_ay_kutimid.htm [accessed 27.06.2006].

Helander, Bernhard 1998. 'The Emperor's New Clothes Removed: a Critique of Besteman's 'Violent Politics and the Politics of Violence'. *American Ethnologist*, 25/3, 489–91.

——— 2003. *The Slaughtered Camel: Coping with Fictitious Descent among the Hubeer of Southern Somalia*. University of Uppsala Press.

Heyer, Sonja 1997. *Staatsentstehung und Staatszerfall in Somalia: Dezentralisierungsmodelle jenseits des Staates?* Working Papers on African Societies, 23. Berlin: Verlag Hans Schiler.

Hoehne, Markus V. 2002. *Somalia zwischen Krieg und Frieden. Strategien der friedlichen Konfliktaustragung auf internationaler und lokaler Ebene*. Hamburg: Institut fuer Afrikakunde.

——— 2006. 'Political Identity, Emerging State Structures and Conflict in Northern Somalia.' *Journal of Modern African Studies*, 44 (3), 397–414.

Kapteijns, Lidwien 1995. 'Gender Relations and the Transformation of the Northern Somali Pastoral Tradition.' *International Journal of African Historical Studies*, 28/2: 241–59.

Lewis, Ioan M. 1961. *A Pastoral Democracy: a Study of Pastoralism and Politics among the Northern Somali of the Horn of Africa*. London: Oxford University Press.

——— 1969. 'From Nomadism to Cultivation. The Expansion of Political Solidarity in Southern Somalia.' In M. Douglas and P. Kaberry (eds) *Man in Africa*. London: Tavistock, pp. 59–78.

——— 1972. 'The Politics of the 1969 Somali Coup.' *Journal of Modern African Studies*, 10/3, 383–408.

——— 1977. 'Confessions of a "Government" Anthropologist.' *Anthropological Forum*, 4 (2), 226–38.

——— 1992. *Social Anthropology in Perspective. The Relevance of Social Anthropology*. Cambridge University Press.

——— 1994. *Blood and Bone. The Call of Kinship in Somali Society*. Lawrenceville, NJ: The Red Sea Press.

——— 1998. 'Doing Violence to Ethnography: Some Comments on Catherine Besteman's Distorted Reporting on Somalia.' *Current Anthropology*, 13 (1), 100–8.

Luling, Virginia 2002. *Somali Sultanate: The Geledi City-State over 150 Years*. Piscataway: Transaction.

Marchal, Roland 1996. 'The Post Civil War Somali Business Class' (Unpublished report to the European Commission). Nairobi: EC/Somali Unit.

——— 1993. 'Les mooryaan de Mogadiscio. Formes de la violence dans un espace urbain en guerre.' *Cahiers d'Etudes Africaines*, 33 (2), 295–320.

Menkhaus, Ken 1999. *Middle Jubba Region* (United Nations Development Office for Somalia, 'Studies on Governance' Series no. 7). Nairobi: UNDOS.

Samatar, Abdi I. 1992. 'Destruction of State and Society in Somalia: Beyond the Tribal Convention.' *Journal of Modern African Studies*, 30 (4), 625–41.

Samatar, Ahmed I. 1994. 'The Curse of Allah: Civic Disembowelment and the Collapse of the State of Somalia.' In A.I. Samatar (ed .) *The Somali Challenge. From Catastrophe to Renewal*. London: Lynne Rienner, pp. 3–19.

Schlee, Günther 2002. 'Regularity in Chaos: The Politics of Difference in the Recent History of Somalia.' In G. Schlee (ed.) *Imagined Differences: Hatred and the Construction of Identity*. Hamburg, Münster: LIT-Verlag, pp. 251–80.

——— 2008. *How Enemies are Made: Towards a Theory of Ethnic and Religious Conflicts*. New York: Berghahn.

Wardheer News 12.04.2009. 'The Traveller to Legendary Lands.' WardheerNews interview with Shiela Andrzejewski, Online at: http://wardheernews.com/Wareysiyo/The%20Traveller%20to%20Legendary%20Lands_wdn.pdf [accessed 07.09.2009].

PART I

THE COLONIAL PERIOD AND TODAY

2

REFLECTIONS 1943–1963

John Drysdale

As one of the oldest and longest serving Somali activists—a Somalilander to boot—I have been pressed by Markus Hoehne to write something. I had told him that there were no suitable reference works for my purpose in Hargeysa and anything approaching an academic effort was impossible. Never mind, he said, we would like you as an oldie to conjure up some dregs of the past which most people interested in the Horn know nothing about. This seemed to me to have inspirational logic so I accepted with some trepidation, hoping that my long term memory was still in reasonable shape. I hope it is as I weave away from my beginning to the end of the colonial period with a bit more besides.

I had been commissioned in the Argyll and Sutherland Highlanders in the early 1940s and at my first breakfast in the intimidating Officers Mess, wearing my Argyll kilt, I spied a tall and very beautiful silver sugar shaker. I shook it vigorously on my porridge when a fierce looking major sitting opposite me bristled and said in a broad Scottish tongue, too loudly for comfort, 'We take salt with our porridge here, not sugar.' I was aghast with embarrassment, and sprinkled some salt on my porridge as well to calm the uptight officers around me. It was my first lesson in Scottish table manners.

I was given a platoon to command. I found the 'Jocks' admirable soldiers but I felt too young to be commanding them. The sergeants and the terrifying Sergeant-Major were far too mature and grisly for my comfort. I got no satisfaction from a mirror of my boyish countenance, so on field exercises I would race through bushes and the branches of low-lying trees to get my face well scratched to the point of bleeding. It was a useless exercise.

The paratroops suddenly attracted me and I applied to join them. My mother was horrified, thinking it was a very dangerous option. In deference to her pleading I told my company commander that I had withdrawn my application. He replied, to my second embarrassment that day, 'You can't in war be tied to your mother's apron strings.'

I remained too young looking for an Argyll officer, and in a way I was not unhappy to be one of the many officers at that time to be posted to a secret destination. My father, commanding a Sikh Regiment in the Indian Army and boasting a DSO and an MC from World War One, was back in England encouraging me to make the British Army my profession. As we parted company on my way to the secret posting his parting shot was, 'I suppose you will be a major when we next meet.' It was prescient.

Climbing aboard a troopship with all the smells of a well-washed deck and hot, musty air from below being blown through large, camouflaged funnels, we descended a narrow gangway to huge dormitories with two or three tiers of insubstantial beds. Drinking warm beer in small quotas, playing bridge and deck games for three weeks, fearing an attack by German U-boats, standing in turn on the bows of the ship to alert the bridge of a suspected submarine, was our life at sea.

Rounding the Cape of Good Hope, we guessed we were bound for East Africa or even Egypt. We docked at Mombasa, and in good spirits we clambered aboard a train which took us up and down escarpments for miles on end to a transit camp in cooler Nairobi. Our real destination was still a secret. Less so when thirty military lorries with canvas covers arrived one morning to take us in a direction that pointed to the north-east. The army too dropped a clue. We were each given a paperback called 'Learning Ki–Swahili'. A further clue came from a terse statement from the convoy commander who said we would be examined in Swahili on arrival in three weeks. 'So learn it' was his peremptory, clipped way of speaking. It was becoming obvious that we were destined for the Horn of Africa, probably Somaliland via Mogadishu along the Indian Ocean—the longest coastline of any African country. The roads were sandy, rocky and in places potholed. The terrain was savanna country with flocks of gazelle wagging their white tails at various speeds in harmony with the excellence or otherwise of the nutrients that they were digesting. So long as the wind blew from the front of us it kept us reasonably cool, but as soon as the winding road unkindly brought the wind to our rear, clouds of fine sand smothered the occupants of the lorry and in the cab in front. Our faces and arms turned a sickly brown. It was no joke, and interrupted our Swahili studies.

Mogadishu was a big city, administered by the British Military Administration (BMA). The young Somali police wore tiny Dik Dik horns as cap badges and were commanded by British officers wearing khaki shorts and brass emblems on their shoulder straps. They strutted up and down the broken pavements looking important. Mosques, of course, were everywhere and an oddly placed Cathedral with a bell chiming at the hour testified to the former Italian presence. Mogadishu had been their colony from the 19th century. Being Italian, not British, they rightly plumped for two mighty rivers to exploit banana plantations—the Jubba and the Shabeelle. Britain in Somaliland did not look for rivers—there were none flowing anyway—but for black headed sheep of sweetish mutton which would go by dhow across the Gulf of Aden for the British garrison there. It oversaw a coaling station for British steamers on their way to the Far East. That was Britain's reason for being in Somaliland in competition with the French in Djibouti. The British had a very different approach to life, essentially harsh, even warlike, but practical.

We spent a night at the Italian-owned Croce del Sud hotel. Slender Somali waiters, elegantly dressed in black trousers and white shirts, contrasted with the sarong-clad Somali shepherds we had seen from the dusty tracks with their camels, sheep and goats on the rather worn-looking pastures of Somalia. In contrast too to our tins of bully beef, dry biscuits and warm beer, our fare on the road, poached red mullet, thinly sliced cheeses, ham, soft long bread, olives and glasses of red wine, went down well in the fan-whirling, humid restaurant. Italians look after themselves. 'Why not white wine?' we asked. It goes sour, the waiter told us in Italian, stacked in the hot holds of ships from Italy. The beds on the verandah upstairs were bug-ridden, so our departure the next morning, after a sweaty, wakeful night's 'rest', with a horrible shave in cold water that morning, was itchy and hasty.

We were on our way to Hargeysa through the white gypsum of Majeerteeniya and Laascaanood, until we saw two solid pyramidal hills of granite known colloquially as Naasa Hablood, the 'girl's breasts'. The hills were on the north side of the valley of Hargeysa, known among Somalis as the valley where the elephants (there were only three then) ripped up the vegetation. On the opposite side of the brown, sandy river bed was the airport. The town, almost entirely composed of single storey white-washed bungalows, stores and shops on one side of the valley, had only a few trees for shade but scores of donkey carts with forty gallon drums carrying water from house to house lined the roads, upsetting the flow of minor traffic. Somalis, wearing second-hand colourful clothes known in Somali as 'Who Dead?', graced the otherwise dust-laden streets in a sparkle of real colour. The men wore chequered sarongs with a shawl over their shoulders in the dry, colder weather of December. The beautiful women wore long garments of the brightest colours and stood in groups like flower beds.

The convoy drove to a camp of double sided tents for each of us, with a large tent that served as a mess. A notice explained that we were to report to the Adjutant the next morning. The oral examination in the Swahili language was upon us. Fortunately the Adjutant, we soon discovered, had only an approximate knowledge of the language himself, and we all passed with flying colours. That particular absurdity was repeated when we were introduced to our respective platoons of very young Somali soldiers who had joined the First Somali Battalion, having been camel herders before they were recruited.

As British officers we naturally wished to communicate with our 'men' (not 'boys' as our fathers' generation would have called them, whereas we followed the post-war fashion of democratic speak), especially our Somali non-commissioned officers, the backbone of any infantry regiment. But our soldiers spoke and understood one language only—Somali. To teach them English was off the agenda as being too difficult. Swahili was the option. Having 'learned' Swahili we were expected to teach our Somali soldiers the language, not English. There was resistance to it. British officers did not understand why.

A little later they encountered an equally mystifying prejudice. The Quartermaster's store in the battalion, which was run by a British NCO, was sent khaki shirts in bulk for our soldiers. They had no collars. They were registered in the Quartermaster's ledger as 'Shirts Murduf'. There were a few senior soldiers in the battalion who were familiar with some English, having served in the British Protectorate's Somaliland Camel Corps. They had beady eyes on anything that smelled of anti–Somali culture. They misread the word 'Murduf' to mean 'native'. So these were 'shirts native' without collars. A bad combination. The rumour had it that the British were turning Somalis into 'natives'. It spread throughout the Battalion. They mutinied. Bewildered officers could not understand the problem.

Our soldiers' uniforms originated in East Africa; they had a mystifying contradiction known as 'long shorts'. These were calf-length cotton trousers with a sleeved tunic to match and no collar. Somalis hated them also, as they hated any collarless garment, especially one described as 'native'. The prejudice was all to do with the Somali aversion to being treated as 'slaves'. Somalis pride themselves that they have never been slaves in their history. To the Somali eye, up until their independence in 1960 when the T-shirt was invented, a garment without a collar had slave connotations. So the 'Shirts Native' were never issued from the Quartermaster's store and the soldiers went happily back on parade. 'Slaves' are not mentioned by Somalis in public any more but in the Somali way of thinking then, and perhaps even to this day, there was always an unspoken distinction between Somalis and those who were, regrettably, enslaved (and who were marked out by their hair and noses), leading in older days to the mild Somali protest, 'We are not Africans'. For similar reasons, Swahili lessons never took off.

Weapons training, on the other hand, was a cinch even for the former camel herders. They broke all records for stripping and reassembling the complicated, multi–part Bren Gun for cleaning—faster than my Jocks in Scotland. This was my first revelation about the cultural diversity of the Somali camel herder. Somalis seemed to have unique characteristics and in later years when they were sent to Aden or the Sudan for secondary education, which did not then exist in Somaliland, they repeatedly came top of the form until the subject got boring.

To go to a modern war without being able to communicate with one's soldiers was, to me, a frightening thought. With only a notebook and pen I set about developing an orthography for the Somali language in order to learn it. My tool for the job was my not very good but adequate schoolboy Latin. It did at least give me the Latin alphabet, pronunciation and, above all, grammar. I set about it with earnest endeavour once I had arrived in Sri Lanka on the way to the Burma campaign as a captain in charge of mortars. It was too close to war to delay my studies.

One result was that a rumour spread among the higher ranks that I was a Somali speaker. This was entirely false; I was still trying to master the conjugations of what appeared to be irregular verbs, and the twenty vowel sounds (I could only find ten) with the horrible 'dh' were a menace. With a spoon in my mouth and a mirror I managed to adjust my tongue to imitate the 'dh' in the end.

We were preparing to leave Sri Lanka and our Brigadier was arriving to bid us farewell. The whole battalion was on parade, with officers standing in front of their charges. Without notice, my Colonel called me to the dais and ordered me to translate into Somali what the Brigadier was about to say. I wanted to escape but there was no way out. I tried lamentably to translate, sensing through the corner of my eyes and ears turbulence in the ranks, the shifting of positions and much murmuring. I gave up, turned about, apologising to the Brigadier, saluting and marching back to my post, blushing furiously and unhappily. I made sure it would not happen again.

We had several skirmishes and minor battles in Burma before we braced ourselves for our last and biggest battle of all at a village called Letse, not far from the Irrawaddy river. We were in a 'box', meaning a circular position with all round protection. The Japanese had surrounded us in the evening and were bent on destroying us. They fired their guns and mortars through open sights along our perimeter to raise our fire so that they could identify our exact defensive positions before they attacked. They knew our weakness, which was poor fire discipline. They attacked all night. We pounded them with artillery from Indian gunners under our command, and fired our six mortars at very close range with the barrels almost vertical. Every rifleman was fully alert, firing at the enemy whenever they advanced towards our positions, until dawn broke and the Japanese retreated, leaving the dead and wounded lying all over the place—except for their commander. He stood on top of a hillock facing our soldiers in their trenches who watched immovably, silently, as the commander pulled a grenade from his pouch, brought it to his chest and pulled the ring in shame for his defeat.

Throughout our campaign our Somali soldiers had the courage of lions; never did they leave our officers or soldiers wounded in battle without going out under fire to carry them home. As one officer in a neighbouring Battalion told us afterwards, 'We wish we had been with your Somalis'. We went home to Somaliland leaving behind, distressingly, many killed and wounded, but proud of our gallant regiment. The British officers and NCOs who were left went to a modest public house in London on the last Friday of October for countless years as a reunion of the brave, and in remembrance of the fallen—until there were almost no more left of us alive in Britain.

On my return to Somaliland from Burma, I found myself motoring to Ceel Waaq in Kenya's Northern Frontier District. It reminded me of a comment I had read by Sheikh Maxamed Cabdille Xassan, erroneously known as the Mad Mullah of Somaliland. In a published letter he wrote to 'the English People' in 1903, he said, 'If the country was cultivated and contained houses or property it would be worth your while to fight. The country is all jungle and that is no use to you. If you want wood or stone you can get them in plenty. There are also many ant-heaps. The sun is very hot. All you can get from me is war, nothing else.' Sheikh Maxamed's succinct description of the Sahel country, which stretches from Senegal in a band south of the Sahara, through Eritrea, down the Somali peninsula to Kenya's Northern Province of old, is pretty accurate.

Ceel Waaq (meaning God's Well)—a large Somali camel watering hole—lies half way along the old Jubbaland provincial boundary of 1918 between Mandera and Wajir. The modern day attraction of Ceel Waaq is a fort, built in haste by the Kenya government when it feared trouble in 1960, the year Italian Somaliland and British Somaliland united as one Republic. It feared trouble because of the strong influence of the Somali Youth League of Italian Somaliland, which had encouraged the belief throughout the Horn of Africa, among Somali–speaking nomads and political leaders alike, that a wider cultural unification, known as Greater Somalia, was desirable and inevitable. The influence had spread to the Somalis of Kenya's Northern Frontier District. Across their border with Somalia, the reconstruction of the Kismaayo port and construction of a meat canning factory, developed by Americans and Russians respectively, were impressive looking developments from which some parts of the Kenya province might prosper. The cattle trade would come to compete with the Republic's Italian induced banana exports, then 44 per cent of the export trade. Both enterprises eventually collapsed, like Somalia itself. But they encouraged a belief in the large, desolate, under-developed district in Kenya that Somalia and its ideals were a reasonable bet.

With my appointment by the Somaliland Protectorate Government in 1955 as British Liaison Officer for the whole of the Haud and

Reserved Area (25,000 square miles, the size of Belgium) I was stationed in Ethiopia's southern province of Jigjiga. I became immersed in the politics of Somaliland, Somalia, Kenya, Ethiopia and Eritrea.

The nub of a developing political crisis consisted of Britain's partial favouring of a Greater Somalia, France's support for Italy's return to her former colonial possession, and Ethiopia's intensification of its claim to Italian Somaliland and thus the long shores of the Indian Ocean. The Ethiopian Government carried its lobbying to the United Nations, which was sympathetic because of Italy's earlier invasion and first colonial occupation of Ethiopia. In Addis Ababa, Ethiopia staged demonstrations outside foreign embassies to impress foreigners with the 'affection' that Somalis had for 'their mother country' Ethiopia.

With the arrival in Mogadishu of a United Nations Four Power Commission to ascertain the wishes of the people, since the former colonial power, Italy, had been defeated by British Commonwealth forces, matters got out of hand, resulting in the deaths of 51 Italians and 17 Somalis. It became evident that Ethiopia supported the Somali desire for unification provided that the territories formed part of the Ethiopian empire, as Eritrea did from 1952. Britain's demarche was defeated by Russia and (nationalist) China. Ethiopia's coveting of the Indian Ocean coast failed to impress the powers. Italy and France won the struggle. By 1949, the United Nations General Assembly placed Italian Somaliland under United Nations Trusteeship for ten years with Italy as the administering power. Independence was forecast for 1960.

The Italians, joyous to be back again in what they called 'their Somalia', were full of energy and earnestness to carry out the United Nations' mandate for their colony. They were lively and generous; they always had a glass of Italian red wine in their hands when one visited them. They appointed Italian District Commissioners, who were trained lawyers, so that they played by the book where they could not be seen to be making money on the side, with enthusiastic Somalis always ready to please—provided there was a backhander. They cherished the 'beau' in Somali culture, the longing to look clean and smart in public places—Italian suits and ties worn by Somali officials, splendid uniforms for the police—but they had no great enthusiasm for the bedrock of Somali culture and society: the elders. These were not particularly beautiful but they could wisely keep the inevitable clan system together, speak classical Somali, know their history and recite their poetry with perfect scansion and alliteration—no mean achievements—to magical effect. Why the clan system? Because it is an ancient system of honest justice through democratic consensus that has proved itself over generations to be wholly commensurate with the nomadic life-styles of those in the majority: the Somali pastoralists. Capital punishment was and is rare, collective punishment is the norm, with a livestock tariff of wickedness which the extended family of the miscreant must adhere to, if found guilty, and give handsomely to the aggrieved party in recompense. Otherwise revenge will be taken and armed strife will develop, possibly far and wide. That is the nature of pastoralism in the Horn.

The remains of Italy's fanciful second attempt at ruling Somalis proved in the end to be constitutionally and culturally opportunistic, certainly, but quite disastrous as a political mould for modern Somalia. The elegance of a collar and tie persisted long after independence in 1960. Those who looked good in this uniform of sophistication looked down on the sarong wearers, and this is the origin of the plight and the blight of Mogadishu today. They should go back to their consensus-living culture which gives people rights and condemns the heathen.

My concern as British Liaison Officer in Jigjiga for five years was the motivation of the Ethiopian Amhara civil servants with whom I had to do business. They could put on a pleasing face if they felt you were on their side. If not they could be quite nasty behind your back. Our problem arose out of the Anglo-Ethiopian Agreement of late 1954. This was hatched in the Colonial Office in London and had the Royal stamp of approval from the Queen, who rewarded Emperor Haile Selassie with a rare state visit to London. In a gilded carriage drawn by fine black steeds with mounts in gold and scarlet tunics and plumes as headgear, Haile Selassie drove to Buckingham Palace for a sparkling banquet. The agreement was truly awful. It allowed Ethiopia to declare the Somaliland clans, grazing their livestock under the 1897 agreement for the Reserved Area and the Haud, to be Ethiopian subjects. By so doing, Ethiopia emasculated the 1897 agreement and rendered our legitimate operation to safeguard our pastoralists, grazing and watering their livestock in the Haud, dangerously ineffective.

Why was this done? The explanation among diplomats was Ethiopians' sensitivity about their sovereignty. That was true. The 1897 agreement was an outrage to most Amharas. It allowed us, British and Somali civil servants with clan police in uniform, to go anywhere in the Haud, arresting marauders if necessary and taking them to Somaliland to be tried. Our uniformed police cocked snooks at the aggressive Ethiopian military and were generally a little bumptious. At the level of senior officials we were always excessively polite, but behind the scenes the Amharas deeply resented our intrusiveness.

I decided to read something about Ethiopian history. The problem became obvious. There are two traumatic events in the Ethiopian calendar which run through the Amhara and Tigrean veins as if they were some genetic caution about the nation's security. These are the conquest of part of Ethiopia for fifteen years by a Somali, Ahmed Grañ (or as Somalis call him Axmed Gurrey, the 'left-handed'), from 1527, and the fact that Lij Yasu, whose *de facto* reign as Emperor of Ethiopia extended from 1911 to 1916, was close to Islam, married a Muslim wife and entertained close relations with Maxamed Cabdille Xassan of Somaliland. He was finally deposed and succeeded by Ras Tafari, the future Emperor Haile Selassie (crowned 1930). These two traumas are a constant reminder of what can happen to Ethiopians if they rest with their swords in scabbards. Hence Ethiopia's ready acceptance of the American prompting to fight the Islamic Courts Union in Mogadishu in 2006, for fear that those Islamists would creep to the borders of Ethiopia and do horrible things.

The independence given to British colonies in the late 1950s and early 1960s was an unexpected turn of events for Ethiopia, and not altogether a welcome prospect. The reality came to light when I was visiting Diredawa for a little shopping. I was lunching alone at a nice hotel when I saw from my table the glass door of the restaurant opening. The Governor of Adal and Issa came in, mopping his brow, sweating profusely. He came to my table with a worried look on his face. 'What's happened?' I asked. 'A terrible thing has happened,' he replied. He went on to explain that the first independent Ghana delegation to Ethiopia had arrived that morning, including Kwame Nkrumah. They had arrived by air in Diredawa because they could not land at the high altitude of Addis Ababa airport. They had to transfer to another aircraft. He met them carrying their suitcases. They retired to the wash room.

'I was appalled', he said with tears in his eyes, 'they emerged from the wash room wearing native clothes'. 'You mean their gold and orange Kente clothes?' I asked. 'Their native dress.' he repeated. 'I told them to change into morning dress with top hats, but they refused. His Imperial Majesty was going to meet them at the airport. He will be angry with me for letting them arrive in native clothes.' I was flabbergasted by his ignorance of Ghanaian customs. Having worked in Ghana I knew how beautiful and valuable Kente cloth is. I was speechless.

Much later the Emperor had evidently been tipped off about 'native' practices in Africa. All non-Ethiopians of African origin, especially Somalis, were referred to in conversation with me as 'natives'. This outmoded talk clearly had to change in Ethiopia if they were going to present a pan-African image. It did change with the erection of a pan-African Conference Hall where the Organisation of African Unity subsequently held office and met, and still meets (as the African Union), without top hats.

Somaliland's independence in 1960, to coincide with the end of Somalia's United Nations-inspired mandate in the same year, was not agreeable to the British government, which had in mind Somaliland's independence at least three decades away. Somalilanders forced the issue. Britain's weakness over Somaliland's constitution-making began in 1956 when the Parliamentary Under-Secretary of State for Foreign Affairs, Douglas Dodds-Parker, visited Addis Ababa and offered, on behalf of the British Government, to purchase the Haud and Reserved Area. The offer received a hostile reception from Ethiopia and aroused even more suspicion as to Britain's real intentions. Either Britain was for Ethiopia or against Ethiopia; evidently it was the latter. This was confirmed in the Ethiopian mind a month later by a visit to Somaliland by the Under Secretary of State in the Colonial Office. He made a statement to Somaliland's political leaders in Hargeysa, indicating early self-government as the aim. As to the future, he revealed a sympathetic attitude to the known aspiration of the British Somalis for ultimate union with Somalia.

The speech was received by the Somaliland politicians with indignation and dismay. This was due to the absence from it of any mention of the Haud and Reserved Area. The Somali hope was that the British Government would have secured a new agreement with the Ethiopians, producing at least the *status quo ante* the recent agreement.

The effect of this speech on the Ethiopians was to increase their anxiety about the future independence of Somaliland and its possible merger with Somalia (which was in fact to occur on 1 July 1960). The Emperor flew to the Ogaden and in a public speech he neatly turned the concept of Greater Somalia to his advantage. 'Our country would thereby become yet stronger and larger,' he announced. On the forthcoming independence of Somalia, the Emperor said its people should remember 'We are united by race, colour, and economics; and we all drink from the same great river.' The speech was received in Somaliland and Somalia with derision.

The Somaliland political leaders were displeased with the British Government's poor performance in retrieving their grazing rights from the wrongful agreement with Ethiopia. It was wrong of Britain to have declined Somaliland's request to take the issue to the International Court of Justice (ICJ) at The Hague. It left a very bad feeling in Somaliland towards Britain, which had the effect of pushing London hard to scrap its ideas of Somaliland joining the Commonwealth on independence and of delaying Somaliland's independence beyond the date of Somalia's independence in 1960. The British Government, caught, as was becoming usual, between loyalty to Ethiopia and loyalty to the Protectorate of Somaliland—a constant fight between the Colonial Office and the Foreign Office—acceded to Somaliland's final demands and offered modest aid. This however was cancelled when the Somali Republic broke relations with Britain in 1963 over the decision by Britain not to grant Somalis in the Northern Frontier District of Kenya union with Somalia. Britain, for the most part, over the years had sided with Ethiopia, unsurprisingly, and has done so ever since.

As a final reflection on the past, it seems appropriate to paraphrase comments I made in my book *Stoics Without Pillows* which was published in the year 2000. I wrote then that to Colonial officials in Hargeysa, the ten-year period of grace before Somalia was to become independent was a long way off. 'No need to worry' was the prevailing attitude. And if the word 'self-government' crossed their lips, there would be much shaking of heads in the government secretariat in sheer disbelief. Somalis could not, it was thought, manage their own affairs after only a decade of experience. Conventional wisdom spoke of thirty years before Somaliland would be ready for self-government, compared with, say, the Gold Coast (Ghana).

As a Colonial Service Administrative Officer in the early 1950s, I arrived on transfer from Ghana to Somaliland. I spoke enthusiastically to the Chief Secretary about Ghana's rapid progress towards self-government. My remarks were met with incomprehension and dismay. The minds of senior Colonial Officers then were dominated with eradicating communism. The Somali Youth League (SYL) was considered communist-backed. Communism, the Government maintained erroneously, was at the core of Somali political agitation.

The SYL, in fact, was having difficulties in sustaining its appeal as the party of all Somalis. The problem first arose in 1948 when the Somali National League was formed, though it maintained friendly ties with the SYL. The reason for its formation was unhappiness with the clan composition of the SYL in Mogadishu which was the very antithesis of Somali unity.

The proliferation of clan-based political parties in the south and the north, though the formation of political parties was designed to curb this, pointed to unspoken but entrenched concerns about representational interests in the transition from open, traditional systems of rudimentary governance, based on consensus, to semi–opaque systems of modern governance, manoeuvred by individuals whose mandates were determined by political party policy, rather than by clan consensus. Professor Hussein M. Adam has pointed out that Somali society shows how absolutely inescapable is the authority of tradition and custom (*dhaqan*) over the functioning of society. In the run up to Somalia's date of independence, 1 July 1960, Prime Minister Cabdullahi Ciise Maxamuud (a close ally of General Caydiid who had a portrait of Cabdullahi in his office in Mogadishu) legislated for a diminution of traditional practices in keeping with the SYL's conviction that clanism was politically divisive in terms of nation building. According to Professor I.M. Lewis, Cabdullahi modified the procedure for applying collective punishment to control inter-clan feuds, placing a stronger burden of responsibility on the individual criminal.

The real threat to the SYL came mainly through the wide cleavage between Darood and Hawiye supporters. There was an underlying struggle for clan power with the scales tipped by Italian influence in favour of Cabdullahi Ciise, a Hawiye. Leading Darood (Majeerteen) politicians broke from the SYL in a mood of pique at the Prime Minister's moderate policies. They formed a caucus in the Croce del Sud hotel and, to the dismay of the Italian administering power, considered asking the United Nations for a postponement of Somalia's independence. By April 1960, the Darood were back in the SYL fold, having come out on top in an agreement with the Hawiye and the Italians.

Under a new constitution in Somaliland an election in April 1960 gave the Somali National League, led by Maxamed Ibraahim Cigaal, pride of place. Cigaal became Leader of Government Business in the country's first Legislative Council. The formation of a government which was to have a life of four months only before merging with Somalia was hardly time enough for him to learn the ropes of governance, unlike Cabdullahi Ciise who had had four years as prime minister.

The mood of Somalilanders at that time was excitable. A matter of deep distress influenced decisions. Echoes from the six–year-old decision by the British Government to hand back the Haud and Reserved Area to Ethiopia, which still rankled, resonated throughout Somaliland. That decision was considered a betrayal of earlier Anglo-Somali agreements, and acknowledged as such by most of the British officials serving in the Protectorate at the time. Many Somalis believed that had it not been for the transfer of the Haud and Reserved Area to Ethiopia there would not have been a desire to unite with Somalia, which was driven by the unrealistic thought that a Greater Somalia would secure a return of these territories.

After Somaliland's elections in 1960, Cigaal with some colleagues visited Mogadishu where I was Oriental Secretary at the British Embassy. We had lunch together. I gave Cigaal a rundown on the political situation in Mogadishu. He was very surprised, even shocked, to hear that the SYL government had already decided that Cabdirashid Cali Sharmaarke (Darood) would replace Cabdillahi Ciise as Prime Minister, and that Cabdirisaq Xaaji Xuseen would become Interior Minister. The reason for the choice of Cabdirashid, rather than the charismatic Cabdirisaq, was simply that the former had an Italian doctorate, which it was thought, incorrectly, would elicit greater confidence in the government from foreign embassies.

The visit of Cigaal and his colleagues was for 'unity talks'. When they were asked by the southerners if Somaliland had any preconditions for union, they replied that they had none. Thus the south got away with the lion's share of all senior appointments, offering Cigaal, the prospective Prime Minister of Somaliland, only the Ministry of Education. At a British cabinet meeting in April 1960, the consensus was that 'The Foreign Office is only interested in Union to the extent that to oppose it might give Nasser or the Russians a chance to fish in troubled waters. We would prefer the Protectorate to develop on parallel lines to Somalia towards independence, working under our guidance for "close association" with Somalia and normal relations with Ethiopia.'

Curiously, it developed in this way after Somaliland's resumption of its sovereignty on 18 May 1991. It might have been 30 years sooner if Britain had not thrown away the Haud and Reserved Area to Ethiopia, which breached Britain's earlier agreements with Somalilanders, without even seeking a legal opinion from the ICJ at The Hague, as the Somalis had requested. Britain had the notion that the Emperor, who had lived in Britain during his exile where he was well looked after, and was brought back to his throne by Britain's reconquest of Ethiopia from Italian rule, would have had the decency to help Britain out over the Haud and Reserved Area. The offer by Britain to purchase the territory, which was a semi–arid grazing ground of no economic use to Ethiopia, was thought to have been reasonable. But that was a misreading of Ethiopia's greater interest, which was to acquire the shores of the Indian Ocean.

Somaliland's history has been characterised by succeeding raw deals, and now that Somalia has proved to be a very unreliable ally of Somaliland, the time is ripe for Britain, in the light of its regrettable historical decisions, to recognise the restoration of Somaliland's sovereign status which it granted in 1960.

3

BENIGN NEGLECT VERSUS *LA GRANDE SOMALIA*

THE COLONIAL LEGACY AND THE POST-COLONIAL SOMALI STATE

Gérard Prunier

Introduction

In 2009, the southern part of Somalia endured its nineteenth year of anarchy since the collapse of the Siad Barre dictatorship in 1991, while the former British Somaliland, which seceded in the borders of the British Protectorate from collapsing Somalia in May 1991, enjoyed its twelfth year of peace since the ending of internal militant conflict in 1997. Somewhere in between, Puntland, the old *Migiurtinia* of the Italian days that was established as autonomous regional state in 1998, tottered on in a semi–coherent state (Menkhaus 2007; Bradbury 2008; Hoehne 2009). This essay, while not pretending to *explain* that situation exclusively in terms of colonial policies, will try to evaluate the ways in which such policies have contributed to this contrasted state of affairs within the confines of a single, largely culturally homogeneous society.[1]

Comparing the structures and motivations of the British and Italian conquests

Britain had no interest in the Somali coastline except that of ensuring the freest passage of its shipping lanes towards India and preventing its occupation by potentially hostile European powers. As long as Egypt was willing to fill the space London had no desire to handle the region directly. However, a problem arose in 1884 when the Sudanese Mahdiyya forced the Egyptians to evacuate the coast and its hinterland.[2] In the meantime Britain had occupied Aden to use it as a major coaling station on the way to India (Gavin 1975: 1–39) and Aden depended on the Somali coast for its food supplies as well as for the sustenance of its local commerce. London was afraid that French occupation of the Somali coast could interfere with Aden's situation and, between 1884 and 1886, reluctantly entered into a series of bilateral treaties with various Somali 'chiefs' who were willing to accept a light protectorate. The new territory was to be administered from Bombay in the most distant manner: '[t]he primary objectives of the Government are to secure a supply market, to check the traffic in slaves and to exclude interference of foreign powers. It is consistent with these objectives and with the protectorate, which the Indian government has assumed, to interfere as little as possible with the customs of the people and to have them administer their own internal affairs' (Brockett in Samatar 1989: 31). In other words, the expression of British imperialism in what came to be known as British Somaliland was essentially reactive, driven by long distance trade concerns and indifferent to the territory itself.

This was in sharp contrast to the Italian outlook. Italy, which had existed as a country for barely fifteen years in the early 1880s, had no empire and was unused to dealing with foreign domination. But it was driven to acquire colonies by a combination of factors completely different from those motivating the British. A newcomer in the European 'concert of nations', it nervously pursued an ambition for a respected role it was not sure the other powers were ready to accept. This ambition was driven by a mixture of cultural and diplomatic frustration coupled with idealised memories of the Roman Empire and attendant fantasies of *missione civilizzatrice*. Reinforcing this syndrome was an actual and pressing problem of overpopulation, which caused the newborn country to haemorrhage towards the 'new world', particularly from the economically destitute *Mezzogiorno*, thus losing a vast human potential (Miège 1968: 40–5).[3] *La conquista dell'Impero* became an ideology supposed to solve major problems of national consciousness and of practical economics, from a position both of no experience and of major emotional investment. In addition, Italy was poor and its yet-to-be-conquered empire was seen a source of enrichment—through commerce, resource exploitation and transfer of population costs—which was brandished by the first 'imperialists', Pasquale Mancini and later Francesco Crispi, as the basic legitimating factor of their policies. All this added up to a form of imperialism, which was seen as organically necessary, almost to the point of national survival, largely ignorant of real geopolitics, and irrationally acquisitive . For these reasons the instruments of the two projects, British and Italian, were bound to differ quite widely.

London's measured detachment towards its Somali protectorate was due to the adaptive and variegated nature of British colonialism. British colonialism was ductile, adapted to its needs, combining grand strategic views with considerable short-term pragmatism. It could run from a hands-on forceful occupation at the service of a settler economy, as was the case in Kenya, to an abstract and absent-minded distant administration as in the Southern Sudan. Obviously, Somaliland belonged to the latter category. Since the Protectorate was not supposed ever to pay for itself, it was of course to be run with the strictest economy. Its role was to keep the French out, intimidate the Abyssinians and send sheep and camel meat to Aden. Such a mission was fully compatible with a very limited level of imperial involvement and with a continuation of most of the social, judicial and even political practices of Somali culture—as long as those did not interfere with the core diplomatic and strategic role attributed to the territory.

The Italian involvement was different. At first, seized by its own version of *Torschlusspanik*,[4] Italy rushed into imperial action without any clear strategic plan. The main impression was one of confusion. Rome thought of invading Tunisia, of occupying Tripoli, of piggybacking the Egyptian occupation of northeastern Africa, and it asked for German support in case it had to fight France in North Africa (Zaghi 1955 *passim;* Miège 1968: 47–52). This resulted in several military mishaps, mostly in Abyssinia.[5] The situation was not much better in Somalia where Italy, since its financial means were limited, had conceded the care of its expansion to a private chartered company, the Filonardi Company. In 1896, threatened by local uprisings, by the disloyalty of their Arab auxiliaries and by an Ethiopian invasion, the company's troops were massacred at Lafole. Italy reorganised its precarious hold on the southern Somali shore, creating another chartered company, the Benadir Company. Accused of tolerating and even secretly supporting the slave trade, the Benadir Company caused a major political and diplomatic scandal and had to fold up by 1905. As a result Rome was finally forced to take over and undertake the direct administration of what the Company had controlled—a small area around Mogadishu and the lower course of the Webi Shabeelle.

Before 1905, short of means, short of money and short of men, the Benadir Company had practiced a very indirect form of administration. In theory the Italian Government was committed to a more direct approach, which was the only way to foster the ambitious vision the colonial party had of the *Conquista dell'Impero*. But in practice the means put at the disposal of the government's administration were not much more effective than what the employees of the Charter Company had had; and this at the same time as efficient economic results were asked from the new government administration (Hess 1966: 87–111). The contradictions were massive and they were solved by various ways of cutting corners and replacing reality with rhetoric: slavery was officially condemned but often practically tolerated when it helped economic returns; government agents were 'chosen' but were often the same traditional leaders the Benadir Company had used; 'protectorates' were declared over Obbia and the Migiurtinia but were not turned into reality; violence was randomly used to extract compliance from the populations and money was paid to 'pacify' those who were reticent to comply; in other words, as the great historian of Italian colonisation Angelo Del Boca remarked, the *missione civilizzatrice* was often reduced to *politica forte e corruzione* (a strong arm and corruption policy) (Del Boca 1976 Vol. I: 803–13).

The British Somaliland situation was both comparable and notably different. The means were equally limited and the Aden authorities who ran the Protectorate spent even less money on it than Rome did on the South. But there was no grand vision of a civilising mission. On the contrary, the role assigned to the British residents at Seylac, Bulhar and Berbera was described as 'parental' and they were asked to interfere as little as possible with the functioning of the local clans. The police force at their disposal numbered about one hundred men. There was no attempt to transform the local economy or extract benefits from it and, apart from collecting custom duties in the harbours, the main economic role of the British agents was to help the local caravan and trade fair organisers so as to protect them from raiders (Lewis 1980: 44–9).

The two colonial experiences

So, even if the motivations and the emotional and political context of the British and Italian presence in Somalia were completely different, they did not amount to a full-fledged form of 'colonisation' if by this word we understand a foreign-controlled form of social transformation and economic development for the benefit of the motherland. Even so, both durably affected the society over which they were superimposed. But there were fundamental differences between the two styles of colonisation. In Somaliland 'indirect rule'—the key doctrine for British colonial administration in Africa—was intended to create a system of stable governance and limit resistance to colonialism by reinforcing traditional forms of authority. In most colonies this approach rested on the presence of chiefly authorities. As these did not exist in Somali society a different strategy was required. In Somaliland the British made senior elders of the *diya*-paying groups part of the state system by bestowing upon them the title of chief (*caqil*), providing them with a government stipend and giving them limited judicial and revenue-collecting powers (Lewis 2002: 105; Bradbury 2008: 28).[6]

This opens the question of the true impact of this system of indirect rule over Somali society. Bradbury (2008: 28–29) discusses two theses in detail: that the British policies deeply transformed Somali native institutions (as Samatar 1989 argued) and, on the contrary, that they did not alter the political structure of pastoral society (as Lewis 1980 and 2002 maintained). The answer is simple: they did both. How? To understand the point we have to go back to the simple distinction made by Ralph Linton (1945) between manifest function and latent function in social phenomena. A bishop can for example be made a member of the board of directors of a company. His manifest function will be to read reports, attend board meetings and vote. But his real (latent) function will be to reassure shareholders as to the honesty and morality of the firm. In the same way time can change the role of an institution, and looking at the role of the British Parliament from the time of Magna Carta to our time is to undertake a study in institutional transformation: nevertheless, 'the parliament' it remains. In a similar way the *diya*-paying groups of Somali society lovingly detailed by Ioan Lewis (1961) were not kept intact and untouched by British intervention, but neither were they destroyed; they survived by becoming something else. The pre-Protectorate clan leadership used to manage kinship relations and pastoral resources; under the British it entered the domain of broader legal action and the management of political and economic entitlements (Hoehne 2006). *But it did not do so entirely in the spirit of its old self.* For better or worse there were District Commissioners and District Courts and there was a constant interpenetration of Western standards of law with those of customary law. To understand the nature of the relationship—and to differentiate it from what was happening further south—it is necessary to remember that the British legal system itself is to a large extent a form of customary law, radically different from the principles of Roman Law which underpin the legal systems of all the Latin nations (and a few others).

So, although the British could be seen and gauged as operating on another plane which was presented as better or finer than the Somali one, it was not a *different* one. It was another system, with points of contact, some contradictions, continuities and possible transfers. In spite of the huge gap created by the lack of literacy and by the principle of collective responsibility, there was no radical ontological contradiction between the operating systems of the two cultures. Clan elders and leaders were wedged in the British system. They did not substitute themselves for it, nor did the British system replace them. The two met along a jagged line, partly blending, partly excluding, which of course did involve a fair transformation, extension or adaptation of some of the 'traditional' aspects of customary law.[7] It is to some degree in this silent cross-fertilisation that the roots of the post-1991 Somaliland experiment can be found.

The situation was very different in *Somalia Italiana*. World War One was a period of neglect for the colony and in 1920 Rome estimated that only about 30 per cent of Somalia was under its effective control. The northern Sultanates of Obbia and Migiurtina (Majeerteeniya) were legally only distant protectorates. But most of the areas populated by Hawiye clans were in fact independent and the Italian army barely controlled the area around Belet Weyn. The governors in Mogadishu had been deprived of means and were content with letting things be.[8] But from 1922 Italy had a new regime, *il Fascismo*. And Fascism, before being a clearly thought out political doctrine, was first and foremost 'a new style' (Del Boca 1979 Vol II: 51). Among the characteristics of this new style were spectacular displays of theatrical virility, authoritarianism, constant harking back to the glories of the Roman

Empire, a preference for violence as a way of resolving contradictions, and the promotion of Italians as *il popolo del destino*, 'the people chosen by fate' (to achieve greatness). It was not racism *per se* (this was more a trait of the later version of Fascism embodied by German National Socialism) but rather a worried and insecure bid for *la grandezza della razza*, 'the greatness of the race'. The Nazis felt sure of their superiority[9] but the Italian Fascists were just hoping to be superior. This made for an attitude of constant posturing, of macho chest-beating, of bombastic pronouncements, which it was tempting to buttress by shooting untrained spear-wielding nomads.

On 23 October 1923 a man who perfectly embodied this syndrome became the new Governor of *Somalia Italiana*. Cesare Maria De Vecchi Di Val Cismon was a war veteran, a close associate of Benito Mussolini and a founder of the *Fasci di Combattimento*, who boasted about being a true *Squadrista* (member of a Fascist street fighting group). Sporting a shaved skull and huge moustache, he deliberately cultivated the look of a mediaeval brigand. As soon as he arrived in Mogadishu he announced disgustedly that 'everything had to be restarted all over again' because the government's policy in Somalia was 'not only not Fascist but marked by pacifist and Masonic liberalism' (De Vecchi 1935: 25).[10] True to his word, he soon got authorisation from Mussolini to start what Italian colonial historians have called 'the second conquest of Somalia' (Del Boca 1979 Vol. II: 51). This was done with all the necessary Fascist vigour. One of the formulae frequently found in the bombastic and self-serving memoirs he wrote seven years after the end of his governorat, is *senz'altro passato per le armi*—'shot by firing squad without any further ado'. During his mandate Rome brought the disputed Sultanates of Obbia and Migiurtina under its close control, recovered by diplomacy the *Oltre Giubba* (Jubaland)[11] in 1925, and generally terrorised the population. Even Mussolini got worried because he was trying to play a respectable role in the European diplomatic scene and he thought that De Vecchi's administration had earned him *una fama di macellaio* ('the notoriety of a butcher') (Del Boca 1979 Vol. II: 69).

But how did this play out in terms of the relationship between the Italians and the Somali traditional clan system? There again we have to go back to Linton's view of the functionality of social structures. On the surface, De Vecchi kept many of the forms of apparently indirect relations between the colonisers and the colonised. But, as one of his own subordinates remarked, 'as far as I can see, the authority of the clan elders and assorted chiefs is by now completely absorbed by the government and most of them, perhaps even all of them, have by now been reduced to being simply decorative figures' (Giuseppe Bottazi, quoted by Del Boca 1979 Vol. II: 91). In a memo to De Vecchi Bottazzi nevertheless recommended that 'for historical reasons' and 'because of traditions', these positions should not be abolished, especially since 'there are not so many of them' and 'their miserable salaries are not much of an expense for the colony' (ibid.). This had far-reaching effects and another of De Vecchi's subordinates remarked later: 'deprived of any real role, frustrated of any remaining prestige, reduced to the level of purely practical laborers [...] the Somali we were dealing with were increasingly turning to religious mysticism' (Pini 1967: 54–5).[12]

The basic difference between the Italian policies and the British policies—apart from the use of violence—had to do with the 'latent role' or 'latent function' ascribed to the native social group. It was not because the British had such a glorified vision of the Somali or were more democratic (even though they were); it was rather due to the perspective of colonisation itself, to what this particular group of *gaal* (unbelievers) had in mind. The British were rationally trying to make a system of long-distance commercial exploitation work; they were 'imperialists' in the modern Leninist sense. For them the Somalis were just a collateral factor tied to the food supply of a coaling station on the way to India. So they had to be treated with kid gloves (or killed if they rebelled, but only in so far as was temporarily necessary), because this was the best way of making them, if not happy, at least harmless.[13] Safeguarding native clanic institutions went a long way in reducing costs and minimising administrative trouble. The 'development' of the Protectorate was of course the least of their concerns.

Not so with the Italians. They were displaying what a liberal Italian critic of his country's colonial past called 'a form of provincial militarism, of anachronistic megalomania coming from a country which in many ways was only partly European' (Iraci 1969: 64). In this way Italy can be seen as a backward semi–industrial country which had been humiliated by its treatment at the hands of its co-victors in 1919–20 and which gave itself to Fascism in a kind of compensatory psychodrama aimed at restoring a fantasised Roman past.[14] The result was an archaic form of colonisation where the Somalis were the living proof of the White Man's superiority and therefore *had* to be politically and administratively disempowered, even if the process served no purpose, even if it was actually harmful to the *real* economic interests of the coloniser. This is why Angelo Del Boca is able to contrast the colonial projects (and ultimate failure) of Duke Luigi di Savoia who ran the Società Agricola Italo-Somala (SAIS) in the 1920s in the hope of developing a modern industrialised form of agriculture (Del Boca 1979 Vol. II: 85) with the neo-latifundist policy of De Vecchi and his development of banana cultivation on 40,000 hectares of land between the Webi Shebelle and Merka. In one case production, slow and difficult, but of a needed resource (sugar); in the other a single crop, quick and spectacular in its results, of a luxury item (bananas) for which the Italian consumer ended up paying twice the price of the same product, of better quality, imported from the Caribbean.[15] But the first policy required patiently gaining the collaboration of the Somalis, while the second could be carried out by hired labour and former slaves.[16]

The decolonisation process

In spite of its military defeat, Italy was to find itself in the paradoxical position of retaining its Somalia colony anyway. The process by which the fate of the Italian colonies was negotiated after 1945 was extremely complex (Rossi 1980) and we will not examine it here in detail. But to summarise it, we can say that after a first period during which the British Foreign Secretary Ernest Bevin tried to create a Greater Somalia federating all Somali people (Lewis 1980: 124), the project was abandoned in June 1948 when Italy managed to lobby the United Nations General Assembly to be given back its old colony, even getting the support of Ethiopia by helping Haile Selassie recover the Ogaden.[17] From 1946 onwards, Rome started to plot its return to Somalia, a bizarre policy which, exactly like in 1919–20, was a consequence of Italy's ambiguous status in the recent war. In 1919 Italy knew it had been defeated at Caporetto and that the only reason why it could sit at the table on the side of the victors was the salvage operation of 1918 carried out by the French and the Americans, leading to the foreign-driven victory of Vittorio Veneto. Similarly, after 1943, Hitler's former ally had been turned into a 'victorious power' through the Badoglio sleight of hand. There again the humiliation was massive since Badoglio was no De Gaulle but a former Marshal of Mussolini who had been one of the brutal actors of *la conquista dell'Impero*. As a result the 'democratic' Italian government wanted to regain at least one of its former colonies to be politically and culturally vindicated and, since neither Libya nor Eritrea were possibilities, its efforts focused on Somalia which many people saw as kind of *res nullius*.

Logically its main enemy was the Somali Youth League (SYL) which had been created in Mogadishu under British protection in May 1943, in line with London's post-war pan-Somali plans. The SYL was a strong and fairly well-organised nationalist movement and therefore stood in the way of Rome's plans. Italian agents, working undercover within the framework of the Four Power Commission,[18] organised pro-Italian groups in the loosely-coordinated Conferenza and also helped start the Hizbia Digil Mirifle Somali (HDMS), a clanic party based on the Southern Rahanweyn (Digil Mirifle) clans.[19] The Italians exploited the cultural differences between the Rahanweyn and the 'truly nomadic' northern Somali clans,[20] picturing the SYL as a 'nomad', mostly Darood organisation. The result was disaster. On 11 January 1948 Italian agents in Mogadishu organised a pro-Italian rally on the occasion of a Four Power Commission delegation's visit to the city. In the purest *Squadristi* style they brought armed goons into town and attacked a parallel SYL demonstration. This turned into a massacre, with over fifty Italians killed, fifty wounded and dozens of Somalis, either SYL or Conferenza, left on the ground. Not only did this not slow down Italian subversive activity, it spurred it into new excesses. Rome's agents took advantage of clanic dissensions within the SYL and deepened them, often with money (Del Boca 1984 Vol. IV: 202–3). In order to guarantee 'peace and order' Italy was asked to create a so-called *Corpo di sicurezza* which was put together from a motley collection of locally raised militias or *bande*. The booklet containing their instructions was a direct copy of the old Fascist *Guida practica per l'ufficiale destinato in Africa Orientale* which depicted the local Somali as 'the enemy ... which, in case of a clash, should be prevented from fleeing and attacked relentlessly till its complete destruction' (*Direttive per l'impiego delle truppe metropolitane in Somalia* quoted in Del Boca 1984 Vol. IV: 213). The tone was set.

On 21 November 1949 the UN finally decided to bring Italy back officially to Somalia for ten years under the name of Amministrazione Fiduciaria Italiana della Somalia (AFIS). The proposal was somewhat surrealistic as the project required the recycling of many former Fascist administrators and called for the recruitment of new cadres from Italy who, in the lean post-war years, saw the job mostly as a chance for economic promotion (Del Boca 1984 Vol. IV: 201–69). During those ten years the AFIS' record in promoting any kind of potentially workable post-independence government was not remarkable. One of the key reasons was that Italy was trying to stay on beyond the 1959 deadline set by the UN. In Del Boca's words (ibid.: 221), most of the AFIS personnel was *ancorato al passato* ('anchored in the past') and desperately tried to turn the clock backwards. In order to further *nostre interesse* ('our interests', a formula compulsively present in the AFIS reports to Rome in Italian, not those written in English for the UN) AFIS officials kept selecting and backing tribes—that is, clans or subclans—which were *filoitaliani* ('pro-Italian'). These included the Rahanweyn of the HDMS of course, but also the Somali Bantu, various small coastal clans like the Biimaal and, among the larger clan families, those like the Marrexaan among the Darood or several Abgal groups among the Hawiye who proved open to blandishments, often of a financial nature. In the same way the economics of the AFIS largely consisted of a return to De Vecchi's compulsive development of inefficient and expensive banana cultivation, 100 per cent dependent on the subsidised Italian market (Karp 1960: 87–103).

Strangely enough this attitude was more a kind of *cultural* bias among the Italian personnel than a deliberate policy choice in Italy, once the initial years of post-1945 anguish had receded into the past. As time went by administrative directions became more and more moderate, the political outlook towards the SYL started to open up, and the top AFIS leadership began to take a longer look at the probability of independence. Paradoxically, in his last report sent to Rome before leaving his position (September 1952) the AFIS boss Giovanni Fornari listed among the negative forces endangering the future of an independent Somali state the Italian community in Somalia, adding somewhat listlessly: 'It is so difficult to transform a set mentality in the space of a few years' (quoted by Del Boca 1984 Vol. IV: 237). The mark of Fascism would take a long time in wearing off and, although it would be exaggerated to see it as the main cause of contemporary Somalia's problems, its role in their etiology cannot be neglected.

Conclusion: styles of colonialism and the Somali culture

The difference in treatment of the two Somalias by their British and Italian overlords was essentially a problem of differential European political culture. If we go back to the 1880s, the difference had to do with the essential nature of the two nations. Britain was a once barbarian land which was contemporaneously on top of the world of its time. Italy, on the contrary, was the distant inheritor of the first great European power which had been for centuries divided, looted, occupied and subjugated by foreigners. In the 1880s it had been reborn for only ten or fifteen ten years, after more than half a century of struggle. As a result each country had a political *ethos* of a completely different nature: self-confident to the point of arrogance in the case of the British, given to self-doubt and a burning desire to compensate for years of humiliation in the case of the Italians. In addition the British saw 'their' chunk of the Somali space as a very secondary piece of real estate which would never be anything more than an appendage to the much larger scheme of 'Empire'. For the Italians, every little bit of territory was, more than a frequently disappointing territorial reality, a symbol of recovered greatness. And greatness had no price; it was qualitative, not quantitative. This is what Fascism later superimposed itself on. The Fascist system, in Italy itself, was a brutal and almost desperate attempt at resolving the Italian quandary through what Carlo Zaghi called 'a gigantic and proliferating bureaucratic machine' whose extension overseas 'had neither the means, nor the adaptability nor the realism of British colonialism' (Zaghi 1980: Vol. II: 1052). Delusional in its perception of reality, driven by a thirst for collective vindication, unsure of itself and therefore unnecessarily brutal in its application, Italian colonialism was very far from the rationally exploitative view of Hilferding and Lenin. It was a dream of lost glory, a showy display of panache aiming at a collective therapy of the national soul.

The Somalis' clanic divisions and their openness to bribery made them an easy tool for the aggressive Italian paranoia which was not aimed at harming them but simply used them for reasons even their masters were not fully aware of. Compared with these painful antics, British colonisation of the Somalis (but was it actually colonisation?) appeared banal and ordinary: a form of no-nonsense benign neglect rationalised into official policy. Italy spent a lot of money and effort beating the Somali into submission, destroying in the process the capacity they had developed to manage their home-grown disorder.[21] Meanwhile Britain, almost absent-mindedly, under-managed Somali democracy, and thus kept its delicate mechanics operational—more by oversight than by design. Today's forms of differential social situations in Somalia have tended to mirror their distant colonial blueprints, self-reliant in one case, suffering and hardly capable of internally-driven stabilisation in the other.

Notes

1. Editors' note: On variations in Somali culture that throughout colonial and post-colonial times, and most dramatically since the outbreak of the Somali civil war, impacted on the differential chances of power and resource sharing as well as survival in Somalia, see the articles by Mukhtar and Luling in this volume.
2. 1884, the year of the Berlin conference, can be considered as a major turning point for regional geopolitics since it also fostered a sudden Italian interest in the area and revived France's dormant interest in its Obock station. It also alerted the future Emperor Menelik to the dangers of European encroachment.
3. *Mezzogiorno* refers to the underdeveloped south of Italy.
4. 'Fear of the closing gate'; this was the concept developed by the German imperialist party during the 1880s in reaction to British and French colonial expansion, which it managed to communicate to Chancellor Bismarck, causing him to call the Berlin conference in 1884.
5. The massacre of the Giulietti column in 1881, the Dogali defeat in 1887 and of course the battle of Adwa in 1896.
6. The title is an Arabic one. It was already mentioned in Burton's first footsteps (1854), and it is quite possible that it had been introduced by some Egyptian emissaries who explored the Somali Peninsula coming from the port of Massawa.
7. Actually, even if this sounds like a paradoxical opinion, I am not sure that the system of Islamic Shari'a is easier to reconcile with the Somali *Xeer* than British Common Law was. Its canonical rigidity is higher and its jurisprudence less open to interpretation (*ijtihad*), a word which has dubious connotations in Arabic.
8. In addition the uprising of Maxamed Cabdille Xassan, although mostly aimed at the British, had drained a good deal of the colony's limited means.
9. And, in a different way, so were the British. So sure were they of their innate superiority that the British never felt they had to *prove* anything. The Italians, on the contrary, kept boasting about *la forza, la grandezza, l'Impero, l'opera dell'Esercito* (the achievements of the army), including in official reports, as if not too sure about all what they were bragging about.
10. 'Masonic' refers to the Freemasons, a secret association which was considered by Fascists to be, along with the Jews, the great source of evil among the nations.
11. The British detached that territory from the Kenya Colony to try assuaging Mussolini's frustrations about the post-World War One peace negotia-

tions. The deal was negotiated directly between Rome and London; De Vecchi only dealt with the results.

12. This and all following translations from Italian to English are mine.
13. London lamented the revolt of Maxamed Cabdille Xassan mostly because it forced the Colonial Office to spend much more on military operations than the colony was intrinsically worth.
14. We should not forget that when Mussolini took power in 1922, Italy as a modern unified state was only 52 years old. Today, the survival of Fascism as a kind of folklore in the *Mezzogiorno* is a constant reminder of this archaic and literally reactionary past.
15. During the post-war years, AFIS managed to produce bananas at 30 per cent more than the market price of Caribbean ones. Even later Rome used the ACP measures of the European Union to keep subsidising this uneconomic production.
16. Many of the banana workers belonged to marginal clans or were Coastal Bantus, i.e. not really Somalis in anthropological terms.
17. Until September 1948 the Ogaden remained under the British Military Administration.
18. The UN-sponsored body in charge of dealing with the former Italian colonies.
19. Back in the 1940s the Rahanweyn were called Digil Mirifle.
20. They also recruited Somali Bantus into the Conferenza, often former banana plantation workers.
21. Democracy and conflict in Somali society go hand in hand. But the forms of democratic conflict resolution the Somalis have inherited from their ancestors are collective rather than depending on a one-man one-vote process. This is why they are more fragile, because a broad social consensus is always harder to achieve than a simple arithmetic plurality. The Italian bull-in-the-china-shop variety of colonialism wrought havoc on the constitutive elements of that social consensus. Interestingly, the re-creation of the old *akil* positions by Siyad Barre in the 1970s (under the name of *nabaddoon*) was a late acknowledgment of what had been lost.

References

Bottazzi, G. 1924. 'Relazione anno solare' (unpublished Manuscript, Del Boca Fund, Milan).

Bradbury, Mark 2008. *Becoming Somaliland*. Oxford: James Currey.

De Vecchi Di Val Cismon, Cesare M. 1935. *Orizzonti d'Impero: cinque anni in Somalia*. Milan: Mondadori.

Del Boca, Angelo 1976. *Gli Italiani in Africa Orientale. Volume I. Dall'unita alla marcia su Roma*. Bari: Laterza.

——— 1979. *Gli Italiani in Africa Orientale. Volume II: La Conquista dell'Impero*. Bari: Laterza.

——— 1984. *Gli Italiani in Africa Orientale. Volume IV: La nostalgia delle colonie*. Bari: Laterza.

Gavin, R.J. 1975. *Aden under British Rule (1839–1967)*. London: Hurst and Co.

Hess, Robert L. 1966. *Italian Colonialism in Somalia*. University of Chicago Press.

Hoehne, Markus V. 2006. *Traditional Authorities in Northern Somalia: Transformation of Powers and Positions*. Halle/Saale: Max Planck Institute for Social Anthropology, Working Paper No. 82.

——— 2009. 'Mimesis and Mimicry in Dynamics of State and Identity Formation in Northern Somalia.' *Africa*, 79 (2), 252–81.

Iraci, Leone 1969. 'Per una demistificazione del colonialismo italiano: il caso della Somalia.' *Terzo Mondo*, 3, 37–67.

Karp, Mark 1960. *The Economics of Trusteeship in Somalia*. Boston University Press.

Lewis, Ioan M. 1961. *A Pastoral Democracy: a Study of Pastoralism and Politics among the Northern Somali*. Oxford University Press.

——— 1980. *A Modern History of Somalia*. London: Longman.

——— 2002. *A Modern History of the Somali: Nation and State in the Horn of Africa*. Oxford: James Currey.

Linton, Ralph 1945. *The Cultural Background of Personality*. New York: D. Appleton.

Menkhaus, Ken 2007. 'The Crisis in Somalia: Tragedy in Five Acts.' *African Affairs*, 106 (204), 357–90.

Miège, Jean-Louis 1968. *L'impérialisme colonial italien de 1870 à nos jours*. Paris: SEDES.

Pini, Ugo 1967. *Sotto le ceneri dell' Impero*. Milan: Musia.

Rossi, Gian L. 1980. *L'Africa italiana verso l'indipendenza (1941–1949)*. Rome: Giuffre.

Samatar, Abdi 1989. *The State and Rural Transformation in Northern Somalia (1884–1986)*. Madison: University of Wisconsin Press.

Zaghi, Carlo 1955. *P.S. Mancini, l'Africa e il problema del Mediterraneo (1884–1885)*. Rome: Gherardo Casini.

——— 1984. *La conquista dell' Africa: studi e ricerche*. (Two volumes). Naples: Istituto Orientale.

PART II

CLAN POLITICS, PASTORAL ECONOMY AND CHANGE

4

SPECULATIONS ON THE HISTORICAL ORIGINS OF THE 'TOTAL SOMALI GENEALOGY'

Lee V. Cassanelli

Introduction

In 1957, I.M. Lewis wrote *The Somali Lineage System and the Total Genealogy: a General Introduction to Basic Principles of Somali Political Institutions*. Based on his first extended period of field research in the Horn, this 140–page typed report (Lewis 1957) was circulated among members of the Somaliland Protectorate government but was never published.[1] Although Lewis later (Lewis 1994: 13) expressed regret for the report's 'pompous' title, its 'shamefully patronizing' tone toward local administrators, and its 'arrogance' which he had 'learnt to cultivate at Oxford', I have always considered 'Total Genealogy' a pioneering and thought-provoking study. It laid the foundation for much of what we know and how we think about Somali social organisation. It highlighted the dynamic aspects of the segmentary lineage system, a theme Lewis would return to in many subsequent writings. It contained the first detailed account of the political parties, which had emerged after World War Two to demand Somali independence, and so is of considerable value to historians.[2] 'Total Genealogy' also included a perceptive discussion of the complex role of Islam and of Somali religious leadership in the rise of Somali political consciousness (Lewis 1957: 129–34) which has proven to be quite prescient in light of recent developments in Somalia.

Any of these topics would be apt for a book of essays recognising Professor Lewis' distinctive contributions to Somali Studies. But here I want to explore the somewhat more elusive subject of the origins of what Lewis called the 'total Somali genealogy'. This is the genealogical map which embraces virtually all Somalis and at its most remote level links them to a putative common ancestor, usually identified as 'Aqiil Abu Taalib, a son of Abu Taalib who was uncle and father-in-law of the Prophet Mohamed (Lewis 1957: 75). The total genealogy allows individual Somalis to situate themselves on a single 'family-tree' and to identify how closely or distantly the contemporary lineages to which they belong are related to other lineages, other branches of that tree. In this way, it serves to reinforce the belief that Somalis are one people with a shared origin and a shared history, while at the same time delineating the cleavages which frequently divide Somalis in matters of politics and everyday social life. The total genealogy thus provides a mental map which enables Somalis—and the 'experts' who study them—to explain both the solidarity and the segmentation which have characterised Somali society through much of its recent history.[3]

Genealogical reckoning as a means of ordering social relations is quite common in human history, particularly among peoples (like the predominantly pastoral Somalis) who are widely dispersed on the ground or who have never shared subject status or citizenship in a single state. But the idea of an all-encompassing genealogy, one which represents an entire 'nation', seems highly unusual and warrants some historical reflection. Jon Abbink (2009: 1) has called the development of this genealogical system a 'major cultural achievement of the Somali people'. Yet no one has purported to explain when and how such an intellectual model might have come into being. Lewis himself notes (1957: 4) that 'such a study would be of interest in throwing light upon the relatively unexplored subject of the historicity of lineage systems'; but in 'Total Genealogy' he limits himself to consideration of 'the various, often contradictory, genealogical claims as *contemporary social facts* [my emphasis] and does not attempt any historical assessment of them' (ibid.).[4] Most scholars have taken a similarly 'presentist' approach to the genealogical question. Indeed, given the many roles both positive and negative that clan and lineage identities continue to play in contemporary Somali society, it is not surprising that specialists have tended to focus on the 'outcomes' rather than the 'origins' of genealogical thinking in Somalia.[5]

There is considerable disagreement among scholars over the historical value of Somali genealogies in general. Until very recently, most

Somalis learned and transmitted their family and lineage genealogies via the oral tradition. Because such orally-transmitted knowledge is prone to selective remembering and forgetting, and subject to manipulation for demographic or political reasons, its value as a source for reconstructing the past has been seriously questioned (see e.g. Abbink 2009: 1–5; Mansur 1995).[6] Lewis has given us several examples of such distortions. For example, he observes that present-day genealogies tend to mirror the relative numerical size of contemporary clans on the ground: 'the genealogies of numerically large lineages [...] are longer than those of smaller and weaker groups' (Lewis 1994: 100). When Somalis trace the genealogical structure of a clan or lineage, they 'invariably follow through first the proliferation of the largest and most important segments and then return to describe the genealogies of smaller collateral segments. Here priority is given to lineage strength, not to order of birth' (ibid.: 101). He adds that 'over the generations [...] through the correlation which Somali see between genealogical span and historical strength, the pedigrees of small groups are telescoped or foreshortened more than those of large and powerful lineages. To this extent within Somalia, genealogies preserve a distorted record' (ibid.: 106).

At the same time, Lewis argues (1962; 1994) that, at least where the ancestors of existing clans are concerned, the genealogies track real historical persons. It is only 'at the point where Somali trace descent from Arabia outside their own society [that] a strong mythical component enters into the genealogies which is not present at the lower generational levels' (Lewis 1962: 47). In other words, while the genealogies of specific clans represent genuine historical forebears (even where some generations may have dropped out or been telescoped), those which purport to link the clan founders to a more remote set of common ancestors from Arabia are in all likelihood mythical, intended, it appears, to glorify the antiquity or the religiosity of the clan in question. This conclusion has come to represent the scholarly consensus on the historicity of Somali genealogies.

If the upper (more ancient) portions of the Somali family tree are indeed intellectual constructs, then who formulated them? When, why, and how did the total genealogy come into being? For a historian these may seem like obvious questions; but they are extremely difficult to answer with any certainty. There is simply no evidence from pre-colonial times to enable us to ascertain how Somalis conceptualised and utilised genealogies in the past, so seeking their historical origins may appear a somewhat fruitless (if not antiquarian) exercise. What we do know is that genealogical thinking continues to pervade modern Somali discourse, even in the face of powerful competing ideologies. But whereas nationalist, pan-Somalist, regionalist or Islamist formulations of Somali solidarity have struggled with only partial or short-term success in capturing Somalis' imaginations, the genealogical idiom continually (and for some 'perniciously') informs the way most Somalis think about themselves and act towards others in both the private and public spheres. Even if the 'total genealogy' can be considered a '*metaphoric, symbolic construct* [...] nevertheless it is constantly referred to by Somalis and by scholars concerned with their rich history and culture' (Abbink 2009: 3, italics his). This suggests that Somalis' sense of who they are is deeply grounded in a historical experience of thinking and acting genealogically.

In the remainder of this essay, I want to speculate on when, how, and why local family and lineage genealogies came to be assembled into a more comprehensive Somali 'national' genealogy, and to attempt to identify at least in a general sense the historical 'agents' behind this intellectual process. While we cannot pinpoint these processes with chronological precision, we may at least propose a plausible interpretation of how such a remarkable genealogical model came into being.

Possible origins of genealogical elaborations

Colonial sources. The 19th-century European travellers who first recorded the genealogies of particular Somali clans provide no evidence for the existence of an overarching genealogical scheme which tied all the clans to a single founder (see e.g. Cruttenden 1849; Gullain 1856; Burton 1856; Robecchi–Brichetti 1899). While Burton (1856) reports traditions of a common founding father of the Isaaq and northern Darood clans, he does not provide any genealogical data to support the connection. Luigi Robecchi–Brichetti (1899: 191), who compiled detailed genealogical charts for most of the major clans, noted of the Habr Ghedir that they 'find their place with the others in the common tree.' This hints at the possibility that Somalis had a concept of the 'total genealogy' at the end of the 19th century; but it may equally be an inference that Robecchi–Brichetti himself drew from the many closely-related origin stories he heard from his local informants (ibid: 366–92).

In the early 20th century European colonial writers began to assemble the various local genealogies they had collected into comprehensive charts which embraced all their Somali subjects (see e.g. Caniglia 1921; Colucci 1927). It was under colonial rule that the 'total genealogy' appears to have become the implicit paradigm for understanding the organisation of the Somali people (though it remained for Lewis to set it out explicitly in his 1957 report). By situating the region's many lineages and clans in a common framework, the European authorities could make sense of the Somalis' complex and often contradictory claims to Arab ancestry. Like the creation of 'tribes' elsewhere in colonial Africa, the use of an organising principle such as the 'total genealogy' helped bring conceptual and administrative order to an unfamiliar social terrain.[7]

The foregoing argument might lead one to conclude that the incorporation of local Somali genealogies into a coherent 'total genealogy' was the product of colonial administrative consolidation, a European intellectual construct superimposed on Somalia's local genealogical traditions to bring unity out of diversity.[8] However, there are other possible explanations for the appearance of the 'total genealogy' at the start of the 20th century. Rather than assuming that it was a Western 'invention', we need to look at the sources of information which European authors drew upon. Those sources invariably were local Somali genealogists and interpreters, all of whom were Muslims and many of whom were already literate in Arabic or had access to Arabic manuscript versions of their family genealogies. This small group of local literati were very influential in brokering the transfer of local knowledge, including genealogical knowledge, to foreigners. They served as the primary informants for most 19th-century European travellers (Cassanelli 2006) as well as for the earliest colonial administrators. In his excellent study of the local religious elites along the Benadir coast, Scott Reese demonstrates how prominent families often produced written genealogies to bolster their religious pedigrees and convince colonial authorities of their political legitimacy (Reese 2008: 65–80). From this evidence, we can infer that the compilation of local genealogies (and possibly their amalgamation into more comprehensive 'trees') was in all likelihood a joint project of Muslim intellectuals and early colonial administrators, drawing on a combination of oral and written sources.

Islamic sources. Even before the onset of colonial administration, there are grounds to suspect that genealogical elaboration had been occurring in Somali society. Conditions during the second half of the 19th century were particularly conducive to the reworking of social relations and the reformulation of genealogical identities. During this period, ideas of Islamic reform swept the wider Islamic world and began to circulate in Somalia. Notions of an *umma* (community of believers) in need of spiritual renewal found a ready audience among Somalia's pious literati, who viewed many of their countrymen as lax Muslims at best. At the same time, large-scale population displacement and political realignments in the Horn had exacerbated local conflicts over natural and social resources, and the task of mediating these conflicts typically fell to men of religion (Lewis 1955; Lewis 1956; Lewis 1994; Cassanelli 1982; Helander 1999). The convergence of these two processes created conditions where a message of Islamic renewal could take hold. To the religiously committed, all Somalis were primarily Muslims, but Muslims constrained by allegiances to kin and clan. Many local reformers acknowledged the existence of these parochial identities and sought to transform them from within. For the reformers, the 'tribes' of Somalia (like those of pre-Islamic Arabia) could become vehicles for the spread of the new dispensation (Reese 2008). What better way to represent a new *umma* of Somali speakers than a genealogical model that tied all Somalis ultimately to the family or companions of the Prophet?

The assimilation of Somali Muslims into the wider community of Islam was no doubt aided by the rapid spread of Sufi religious orders (*turuq)* in Somalia during the 19th century. In addition to preaching, *tariqa* leaders founded religious settlements *(jameecooyin*) in the interior of Somalia, which attracted adepts from many clans. According to Ali Hersi (1977: 249), the more learned adherents of these orders 'waged a vigorous campaign against the Somali social system of lineage and clan affiliations which, they pointed out, was the cause of many impious acts and the basis of pastoral turbulence. They sought to create a harmonious community in the place of fissiparous tribalism.' Noting the multi–clan composition of many of the early *jameecooyin*, Hersi argues that their members 'voluntarily renounced their clan ties and loyalties and came to identify with their *tariqa* community' and 'as proof of their radical break with the traditional tribal order [...] considered themselves—even addressed each other—as brethren (*ikhwan*)' (ibid.: 250). While Hersi adduces little direct evidence from the 19th century, his observations are consistent with what we know of *tariqa* organisation in later times.

The probable impact of the Sufi 'revival' on Somali genealogical thinking is nicely summarised by Helander (1999: 46), although he too bases his analysis on recent ethnographic observation:

> [M]embers of the *jamea* (Sufi religious settlements) often chose to replace their clan genealogies with religious ones known as *silsilad* (lit. 'chain') consisting of sheykhs within the order who taught the founder of the settlement and his teachers in turn, right back to the Prophet Muhammad and even to earlier biblical prophets. These genealogies, while constructed, often replaced the clan genealogies (equally constructed) and were often committed to writing, thus acquiring a certain sanctity. This was probably an important factor in explaining why even secular Somali genealogies also claim descent ultimately from the Prophet's Quraysh lineage. The entire process helped instill the idea of a people with a common ancestry and religious heritage [italics in the original].

Keeping in mind the turbulent circumstances under which these Sufi leaders (and their more orthodox counterparts) often lived and worked, their ability to provide conceptual maps to help local Somalis navigate through changing social, political, and religious conditions gave them a high profile.[9] The vision of a more inclusive community fitted very comfortably with Islamic reformist ideas of enlarging the *umma* through the incorporation of Muslims from diverse 'tribal' or 'ethnic' communities.[10] This vision was most dramatically expressed in the early 20th-century Dervish movement of Maxamed Cabdille Xassan, who used Islamic rhetoric in his effort to unite his countrymen against the infidels; but it is also evident in the more peaceful proselytism of Sheikh Aweys and other Sufis who sought to implement their own versions of Somali solidarity in an Islamic framework. The cumulative effect of these calls for unity furthered the identification of local Somalis with their co-religionists elsewhere in the Peninsula and almost certainly made at least some of them receptive to the notion of a more inclusive genealogy.

What enabled these reformist ideas to penetrate the consciousness of rural Somali was the engagement of local sheikhs in the continual process of mediating local clan disputes. By reminding contending parties of their common Islamic identity, the sheikhs sought to bring local *xeer* into greater conformity with Islamic practice. The resolution of local disputes typically involved washing the ink from a Quranic *loox* (writing tablet) and distributing the holy water among the contending parties while invoking the name of Allah (see e.g. Cassanelli 1982: 122–32). These same mediators were also often keepers of local genealogies, and were probably instrumental in using them to persuade feuding lineages that they shared a common (Muslim) ancestry. By bringing the combatants under a common genealogical umbrella, these religious intermediaries helped lay the foundations for a broader Somali Muslim consciousness, even if they failed—as they invariably did—to establish lasting peace on the ground.

Although we can probably never know the precise mechanisms by which Somalis came to see themselves as a single people, it seems that local Muslim intellectuals played a major role as agents in that process. By 're-imagining' the chronically divided Somali communities as part of the greater *umma*, and by bringing Somalis into the universal and inclusive narrative of Islamic conversion and reform, they provided an alternative to the clan-based model of history and identity.[11] Clan narratives had been preserved chiefly through oral tradition and poetry; the reformist vision employed written texts (including genealogies) to promote its appeal for a new solidarity. In this regard, Professor Lewis' observations on the role of literacy in modern Somalia are apropos. Noting how the expansion of Arabic literacy in 20th-century Somalia had tended to encourage the 'mythologizing process' in the elaboration of local genealogies and the validation of Somali claims to Arab origins, Lewis (1994: 105) identifies a process that was almost certainly operative in the 19th century as well, when the prestige associated with writing in Arabic greatly assisted the spread of reformist ideologies. Elsewhere, Lewis (2001) notes how literate (urban) elites were contributing to the modern 'manufacturing' of religious ideologies and theologies which underpinned popular Somali belief, again pointing us to a possible parallel with the role of earlier religious elites in helping their countrymen forge new religious identities. I would go even further and contend that the roles Lewis attributes to Islamic learning and literacy in modern Somalia are not simply analogous to intellectual processes at work in earlier centuries, but in fact direct continuations of those processes.

It may well be that the process of re-imagining a larger Somali community began even earlier than the 19th century, although the hard evidence for previous centuries is even scantier and more circumstantial than that for the 19th. Hersi, for example, suggests that the migration of Sada-Ashraf families from the Hadhramaut and their resettlement in the Horn in the later 16th and 17th centuries stimulated an early-modern religious revival. The claims of these immigrants to noble birth and powerful *baraka* made them welcome among local

Somali Muslims. Having been initially attracted to the Horn by the opportunities to participate in the religious wars against Christian Ethiopia, and later driven there by drought and internal warfare within Arabia, these Hadhrami immigrants worked as preachers and missionaries for their faith. If they did not consciously promote efforts to link the ancestors of their host Somali families to the noble lineages of Arabia, their presence and example may well have prompted local intellectuals to do so (Hersi 1977: 235–41).[12] While Arabic sources containing Somali genealogical records from the 17th and 18th centuries may yet be discovered, we can for the moment only speculate on how early the process of incorporating local into universal Islamic genealogies began.

Functional and historical explanation of genealogical consciousness

One important question remains. If, as I have attempted to argue, the intellectual roots of the 'total genealogy' lie in the pre-colonial era and are associated with the spread of Islamic literacy and religious mediation, both of which have increased in modern times, why were so few Somalis familiar with it? As Lewis observed in 1957, while Somalis of both sexes will know their genealogy up to their clan and usually clan-family ancestors, and while elders (*odayaal*, *cuqaal*, *saladiin*) 'will generally know the genealogical relationships between their clans and other clans of the same clan family, very infrequently is knowledge found of or interest [expressed] in the relationships among the various clan families which make up the total genealogy. [Moreover] the relationship between Samaale and Sab—Somali kinship in its most extensive and remote sense—is unknown in northern Somaliland' (Lewis 1957: 71–2). Iye's research among the Ciise yielded a similar conclusion:

> Chez les Somalis, les généalogies en général ne dépassent pas l'éponyme qui est à la base de la confédération tribale du clan. C'est-à-dire qu'aucune généalogie ne se proclame de l'ancêtre commun à tous les Somalis. Ainsi les généalogies des clans, tribus et confédérations somalis semblent ignorer complètement l'unité de ce peuple et ne revendiquent pas leur affiliation à l'ancêtre Somali par exemple. En d'autres termes, si la conscience de l'appartenance à l'ensemble Somali est forte elle n'est nullement reprise par les généalogies qui elles s'arrêtent à l'éponyme du fondateur du clan (Iye 1990: 113).

Lewis' explanation for the very limited knowledge of the total genealogy in northern Somalia is a resolutely functional one: because knowledge of the total genealogy is not important to Somalis in their management of political affairs, there is no need for most of them to learn it. Furthermore, 'since the total genealogy is unknown it is of no social significance there' (1957: 72). In contrast, Lewis found that in the south 'knowledge of the total genealogy appears to have a greater currency' (ibid.). This he attributed to the fact that representatives of virtually every clan can be found in the south, and consequently there has been more interaction among members of different clans, particularly in the cosmopolitan capital of Mogadishu (ibid: 72–3). He adds that 'in any case, there are many sheikhs and secular historians who possess Arabic MSS [manunscripts] in which the total genealogy is recorded' (ibid). This simple observation reinforces our argument that knowledge of the total genealogy seems to be associated with a degree of Islamic literacy and carries greater importance in settings where lineages and clans unfamiliar with each other come into contact.

On the other hand, if we presume that the total genealogy, which links Somali clans to a common Arab/Islamic ancestor, functions solely to enhance the status and embellish the pedigrees of individuals and lineages by tying them genealogically to the Qurayshitic lineage of the Prophet Mohamed, then the total genealogy becomes simply another component of Somalis' Islamic identity, grounded less in history than in faith and belief. Yet, the incorporation of a universalist Islamic dimension into Somali genealogical consciousness must also be considered a *historical* phenomenon, the product of intellectual and social processes that were rooted in the experiences and encounters of individuals and communities in specific times and spaces. Without denying the fact that lengthy genealogies often reflect present-day power relations rather than past realities, we need to pay attention to the historical role that Islamic intellectuals played in broadening Somali genealogical horizons as they sought to expand the *umma*. Even where holy men attempted to accumulate *baraka* for themselves or their lineages by claiming descent from religiously prestigious forebears, they set an example for more secular Somalis of a new more inclusive identity.

In suggesting that the total genealogy was part of a long-established Islamic project to bring Somalis to a higher level of religious consciousness, I am not denying the reality that genealogical claims to Quraysh ancestry often serve (today as in the past) narrow political or sectarian interests, or that clan leaders, authoritarian regimes, or militant reformers might have less noble reasons for embracing the idea of a single genealogical nation. However, the incomplete realisation of this project should not automatically be taken as evidence that its proponents were ill intentioned or insincere. If anything, by using the notion of a 'total genealogy' to promote the spread of Islamic reform in Somalia, Somali Muslim intellectuals helped perpetuate genealogical thinking in the collective public life of the country, reinforcing its parochial tendencies even as it sought to transcend them. For most of the 20th century, Somali Sufis, scholars, and local clan intellectuals found that Islamic identity could coexist with clan loyalty, however uneasy that relationship might be. With the collapse of the Somali state and the spread of anarchy in the past two decades, a new generation of reformist Muslims has appeared on the scene to call Somalis to join the community of believers. Some of them—labelled 'radicals' or 'fundamentalists' in the popular press—appear to have turned away from the genealogical model as a basis for inclusion in the *umma*. By desecrating Sufi shrines and (by extension) the *silsilad* of those who are buried in them; by attacking religious leaders and pious elders who may not share their vision of proper Islamic practice; and by using violence and intimidation to attract adherents, these new reformers (or at least their leadership) appear to reject the call of clanship and the power of genealogical ancestry and to replace them with a stark, literalist reading of Islam. Earlier generations of Islamic reformers strove to overcome the 'tribal' mentality of Somalis by offering a more inclusive genealogical vision; whatever success they had was only temporary, partial, and clearly reversible. Only time will tell if the new reformers—for whom the total genealogy has scant importance—will enjoy any greater success.

Notes

1. The text on the 'Total Genealogy' followed Lewis' well-known *Peoples of the Horn of Africa* (1955), which was based entirely on library research, and preceded his seminal book *A Pastoral Democracy* (1961) based on his Oxford DPhil thesis.
2. Lewis (1958) elaborated on these parties and their agendas in his double article on *Modern political Movements in Somaliland*.

3. Virginia Luling noted that kinship continues to form the organisational framework for contemporary Somalis: 'as well as being the framework within which people organize their lives and compete for resources of whatever kind, it also provides a scheme which *explains* why the various groups are where and what they are' (Luling 2006: 471, italics hers).
4. Though as we see below, Lewis was not uninterested in the question of 'genealogy as history', and in several subsequent articles (Lewis 1962, 1994) provided important insights into the historical factors which shaped the contemporary genealogical system.
5. For a provocative critique of 'a-historical' approaches to Somali thinking about clanship, see Kapteijns (2010).
6. E.E. Evans-Pritchard, Lewis' mentor at Oxford, described this process of 'selective remembering' with regard to Nuer genealogies as 'telescoping' (Evans-Pritchard 1982 [1940]: 199–200)
7. This argument is developed in Kapteijns (2010).
8. Ali Jimale Ahmed (1996: 113) notes: 'Since no one has documented a chronology of Somali national consciousness beyond what seems to be its genealogical manifestation, we cannot really demonstrate that all Somalis saw themselves as one people…before colonialism.'
9. This appears similar to the ways in which the *Xeer Ciise* evolved to help stabilise social relations in fluctuating demographic and political circumstances, as reconstructed by Ali Moussa Iye (Iye 1990).
10. As Scott Reese (1998) shows, this is clearly the argument of Sharif Aydarus in his eclectic 1954 history of the Somalis, which attempts to incorporate Somali clan histories into the broader (universal) sweep of the history of Islam. While Aydarus' *Bughyat al-Amal* is a 20th century reconstruction, it represents a world view rooted in a long Islamic intellectual tradition, one which probably informed Muslim reformist thinking in the 19th century and perhaps much earlier.
11. Similar processes of rethinking identities in a Muslim idiom appear to be at work in the contemporary Somali diaspora and, most obviously, in Somalia itself, despite the many divisions within the Islamist movement.
12. Ali Moussa Iye (1990) offers a challenging alternative explanation which locates the origins of modern Somali clan identities in the 16th century, following the decline of the mediaeval Islamic sultanates of Adal and Ifat and the eclipse of the Islamic legal structures they had propagated. To meet the challenges of a society which had become demoralised and 're-tribalised,' local elders had to find a system which bound the scattered subjects of these collapsed states together. They did so, according to Iye, by forging ties of cooperation and collective responsibility, using extended clanship (genealogy) and contract (*xeer)* to help stabilise social relations. The outcome, following long and laborious negotiations, produced the Ciise clan confederation and the *xeer* or customary law which served to regulate relations among its members.

References

Abbink, Jon 2009. *The Total Somali Clan Genealogy (Second edition)*. ASC Working Paper 84, Leiden: African Studies Center.

Ali Jimale Ahmed 1996. *Daybreak is Near. Literature, Clans and the Nation-state in Somalia*. Lawrencville NJ: The Red Sea Press.

Burton, Richard 1856. *First Footsteps in East Africa*. London: Longman, Brown, Green & Longman.

Caniglia, Giuseppe 1921. *Genti di Somalia*. Munich: Verlag der M. Rieger'schen Universitäts-Buchhandlung.

Cassanelli, Lee V. *The Shaping of Somali Society*. Philadelphia: University of Pennsylvania Press.

——— 2006. 'Tradition to Text: Writing Local Somali History in the Travel Narrative of Charles Guillain (1846–48).' *Journal of African Cultural Studies* 18 (1), 57–71.

Colucci, Massimo 1924. *Principi di diritto consuetudinario della Somalia italiana meridionale*. Florence: Società Editrice 'La Voce'.

Cruttenden, Charles J. 1849. 'Memoir on the Western or Edoor Tribes, Inhabiting the Somali Coast of North East Africa. Part 1.' *Journal of the Royal Geographical Society*, 19, 49–76; Part 2: *Transactions of the Bombay Geographical Society* 8, 177–210.

Evans-Pritchard, Edward E. 1982 [1940]. *The Nuer: A Description of the Modes of Livelihood and Political Institutions of a Neolithic People*. London and New York: Oxford University Press.

Guillain, Charles 1856. *Documents sur l'histoire, la geographie et le commerce de l'Afrique orientale*. 3 vols., Paris: Arthus Bertrand.

Helander, Bernhard 1999. 'Somalia.' In D. Westerlund and I. Svanberg (eds), *Islam Outside the Arab World*. London: Palgrave Macmillan, pp. 39–55.

Hersi, Ali A. 1977. 'The Arab Factor in Somali History' (unpublished doctoral dissertation, University of California, Los Angeles).

Iye, Ali Moussa 1990. *Le verdict de l'arbre*. Dubai: International Printing Press.

Kapteijns, Lidwien 2010 (forthcoming). 'The Clanship Paradigm in Somali Studies: A Critique.' Northeast African Studies 11 (1).

Lewis, Ioan M. 1957. *The Somali Lineage System and the Total Genealogy. A General Introduction to Basic Principles of Somali Political Institutions*. Hargeisa: Somaliland Government.

——— 1958. 'Modern Political Movements in Somaliland. (Parts 1 and 2).' *Africa*, 28 (3), 244-61 and (4), 344-64.

——— 1962. 'Historical Aspects of Genealogies in Northern Somali Social Structure.' *Journal of African History*, 3 (1), 35–48.

——— 1994. *Blood and Bone. The Call of Kinship in Somali Society*. Lawrenceville, NJ: The Red Sea Press.

——— 2001. 'Saints in North East African Islam.' In B.S. Amoretti (ed.), *Islam in East Africa: New Sources*. Rome: Herder, pp. 227–40.

Luling, Virginia 2006. 'Genealogy as Theory, Genealogy as Tool: Aspects of Somali "Clanship".' *Social Identities* 12 (4), 471–85.

Mansur, Abdalla O. 1995. 'The Nature of the Somali Clan System.' In A.J. Ahmed (ed.), *The Invention of Somalia*. Lawrenceville, NJ: The Red Sea Press, pp. 117–34.

Reese, Scott 1998. 'Tales which Persist on the Tongue: Arabic Literacy and the Definition of Communal Boundaries in Sharif 'Aydarus's "Bughyat al-Amal".' *Sudanic Africa*, 9, 1–17.

——— 2008. *Renewers of the Age. Holy Men and Social Discourse in Colonial Benadir*. Leiden: Brill.

Robecchi Brichetti, Luigi 1899. *Somalia e Benadir*. Milan: Carlo Aliprandi.

5

TRADE, LINEAGES, INEQUALITIES

TWISTS IN THE NORTHERN SOMALI PATH TO MODERNITY

Luca Ciabarri

Introduction

Addressing the topic of social change in Somali areas, trade and transformations brought about by trade occupy a conspicuous place in scholarly literature. In particular, there has been extensive debate on how trade is organised along kinship lines mirroring the segmentary organisation of society and how changes in trade organisation could eventually transform or affect social structure. Professor Lewis' article on *Lineage Continuity and Commerce in Northern Somaliland* (originally published in 1962, and revised and re-published in 1994) has been highly influential in this respect.[1] His findings have been picked up and later challenged by scholars focusing on transformations in the countryside induced by livestock trade and on elite formation. The growing commercialisation of livestock in the international market was seen in fact as the determining factor that initiated a set of transformations within the nomadic part of Somali society and in the social relationships between rural pastoralists and urban businessmen, resulting in increased inequalities and social differentiation.

Livestock trade, in a society seen as predominantly pastoralist, took on the role of reflecting the whole set of transformations occurring during the modernisation process. This was all the more true with regard to the northwestern Somali region, currently referred to as Somaliland, but, given the past tendency to extend the pastoral model to the whole of Somali society (Ahmed 1995), it also worked to some extent as a general model. Indeed, besides contributions related to north and central Somalia (Swift 1979; Aronson 1980; Samatar 1989; Samatar *et al.* 1988; Djama 1997; Lewis 1994; Jama Mohammed Jama 2004; Abdillahi 1990; Baumann *et al.* 1993), there is an equally important literature on livestock trade in the region straddling southern Somalia and northern Kenya (Dalleo 1975; Cassanelli 1982; Little 2003), focusing in particular on cross-border movements. Since this discussion has framed the general reflections on social change in northern Somalia, and since trade is here portrayed as deeply entwined with change, a factor that is all the more evident nowadays, it seems to me of special interest to recall its general contents and to highlight those aspects that still offer in my view valuable insights for today's social dynamics.

The discussion has been in terms of a polarity between continuity of social organisation and growing inequalities: I shall argue for the need to reconcile these two features. The debate in fact still bears an unresolved epistemological question. The basic problem, how economic differences are reflected in social organisation, is still relevant and insufficiently addressed with regard to Somali society. This point also strongly resonates with, or actually anticipates, the recent debates on clan and politics which have provided alternative explanations of the civil war events.[2]

In addition, though focusing only on livestock trade and thus setting aside important dimensions of social change, the debate has identified three peculiar problematic areas which represent structural and recurrent transformations of northern Somali society: first, the marginalisation of countryside vis-à-vis town (and the disequilibrium set in motion by the urbanisation process); second, the recurrent readjustments of commercial relationships within a wider regional panorama; third, the mutually constitutive relationships between trade and politics. In the chapter, I will first sum up the discussion on the effects of livestock commercialisation and then briefly show how the post-conflict recomposition of Somaliland revolved around the three dimensions highlighted here. Overall, the development of what Geshekter (1984: 238) saw as the sea-desert connection, and which I would like to represent here in terms of commercial corridors as specific forms of territorial integration, proved to be pivotal in Somaliland state-building and appears as a kind of long-term structure of that specific territory.

Economic changes and social changes: the effects of the commercialisation of livestock

Livestock trade and access to international markets have a long history in northern Somali society and scholars referring to various periods of time (Lewis 1994; Djama 1995; Geshekter 1984; Jama Mohamed Jama 2004) have addressed the topic. I will deal here with contributions that focused on changes after the 1950s and 1960s, including the Saudi Arabia oil boom and the dramatic drought of 1974–75, and authors such as I.M. Lewis, J. Swift, D. Aronson, A. Samatar and V. Jamal.

Though started in colonial times, livestock export acquired tremendous relevance from the 1950s and 1960s onward. On the one hand, the expanding labour migration into the emerging oil-rich Middle East countries increased their demand for meat; on the other hand, and most importantly, the transformation of Hajj rituals into a mass phenomenon operated by the Saudi monarchy created entirely new conditions for export activity. Typically, the export flows reflected the demand and annually had their major peak during the two to three months preceding the Hajj pilgrimage and a second, less relevant peak for the celebrations following the end of Ramadan (*'īd al-fitr*). According to Swift (1979), livestock exports in the 1950s surpassed the exports of hides and skins and at national level soon challenged the banana business, which was actually declining (Samatar 1989). They reached a peak in the 1970s and early 1980s, until political instabilities in the 1980s and declining conditions in the Middle East oil economies contributed to a temporarily downscaling of the market.[3] However, the high prices offered by the Saudis during the Hajj period and the quantities absorbed virtually transformed that market into the unique purchaser, under a regime of quasi–monopsony.[4] On the Somali side Berbera, being the closest port, was by far the main outlet of such trade. Outbreaks of animal diseases since the 1980s, which led Saudi authorities repeatedly to ban any imports from Somali areas, amplified the problem of depending on a single outlet.[5] The Saudi market has thus represented at the same time the strength and weakness of Somali exports.

In view of the dimensions acquired by the livestock trade—in terms of value and number of people implicated—it is no surprise that it became the major entry point for any discussion on social change in northern Somalia. Several factors accounted for this: the peculiarity of the livestock sector involving all segments of society, from the pastoralists to the merchant class (the former metonymically representing 'the countryside' and the latter 'the town'); the fact that it constituted the basic purchasing power of the largest part of society; and, finally, the fact that it represented the largest supply of foreign currency for the state and, through custom duties, a major contribution to the national budget. Scholars who have analysed the responses to livestock commercialisation (Swift 1979; Aronson 1980; Abdiallahi 1990; Baumann *et al.* 1993; Samatar 1989; Samatar *et al.* 1988) focused on two main themes that I will present as 'ecological and social disequilibrium' and 'class analysis and clan behaviour'.

Ecological and social disequilibrium. Under the deceptive cover of a still traditional pastoral sector—labour intensive and wide-ranging transhumance (Swift 1979)—a new landscape made up of reduced mobility, increased inequalities, loss of autonomy, out-migration to town, enclosures of grazing lands and privatisation of water points progressively emerged in the countryside and became particularly evident from the 1960s and 1970s. There were changes in pastoralists' strategies in herd management and access to market, market organisation, and the dynamics of appropriation and use of land and resources. Herd management strategies based on consolidated patterns of mobility and differentiation and splitting of animals into different groups were over time challenged by increasing pressure from the merchants' middlemen and brokers to sell the animals in accordance with the demands of the external market. The very shape of the herds changed, privileging stock for export and minimising stock and herding practices normally included in risk-avoidance schemes or destined for social purposes (Swift 1979). Needing to accumulate a large number of animals in a short time, the big exporters increasingly hired agents (Aronson 1980). These middlemen, purchasing animals over the year, tended to form trade herds that needed water and grazing (ibid.). Phenomena linked to the penetration of a commercial logic—enclosures of common grazing lands, increased hiring of herdsmen, privatisation of water points and construction of water reservoirs (*berkad*) in areas like the internal plateau normally grazed only in limited seasons, distribution and selling of water by trucks—were partly a consequence of this, coupled with the reinvestments by well-off livestock owners residing in town and the rationalisation of production that they were carrying out. Investment in water points by merchants was also a way to attract the pastoralists, in a framework of strong competition between businessmen (Aronson 1980).

The results were a reduction in mobility and an increase in the risk of overgrazing and environmental degradation, the abandoning of traditional internally managed coping strategies for drought and thus increased reliance on external support and, finally, growing inequalities and out-migration to town or abroad. The latter factor was both a consequence and a further cause of pauperisation, depriving pastoral groups of their main wealth (Abdillahi 1990). Overall, a reduction of the flexibility to adjust to variable conditions undermined the resilience of pastoralists, in particular the poorest ones. Indeed the effects of the severe droughts of 1974–75 were seen as partly generated by this set of phenomena (cf. Lewis 1975).

Scholars tried to represent the increasingly unequal relationship between producers and merchants by studying the long-term fluctuation of the terms of trade of livestock prices vs. food prices bought in exchange by the producers (staple food such as rice, sugar, grains). Although with incomplete historical data, J. Swift (1979) showed a declining long-term trend for pastoralists. In the ensuing discussion, Lewis (1994) argued, referring to Vali Jamal's studies (Jamal 1988), that the bonanza of the Saudi market since the 1950s and the money that the workers in the oil countries started to remit home in the 1970s kept conditions favourable for pastoralists as well. All the authors, however, agreed that the 1980s inaugurated a long period of falling prices and declining conditions. Inflation and the faster increase of import products with respect to export, more than a simple fall in stock prices, were the key factors shaping the whole dynamic. Apart from terms of trade, however, disadvantaged relations were also evident in the fact that pastoralists lacked any control over market prices and credit (Aronson 1980: 20).

Another point of discussion regarded the off-take of animals from pastoralists' herds, considering the huge increase in exports on the one hand and the still subsistence-oriented behaviour of the pastoralists on the other. Among the points highlighted,[6] the progressive enlargement of the purchasing area (gradually including central Somalia and a larger portion of Ethiopian regions) seems particularly relevant, as environmental degradation was more pronounced in the export areas than in those zones less involved with trade (Aronson 1980).

In general, particularly in the contributions of Swift (1979) and Samatar (1989), the analysis was encapsulated into a subsistence/market oriented bi–partition, and their efforts were directed to capturing that particular turning point. More recent and historically oriented approaches have emphasised the ability of pastoralists to readjust constantly to shifting conditions. Access to market in this respect is an option for Somali pastoralists and a decisive factor in coping with drought. Pastoralists' organisation actually keeps track of the succession of these historical contingencies (Little 2003). Even though, in the background, a cumulative and radical transformation continues and the current landscape and practices are very different from those of the past,[7] the above mentioned transformations can be seen in general as adjustment to the peculiar and exceptional requirements of the Saudi Arabian demand, in a context where Somalia, as pointed out by Aronson (1980: 14), 'deepened its status [...] as a satellite to the galloping capitalist economies of the Arabian peninsula.' In this respect, the contemporaneous out-migration towards the oil-rich Gulf economies (Mohamed Salih 1992) represented the second facet of the same phenomenon.

Class analysis and clan behaviour. Authors such as Abdi Ismail Samatar and Dan Aronson brought the issue to a more general level, pointing to a precise divide in the set of inequalities described and to the formation of a differentiated class of merchants and businessmen whose interests were closely connected to state administration. They advocated a shift of analysis from lineage organisation to class and state structures: the effects of the internationalisation of livestock trade have broken, in their view, the unity of lineages and constructed more important rapprochements between traders and parts of the state. Aronson (1980) stressed the common interests of the state and the merchant class. From the state's side such interests relied on hard currency earnings and, through the so-called *Franco Valuta* system, on food imports financed and managed by the exporters, thus saving the state's expenditure capacity for other purposes (ibid.: 20). The relationship was so beneficial as to constitute a real alliance. Yet we must add that such a picture only holds true in the north until the early 1980s and was later overturned by political developments. The proliferation of informal circuits in that period vividly reflects the transfer of much of the economic dynamics and struggles to this shadow zone, wherein both government and businessmen participated. This factor, not taken into account in these analyses, would later give the major clues for understanding the civil war dynamics of the early 1990s, as well as explaining Somali resilience in the post-collapse environment (Reno 2003; Marchal 1996).

In Samatar's (1989: 154–62) description, the merchant class does not appear so homogeneous and united. It is rather composed of different strata of merchants, each one having different interests (he identified 923 export traders operating in Berbera, but only 29 had a dominant position) and in constant competition with each other. In this competition, related to business and to access to the state, the upper class composed of merchants and state bureaucrats tries to acquire the support of their clan group via patronage and manipulation in order to secure a large consensus. This, to put it briefly, corresponds to the definition of clanism given by the author. The critical reference here was the general picture of northern Somali society presented by Lewis (1961 and 1962). In his 1962 article, Lewis portrayed life in the new and emerging towns of Somaliland and the trade activity as strongly shaped and, so to speak, infiltrated by the clanship logic that characterised traditional pastoral society. According to Lewis, the social organisation of pastoralism, based on the clan system, was transferred to the town (and to the state). As reasserted in the 1994 update and in successive publications, the cleavages created by changes in livestock production and the development of the colonial and post-colonial state were somehow re-absorbed into the clan dynamic and its web of reciprocal obligations, instead of the other way around.

The cause of disagreement was the interpretation and representation of the Somali process of social change. New actors came into view, linked to international trade or state administration (and, for instance, to the army, international assistance, or the constitution of migrant communities abroad) and all of them were engaged in new arenas and dynamics: how were these novel dimensions affecting corporate groups? If analysts were applying class logic, were the actors doing the same? The debate highlighted a different way to assess the effects of inequalities and divergent interests on corporate groups: on one side an emphasis on persistence and on the paramount role of segmentary lineage logic, and on the other an effort to see how economic cleavages were replicated in social and political structure. But despite the differences, the two positions also shared a similar theoretical frame vis-à-vis social change, centred on a 'two systems' narration. In Lewis' account, even though he extensively described new evolutions and trends in both politics and the economy, these are seen in opposition to lineage structure, as belonging to a different logic. The point thus was to see which of the two prevailed, or the mutual disturbances and incompatibilities. For Samatar and others, clanism was a deteriorated and corrupted form that was opposed to a somehow pure and original pre-colonial model. In his view agency resided solely in the new elites, and their relationship with clan was one-sided and characterised by manipulation and clientalisation.

In spite of these limitations and the common criticism of the theoretical framework to which they refer,[8] it is nevertheless difficult to evade both the aspects of continuity on the one side and inequality on the other that the two positions were pointing out. Framed along these two axes, the debate still raises important questions regarding relations between the economic and social domains. How do changes in one domain affect the other one? Somehow, it seems extremely difficult in the Somali context to extricate the complex dynamic of resource competition, group formation and group mobilisation from a bi–polar model.[9] The recent debates on clan and politics referring to the civil war events have followed this scheme; they continue to tackle the same unresolved questions.

The nationalistic elite who announced in the early 1960s the advent of modernisation and development also shared a bi–polar model. Looking back at dynamics on the ground, however, one would see that the reproduction of clan dynamics both under the civil government and under the Siyad Barre dictatorship later on occurred within the so-called 'modern' pole. Lineages—leaving aside their implication at the level of personal identity—have always been a paramount and most efficient organising factor in politics and equally extremely efficient in providing jobs, economic assistance and business opportunities.

Whereas growing inequalities were and are apparent, the social and cultural translation of these remains problematic. Factors that have historically pushed for their reabsorption into clan dynamics were related to struggles over personal security and protection, economic redistribution and political inclusion. At the same time, under the influence of internal competition for power or struggles against marginalisation, of shifting equilibriums and the turning of horizontal relations into vertical ones, relationships based on lineages were also modified. Reabsorbed into lineages, social change is re-inscribed in genealogies as pointed out in Djama's study (1995). However, the opposite is also true: as an organisational force lineages do create dynamics. Clarifying these points means engaging with a processually oriented and historically focused ethnography of the articulations, rapprochements, entanglements and disentanglements between the various elements at play and with reference to specific areas of interaction.

Continuities and inequalities in post-war recomposition

Besides theoretical aspects, there are also relevant empirical reasons for reviewing the debate on trade and social change. Several features of trade in northern Somalia distinctively emerge. First, trade is located at the core of the social change process. As a major force of accumulation, it is actually seen as the locus of social change, shaping and transforming several dynamics. It has historically mediated the interface between local and international actors, and produced internal territorial integration and shaped the forms of territoriality (Ciabarri 2007). It has modified people's habits and consumption patterns and, as seen in the role of the merchant class, contributed to structuring of the political realm. As stated in the introduction, the debate has identified structural and recurrent transformations of northern Somali society regarding three main connection points: town/countryside, external/internal markets, and trade/politics. Looking at the creation and consolidation of Somaliland, all these dimensions are evident. In Somaliland, the very fast urbanisation process and the internationalisation of society characterise post-conflict dynamics. Conditions in the countryside have changed dramatically. The conventional references to pastoralism as the 'dominant system of production', which still employs 'the largest part of the population' (APD 2009: 2), are rather doubtful. Despite the long discussion on the topic, there is a big shortage of in-depth and detailed research. Yet, there is significant evidence that substantial changes are underway. Recent reports (APD 2002, 2009) point to land grabbing, erecting of enclosures, proliferation of private water points, deforestation induced by charcoal production, sedentarisation, and growing identification between territory and specific sub-clans. Mounting land conflicts are the result of this rush to land appropriation (APD 2009). Besides the legacy of war and related displacement of population and the uncertainty of land ownership and users' rights, the prolonged ban on Somali livestock by Saudi Arabia partially accounts for such problems.

Interestingly, the same idea of being on the brink of a critical alteration of equilibriums that characterised the older debate on livestock commercialisation is expressed in the literature today. Indeed, such a representation can be also placed in a much longer continuity, if, as Jama Mohamed Jama (2004) brilliantly demonstrated, the same issues were significantly at the core of British colonial officers' anxieties and of public debates at that time. Land grabbing and proliferation of water points in the internal plateau, partly encouraged by the British administration, were described as a reaction to the destabilisation due to the colonial war waged against Maxamed Cabdille Xassan and further conflicts. How can this be understood—as recurrence in local social change representations or recurrence in crisis patterns? Surely, reliable census data today would challenge the longstanding perception of pastoralism as by far the dominant system of production. Patterns of continuity in social change thus regard not only the role of lineages but also the very dynamics of transformation. This is even truer with regard to the two other dimensions mentioned above: the recurrent readjustments of commercial relationships within the wider regional context and the mutually constitutive relationship between trade and politics. I set out now to 'test' these assumptions by discussing in general lines the process of recomposition that eventually led to the formation of Somaliland in the early 1990s.

Reconfiguration of regional markets. While the general contours of the process, taking the perspective of trade relations, have been already pointed out (Marchal 1996, 1999; Bradbury 2003; Ciabarri 2007) and will only be recapitulated here, I would like to stress in particular how a specific form of territorial integration, the commercial corridor, was at the core of such dynamics. The military and political path, which has led to the formation of Somaliland, has received much attention by commentators and scholars (Compagnon 1992; Farah and Lewis 1994; Bradbury 2008). As noted by Bradbury, Somaliland is in this respect essentially a political community originating from the struggle against the central government and consequent war (2008: 50). In addition, however, a 'commercial factor' was at work and proved to be extremely relevant to such dynamics as the stabilisation of the territory, state-building, formation of centres of economic and political power within the new polity and Somaliland's relations with its neighbours.

Three nearly simultaneous political crises—state collapse in Somalia, regime change in Ethiopia, internal instability in Djibouti—coalesced to create new opportunities from the point of view of business. This in turn created the conditions for the emergence of a new business class in Somaliland. Finally, the business dynamics were 'captured back' by a specific political project designed under the guidance of Maxamed Xaaji Ibraahim Cigaal who served as president of the new polity from 1993 until his death in 2002. Two levels of business need attention. One involved big import traders previously based in Djibouti, the other small and medium businessmen importing diverse kinds of items from countries such as Yemen, Dubai or the Far East; among them, many started or restarted business taking advantage of the economy which developed throughout the 1990s in the Ethiopian refugee camps hosting Somalilanders who had fled during the war (Ciabarri 2008). After 1997, together with others, they played a leading role in the reconstruction business that progressively unfolded in Somaliland.

State collapse in Somalia created a completely new social environment. From an economic point of view, this meant a dramatic shift from an environment characterised by heavy state intervention to one entirely free and non-regulated.[10] In the North, the war and the reopening of the port of Berbera liberated by the Isaaq/Ciise Muuse militias of SNM (early 1991) potentially disclosed a new internal market, with regulations and taxation no longer in force, no competition from external actors, and a privileged access to the much larger and remunerative Ethiopian market. The end of the Mengistu regime in Ethiopia in May 1991 meant the reopening of a border previously highly patrolled because of the wars fought in the past between Somalia and Ethiopia. In reality, relationships along the boundary started to change in 1988 with the establishment of the refugee camps. This created smoother relations between Ethiopian authorities and the Somaliland populace. The existence of the refugee camps created business opportunities in the long run. Food aid was exchanged to obtain other much-needed goods. Later exchanges involved much more sophisticated goods, and the refugee camps operated as a kind of umbrella to cover cross-border trade. After the fall of Mengistu the new Ethiopian elite kept a benevolent attitude towards peripheral areas and continued the process of rapprochement, allowing, and to a certain extent probably benefiting from, the cross-border trade as long as the refugee camps remained in place (until the early 2000s).

Traders from northern Somalia who had previously had their centres of business in Mogadishu and whose businesses, because of political patronage, credit or protection, had been linked to the state remained entrapped in that net. They did not get credit any longer; their property was either destroyed or looted. Some of them migrated abroad or just retired from business; others needed time to recover and reappeared only later. A group of Isaaq businessmen based in Djibouti, who had direct links with Somaliland, with the groups that were controlling Berbera (on the basis of past commercial relationships and/or shared clan membership) and in some cases also with the SNM, having backed the rebellion during the war, proved to be better equipped to take up the new opportunity. This group was formed by businessmen who had built their careers in Djibouti, in some cases since the 1950s-60s, in other cases after Siyad Barre came to power in Somalia in 1969. They chose Djibouti as the centre of their business and developed there important companies involved in the importation of basic foods, in particular after Djibouti's independence. Linked to Somaliland, they could also continue relying on credit given by Djibouti banks and had been protected from the destruction and loss of resources which the war brought about in Somalia. On the contrary, they could profit from this same destruction. Together with another prominent businessman (linked to them via a commercial alliance), this group played a dominant role in the economic expansion of exports of livestock and imports of commodities in exchange, which promptly resumed in 1991. After the partial decrease in 1992 (due to internal fighting over the control of Berbera port—a conflict that was named 'the sheep war') the new livestock boom continued until 1998, guaranteeing enormous profits and reaching unprecedented proportions. Berbera port alone surpassed the peaks of the 1970s.[11] Here Djibouti traders and those linked to them acquired market supremacy.

A new ban imposed by Saudi Arabia in 1998 and again from 2000 onward cooled down the trade. With few exceptions, the big businessmen returned to their 'core-business' of importing staple food. Livestock was for them a commodity they dealt with as long as conditions were good. In times of stress they simply abandoned the sector. Currently these businessmen are, for instance, involved in importing construction material, a lucrative business today. As mentioned, this general reconfiguration of market relations involving the whole regional framework intersected with the political trajectory of Somaliland.

Trade and politics in Somaliland. The success of Maxamed Xaaji Ibraahim Cigaal resulted from his ability to bring the revenues of the port of Berbera under the umbrella of the state. It was precisely the failure to carry out this move that had brought about the downfall of the previous government, led by Cabdiraxman Axmed Cali Tuur. His attempt to control Berbera port led in 1992 to an internal war between his government and the local militia belonging to the clan predominantly inhabiting the Berbera area, the Ciise Muuse. The confrontation immediately turned into a war between Tuur's clan (the Habr Yonis) and the Ciise Muuse (plus some allies), with the latter claiming a right to control Berbera. Later, after being elected president at the clan/community-conference (*shir beeleed*) in Borama in 1993, Cigaal, who himself belonged to the Ciise Muuse, managed to establish the control of the state over the port. The key to his success was a commercial pact with the prominent businessmen above mentioned, belonging to his larger tribal group (Isaaq/Habar Awal). These businessmen financed the demobilisation of the militias through distribution of food rations in exchange for tax exemption. They also provided loans to the administration (as well as money for Cigaal's political battles) and support for the printing of the new national currency, the Somaliland Shilling, that was introduced in 1994 (Bradbury 2008: 112). On the side of the businessmen, the advantage was purely commercial, giving them the chance to operate in a pacified environment. The demobilisation of the militias also implied removal of most of the roadblocks.

The support given by this group to the state became a founding characteristic of both market and state organisation in Somaliland. Direct negotiations and a regime of exemption characterised the relationship between state and big business. Furthermore, the pact resulted in a specific encapsulation of port incomes involving the local administration and the presidency in a non-transparent budget. Declared a public asset, Berbera Port Authority was created as an autonomous body directly under the president's office (Bradbury 2008: 111). The pact thus laid the foundations for two kinds of monopolistic positions: on one side that of the businessmen with respect to the internal market, and on the other that of the presidency with respect to the other constitutional powers.

Behind the 'big businessmen', medium and small traders as well as middlemen at various levels operate too. Some of them started their businesses in the refugee camps; others had family assets or collected money through the diaspora or in partnership; others, again, belonged to those who in the 1980s invested in the informal circuits, generally linked to the Gulf countries, where trade was interlinked to remittances.[12] Particularly after 1997, when political problems related to the 1994–95 airport war, to the drawing of a new constitution, and to the new presidential mandate were finally settled (Renders 2006), their activities, based on imports typically from Dubai and the Far East, and services such as money transfer, telecommunications and transport, joined up with the process of reconstruction of the country to shape a long-lasting economic boom centred on the major towns. Through a set of multiplier effects, these forces are now producing a unique urban landscape, and shaping Somaliland in new forms as a territory and a community. Operating along the commercial corridors crossing Somaliland and linking it to Ethiopia on one side and the Middle and Far East on the other, the import activity also nourishes a considerable informal trade with Ethiopia. Not only food but also the latest electronic equipment, furniture, household appliances, computers and TVs are traded.

The pivotal elements of this economy are, first, the major cities—Hargeysa, Burco, Boorama—whose populations have roughly tripled since the pre-war period. Building a new life after the civil war was perceived as easier in town than in the countryside. Similarly, the return of the population from the Ethiopian refugee camps and from the further diaspora in the Western countries and the Arab states focused primarily on the big cities rather than on smaller villages and the countryside. Secondly, there is the post-war reconstruction business, involving houses, transport and services. Some of the cities, such as Hargeysa and Burco, had been extensively destroyed during the civil war and required rebuilding. New houses are also built for the new inhabitants and for those still living abroad, for a future return or for investment, expanding the boundaries of the cities on an unprecedented scale. Thirdly, the new remittance economy (Jamal 1988; Ahmed 2000) generated by the war diaspora (Farah *et al.* 2007; Kusow and Bjork 2007; Lindley 2009). Remittances, of course, are sustaining all these investments. Their effect, however, is multiplied because of the specific receiving environment—the open border with Ethiopia, limited taxation, post-war opportunities and post-war reconstruction. The material results of these interconnections are building activity, extensive development of information technologies and vibrant cross-border trade.

Of course, under the present conditions of a remittance economy and the circumstance of a prolonged livestock ban, import activity is all the more important and central. Imports and import companies dominate the contours of current economic activity. Mirroring the web of agents that radiated from Berbera in search of export livestock, an equivalent web of brokers is radiating from Somaliland to the new business hot spots for the importation of consumer goods, such as Dubai, Thailand and now especially China. The interlacing of all these combined factors has created the foundations for a transit or entrepot economy (Little 2003) and a commercial state (Ciabarri 2007) based on a combination, along the market chain, of low taxation, smuggling, and legal as well as informal tax–free areas. Somehow, an unintended form of readjustment from the narrow dependency on the Gulf zone unfolded, most of all with the emergence of Ethiopia as a fundamental market and the consequent need to find new political arrangements with the cumbersome neighbour. Similarly, the labour diaspora previously concentrated mostly in the Middle East countries became a forced diaspora following the war. Somalis now reside, literally, all over the world.

With all this, the debate on social change, which previously focused narrowly on the livestock trade, is now more and more widened. It potentially involves such topics as the effect of the diaspora and remittance economy, for instance on consumption practices, lifestyles and dynamics of emulation, as well as topics like religious change, thus mirroring the further pathways taken by Somali modernity. Nonetheless, the axes of continuity and inequality will remain central to the debate. Continuity is for instance apparent in the globalisation of the segmentary logic, permeating and regulating the web of connections that links traders and brokers over and across the continents. Inequalities are even more noticeable looking at the formation of monopolies of power in economy and politics, and at the substantial differences in access to the internationalisation process and to international mobility that persist and increase between the inhabitants of Somaliland.

Notes

1. If not indicated differently, I will use the 1994 version throughout the chapter.
2. I am referring to the well-known disputes involving such authors as C. Besteman, V.L. Cassanelli, B. Helander, I.M. Lewis, and Ah.I. Samatar. Schlee (2002 and 2008), who discussed the clan/politics issue in terms of resources vs. actors, has recently expressed the need to combine the two dimensions into a single analysis.
3. However, considering only sheep and goats, northern Somalia's specialisation, the peak was reached in 1972 (1,635,000 head) and there was no recovery after the 1974–75 drought (Samatar 1989: 123) until the economic rally of the 1990s—see last paragraph.
4. Egypt, the United Arab Emirates and Yemen are other markets. During the Hajj mainly sheep are sold, though trade normally includes also cattle and camels.
5. Bans were established from 1984 onward on cattle and later on in 1998 and again from 2000 onward including sheep and goats.
6. These were an increase in animals number due to augmented veterinary assistance, pastoralists' out-migration, and a more efficient herding management and purchasing organisation
7. Indeed, transformations in the countryside are related to larger phenomena, such as the attraction exercised by big towns, in terms of salaries, lifestyles and better medical and education services. Modernisation policies also played a role. If many sources indicate the 1974–75 drought as the time of exit from pastoralism, others for instance also point to the unintended effects of the quasi–contemporary literacy campaign as crucial factor. At the same time environmental degradation was caused, as always, not only by economic but also by political factors (Markakis 1993; Jama Mohamed Jama 2004; APD 2002, 2009).
8. Such as the normative stand of the British functionalist school, and the use of too large aggregates—class, state—with limited empirical reference of the political economy approach.
9. Djama (1997) correctly pointed out some technical questions that prevented further advances: in particular the extreme difficulty of carrying out field research in the Siyad Barre period (and I would add during the civil war as well) and the ban on clan references at that time. A further factor may be the peculiarity of the clan system as a form of knowledge that constantly, in front of empirical facts, confirms itself and potentially can wrap up in a logically conclusive form any social dynamics.
10. Editors' note: On the existing informal economy and its contribution to coping with statelessness after 1991 see Healy, this volume.
11. According to the Somaliland Chamber of Commerce, the number of sheep and goats exported from Berbera exceeded two million.
12. From these circuits other 'big names' of the Somaliland economy emerged, involved in money transfer, telecommunications and air transport. They

are now international companies operating in various markets in the Somali lands and elsewhere.

References

Abdullahi, Ahmed M. 1990. *Pastoral Production Systems in Africa: A Study of Nomadic Household Economy and Livestock Marketing in Central Somalia*. Kiel: Wissenschaftsverlag Vauk.

Ahmed, Ali J. (ed.) 1995. *The Invention of Somalia*. Lawrenceville, NJ: The Red Sea Press.

Ahmed, Ismail 2000. 'Remittances and their Economic Impact in Post-war Somaliland.' *Disasters*, 24 (4), 380–9.

Aronson, Dan 1980. 'Kinsmen and Comrades: Toward a Class Analysis of the Somali Pastoral Sector.' *Nomadic Peoples*, 11, 14–23.

APD Academy for Peace and Development 2002. *Regulating the Livestock Economy of Somaliland*. Hargeysa (Somaliland).

——— 2009. *No more 'Grass grown by the Spear'. Addressing Land-based Conflicts in Somaliland*. Hargeysa (Somaliland).

Baumann, Maximilian PO, Jörg Janzen and Horst J. Schwartz (eds) 1993. *Pastoral Production in Central Somalia*. Eschborn: GTZ.

Bohannan, Paul and George Dalton (eds) 1962. *Markets in Africa*. Evanston: Northwestern University Press.

Bradbury, Marc 2008. *Becoming Somaliland*. London: James Currey/ Progressio.

Cassanelli, Lee V. 1982. *The Shaping of Somali Society*. Philadelphia University Press.

Ciabarri, Luca 2008. 'Productivity of Refugee Camps: Social and Political Dynamics from the Somaliland-Ethiopia Border (1988–2001).' *Afrika Spectrum*, 43 (1), 67–90.

——— 2007. *The Commercial Factor in Somaliland State Building and Territorial Integration*. Paper presented at the Tenth International Congress of the Somali Studies Association, Part II, Djibouti.

Compagnon, Daniel 1992. 'Dynamiques de mobilisation, dissidence armée et rébellion populaire: le cas du Mouvement National Somali (1981–1990).' *Africa*, 47 (4), 503–30.

Dalleo, Peter T. 1975. 'Trade and Pastoralism: Economic Factors in the History of the Somali of Northeastern Kenya, 1892–1948.' (unpublished PhD Thesis, Syracuse University)

Djama, Marcel 1995. *L'espace, le lieu. Les cadres du changement social en pays nord-somali. La plaine du Hawd (1884–1990)*. (PhD Thesis) Paris: EHESS.

——— 1997. 'Trajectoire du pouvoir en pays somali.' *Cahiers d'Etudes Africaines*, 146, (37) 2, 403–28.

Farah, Ahmed Y. and Ioan M. Lewis 1997. 'Making Peace in Somaliland.' *Cahiers d'Etudes Africaines*, 146, (37) 2, 349–77.

Farah, Abdulkadir O., Mammo Muchie and Joakim Gundel (eds) 2007. *Somalia: Diaspora and State Reconstitution in the Horn of Africa*. London: Adonis & Abbey.

Geshekter, Charles L. 1984. 'Anti–Colonialism and Class Formation: the Horn of Africa before 1950.' In T. Labahn (ed.) *Proceedings of the Second International Congress of Somali Studies*. Hamburg: Buske, pp. 217–65.

Jamal, Vali 1988. 'Somalia: Understanding an Unconventional Economy.' *Development & Change*, 19, 203–65.

Kusow, Abdi M. and Stephanie R. Bjork (eds) 2007. *From Mogadishu to Dixon: the Somali Diaspora in a Global Context*. Trenton, NJ: The Red Sea Press.

Lewis, Ioan M. 1961. *A Pastoral Democracy: a Study of Pastoralism and Politics among the Northern Somali of the Horn of Africa*. London: Oxford University Press.

——— 1994. 'Lineage Continuity and Commerce in Northern Somaliland.' In I.M. Lewis *Blood and Bone: the Call of Kinship in Somali Culture*. Lawrenceville, NJ: The Red Sea Press, pp. 113–32.

——— (ed.) 1975. *Abaar. The Somali Drought*. London: International African Institute.

Lindley, Anna 2009. 'The Early-Morning Phonecall: Remittances from a Refugee Diaspora Perspective.' *Journal of Ethnic and Migration Studies*, 35 (8), 1315–34.

Little, Peter D. 2003. *Somalia: Economy without State*. Oxford: James Currey.

Marchal, Roland 1996. *The Post Civil War Somali Business Class*. Paris: EHESS.

——— 1999. 'Des contresens possibles de la globalisation. Privatisation de l'État et bienfaisance au Soudan et au Somaliland.' *Politique Africaine*, 73, pp. 68–81.

Markakis, John (ed.) 1993. *Conflict and the Decline of Pastoralism in the Horn of Africa*. London: Macmillan.

Mohamed, Jama 2004. 'The Political Ecology of Colonial Somaliland.' *Africa*, 74 (4), 534–66.

Mohamed, Salih M.A. (ed.) 1992. *The Least Developed and the Oil-rich Arab Countries*. New York: St. Martin's Press.

Renders, Marleen 2006. "Traditional' Leaders and Institutions in the Building of the Muslim Republic of Somaliland.' (PhD thesis). Ghent: Universiteit Gent.

Reno, William 2003. *Somalia and Survival in the Shadow of the Global Economy*. QEH Working Paper Series, 100.

Samatar, Ahmed I. 1989. *The State and the Rural Transformations in Northern Somalia, 1884–1986*. Madison: University of Wisconsin Press.

Samatar, Abdi, Lance Salisbury and Jonathan Bascom 1988. 'The Political Economy of Livestock Marketing in Northern Somalia.' *African Economic History*, 17, 81–98.

Schlee, Günther 2002. 'Régularités dans le chaos: Traits récurrents dans l'organisation politico-religieuse et militaire des Somali.' *L'Homme*, 161, 17–49.

——— 2008. *How Enemies are Made: Towards a Theory of Ethnic and Religious Conflicts*. New York: Berghahn.

Swift, Jeremy 1979. 'The Development of Livestock Trading in Nomad Pastoral Economy: the Somali Case.' In Equipe Ecologie et Anthropologie des Sociétés Pastorales (eds) *Pastoral Production and Society/ Production pastorale et société*. Cambridge Univeristy Press/Paris: Editions de la Maison des Sciences de l'Homme, pp. 447–65.

6

THE QUESTION OF ETHNICITY IN SOMALI STUDIES

THE CASE OF SOMALI BANTU IDENTITY

Ken Menkhaus

Introduction

Of all the contributions to Somali studies made by Professor I.M. Lewis, none has evoked as much passionate debate as his treatment of the role of clan and ethnicity in Somali society and politics. For Lewis' detractors, the prominence he gives clan as a driver of political behaviour and social affiliation is reductionist and primordialist. For others, Lewis' work on clans and clanism is an indispensable road-map of Somali society as they experience it on the ground.

This debate over how to understand clanism and ethnic identity in Somalia frames both academic research and more immediate political and policy discussions in the country. The issue is partly theoretical and academic—the 'primordialist versus constructivist' debate. It is partly a matter of historical baggage, namely the enduring taint of anthropological work conducted on clans and tribes in the service of European colonial administration, and the subsequent efforts of social scientists to distance themselves from open discussion of tribe and clan. But it is also a normative, political, and ideological struggle, in which scholars are torn between a professional allegiance to analytic precision—regardless of its political impact—and a normative commitment to harness their scholarly writing to advance what they believe to be a laudable political objective, be it national unity, peace building, or some other objective. Put another way, the debate over the treatment of clanism partly reflects a disagreement over whether social science research stands apart from or is inextricably part of the political dynamics it attempts to assess. For some, discussion of clanism and ethnic identity is criticised not only because it is believed to be devoid of explanatory value, but also because highlighting clanism risks reinforcing what some activist scholars understandably see as a highly pernicious and divisive force which must be overcome, not enshrined, in Somali affairs. And although analysts and practitioners alike often try to sidestep it, sometimes by using politically correct code-words like 'constituencies', and 'social groupings' or by referring to regional identity as a surrogate for clan, taking a position on how to handle clanism is unavoidable. Not to choose is to choose.

Ironically, the very topic that sparked the most debate arising from Professor Lewis' writings has seen the least progress in subsequent academic research on Somalia. Our ability to produce a more nuanced and accurate approach to clanism and ethnic identity in our explanations of Somali politics has been hampered by what amounts to a false choice, one in which ethnic identity has typically been either clumsily reified or ignored completely, and in which academic exchanges about the question of Somali ethnic identity have at times been vitriolic, frightening off young scholars from taking thoughtfully critical positions on the matter. Even when more nuanced explanations of clanism and ethnicity in Somali history and politics have been produced—and there are a number of noteworthy recent contributions in this regard, including the works of Luling (2006), Barnes (2006), Hagmann (2007), Gundel (2006), and Hoehne (2009), to name but a few—they have had little success penetrating broader political analysis and policy discourse, a problem that is not unique to Somali studies (Chandra 2001: 7).

This chapter does not pretend to resolve the debate, but aspires only to serve as an invitation to others to explore the rich theoretical and empirical space lying between the primordialist-constructivist divide as it pertains to the Somali case.[1] It draws on the rise of Somali Bantu identity as a fascinating case study which appears to both bolster and challenge key tenets of both neo-primordialist and constructivist claims. Its main argument can be summarised as follows. Constructivists are correct to claim that ethnic identity in Somalia is indeed 'constructed', 'invented', and 'imagined', and clanism is far more fluid and flexible than most outsiders realise. But years of political manipulation, warfare, atrocities, ethnic cleansing, and new political configurations (including the consociational system of representation known as the 4.5–formula) have unquestionably mobilised and hardened clan identity to an extent that one cannot conduct a serious analysis of Somali politics at either the national or the local level without treating clanism as one of the main drivers of behaviour.

This is not to advocate a reductionist explanation of Somali politics, which is far too complex to explain by way of any single factor. Nor is it an implicit endorsement of political proposals designed to enshrine or institutionalise clanism in systems of representation and government in Somalia; that too is a vastly complex matter that does not lend itself to simple solutions. My line of argument—that ethnic identity in contemporary Somalia is at once fluid, invented, contested, mobilised, hardened, and central to calculations of survival at both household and political level—is frustratingly ambiguous and deeply unsatisfying for those seeking a more parsimonious explanation of Somali affairs. But it reflects the messy and complex social and political realities of the country. And it is particularly essential to understanding of local level, informal political systems in Somalia, which, in the absence of a functional state for twenty years, are the only political systems in place in the country.

Lewis and the primordialist-constructivist debate

From the early 1960s through the 1980s, Lewis' works dominated the field of Somali studies and served as the point of reference for anything else written on the country. And while his work *A Modern History of Somaliland* (1965), whose most recent and enlarged edition is called *A Modern History of the Somali* (2002), was probably more widely read, it was *A Pastoral Democracy* (1961) that had the most interesting implications for our understanding of ethnic identity in Somali society. The implications of Lewis' portrait of how a stateless society managed 'anarchy'—to deter war, resolve conflicts, and share access to resources—were immediate and profound for those of us studying international relations, a discipline preoccupied by the issue of conflict and cooperation in a context of global anarchy. Clan, of course, was the main unit of analysis in Lewis' work, and the interests and behaviour of clans were central to management of 'anarchy'. Clan identity was inextricably woven into the working of blood-payment groups which deterred crime and resolved disputes. Threats of retaliation by clans provided some modicum of physical protection for clan members. *Xeer* or customary law governed relations between clans in roughly the same imperfect manner that international law and international regimes provide some level of order in international politics. And the strong ethos of mutual obligation within lineages provided households with an invaluable form of social security in a risky production environment.

The primacy of clanism as the bedrock of social organisation in this portrait of Somali society, and the inescapability of lineage identity in Somalia society, certainly qualify Lewis' work as a 'primordialist' interpretation of Somali ethnic identity (Samatar 2003). He seems to have actively invited this label by naming one of his later books on Somalia *Blood and Bone* (1994), a study which for the most part essentialises clan. But it is worth noting that several aspects of his portrait of Somali identity actually serve to support a constructivist interpretation. The first is the central importance of fluidity in clan identity: which clan or sub-clan matters in a Somali's lineage is entirely situational and shifts according to the issue at hand. Secondly, Lewis documents the practice of *sheegat* or adoption into a clan, a phenomenon especially prevalent in the settled agricultural areas of southern Somalia. Thirdly, Lewis' overall portrait of the Somali political culture—one dominated by pragmatism, negotiation, and survivalism in a difficult environment—reinforces the idea that clan identity is used instrumentally by Somali populations seeking to negotiate their survival and access to resources. This too is a central tenet of constructivist theories of ethnic identity.

My own doctoral field research, in pre-war Somalia's Lower Jubba Valley, was not initially informed by considerations of ethno-politics of any sort, though I had read Lewis' works closely. Like most of my peers in the 1980s, I was a product of an academic environment dominated by political economy approaches, and so was trained to approach the question of land, production, and the state through that prism. As a consequence of that socialisation process, I uncritically accepted the dismissal of the earlier scholarship of cultural anthropologists and their fellow travellers in political science who reified ethnic identity and whose writing incautiously echoed the discredited tone of colonial administrators. As a result, in preparing for my fieldwork, I intentionally downplayed matters of clan and ethnic identity, and kept a quiet distance from the ideas and analyses of scholars like Professor Lewis. Of course I was well aware that the communities I was to study in the Lower Jubba Valley were an ethnically distinct and subordinate people known then as the Gosha, *reer-goleed*, or *timo-jareer* (hard-hairs), who as descendents of East African slaves endured second-class status in Somali society. But analytically, I approached these riverine populations as peasants and smallholders, and their plight as one related to exploitation at the hands of a 'state class'.

The realities I encountered on the ground, first in the Jubba valley in 1988 and then in subsequent work in emergency relief in 1991 and in the 1993–94 UN peace operation in Somalia, forced me to reconsider. Clanism permeated political dynamics at the national level, while local level governance and society was almost entirely based on ethnic, sub-clan, and/or tribal affiliation. Of all of my encounters with identity politics in Somalia, none was as dramatic, and none was as impervious to pure primordialist or constructivist interpretations, as the case of the people who came to be known as the Somali Bantu.

Identity politics and the Bantu of the Lower Jubba Valley

Until 1990, Somalia was routinely portrayed as one of the few countries in Africa where nation and state were synonymous, an island of ethnic homogeneity in a sea of multi–ethnic states.[2] The country's collapse into extended clan warfare in 1990, and subsequent international attention to the plight of Somali 'minorities' as principal famine and war victims, shattered that myth. One such minority, the Somali Bantu, attracted special attention. In 2002, 12,000 Somali Bantu refugees in Kenya were targeted for resettlement in the US; they were one of the largest refugee groups to receive blanket permission for resettlement to the US in decades. This policy was based on the conclusion that the Bantu face chronic discrimination, are weak and vulnerable to predatory attacks and abuse by ethnic Somalis, and hence cannot be safely repatriated back into lawless Somalia. For the Somali Bantu, this transformation from a virtually unknown minority to a category of Somali society receiving preferential treatment in international refugee resettlement was an extraordinary turn of events.

Aside from the conventional wisdom that the Bantu are among the most vulnerable communities in Somalia, few observers outside a very small group of Somali intellectuals and foreign area specialists know anything more about this minority group, which is estimated to constitute roughly five per cent of the total population of Somalia. Most international observers and relief agencies would be surprised to learn that the notion of the 'Somali Bantu', which they take for granted, never existed prior to 1991. They would be even more surprised to discover that the ethnic category of Somali Bantu was an inadvertent creation of the international community—specifically, aid agencies and the media. For social scientists who subscribe to constructivist theories of ethnic identity, the case of the Somali Bantu appears to be attractive grist for their mill. It is hard to make a primordialist case for an ethnic identity which is little more than fifteen years old. How an ethnic identity could so quickly and powerfully come into existence, and then harden in such a way that it looks to be a relatively permanent fixture in the Somali political landscape, is the story this chapter traces.

Minorities, ethnicity, and nomenclature in the Somali context

Discussion of the status of minorities in Somalia is complicated by genuine confusion over what actually constitutes a 'minority' in the Somali context. This confusion has been exacerbated by the scramble by Somali asylum seekers to assert minority status (legitimately and fraudulently), in order to improve their chances of being accepted as refugees. In reality, Somalia features a range of different social groups with variable claims on being a minority. One minority category consists of communities which are ethnically non-Somali, meaning that they have no affiliation (client or otherwise) to a Somali clan. This includes several diverse groups, including the southern Somali coastal commercial populations of the Barawan, Reer Benadiri, and Bajuni. Another minority category is that of Somalis who enjoy membership in a clan, but occupy a low status position within that lineage. There are many variations on this complex spectrum of social hierarchy, including occupational minorities—low-caste groups within every Somali clan known variously as the Yibir, Midgaan, and Tumaal, which have historically been linked to 'unclean' occupations such as hair-cutting and metal-work. A third group are lineages which are considered 'commoner' (*boon*) as opposed to 'noble' (*bilis*). Among the Rahanweyn clan-family, Bernhard Helander estimated that up to

30 per cent of the population falls into the category of *boon* (Helander 1996: 51–2). A final group in this category are *sheegat* or adopted clan members in various stages of absorption. The use of *sheegat* is especially common in southern Somalia, where high rates in migration occur and where newcomers must seek protection by adopting the identity of more powerful local lineages (Helander 2003).

Nomenclature for these minority groups in general, and for the Bantu in particular, has been an additional source of confusion. This is partly because the Bantu, like many minority groups, have always been named by others. Only two group names currently carry no pejorative connotations. The first, 'Bantu', is a label applied to the group by foreigners since 1990, and quickly adopted inside Somalia. Ironically, only one so-called Bantu community, the Mushunguli people of the Lower Jubba valley, actually uses a Bantu language, so this linguistic appellation is somewhat misleading. In fact, some Jareer communities, particularly those in the Middle Shabelle and Hiran regions, are resisting use of the new term Bantu on grounds that they have never spoken a Bantu language. The second name, Jareer, is a more accurate group name, as it alludes to the one feature distinguishing the Somali Bantu from ethnic Somalis—namely, their tight or hard curled hair. The term *jareer* is now widely used by the Somali Bantu themselves, and carries no pejorative connotations; indeed, the name is employed with a certain sense of pride, perhaps because of its double meaning (suggesting both hardness of hair and hardness of the people themselves).

The unlikelihood of Somali Bantu identity

The rise of Somali Bantu identity is remarkable not only for its rapidity, but also because the community possesses almost none of the features typically associated with a cohesive ethnic group. First, Somali Bantu communities share no common language or dialect. Because most of the Bantu population is concentrated in the inter-riverine area of the south, the most common language used by Bantu is the *Af-Maay* dialect associated with that region and with the Digil-Rahanweyn. But some Bantu communities, such as the Makanne in Hiran region, speak *Af-Maxaa*, or 'standard' Somali (see Mukhtar in this volume on language differences and politics). One Bantu group, the Mushunguli of the Lower Jubba valley, retains a Bantu tongue (*Ki–Zegua*) as its first language. Finally, a stretch of riverine Bantu communities in parts of the Middle Jubba region use *af-Maay* as their first language but understand Swahili.

The Bantu also share no common geographical homeland in Somalia. Although they are concentrated along the Jubba and Shabelle rivers in southern Somalia, they are also numerous in the inter-riverine regions of Bay and Bakool, and even exist in very small numbers (mainly as fishermen) in northern coastal towns. Urban migration starting in the 1970s increased the number of Bantu living in Mogadishu and Kismaayo. Massive displacement caused by war and state collapse in the 1990s has dramatically increased the outflow of rural Bantu to large cities, where they hope to secure access to aid. Displaced Bantu are now thought to be the single largest group in Kismaayo. Economic duress has also led to a small but growing migration of Bantu into central and northern Somalia, where they work in towns as casual labourers.

The Somali Bantu have no shared history. One portion of Somali Bantu are descendants of East African slaves brought to Somalia in the 19th century, while others are 'first people' predating the Somali expansion into southern Somalia centuries ago (Cassanelli 1982). In some cases, a Bantu community's origins are clearly known—the Makanne of Hiran region are an aboriginal group, while the Mushunguli of the Lower Jubba are descendants of enslaved Zegua people of northern Tanzania. But in other cases aboriginal Bantu and descendants of slaves are mixed in common lineages, especially in the Lower Shabelle region, among for instance the Jiddu, Biimaal, and Geledi clans (Luling 1984). Because the history of enslavement carries a stigma, some Bantu claiming aboriginal status are unenthusiastic about embracing a common identity with Bantu descended from slaves.

In addition, Bantu communities are internally subdivided by the status of their affiliation within Somali lineage system. Some have tribal identities outside the Somali lineage, while others are fully assimilated in a Somali clan. Those retaining separate tribal identities include both aboriginal groups and descendants of slaves. In some instances, Bantu communities retain a distinct tribal identity but have developed an association or federation with a nearby Somali clan, usually as a client of some sort (Lewis 1955: 39–42, 127). These associations with Somali lineages can range from minimalist (mainly ritualistic acknowledgement of a *suldaan*) to substantial (*diya*-paying obligations), and can shift in significance over time. One of the more intriguing political aspects of the recent mobilisation of Bantu ethnic identity is the extent to which this will weaken some of the federated relationships which many Bantu groups have with Somali clans.

Finally, those Bantu which have retained a distinct group identity (either autonomous from Somali lineage or as a federated group within a lineage) are themselves divided into distinct units which play a far more functional role in their everyday lives than does their Bantu identity. In the Jubba valley, they include the Mushunguli, the Shambara (which in turn is subdivided into up to twelve East African tribes such as the Yao and MaKua), and the Gabaweyn (an aboriginal group in Gedo region). These highly localised social identities are the basis for systems of mutual obligations, customary law, allocation of land, and other forms of local governance.

The picture which emerges from this portrait of the Somali Bantu is that of a highly diverse group with no shared history nor, until recently, even any shared knowledge of one another. Most of these groups lived in riverine or inter-riverine enclaves and had few opportunities for meaningful contact with one another. Their enthusiasm for a common Bantu identity varies, with Jareer from the Jubba valley much more assertive about the identity than Jareer from the upper reaches of the Shabelle river. The tie that binds them is above all else the discriminatory attitude of ethnic Somalis towards countrymen with an 'African', as opposed to Somali, ethnic heritage. They are a distinct group because the dominant ethnic group in the land treats them so.

This portrait also underscores the fact that Somali Bantu identity is a cross-cutting ethnic label, one of several social identities which a Somali Jareer can invoke. A Somali Jareer can now simultaneously embrace identity as a Somali (by citizenship), as a member of a Somali lineage, as a member of a Bantu group federated to that Somali lineage, and as a member of the 'Somali Bantu'. Each of these identities can carry costs and opportunities, depending on the situation at hand. As Lewis has extensively documented and as constructivists would persuasively argue, Somalis—and Somali Bantu—are adept at using identity politics as a tool to advance their interests.

History of the Somali Bantu in the 20th century

In the pre-colonial era, the status of the Somali Jareer was very low. There were exceptions. Some freed slave (*watoro*) communities established themselves in the forested riverine areas of the Lower and Middle Jubba. Some aboriginal Bantu groups, such as the Makanne and Shidle, maintained considerable cohesion and were powerful enough to maintain political autonomy from, and minimise predatory raids by, surrounding pastoralists.[3] But most Somali Jareer lived in a state of either enslavement (especially along the lower Shabelle river, in the 19th century) or serfdom.

The arrival of colonialism, and the gradual establishment of a central administrative state, changed but did not necessarily improve this situation. The most dramatic improvement was the abolition of slavery by the Italian colonialists. But colonial law never interfered with traditional practices of serfdom imposed by powerful Somali lineages on the Bantu. And by the 1920s the colonial authorities began expropriating riverine land for Italian plantations, setting in motion a long process of state-sponsored land alienation which hit Bantu farming communities especially hard. In tandem with land expropriation were state policies designed to coerce labour from Bantu villages onto the plantations. This eventually produced the infamous *colonia* period of forced labour from 1935 to 1941 (Menkhaus 1989: 252–62).

In the 1950s, as Somalia was prepared for independence under the tutelage of a UN Trusteeship, Somali Jareer were under no illusions that the transition from colonial to post-colonial state would improve their situation. The Somali Bantu feared that an independent state dominated by ethnic Somalis would perpetuate and even worsen the exploitation visited on them by the state. This fear was shared by other weak clans and minorities who formed a coalition in the Xisbia Dastuur Muustaqiil Soomaali (XDMS) political party opposing the dominant Somali Youth League (SYL). For the Somali Bantu, choosing to support the SYL was not even an option, as the SYL's early membership criteria excluded non-Somalis (Menkhaus 1989: 298). Although the SYL earned the reputation as the nationalist party and Xisbia is remembered as 'tribal', from the perspective of the Bantu the SYL's chauvinistic version of nationalism appeared to be more exclusive than inclusive. At the core of Somali Bantu political anxieties over an independent state was land. The colonial era had already served notice that commercial agriculture placed a high value on irrigable riverine land; a significant portion of Bantu farmland had been expropriated without compensation along parts of the lower and middle Shabelle river valley, and in the lower Jubba region. The Bantu recognised early on the paradox that they, a powerless social group, occupied riverine land which was increasingly viewed as a valuable asset. It would not be long before that contradiction would be resolved by further land grabs. The only solution the Bantu could see was some sort of political autonomy from the more powerful Somali clans, a position which coincided with the Xisbia platform calling for a federal system guaranteeing 'full regional autonomy' (Castagno 1959: 359). Ominously, the SYL promptly denounced this proposal as 'high treason' (Castagno 1964: 534).

In the 1970s and 1980s, the Bantu's worst fears were realised, as state-sponsored land expropriations dispossessed one Bantu village after another of valuable riverine land. The state farms also triggered a major settlement of ethnic Somalis employed by them into Bantu areas, which was viewed locally as a form of internal colonialism. A second form of land expropriation was via individual abuse of land registration laws. This massive land grab in the 1980s, in which Bantu villagers were dispossessed of thousands of hectares of prime farmland by Somali civil servants and others who manipulated a process of land registration to take legal deeds of land they had often never seen, is extensively documented elsewhere (Besteman and Cassanelli 1996; Menkhaus 1989). What is important for our purposes is simply to observe that the state served not as an instrument of protection and rule of law for the Bantu, but rather as an instrument by which powerful ethnic Somalis expropriated the Bantu's land, not by force of arms but with bureaucracy and legal documents. By the late 1980s, most Jareer communities in Somalia found themselves weaker, poorer, and worse off than at any time in history.

The post-1990 crisis and the rise of a Bantu identity

The crises of state collapse, protracted warfare, lawlessness, and famine in the early 1990s hit Bantu Somalis as hard as any social group in the country. When residual government forces (mainly of the President Siyad Barre's Marrexaan clan) fled Mogadishu in January 1991 to the Kismaayo and Gedo region, they looted and attacked inter-riverine communities as they passed. It was the first taste of two years of repeated attack, occupation, looting, assault, and forced labour imposed on a 'shatter zone' of mainly farming communities between Mogadishu and the Jubba valley. The militias of the Hawiye clan's

United Somali Congress (USC) and the Darood clan militias in the Somali Patriotic Movement (SPM) and Somali National Front (SNF) increasingly fought not so much to win but to gain control of villages in order to loot them.

The lawlessness and atrocities associated with this period are well known, and need not be detailed here. What is important to underscore here is that the groups which suffered most from this period of banditry, warfare, criminality, and eventually starvation were the weak, largely unarmed clans and social groups in the riverine and inter-riverine areas. The Bantu were prominent members of this class of victims, looted and assaulted by all sides and with no means of protecting themselves. Even Jareer who had affiliation in a Somali clan were afforded little protection; indeed, Jareer were often looted by their own Somali clan members, and were denied access to emergency relief by clan elders and leaders from more powerful lineages. Food aid had become a principal target of looting, and those who were starving were the bait that attracted the emergency relief. Even during the UNOSOM intervention, Somali militias jostled for control over Bantu internally-displaced persons (IDP) camps, in order to divert the food aid delivered there. Now that they were dispossessed of all they had, the Bantu's destitution itself became a commodity to exploit.

International relief agencies operating in the famine of southern Somalia in 1991—mainly the International Committee of the Red Cross (ICRC) and a handful of NGOs—were quick to realise that food aid was failing to reach certain social groups, chief among them the *jareer*. Reports identifying 'vulnerable groups' in the famine began to make reference to the 'Bantu', shorthand for the Somali farmers with black African physical features who were descendants of Bantu-speaking slaves (Menkhaus 1991). As media coverage of the famine intensified in 1992, journalists appropriated the term from aid agencies, and dozens of stories were filed about the racial dimensions of the Somali famine. In the eyes of the external world, if not yet inside Somalia, a new ethnic category was taking shape.

Among the mainly Western relief workers, a sense of outrage grew at what appeared to be the complete indifference of ethnic Somalis to the suffering of weaker groups such as the Bantu. The outrage eventually led to a chorus of calls for armed intervention. But the question 'how can you starve your own people?', which was sometimes directed by reporters at militia and clan leaders, was based on a false premise.

The Bantu and other low-status groups were not 'their own people'; in the logic of lineage-based societies, these groups were 'others' for whom they bore no particular responsibility.

This point is critical, because it suggests that the virtual holocaust visited upon low-status groups such as the Jareer in 1991 and 1992 was not just a tragic result of warlords and young gunmen run amok; it was also the result of conscious decisions by clan elders and militia leaders over who lived and who died, an 'allocation of pain' which reflected the ethics and logic of the existing social order in crisis, and which betrayed the fact that low status members of the clan simply did not matter enough to live. For our purposes, it also underscores the point that, while 'being Bantu' is very much a constructed ethnic identity in contemporary Somalia, it was hardly inconsequential. Who you were and what lineage and ethnic category you fell into was literally a matter of life and death in southern Somalia in 1991–92.

For the Jareer, the horrors of the Somali war and famine became the source of a deep store of grievances against the rest of Somali society and were an important catalyst for the mobilisation and hardening of a Somali Bantu identity. But the rapid and dramatic rise of Bantu identity in Somalia has been fuelled by other factors as well. One is economic. The relief agencies' practice of identifying vulnerable groups and trying to target them for privileged assistance set a precedent with important local repercussions—it conferred an economic value on being Bantu. Since international aid was one of the few sources of sustenance and employment in southern Somalia in those years, this was not inconsequential. Once the famine ended and aid agencies could devote more attention to rehabilitation or post-conflict assistance, being Bantu had the *potential* to mean getting privileged access to whatever resources were being doled out—food-for-work, training, education, jobs. In some cases, militias have been clever enough to recognise the economic value accorded to the Bantu and use them as bait for aid programmes. One of the most distressing and recurring instances of this predatory behaviour is control over Bantu IDP camps in major cities, which attract food aid that 'camp managers' divert.

Another factor reinforcing the rise of Bantu identity is political. Ever since the UN peace operation entered Somalia in 1992, external diplomats have sought to convene representatives of Somali society to broker an accord over national reconciliation and the revival of a central government. During UNOSOM, political factions—thinly disguised clan entities—were the preferred units of representation of the Somali people. To ensure a place at the bargaining table, where coalitions were formed and positions of power allocated, Somali clans scrambled to establish factions of their own. The Bantu were no exception. In early 1992, a group of Jareer intellectuals and political figures established the SAMO (Somali African Muki Organisation) faction as the exclusive voice of the Bantu/Jareer people. SAMO became one of the fifteen signatories to the Addis Ababa accords of March 1993. Though the UN and the international community understood that SAMO was a weak faction without any militia power, there was general sympathy for the Bantu and an inclination to insist that they be included in political negotiations. SAMO had, in other words, what most of the other factions lacked—a certain cache of political legitimacy, simply by merit of representing the vulnerable. Regardless of the fate of SAMO (and factions in general, which quickly faded in importance by the late 1990s) there was now a group of Bantu urban political elites and intellectuals with a strong vested interest in mobilising and maintaining a distinct Bantu identity. In more recent years, this political mobilisation has helped to routinise representation for Somali 'minorities' in national reconciliation talks. They are the '.5' in the '4.5' formula which is used to allocate positions in talks and transitional governments by clan, a practice which, for better or worse, has become enshrined in Somali politics since the late 1990s.

Bantu identity also gained currency as a result of international refugee resettlement and asylum policy. In the early and mid-1990s, a claim of minority status was very effective for Somalis seeking asylum in the US, Canada, and Europe, where there was a general, but very thin, understanding that minority groups were at special risk inside Somalia. This again placed a value on 'being Bantu' (or Barawan, or Midgaan). The recent programme for Bantu refugees in Kenya to be resettled in the US placed even higher value on 'being Bantu', since resettlement papers are one of the most prized possessions in a country which lives mainly off remittances sent home by its large and growing diaspora.

Finally, Bantu identity was mobilised by the UN peacekeeping intervention itself, through a sort of accidental 'Bantu conscious-raising' syndrome. It is impossible to gauge how significant this factor is, but in 1993 the arrival of heavily-armed African-American Marines, followed by black African UN peacekeeping forces, made an indelible impression on Jareer populations. For Somali Bantu who had always been treated as second class citizens, the sudden encounter with hard hairs who wielded real power—in the US Marines, in the UN peace-keeping coalition, and in the UN diplomatic corps—was an epiphany.

The reaction of ethnic Somalis to the mobilisation of Bantu identity was predictable. A small group of intellectuals and civil society leaders were frank about what they called the 'race problem' in Somalia. But the bulk of the political leadership, and some intellectuals, either dismissed the Bantu issue altogether or reacted defensively. Somali lineages which have significant numbers of Bantu minority members had the most to lose from this new claim on identity and loyalty, and were the most reluctant to allow a separate Bantu representation by SAMO. One leading Rahanweyn political figure, Cabdulqadir Maxamed Aaden 'Soppe', said in a 1994 interview in the Somali newspaper *Runta* (The Truth) that the Bantu 'don't exist' and were a creation of UNOSOM.[4] Bantu grievances are frequently met with resentment and counter-grievances; nearly every Somali clan and social group feels deeply aggrieved over losses and injustices it has suffered, and is reluctant to concede that others are worse off. By universalising victim status, Somali clans which played a role in the plight of the Bantu absolve themselves from responsibility.

Conclusion

The case of Somali Bantu identity since the early 1990s cannot be adequately explained by pure primordialist or constructivist theories of ethnic identity. While Bantu identity is on the one hand a very recent social construction, a variety of factors have contributed to the 'hardening' of the identity, so that we can expect it will remain an important part of the Somali social and political landscape for the foreseeable future. In the highly uncertain and insecure environment of Somalia, however, the Somali Bantu will continue to treat Bantu identity as the equivalent of a second passport, as one of several social identities to be invoked only when it confers tangible benefits and does not entail risk. In this sense, Bantu ethnicity in Somalia is not unlike Somali clan identity—a flexible tool designed principally to manage risk in a very dangerous environment, to maximise personal security and access to resources in a context of scarcity, violence, and lawlessness.

The self-evident conclusion from this case is that scholars must take ethno-politics in Somalia seriously, and treat it openly, but without essentialising clan and ethnic identity. It is in the rich and complex space between primordialist and constructivist theories that clearer explanations of the place of ethnic identity in Somali affairs will be produced. This is especially important in light of a growing interest on the part of both policy-makers and academics in local informal governance systems and their potential role in peace-building and state-building. It is at the local level where informal governance systems in Somalia are often most directly, and in some cases unavoidably, tied to clan and ethnic identity (Hagmann 2007; Gundel 2006; Menkhaus 2007).

For political scientists, the specific challenge is to consider the question of clan and ethnic identity in Somalia through the prism of the fundamental question 'who acts?' This is a problem of political science across the discipline, where a considerable body of research on mediation, civil war, post-war systems of representation, and other topics has been built on the assumption that ethnic groups are more or less cohesive units with coherent interests. For these research communities, constructivist critiques constitute a major challenge to the enterprise (Laitin 2001; Wilkinson 2001). In our models of Somali politics, can clans ever be said to 'act'? Or, alternatively, is clanism only one of a number of interests and forces that help shape the behaviour and decisions of other political actors? Who, in that case, are those other actors? And under what circumstances does clanism carry special weight as a driver of political behaviour?

It may seem outrageous that such elementary questions could be posed of an important field of Somali studies. And yet, political scientists are confronted with an unprecedented analytical challenge in Somalia, where the state—our conventional unit of analysis—disappeared twenty years ago, as did the formal economy, creating vexing complications for political economy analysis as well. Fortunately, the disciplines of history and anthropology afford us at least some tools of use in making sense of this brave new world. But the seismic changes that have transformed much of Somali politics and society since 1991 have left us all struggling with elementary questions, and with a paucity of both information and tools to answer them. If nothing else, this should inject a tone of humility and open-mindedness in our debates about the place of clan and ethnicity in Somali politics.

Notes

1. This chapter does not attempt to summarise the rich theoretical literature on ethnicity and ethno-politics. For one useful summary of the state of the debate on theories of constructivism, neo-primordialism, and their application to broader political and conflict analysis, see the short pieces collected in the Symposium 'Cumulative Findings in the Study of Ethnic Politics' of the Fall 2001 American Politics Science Association *Comparative Politics Newsletter* (Chandra 2001; Lijphart 2001; Laitin 2001; Wilkinson 2001: Van Evera 2001).
2. This section of the chapter summarises a more detailed analysis of the Somali Bantu available in Menkhaus (1989 and 2003).
3. My occasional use of the term Bantu in this section covering the pre-1991 period is of course somewhat 'anachronistic'. It serves to avoid a rather confusing mass of different group names and reflects a sense that 'Bantu' is now the accepted group designation.
4. Author's field notes, August 1998.

References

Barnes, Cedric 2006. 'U dhashay–ku dhashay: Genealogical and Territorial Discourse in Somali History.' *Social Identities*, 12 (4), 487–98.

Besteman, Catherine 1999. *Unraveling Somalia. Race, Violence and the Legacy of Slavery*. University of Pennsylvania Press.

Besteman, Catherine and Lee V. Cassanelli (eds) 1996. *The Struggle for Land in Southern Somalia. The War behind the War*. Boulder: Westview Press.

Cassanelli, Lee V. 1982. *The Shaping of Somali Society*. Philadelphia: University of Pennsylvania Press.

Castagno, Alphonse A. 1959. 'Somalia.' *International Conciliation*, 522, 339–400.

——— 1964. 'Somali Republic.' In J. Coleman and C. Rosberg (eds), *Political Parties and National Integration in Tropical Africa*. Berkeley: University of California Press, pp. 512–59.

Chandra, Kanchan 2001. 'Cumulative Findings in the Study of Ethnic Politics.' *American Political Science Association Newsletter*, 12 (1), pp. 7–11.

Gundel, Joachim 2006. *The Predicament of the 'Oday'. The Role of Traditional Structures in Security, Rights, Law, and Development in Somalia*. Nairobi: Oxfam/NOVIB and Danish Refugee Council.

Hagmann, Tobias 2007. 'Bringing the Sultan Back. Elders as Peacemakers in Ethiopia's Somali Region.' In L. Buur and H. Kyed (eds), *Recognition and Democratisation. New Roles for Traditional Leaders in Sub-Saharan Africa*. New York: Palgrave, pp. 31–51.

Helander, Bernard 2003. *Slaughtered Camel. Coping with Fictitious Descent Among the Hubeer of Southern Somalia*. Uppsala: Uppsala Studies in Cultural Anthropology, 34.

——— 1996. 'The *Hubeer* in the Land of Plenty: Land, Labor, and the Vulnerability Among a Southern Somali Clan.' In C. Besteman and L. V. Cassanelli (eds), *The Struggle for Land in Southern Somalia. The War behind the War*. Boulder: Westview Press, pp. 131–43.

Hoehne, Markus V. 2009. 'Mimesis and Mimicry in Dynamics of State and Identity Formation in Northern Somalia.' *Africa*, 79 (2), 252–81.

Laitin, David 2001. 'The Implications of Constructivism for Constructing Ethnic Fractionalization Indices.' *American Political Science Association Newsletter*, 12 (1), 13–17.

Lijphart, Arend 2001. 'Constructivism and Consociationalism.' *American Political Science Association Newsletter*,12 (1), 11–13.

Lewis, Ioan M. 1955. *People of the Horn of Africa. Somali, Afar, and Saho*. London: International African Institute.

——— 1961. *A Pastoral Democracy. A Study of Pastoralism and Politics Among the Northern Somali of the Horn of Africa*. Oxford University Press.

——— 2002 [1964]. *A Modern History of the Somali*. Oxford: James Currey.

——— 1994. *Blood and Bone. The Call of Kinship in Somali Society*. Lawrenceville, NJ: The Red Sea Press.

Luling, Virginia 1984. 'The Other Somali–Minority Groups in Traditional Somali Society.' In T. Labahn (ed.), *Proceedings of the Second International Congress of Somali Studies*. Hamburg: Buske, pp. 39–55.

——— 2006. 'Genealogy as Theory, Genealogy as Tool: Aspects of Somali 'Clanship'.' *Social Identities*, 12 (4), 471–485.

Menkhaus, Ken 1989. 'Rural Transformation and the Roots of Underdevelopment in Somalia's Lower Jubba Valley.' (PhD dissertation, University of South Carolina)

——— 1991. *Report on an Emergency Needs Assessment of the Lower Jubba Region, Somalia*. Nairobi: World Concern, July.

——— 2003. 'Bantu Ethnic Identities in Somalia.' *Annales d'Éthiopie*, 19, 323–39.

——— 2006. 'Governance without Government in Somalia: Spoilers, State Building, and the Politics of Coping.' *International Security*, 31 (3), 74–106.

——— 2007. 'Local Security Systems in Somali East Africa.' In L. Andersen, B. Møller and F. Stepputat (eds), *Fragile States and Insecure People? Violence, Security, and Statehood in the Twenty-First Century*. New York: Palgrave, pp. 67–98.

Samatar, Ahmed 2003. Review of Lewis, I.M.: A History of the Somali. *H-New Reviews in the Humanities and Social Sciences*.

Online at http://www.h-net.org/reviews/showpdf.php?id=8552 [accessed 31.08. 2009].

Van Evera, Stephen 2001. 'Primordialism Lives!' *American Political Science Association Newsletter*, 12 (1), pp. 20–5.

Wilkinson, Steven 2001. 'Constructivist Assumptions and Ethnic Violence.' *American Political Science Association Newsletter*, 12 (1), 17–20.

7

THE POLITICAL ANTHROPOLOGY OF 'PASTORAL DEMOCRACY'

SCOPE AND LIMITATIONS OF A POLITICAL ECOLOGY

Marcel Djama

Introduction

For more than two decades, the works of I.M. Lewis have given rise to a series of controversies and criticisms which reflect a renewed vitality in Somali studies (Samatar, 1989; Besteman, 1996; Besteman, 1998). At the same time, it should be noted that the analytical framework and categories popularised by Lewis—which depict Somali societies as being fundamentally governed by clan-based allegiances and resistant to any form of authority emanating from the state apparatus—remain widespread both within the scientific community and among aid agencies, NGOs and international organisations active in the country. It would even appear that this vision of politics has been adopted by a number of Somali intellectuals and is shared in popular thinking, while the context of armed violence and the absence of a functional government since 1991 can only give credence to this point of view.

The brilliant academic career of I.M. Lewis has doubtless helped to consolidate an undeniable ethnographic authority acquired through his involvement in the field. Beyond Somali studies, I.M. Lewis is a recognised anthropologist who has occupied top-flight academic positions. He is held in high esteem by his peers both for his comparative works in the field of religious anthropology (Lewis 1971 and 1986) and for his considerations on the contemporary role of anthropology (Lewis 1985).

Returning to Somali studies, I nevertheless feel that one of the characteristics (which is both a strength and weakness) of the interpretative framework developed by I.M Lewis lies in the fact that the political institutions that he shows us are largely determined by the ecological variables and technical characteristics of nomadic pastoralism in northern Somalia. This is of course the main thread of *Pastoral Democracy* (up to and including the title), his major work on the northern Somali pastoralists.

I believe that one way in which an author and his publications can be celebrated is by discussing his work. In the following pages, I intend to review the role of the ecological variable in interpreting the political system of the nomadic herdsmen of northern Somalia. In the first section, I will discuss this point on the basis of a reading of *Pastoral Democracy*, while in the second section I will review the blind spots of this interpretative framework.

The political ecology of Pastoral Democracy

As with all works, those of I.M. Lewis, and more particularly *Pastoral Democracy* which remains his major ethnographic book, must be understood with regard to an intellectual context and a theoretical framework once dominant in social anthropology: structural-functionalism. The intellectual project of this school of thought organises the divisions of the real world and the type of question selected by the author. Briefly, structural-functionalism views societies as being governed by institutions whose aim is to maintain social order. In a work devoted to the history of social anthropology, Lewis (1985: 56) refers to the structural-functionalism of the anthropologist Radcliffe Brown (1881–1955) who was its main theorist: 'It is only within and in relation to this 'structure' that institutions have functions to fulfil. Their primary purpose is the conservative one of helping to sustain and maintain the existing order of things. Thus, for the structural functionalist we may say that the ends (social solidarity) always justify the means (social institutions).' In analysis of the political field, this approach favours the study of the institutions which work to maintain social order: the emphasis is firmly placed on the functions of political regulation (legal or customary framework, methods of solving conflicts, the political dimension of kinship and alliance etc.).

This theoretical framework also served to develop a typological approach to the forms of political organisation in non-Western societies, which can in particular be found in the now classic book edited by Meyer Fortes and E.E. Evans-Pritchard (1940), *African Political Systems*. The political institutions of a certain number of African societies are distributed according to a radical opposition between state-based societies and societies without state, and analysed through explanatory variables such as demography, ecology and modes of production. I.M. Lewis' analysis of political systems follows this academic tradition.

The political organisation observed among the northern Somali pastoral nomads reflects a type of segmentary society without state, characterised by the absence of any form of central authority. However, the Somali system also presents a number of particular features. First, the socio-political units which are formed within the framework of genealogical kinship are not stable: they can be formed at varying levels of genealogical segmentation. Moreover, they are subject to no specific terminological designation. The term '*tol*' (translated by 'sew') refers to the principle of patrilineal descent without distinguishing levels of segmentation between the clan and the individual.

Nevertheless, in practice, Somalis distinguish social formations linked to an ancestor situated in an intermediate position between the macro-sociological level of the clan and the individual. Lewis' main contribution is to have succeeded in reconstructing the mechanisms underlying the formation of these intermediate levels by demonstrating that the isolated groups only existed in their relationship to other equivalent socio-political units. At the core of the system of patrilineal descent, two criteria contribute to the formation of politically significant groups. The first—which Lewis referred to as the 'size factor'—is based on Somali representations whereby the equivalence in status of the lineages does not refer to the same genealogical position but to their demography. This element goes beyond the simple structural mechanics of the formation of social groups, as in practice it creates an egalitarian logic: the social units are not placed in a predefined genealogical order and perceived as immutable, which generally gives rise to hierarchical formulae. Within such circumscribed segments, a second principle is at work to strengthen the cohesion of the groups on a contractual basis: it involves customary agreements (*xeer*) made at certain times in the context of military operations or through allegiances developed to pay compensation in the event of homicide (*mag*).[1]

These two processes of lineage-based cohesion (*tol*) supported by occasional contracts (*xeer*) contribute to the formation of socio-political units which are never definitively fixed, instead remaining fluid. Lewis thus identifies three levels of solidarity in the genealogical framework, which he conceptualises using analytical categories—the clan and the 'primary lineages'—or descriptive categories, the 'dia-paying groups'. The balance of power between social groups will thus develop with a view to confronting socio-political units whose status is assumed to be equivalent (that is, units with the same demographic weight) and, according to an additional line of opposition, the members of a kinship group may fight against one another in the course of a conflict but will join forces against another more distant group in genealogical terms. The model developed by Lewis fundamentally remains a structural model of political equilibrium.

The second particularity of the Somali segmentary model is that the socio-political units thus formed have no real territorial base, unlike the archetypes of segmentary societies without centralised government highlighted by anthropologists adhering to the structural functionalist school of thought. This distortion in relation to the classic functionalist framework—largely defended by Lewis as due to his desire to reflect the empirical reality—leads him to prefer to apply the notion of 'clan' rather than that of 'tribe' when referring to the largest socio-political units.[2] The author of *Pastoral Democracy* indeed notes the existence of a certain coherence in the territorial distribution of the clans of northern Somali herders, although this does not contribute to the identification of social groups or to the formation of the political bond. It is here that the contract (*xeer*) bridges the gap by appearing in the Somali system as the secondary principle which strengthens the cohesion of the kinship groups in the same way as residency does in other segmentary societies.[3]

Lewis believes that the absence of a territorial basis for the political bond results from the local form of pastoralism and, more broadly speaking, from the ecological conditions specific to northern Somalia. These conditions impose irregular forms of transhumance linked to the unpredictability of the rains. The same phenomenon prevents any form of appropriation—either individual or collective—of the pastoral resources, in particular pastureland.

By identifying such a strong correlation between the political institutional models and the technical economic form of nomadic pastoralism in northern Somalia, itself determined by environmental factors, I.M. Lewis introduces an analysis of political events in Somali societies that has had lasting influence. For example, one of the first Somali historians, Ali Abdirahman Hersi (1977: 177–8), saw the possibility of a central political authority among nomadic Somali herdsmen as culturally inconceivable: 'To the Somali pastoralist, forever on the move …, a state of chiefdom with central political authority meant nothing, as indeed it does not even today. The idea itself was an unthinkable anathema. Besides the nomadic mode of existence there was one other factor which militated against the formation of states structures in Somaliland: the poverty of the Somali environment.'

Furthermore, Lewis interprets the variations in the segmentary political system that he observed in other regions of Somalia (in particular the southern regions of Benaadir or the banks of the Jubba and Shabeelle rivers) as the result of transformations linked to the herders' increasingly sedentary lifestyle and the cultural contribution of the Bantu communities who have moved into this area (Lewis, 1969). Returning, in a subsequent work, to the regional variations in the segmentary model of the northern Somali pastoralists presented as an archetype, he explicitly cites the weight of the ecological variable: 'in examining southern Somali structures we are also tracing, to an extent that would be difficult to measure exactly, the modification of the nomadic way of life in new ecological circumstances' (Lewis, 1994: 148).

The political ecology of *Pastoral Democracy* is also echoed far beyond the Somali context. It has inspired many studies on the ecology of pastoral societies (Salzmann, 1967; Dahl, 1982), some of them grounded in Marxist theory.[4]

The foundations of politics: pastoral production versus trade circulation

Numerous objections have been raised to the positions adopted by Lewis, regarding both the role he attributes to the segmentary system and its relevance as an interpretive basis for the contemporary political situation.[5] Two main weaknesses stand out: first, the institutions described by Lewis do not reflect the diversity of political structures observed throughout the pre-colonial, modern and contemporary periods in Somali societies. Second, the focus of the political model on both the ecological constraints and the particularities of pastoral production is only partial in nature, insofar as the author takes into account only a part of the resources that can be mobilised for political ends. The institutions studied by Lewis emphasise the means of regulating the relationships of social production in the pastoral domain in a context of low economic and political pressure on producers. They mask the multifunctional nature of the pastoralists' activities, in particular the important and ancient role of trade circulation in shaping political structures.

Historians would extend the vision of the Somali political field beyond the *Pastoral Democracy* model, in particular in Lee Cassanelli's works (1982) devoted to the history of the pre-colonial political structures of the successive Ajuraan and Geledi sultanates observed between the 16th and 19th centuries in the hinterland of what is now southern Somalia. Adopting a regional analysis framework and comparing traditional oral sources with the written documentation available, he analysed the centralisation processes of political power resulting from both external factors (the role of Islam, long-distance trade) and internal factors (local forms of Islamic religious mysticism, mobilisation of the military potential of the pastoral clans).

Another example can be found in W.K. Durrill (1986) concerning the changes in the consolidation strategies of the Majeerteen sultanate on the eve of Italian colonisation. After a period of mixed fortunes, the Majeerteen sultanate, dating back to the 16th century (Hersi, 1977: 212), found a new lease of life at the beginning of the 1800s under the direction of the senior branch of the Cismaan Maxamuud fraction of the clan. The increase in power of the latter was initially based on its monopoly over a surprising resource—the plundering of ships surprised by the terrible currents off Cape Guardafui and wrecked on the Somali coast. This plundering was only one episode in the maritime trade which developed in the Red Sea and in which the first sultans played an active part. One such sultan, Maxamuud I who reigned from 1809 to 1818, took control of the main ports of the Majeerteen coast. His eldest son, who succeeded him in 1818, intensified trading activities, developed the production and trade of aromatic gums and incense and oversaw the construction of fortifications to protect the coastal bases captured by his father. The arrival of the British in Aden in 1839 contributed to consolidating the power of the sultan, who negotiated an agreement providing for the protection of British sailors shipwrecked on the Majeerteen coast and the right to supply livestock to the British garrison.

These two examples demonstrate processes of political centralisation which do not comply with the model proposed in *Pastoral Democracy*. They highlight the role in the development of political structure of outside intervention and of alliances between the military strength of pastoral clans and trading cities or centres. However, the work of historians has the particular merit of identifying the political resources that can be mobilised beyond the pastoral framework: in particular, while the works of Lewis emphasise production relations, these works identified the ancient and politically decisive role of trade in creating power bases.

It may be objected that these political situations arise in Somali regions which differ, from an ecological point of view and with regard to the resources available, from the northern Somali lands studied by Lewis. Nevertheless, the first European impressions of northern Somalia paint a much more diversified picture of the political models in place. At the opening of *Pastoral Democracy*, Lewis quotes the expression of the explorer R.F. Burton, who described the Somali nomadic pastoralists as 'a fierce and turbulent race of Republicans'. Burton contrasted the political world of the 'Bedouins' and that of the city dwellers (Seylac, Harar) governed by despots whose mechanisms of government he compared to those in force in the great oriental cities (Burton, 1910: 96). However, he also presented these two types of government as situations which shaped the political experience of the nomadic pastoralists. When speaking of these herders, he wrote: 'Every free-born man holds himself equal to his ruler, and allows no royalties or prerogatives to abridge his birthright of liberty. Yet I have observed that with all their passion for independence, the Somal, when subject to strict rule as at Zayla [Seylac] and Harar, are both apt to discipline and subservient to command' (ibid.: 127).

While a certain degree of caution is necessary in relation to Burton's categories of analysis, I believe that it is important to retain this idea that the political experience of the northern Somali pastoralists goes beyond the institutions described in *Pastoral Democracy* and that the mechanisms of political regulation in the pastoral sphere cannot be identified as the dominant and decisive political principles in all circumstances.

Burton also described the economy of the Somali nomadic herders as a diversified economy combining pastoral production activities, essentially governed by non-market relations, and market activities relying on the commercialisation of non-pastoral products and the sale of military services for protection of the trade caravans. Thanks to their mobility and military capacity, the herdsmen assumed the dual role of providing protection and acting as brokers for the trade caravans travelling between the coast and the cities inland, in particular Harar. This brokerage activity was performed by the *abbaan*. Burton (ibid.: 74–5) defined the *abbaan* as 'a broker, an escort, a commercial agent and an interpreter'. The *abbaan* responsible for ensuring the protection of the caravans is primarily an elder (*oday*), in both senses of the word as understood by the Somalis. He is the head of a family (*odayga reerka*) satisfying the criteria which, in the pastoral sphere, authorise individuals to participate fully in the public affairs of the group to which they belong: that is, having a household (*xaas*) and a herd (*xoolo*). He is also a notable, that is, an individual who is distinguished within his group through his wealth, measured in livestock, and his fighting or oratory skills (ibid: 127). The *abbaan* is thus an elder who has transformed the prestige acquired in the field of pastoral production into a highly strategic role of broker and protector in the field of trade circulation. In doing so, he strengthens his status and makes it permanent in a way that he could not by pastoral activities alone. Furthermore, his role as a protector, linked to the influence he exerts over the group to which he belongs and his capacity to mobilise it, is only effective if he redistributes a proportion of the goods acquired in performing his task: to be efficient, he must develop some kind of patron/client relationship with the members of his clan and lineage.

Conclusion

The pre-colonial situations described by historians or observers such as Burton are, to a certain extent, echoed in recent times which have been marked by the decline of the central state and the emergence of new powers. The present battles for the control of strategic trade hubs and the sale of armed protection services to traders, NGOs, or other outside operators have historical precedents. We cannot help noticing a form of continuity in political practices, even if it is important to remain attentive to regional forms of political order and above all to the notable political transformations during the long years of violence since 1991.

Somali political dynamics—in all their diversity—would appear to be shaped less by ecology and pastoral production relations than by a combination of factors outside the Somali world (international trade, colonial intervention, the politicisation of Islam, the Cold War, 'the War on Terror', etc.) reformulated in the social and political fabric of Somalia. We believe that this structure of reality already existed when I.M. Lewis undertook his ethnographical surveys that were to result in the publication of *Pastoral Democracy*, irrespective of the ethnographic qualities of this study. The subsequent positions adopted by the author, in particular his fierce defence of an understanding that emphasises the clan factor in the state crisis and the forms of armed violence which have developed, would suggest that he has remained within a structural functionalist theoretical framework which favours a formal and institutional understanding of political mechanisms.

However, while he has remained faithful to his theoretical orientations and firm in his interpretations, I.M. Lewis is in no way a dogmatic thinker. Having had the privilege of completing my doctoral research under his supervision (Djama, 1995), he remains in my opinion the model of an intellectual who cares about the point of view of others, more attentive to ethnographic precision than to dogma.

I have chosen to replace his questions in these initial field surveys—how to characterise the political institutions of nomadic herders in northern Somalia and how these institutions work—by others: how are the populations governed? By whom? By what methods? To what ends? How do the governed organise themselves with regard to the authorities? Theoretical frameworks and formulation of questions that are open to areas of intelligibility of the social world. While neither repudiating its legacy nor refusing to criticise it, we must use the work of I.M. Lewis to reimagine the frameworks of a political anthropology of the Somali worlds.

Notes

1. Lewis often uses the Arabic term *diya*. He refers to groups which are formed to pay or collect the price of blood—thereby engaging their collective responsibility in settling conflicts—as 'dia-paying groups'.
2. Cf. Lewis (1961: 2): 'Since the term 'tribe' is generally taken to connote a stable political and jural group whose members are united in respect of common attachment to territory as such, it is inappropriate to speak of Somali 'tribes'.'
3. Cf. (Ibid.: 300): 'Compared to other segmentary lineage societies where ties to locality supply one of the main strands in the web of government, it

seems that in the Somali system where local contiguity is weak, contract replaces it as a political principle of fundamental importance.'

4. In particular, see the works of the Ecology and Anthropology of Pastoral Societies team who published the book *Pastoral Production and Society* in 1979.
5. Thus he wrote: 'At a more abstract level, the collapse of the colonially created state represents technically a triumph for the segmentary lineage system and the political power of kinship' (ibid. 1994: 233).

References

Besteman, Catherine 1996. 'Representing Violence and "Othering" Somalia.' *Cultural Anthropology*, 11 (1) pp. 120–33.

——— 1998. 'Primordialist Blinders: a Reply to I.M. Lewis.' *Cultural Anthropology*, 13 (1) pp. 109–20.

Burton, Richard 1910. *First Footsteps in East Africa*. London: Longman, Brown, Green & Longman.[first ed. 1856]

Cassanelli, Lee V. 1982. *The Shaping of Somali Society*. Philadelphia: University of Pennsylvania Press.

Dahl, Gudrun 1982. *Suffering Grass: Subsistence and Society of Waso Borana*. University of Stockholm Press.

Djama, Marcel 1995. 'L'espace, le lieu. Les cadres du changement social en Pays Nord-Somali. La plaine du Hawd (1884–1990).' (Doctorate thesis) Paris: Ecole des Hautes Etudes en Sciences Sociales.

Durrill, W.K. 1986. 'Atrocious Misery: The African Origins of Famine in Northern Somalia, 1839–1884', *The American Historical Review*, XCI (2), pp. 287–306.

Equipe Ecologie et Anthropologie des Sociétés Pastorales, 1979. *Pastoral Production and Society*, Cambridge/Paris: Cambridge University Press/Maison des Sciences de l'Homme.

Fortes, Meyer and E.E. Evans-Pritchard (eds) 1987. *African Political Systems*. London: Kegan Paul [first ed. 1940]

Hersi, Ali Abdirahman 1977. 'The Arab Factor in Somali History.' (Unpublished doctoral dissertation) University of California, Los Angeles)

Lewis, Ioan M. 1961. *A Pastoral Democracy: a Study of Pastoralism and Politics among the Northern Somali*. London: Oxford University Press.

——— 1969. 'From Nomadism to Cultivation: the Expansion of Political Solidarity in Southern Somalia.' In M. Douglas and P. Kaberry (eds) *Man in Africa*. London, Tavistock.

——— 1971. *Ecstatic Religion. An Anthropological Study of Spirit Possession and Shamanism*. London: Penguin Books.

——— 1985. *Social Anthropology in Perspective*. Cambridge, London, New York: Cambridge University Press [first ed. 1976]

——— 1986. *Social Religion in Context. Cult and Charisma*. Cambridge, London, New York: Cambridge University Press.

——— 1994. *Blood and Bone: the Call of Kinship in Somali Culture*. Lawrenceville, NJ: Rea Sea Press.

Salzman, P.C. 1967. 'Political Organization among Nomadic People.' *Proceedings of the American Philosophical Society*, 111, pp. 115–31.

Samatar, Ahmed Ismail. 1989. 'Somali Studies: towards an Alternative Epistemology.' *Northeast African Studies*, XI (1) pp. 3–17.

Part IV

ISLAM

8

POLITICAL ISLAM IN SOMALI HISTORY

Hussein M. Adam

Introduction

This paper traces the role of Islam in Somali politics and provides a historical context for the manifestations of politicised Islam within the current Somali crisis. Even though Islam epitomises Somali culture and the Somali experience, Somali historiography is lacking in studies concerning political Islam.

Political Islam has manifested an expansionist as well as a revivalist face. Expansionism involves the spread of religion and the rapid conversion of non-Muslims. Revivalism involves the phenomenon superficially referred to as 'born again' among those who are already converted. In a relatively routine search for personal roots in piety, revivalism reflects an Islamic renewal reformist movement; but revivalism in an angry process of 'rediscovered fundamentalism' implies fanaticism, often spilling over into violence.

On 7 October 1990, the Islamic movement opposed to the military regime headed by the dictator Maxamed Siyad Barre issued a formal manifesto entitled *The Righteous Call*. From then onwards the issue became not whether Islam would play a role in Somali politics, but what type of Islam would play such a role and to what degree.

The social and historical background

Rarely is it remembered that both Islam and Christianity found homes in the Horn of Africa, almost from their very inception (Trimingham

1952; Ahmed 2006). Certain historical episodes point to the introduction of Islam on the northeast African coast before it became firmly rooted in Arabia itself (with a so-called first Hijra around 615 to Aksum); nevertheless, the mass conversions and deepening of Islam among the Somalis seem to have taken place only from the 11th to the 13th century. Lacking a tradition of political unity achieved through a centralised state, Somali nationalism has historically relied on Islamic cultural nationalism (Lewis 1965: 16). Lewis (1956: 150) offered the following summary account of Somali Islam:

> Despite these differences in the jurisdiction allowed to the Shari'a, there is little difference between the nomads and cultivators in the importance attached to the fundamental principles of Islam. Except for a few tribes who have remained relatively sheltered from Muslim influence, the five 'Pillars of the Faith' i.e. the profession of the Faith; prayers; fasting, somewhat irregularly observed perhaps; almsgiving; and pilgrimage seem to be universally practised. Competent witnesses have generally been struck by the devoutness of the Somali tribesman.

Religious associations and rituals, however, tend to be more formal and structured among the settled cultivators and urban populations (ibid.).

Somalis follow Sunni Islam; Sufism greatly influenced their religious practices. Four Sufi orders are especially influential among them: Qadiriyya, Ahmadiyya, Salihiyya, and, less significant in terms of followers, Rifa'iyya. Sufism has given Somalis space to incorporate several aspects of their pre-Islamic customs and practices. For the most part, rural Somalis, especially the pastoralists, have tended to rely on traditional Somali law (*xeer Soomaali)* in regulating most of their lives.

Somali lore divides society into two main groups: the man of religion (*wadaad*; pl. *wadaado)* and the warrior (*waranleh*, literally 'spear-bearer'). The *wadaado* devote their lives to religion and in some sense practice as men of God. A *wadaad* who has acquired considerable religious knowledge is usually referred to as a Sheikh. His duties include teaching elements of the faith and the Qur'an to the young. He conducts marriage cermonies and settles disputes pertaining to matrimony and inheritance according to the Islamic *Shari'a*. People call him to assess damages for injury in cases in which, as stated above, traditional Somali law is applied for historical and practical reasons. In contrast to the position of religious personalities in Shia Islam and even in other Sunni Muslim countries, Somalia is significant in preferring separation of the roles of religious and political leaders (Lewis 1961). Only in very exceptional circumstances would Somalis tolerate the assumption of political power by religious leaders. Ideally, for remaining aloof from politics, men of religion were considered above the rigid bonds of *diya* paying and clan obligations (*diya* is the fine paid for killing someone). In many cases in the past, their lives were spared during periods of violent internecine secular rivalry and conflicts. Accordingly, they were often able to play leading roles as mediators in such conflicts.

Compared with other African peoples, the peoples of the Horn are strikingly similar in many ways. Yet, they also have significant differences. The highlanders of Abyssinia (present-day Ethiopia) who follow an early form of Christianity have developed centralised religious and state institutions and practice agriculture. The coastal peoples, mostly Somalis, have adopted Islam, decentralised polities, and a pastoral way of life. At the same time, the two ecological zones and their peoples complement one another. In normal circumstances, the highlanders conduct their trade through the coastal peoples. Sometimes, however, the Christian semi–feudal rulers of Abyssinia dreamed of an expansion in order to have direct access to the sea for trade and the procurement of arms. They appealed to the Portuguese for help: 'We are a Christian island in an Islamic sea' (Farer 1976: 9).

In 1415 the Abyssinians invaded the large sultanate of Ifat under which came the state of Adal. They decisively defeated the Muslim armies and chased the Sultan, Sad al-Din, to an island off the coast where they killed him in battle. Since he died in holy war, *jihad*, he was later revered as a saint by Somali mystics. The Muslims were avenged by the remarkable leader Axmed Gurrey, the left-handed (or Ahmed Grañ, as the Ethiopians call him) in the second decade of the 16th century. He began life as a famous warrior who later assumed the religious title of Imam. His armies pushed deep into the highlands, inflicting one defeat after another on those who had shed the blood of Sad al-Din and other Muslims in previous wars. He was defeated eventually and killed in 1542 when at least 400 Portuguese bearing firearms joined the Abyssinian armies.

Axmed Gurrey's *jihad* was the high-water mark of such *jihad*s. In the next three centuries or so, they were eclipsed by wars waged by the non-Muslim, non-Christian Oromos in the course of their northward migrations. Oromo migrations drove a wedge between the older antagonists. Early political Islam, therefore, took the form of political propagation and expansion.

Political Islam in modern times

European imperialism served as a catalyst for Islamic revivalism in several parts of the Muslim world: Emir Abdel Kader in Algeria, the Sanusiyya in Libya, the Wahhabis in Saudi Arabia, the Mahdi in the Sudan, and the Sayid in Somalia. From 1899 to 1920 Sheikh Maxamed Cabdille Xassan, popularly known as the Sayid, at the head of his 'Dervishes' waged a twenty-year anticolonial *jihad* against British, Ethiopian, and Italian military forces. With messianic zeal he exhorted all Somalis to return to the strict path of Muslim devotion. Sheikh Maxamed travelled widely in East Africa and the Middle East. He encountered various trends of Islamic resurgence, and drew inspiration from the Mahdists' holy struggle for freedom in the Sudan. During a pilgrimage to Makka he became a disciple of Mohamed Salih (in Somali orthography: Maxamed Salix), the founder of the Salihiyya. This order is remarkable for its puritanical precepts. The founder appointed the Sayid as a deputy and charged him with its propagation among the Somalis (Jardine 1923: 36–8).

Around 1887 he began to teach and preach near Berbera on the north Somali coast where he was incensed to witness the activities of the Christian missionaries operating along the coast under British colonial protection. In 1899 he formally declared *jihad* against 'infidel' domination, and in a letter to the British he wrote: 'If the country [Somaliland] was cultivated or contained houses or property it would be worth your while to fight [...] If you want wood or stone you can get them in plenty. There are also many ant-heaps. The sun is very hot. All you can get from me is war, nothing else' (cited in Drysdale 1964: 32).

Most Somalis admire the Sayid for his defiance of colonial authorities. They differ widely with regard to his historical legacy. He has left a very important, though negative lesson for future Somalis: the violent pitfalls of an embryonic theocratic state founded on a narrow, fanatical, sectarian ideology.

In spite of growing defections of his followers, the Sayid continued to wage wars and to escape from the international coalition of forces ranged against his movement. In 1920 the British took the almost unprecedented step of introducing aircraft in an African conflict when they bombed his magnificent fortress at Taleex. The Sayid escaped, but his forces suffered heavy casualties in the combined aerial and ground assault. Though a defeated man, he died peacefully some time in 1921. Many Somalis feel that his trials and tribulations vindicate the age-old adage: he who holds the holy book should not wield the sword.

The revolutionary radicalism of the Sayid was replaced by the cautious reformism of elders who emerged during the 1920s and 1930s. An example of such a new leader was Xaaji Faarax Cumar, a former colonial civil servant who became active around 1920 (Touval 1963: 65). In spite of his Islamic reformist orientation, jittery colonial authorities did not wish to take any chances and he was exiled to Aden. While there, he actively participated in the formation of the Somali Islamic Association, a cultural organisation with indirect political implications. In some ways Xaaji Faarax's efforts were similar to those of Ben Badis in Algeria. Ben Badis' reformist movement was able to forge close ties with the nationalist movement. Thus the Algerian nationalist party, the FLN (National Liberation Front), came to reflect an Islamic as well as a secular outlook (Vatin 1984: 86). Even though the FLN waged a prolonged revolutionary war for independence, which led it to adopt, in the past at least, a radical version of socialism as political ideology, the Islamic aspect never faded. In fact, it has grown with time to the point where in recent times it has broken away and offers a violent alternative. The banishment of Xaaji Faarax and his Somali Islamic Association seems to have contributed to a similar rupture in linkages between Islamic reformism and secular Somali nationalism that flourished in the 1940s and 1950s.

This was shown in the debate over the question of a script for the Somali language, which demonstrated the impotence of the Somali parliamentary system. The governments elected into power between 1960 and 1969 were unable or even unwilling to resolve the issue of the Somali script. Apart from Islam, the Somali language constitutes the most prized of all things in the Somali national heritage. In restricted circles the Arabic script had long been in use as a medium for writing Somali. The Sayid used it and his arch-rival Sheikh Uways was even able to introduce several technical improvements to this system.

With the parliamentary governments unable to provide leadership and guidance, various personalities and voluntary organisations within Somali's civil society moved to politicise the issue. Among the three who actively advocated an Arabic script for Somali were General Maxamed Abshir, Ibraahim Xaashi Maxamuud, and Maxamuud Axmed Cali. These men and the others who supported the Arabic script for Somali injected notions of political Islam into the wider society during the parliamentary era.

In a 1963 publication in Arabic, *al-Sumaliyyatu bi–lughati l-qur'an* (Somali in the Quranic Script), Ibraahim Maxamuud Xaashi offered several arguments in support of the Arabic script for writing Somali: Somalis are Muslims and the Constitution should be taken seriously since it states Islam is the state religion. Owing to geographic proximity and comprehensive historical contacts, Somali culture and Arabic culture are closely related. Writing Somali in Arabic characters would facilitate these cultural and religious contacts and strengthen relations between Somalis and the rest of the Muslim world. He cited Pakistan, Iran, and Afghanistan as examples of Islamic non-Arab countries that use Arabic characters to transcribe their languages.

Professor Mazrui (1988: 499) argued:

> In Africa since independence two issues have been central to religious speculation—Islamic expansion and Islamic revivalism. Expansion is about the spread of religion and its scale of new conversions. Revivalism is about rebirth of faith among those who are already converted. Expansion is a matter of geography and populations-in search of new worlds to conquer. Revivalism is a matter of history and nostalgia-in search of ancient worlds to re-enact. The spread of Islam in post-colonial Africa is basically a peaceful process of persuasion and consent. The revival of Islam is often an angry process of rediscovered fundamentalism.

Axmed Gurrey's campaigns represented a militarised form of Islamic expansionism, while the Sayid's movement manifested a violent form of 'rediscovered fundamentalism'. Most of the arguments in favour of the Arabic script for Somali were based on a moderate revivalist perspective.

Islam and 'scientific socialism'

The problem of a script for Somali came to be resolved under the military dictatorship of General Maxamed Siyad Barre who instigated a military coup d'état in October 1969. He proclaimed scientific socialism as the official ideology one year later; relations between Islam and the state began to move towards hostilities. But as a consummate politician and manipulator, Barre did not let hostilities get out of hand, at least not during the early 1970s. When launching their first Three-Year Plan 1971 to 1973, the new leaders felt compelled to seek the support of religious leaders to implement their socio-economic programme. In March the government newspaper proclaimed that 'scientific socialism' was the only system compatible with 'our religion'. On 4 September 1971, over a hundred religious leaders were gathered in Mogadishu where Barre urged them passionately and at length to participate actively in the building of a new socialist society. His speech contained a clear warning: either you help us build the scientific socialist society as we have defined it, or you stay out of politics altogether. On this and other occasions (such as Islamic festivals) Barre insisted that religion was an integral part of the Somali world view, but it belonged in the private sphere, whereas scientific socialism dealt with material concerns such as poverty. Religious leaders should exercise their moral influence but refrain from interfering in political and economic matters.

Somalia joined the Arab League in 1974; some religious leaders hoped this step might moderate Barre's 'scientific socialism'. Interestingly enough, and maybe typically of Siyad Barre's policy, Somalia signed a treaty of friendship with the USSR in the same year. Somalia also agreed to host the continental Pan-African Women's Conference in April 1975, to prepare for the July UN World Conference on Women held in Mexico City. In January 1975 Barre proclaimed a new Family Law which gave women the right to inherit property equally with men. Religious leaders were outraged: here finally they found tangible evidence that the scientific socialist state wanted to undermine the basic laws and codes of an Islamic society. Making use of their right to speak within their mosques during Friday noon prayers, 23 religious leaders protested. They were arrested and charged with violating state security, and ten of them were publicly executed on 23 January 1975. Even though most religious leaders avoided open protest, this event marked the beginnings of a silent Islamic opposition movement. Somali religious leaders discovered that the post-Arab League honeymoon had lasted for less than a year.[1]

In July 1976 Somalia launched a new, single party—the Somali Revolutionary Socialist Party (SRSP). Originally intended to facilitate mass participation, the SRSP soon came to serve as a complement to the main spying agency, the National Security Service (NSS). It was also charged with the task of political indoctrination through propagation of the ideology of scientific socialism. The zealots among the party cadres continued to put religious leaders on the defensive. The practice of jailing people for allegedly misusing Islam spread to the regions and increased as time went on. At the Somali National University, for example, some of the lecturers in Arabic and Islamic religion often found themselves in and out of prison, depending on the whims of the party representative to the university.

The regime continued to flex its muscles, domestically and with respect to its 'perennial' enemy, Ethiopia. In 1974 the imperial regime of Ethiopia collapsed. Subsequently, the country was engulfed in power struggles and social upheaval. In 1977, Siyad Barre launched a front to reclaim the so-called Ogaden region of Ethiopia. The Western Somali Liberation Front (WSLF), the Somali guerrillas in this region who enjoyed the clandestine support of Mogadishu, waged a relatively successful guerrilla war against the 'occupying' Ethiopian troops. Pressures from the army and other strata of Somali society prompted Siyad Barre to send the Somali army in support of the WSLF.[2] By the end of 1977 most of the Ogaden had been liberated. The city of Jigjiga was in Somali hands, Dire Dawa was controlled by both sides with Somalis gaining the upper hand, and the ancient Islamic city of Harar was under siege, surrounded by Somali troops and WSLF guerrillas. Simultaneously, the USSR, previously Somalia's main ally, openly embraced the new Ethiopian military regime that had taken a socialist stand, and put pressure on the Somali government to co-operate with it.[3] Nonetheless, Siyad Barre, deeply involved in the Ogaden, abrogated the treaty of peace and friendship signed with the USSR in November 1977. The consequences were dramatic. The USSR and its allies gave unprecedented support to the Ethiopian regime. Consequently, the Somali army and the WSLF were routed by thousands of Cuban and other socialist 'brother-troops' in February/March 1978. Siyad Barre succeeded in realigning Somalia with the USA and the Western powers, and the moderate and conservative Arab block, only in 1980.

Barre, who had hoped to make a historic contribution to the perennial problem of Somali liberation and unification, lost the war and lost his sense of direction, his ideological bearings. For all practical purposes scientific socialism was dead as a ruling ideology, though Barre never admitted this publicly. The stage was set for both ideological confusion and growing societal chaos. Following the *de facto* collapse of scientific socialism, Barre could have attempted to revive the Somali nationalism of the 1940s and 1950s. Instead, he resorted to masked and unmasked forms of clanism and nepotism. As part of his public relations he sometimes appeared with a religious rosary and made the obligatory pilgrimage to Makka, but he ruled out the Numeiri option of resorting to a born-again Islamic political ideology (Cudsi 1984: 36–55). Siyad Barre probably did the Islamic opposition movement a great favour by not appropriating their religiously influenced vocabulary, their symbols, and some of their objectives as a substitute for Marxism-Leninism after 1977. During this period, his attitudes seem to have swung between considering Somali Islam as a paper tiger, to be provoked with impunity, and regarding it as a sleeping giant, to be treated with prudence and caution.

In response to social and economic insecurities the Islamic reaction exhibited various manifestations: (a) a striking increase in religious observance among the people, especially among the urban elites; (b) by comparison with the early days of the military regime, a marked increase in communal religious practices including pilgrimages to the tombs of local saints; (c) visits to charismatic sheikhs for spiritual healing; and (d) enhanced activities among relatively self-reliant Islamic agro-pastoral co-operatives. The regime began to claim that elements of the educated, religiously inclined urban elite had started to form an underground Islamic opposition movement. However, there was no evidence of such a movement during this early period; an examination of the existing evidence leads us to conclude that the Islamic opposition movement developed eventually because of excessive, unprovoked state repression, rather than being deterred by it.

Official provocations led to religious riots and government massacres, which took place in 1989 and 1990. In May 1990 former politicians published a Manifesto condemning the regime. On 7 October 1990, the Islamic opposition movement issued its formal document, *The Righteous Call*, mentioned earlier in this chapter. It offered an outline history that viewed Axmed Gurrey's expansionist *jihad* in a positive light; the Sayid's name was omitted, while the document indirectly acknowledged his radical revivalist movement. As discussed earlier on, this represents Somali ambivalence towards the Somali Dervish movement.

The Righteous Call began with a general endorsement of the previous Manifesto, proclaimed by former Somali parliamentary leaders. Both internal opposition movements espoused non-violence in calling for a dialogue to achieve a peaceful settlement of the civil wars; however, signatories of the call traced the origin of the problem to secular nationalism and blamed not only the Barre-regime but also the parliamentary system for having led Somalis astray. Obviously, they reserved particularly harsh condemnation for Barre's scientific socialism. *The Righteous Call* accepted democracy as the general objective, but insisted on an Islamic *(shura)* parliamentary democracy. Its signatories included several faculty members of the Somali National University, engineers, lawyers, doctors; the document lists 67 individuals bearing the religious title 'sheikh', seven with the title 'Xaaji', and eleven with the title 'Macaalin' ([Islamic] teacher). The Islamic movement in Somalia does not represent a marginal stratum of the elite. The active presence of intellectuals and professionals among them shows that frustrated lecturers in Arabic and Islamic studies were not the only ones leading the catalytic actions. Lay ideologists have considerably helped the movement to develop and mature. An analysis of *The Righteous Call* and its leading personalities indicates its mainstream, Islamic-renewal aspirations. Its rejection of violence is but one aspect of its opposition to radical Islamic 'fundamentalism'.

Political Islam since 1991

Barre's military dictatorship collapsed in January 1991, following guerrilla wars waged by the Somali National Movement (SNM), the Somali Salvation Democratic Front (SSDF), the United Somali Congress (USC) and the Somali Patriotic Movement (SPM). The country was divided as each group took hold of its clan homeland. During the mid-1980s, the SSDF went through an internal crisis, one wing opting to stay rebellious within Ethiopia, another defecting to join Siyad's side in the civil wars. Upon the fall of Barre, the rebellious wing returned and took control of the northeast regions—Bari, Nugal, and a part of Mudug. Cabdullahi Yuusuf emerged as Minister of Defence as the movement also welcomed the former Police Commander General (now also Imam) Maxamed Abshir Muuse as the new SSDF Chairman. One of the more prominent Somali 'fundamentalist' groups, Itixaad al-Islami (Islamic Unity), has strong leaders and followers in these regions. It first succeeded in bringing order to the port of Boosaaso. When chaos broke out as private militias were hired to protect private properties, Itixaad al-Islami took charge, providing efficient services, security, and law and order at minimal cost. It also used part of the funds raised at the port to invest in Islamic charity undertakings. It sponsored a well-organised non-governmental organisation, al-Falah, which maintained and improved services at Boosaaso hospital.

As Itixaad al-Islami gained popularity and influence, it was reported to be starting to buy and store large quantities of arms. Its multi–clan following included supporters from other parts of Somalia. One of its leaders in 1992 was Sheikh Cali Warsame. Others included Maxamed Sheikh and Xuseen Cabdulle. As its popularity and strength increased, tensions between it and the SSDF began to rise. The killing of the first UN medical expert in northeast Somalia was blamed on Itixaad al-Islami. Movement supporters claim that the assassination was the work of the old regional leaders who had been replaced by the former SSDF exiles, who allegedly did it in order to turn the conflict into an SSDF-Itixaad struggle. The SSDF Chair Imam Abshir, incidentally, is an Islamic renewal leader who was one of the most prominent signatories to both the Manifesto and the Islamic Call documents. The name of the Itixaad leader in the Garowe area was Cabdulkadir Gacame, while the leader in the Laascaanood area preferred to camouflage his identity by adopting a PLO-type name, Abu Muhsin. Probably, the most charismatic leader was Xassan Daahir Aweys. The SSDF claims that Itixaad al-Islami used radio communications to plan a simultaneous takeover involving Garowe, Qardo, and Boosaaso. Fighting broke out in June 1992, and for a few weeks Itixaad had the upper hand, but the clan-recruited militias supported by the Ethiopian troops that had been invited by Cabdullahi Yuusuf heavily outnumbered them.

In military confrontations between June and August 1992 between 400 and 600 people lost their lives. The remaining Itixaad forces retreated to the port of Laas Qorey in Somaliland; reports indicate that they later left the port and were based in a smaller nearby settlement. Supporters of the movement claim that it is an essentially indigenous movement that wants to install an Islamic state and Islamic law (*Shari'a)* in Somalia. It intends to respect the rights of non-Muslims, and wants to promote better understanding with the West. Itixaad has received external assistance in the form of Islamic books and scholarships as well as help to construct or repair mosques. Its opponents charge that its external links have involved arms, money and training besides charity and scholarships, singling out a foreign visitor from Saudi Arabia for indirectly assisting the revolt. They believe that radical Islam in Somalia has diverse sources of arms, finance, and training: Sudan, Iran, Egypt, Yemen, Afghanistan, Iraq, and even Saudi Arabia. Following military defeat, the movement allegedly changed tactics and concentrated on gaining power and influence through commerce, educational institutions, health, and religious activities.

Islamic renewal and fundamentalist positions have also gained followings among Somali refugees and exiles in various countries including the USA, Canada, the United Kingdom, Italy, France, Germany, Scandinavia, Egypt, Saudi Arabia and the Gulf States, Ethiopia, Djibouti, Uganda, Kenya, and Tanzania. Unlike during the nationalist, parliamentary, and military-rule epochs, Islam is today poised to play a more prominent role in Somali politics: the issue is, to repeat, how much and what kinds of Islam are compatible (or necessary) for political development in Somalia's future.

Future options for Somali political Islam

The options that seem open for political Islam include:

1. *The civil society strategy*: Among other things, this involves efforts to exercise hegemony in education, health and social services, commerce and financial markets, business, cultural and religious activities. The idea is to influence politics indirectly rather than directly. This is the strategy pursued by the traditional Somali Sufi non-governmental organisations such as Ahlu-Sunna wal-Jama'a and Majma. Wahda emerged in the north at one point in support of the SNM, with a vision of evolving and developing Muslim society in the long run by influencing by example via mosques, schools, clinics, charitable work, trade etc. Indonesia is probably the best example of Islamic civil society influencing the political arena. Many Islamic NGOs emphasise nonviolence to mark their difference from the radicals.

2. *The Islamic courts movement*: Somalia is probably unique in creating Islamic (Shari'a) courts with an armed militia. This option developed as a reaction to the anarchy of Somali wardlordism and from a yearning for a new era of law and order. The Islamic NGOs that emerged in dialectical opposition to Barre's rule enabled the rise of Islamic courts by creating a favourable environment. The movement began with separate sub-clan courts with their own militias. This pragmatic response led to the establishment of sub-clan courts, the mobili-

sation of court militias and eventually a federation. By 2004/5 they decided to amalgamate into the Union of Islamic Courts (UIC). The UIC is in fact an umbrella organisation for a broad range of socio-economic, commercial, political and clan interests. In June 2006, the UIC vanquished the coalition of warlords armed and financed by the US in its war against terrorism. However, it came to confront the UN-sponsored Transitional Federal Institutions (TFI)

Like other such disparate movements, the UIC had two opposed factions—the moderates, and the radicals described below. The moderates are often called reformists. They tend to be more receptive to new ideas, practices, and institutions. They have a vision of Islam and democracy with its principles of limited government, public accountability and rotation of leaders, separation of powers and checks and balances. In their view Islamic Shari'a has to be reinterpreted according the changing needs of modern society. Therefore there is a clash of visions, with the radicals or jihadists despising democracy as the rule of humans as opposed to Islamism, which they believe is rule of God.

3. *The Jihadist option*: This implies aiming at and capturing state power (as in Iran) and installing an Islamist State. The jihadists intend to use any means necessary and tend to glorify violence including political suicides. They reject the power-sharing vision of the moderates. This nonviolent moderate thinking is anathema to the ultra-nationalist elements within the Courts, especially the Shabaab, whose membership is drawn from a broad cross section of Somali clans. Public statements by Shabaab leaders and their UIC allies assert that the Somali *jihad* will continue until it reaches every corner of the Somali Republic. Xassan Daahir Aweys, to whom much of the Court membership looks for guidance, has also implied that the UIC could legitimately take an interest in the welfare of Somalis in eastern Ethiopia. Such statements appear to set the Courts on a collision course with the governments of Puntland and Somaliland, as well as Ethiopia. However, UIC nationalists probably do not envision military expansion so much as encouraging sympathisers within each of these areas to take the lead in challenging the established authorities (Bryden 2006).[4]

4. *The democratic/constitutional approach*: This option implicitly involves power sharing and the willingness of all main actors and the majority of the Somali people to participate in democratic, multi–party

electoral politics and accept constitutional limitations. Turkey is perhaps the best example of this approach. This option, however, was aborted in Algeria in 1992. The window of opportunity to negotiate a power sharing constitutional system was missed in Somalia between June and December 2006. In the Khartoum negotiations between the UIC and the Transitional Federal Government (TFG), the moderates within the UIC led by Sheikh Sharif Sheikh Axmed appeared willing to accept the principle of a multi–party system and elections. From the TFG side, this reconciliation effort was headed by the speaker of the TFG parliament, Sharif Xassan Sheikh. Unfortunately, it soon became clear that both sides were conducting false negotiations. From the side of the UIC, the jihadist minority in ascendancy would not give up their vision of an Islamist state imposed by any means necessary. The militarists within the TFG were encouraged by Ethiopia's readiness and willingness to impose the TFG on the Somali people via military force.

The US global policy of counter-terrorism provided Ethiopia with both diplomatic cover and military assistance, an enabling environment. Within such an atmosphere, the talks and negotiations were doomed from the start. Inviting and relying on Ethiopian troops has posed an insurmountable obstacle to the TFG's ability to gain the support and trust (legitimacy) of the Somali people, because of the perception within Somalia regarding foreign troops, especially those from neighbouring countries which may be biased towards one or more elements of the Transitional Federal Government. The majority moderates within the UIC and the constitutional elements with the TFG have both lost to the minority jihadists (UIC) and minority militarists (TFG). This proves the saying that the people who are moderate are not effective and the people who are effective are not moderate.

Had the constitutional approach succeeded, one could speculate about the checks and balances within Somali society that might moderate the harsh and radical elements within political Islam. Most of these are 'foreign Islamic' elements imported by the jihadists. Somalia does not have a history of radical Islam, except for the Dervish movement at the turn of the 20th century. The majority rural population—the pastoral and agro-pastoral communities—are attached to both Islam and traditional law (*xeer*), without noticing any contradictions. They will probably resist attempts to impose strict Shari'a laws on their age-old traditions. The will and capabilities of the business elite, some of whom have funded the Islamist movement, tend to rein in the radicals and steer the movement towards Islamic moderation. One may surmise that Somali civil society—both at home and in the diaspora—would, with some exceptions, tend to favour a moderate brand of Islam. Many Somali women will continue to strive to protect and promote the human rights they gained during many years of struggle. Jihadists will also encounter the resistance of the youth who resent the banning of *qaad*, films, TV and sports; also, the majority of the traditional Sunni religious leaders who practice a more tolerant form of Islam would prefer the civil society strategy. Violent resistance may emerge because of the politicisation of clan emotions—clanism remains the most potent force within Somali politics and society. There are also international powers that would support moderate Somali Islam. The indigenous checks and balances could only be effective when aggressive foreign troops are kept at bay. But instead of supporting and encouraging such indigenous checks and balances, the advocates of counter-terrorism believe that military repression is the best way to prevent Islamism from growing as a threat to the US and Ethiopia.

The Ethiopian intervention helped radicalise the Somali Islamist movement and its extremist wing, the Shabaab. The UIC leaders sought exile in Asmara in Eritrea where they formed the Alliance for the Re-Liberation of Somalia (ARS). The moderate Sheikh Sharif Axmed sought negotiations with the United Nations-backed TFG. He was eventually elected the new President of Somalia in January 2009, after Cabdullahi Yuusuf of the previous TFG had lost international and Ethiopian support. Sheikh Sharif's former co-leader in the UIC, Xassan Daahir Aweys, refused negotiations with the former enemy (the TFG and Ethiopia), and finally joined the newly established Hizbi al-Islam (Islamic Party). The latter allied with Al Shabaab in April 2009. Both movements currently wage war against the new TFG under Sheikh Sharif. Al Shabaab came to control most of the towns in south-central Somalia. The Somali (civil) war has thus taken on some 'ideological' colouring; it pits the radical (Shabaab and Hizbi al-Islam) against the moderate (Ahlu-Sunna wal-Jama'a) wings of the Islamist movement.

Even though the Somali Islamist movement tries to bridge descent-based divisions through multi–clan coalitions, internal conflicts point to the very limited success in this regard. The current moderate *versus* radical conflict partly reflects the conflict between two Hawiye clans: Sheikh Sharif Sheikh Axmed's Abgaal clan and Xassan Daahir Aweys' Habar Gedir clan. A similar scenario, with warlords as the main actors, was played during the early 1990s, when Maxamed Faarax Caydiid (Habr Gedir) fought Cali Mahdi (Abgaal). As far as the class dimension is concerned, Somalia, like Afghanistan in the 1990s but unlike Pakistan, does not have a professional army and a large middle class to serve as a buffer between radical Islamism and the state.

Notes

1. Editors' note: On the Somali Family Law (1975) and its impact on Islamic revivalism see Abdullahi in this volume.
2. Yet only in February 1978 did Somalia declare war officially.
3. Early in 1977 Mengistu Haile Mariam came to power in a coup and the Soviets rushed to sign a treaty of peace and friendship with his government.
4. By October 2006, it became clear that the Somali jihadists had an upper hand for the moment.

References

Adam, Hussein M. 1968. 'A Nation in Search of a Script.' (MA Thesis) Kampala: University of East Africa.

Ahmed, Hussein 2006. 'Coexistence and/or Confrontation?: Towards a Reappraisal of Christian-Muslim Encounter in Contemporary Ethiopia.' *Journal of Religion in Africa*, 36 (1), 4–22.

Bryden, Matt 2006. Notes. (mimeographed)

Cudsi, Alexander S. 1984. 'Islam and Politics in the Sudan.' In J. Piscatori (ed.), *Islam in the Political Process*. Cambridge University Press, pp. 36–55.

Drysdale, John 1964. *The Somali Dispute*. New York: Praeger.

——— 1994. *Whatever Happened to Somalia? A Tale of Tragic Blunders*. London: Haan.

Esposito, John L. 1980. *Islam and Development*. Syracuse University Press.

Farer, Tom J. 1976. *War Clouds on the Horn of Africa: A Crisis for Détente*. New York: Carnegie Endowment for International Peace.

Jardine, Douglas 1923. *The Mad Mullah of Somaliland*. London: Herbert Jenkins.

Lewis, Ioan M. 1956. 'Sufism in Somaliland II: A Study in Tribal Islam.' *Bulletin of the School of Oriental and African Studies*, 18 (1), 146–60.

——— 1961. *A Pastoral Democracy*. London: Oxford University Press.

——— 1965. *The Modern History of Somaliland*. London: Weidenfeld and Nicolson.

Mazrui, Ali A. 1988. 'African Islam and Competitive Religion: Between Revivalism and Expansion.' (Special issue dedicated to 'Islam and Politics') *Third World Quarterly*, 10 (2), 499–518.

Touval, Saadia 1963. *Somali Nationalism*. Cambridge: Harvard University Press.

Trimingham, Spencer J. 1952. *Islam in Ethiopia*. London: Oxford University Press.

Vatin, Jean-Claude 1984. 'Popular Puritanism versus State Reformism: Islam in Algeria.' In J. Piscatori (ed.), *Islam in the Political Process*. Cambridge University Press, pp. 98–121.

9

WOMEN, ISLAMISTS AND THE MILITARY REGIME IN SOMALIA

THE NEW FAMILY LAW AND ITS IMPLICATIONS

Abdurahman M. Abdullahi (Baadiyow)

Allah directs you as regards your children's (inheritance): to the male, a portion equal to that of two females, if only daughters, two or more, their share is two-thirds of the inheritance; if only one, her share is a half. [...]These are settled portions ordained by Allah; and Allah is All-Knowing, All-Wise. (Qur'an, 4:11)

As of today, Somali men and women are equal. They have the same equality, the same rights and the same share of whatever is inherited from their parents. (Extracts from the speech of the President of the Supreme Revolutionary Council, General Maxamed Siyad Barre, at the Stadium on January, 11, 1975)

According to the Somali News agency, ten persons whom the National Security Court sentenced to the death penalty were executed this morning by firing squad at the public square near the Police Academy. (*The October Star*, 23 January 1975)

The military regime that took power in Somalia in 1969 launched the new Family Law on 11 January 1975. President Maxamed Siyad Barre promulgated this controversial law, which offered 'equality between men and women' including matters of inheritance, in a publicly broadcast speech at the Stadium in Mogadishu. The speech caught the public by surprise, and caused frustration and fear. Nonetheless, public reaction was timid and cautious because of the massive presence of the repressive security apparatus. However, after five days, on 16 January 1975, a few Islamic scholars did have the courage to criticise the law overtly. These scholars condemned the law from the pulpit of the famous Cabdulqadir Mosque in Mogadishu (Abubakar 1985: 158).[1] The location and timing selected for the protest were strategic. The Cabdulqadir Mosque was the epicentre for the emerging Islamic movement, where readings of Quranic commentary (*tafsir)* based on Sayid Qutb's *In the Shade of the Qur'an* were regularly given by Sheikh Maxamed Macallin.[2] Moreover, many Islamic activists and individuals unhappy with the regime and its socialist ideology attended Friday prayers in this mosque.

At the same time, the Mosque was under the watchful eyes of the security apparatus of the regime, suspicious of any signs of opposition under the guise of Islam, with the result that the regime was able to quickly unleash its security apparatus and detain these scholars and hundreds of activists and sympathisers, while others were able to escape. Subsequently, on 18 and 19 January, the National Security Court put the first group of detainees on trial and imposed the death sentence on ten scholars, and jailed six of them for 30 years and 17 others for 20 years (ibid.: 163).[3] Moreover, hundreds detained from all regions were kept in prison without due process. The execution of the ten scholars took place hurriedly within three days after the court ruling, since the scholars abstained from applying for pardon and the President dismissed all appeals for clemency (Abubakar 1992: 159).[4] So, on 23 January 1975, at the Police Academy in Mogadishu, the military regime executed these ten scholars (ibid.: 136).[5]

The motivation for adopting the new Family Law can be traced back to the President's claim that he was seeking to modernise Somali society and promote women's rights. He argued that socialist transformation would be deficient unless women were liberated, through revolutionary legal reform, from the shackles of culture and traditional interpretation of religion. Moreover, the regime claimed that the new Family Law was not contradicting Islam but simply offering a modernist interpretation (ibid.: 126).[6] Conversely, the focus of the Islamic scholars' counter argument was that the new Family Law set the stage for more secularisation of the society by assaulting its most sacred domain—the family. For them, the realm of the family was one of the areas to which Islamic jurisprudence provided detailed rules (ibid.: 126).[7] Therefore, they considered the law as a transgression of Shari'a and a rejection of the Quranic verses, tantamount to explicit apostasy (ibid.: 126–32).

Along these lines, an intense controversy between the Islamic scholars and the military regime broke out on the role of Islam in the state and society. The issue of women was merely the theatre of confrontation between them, suspicious of each other because of the regime's orientation towards socialism. The regime may have miscalculated the implications of the new Family Law, since many secular laws enacted by the state earlier had not attracted any substantial reaction.[8] Conceivably, Islamic scholars were not expecting such harsh treatment for simply stating their Islamic position loudly and clearly.[9] As for Somali women, they were suffering from many consequences of the patriarchal system that both the regime and Islamic scholars upheld equally.[10]

Historians have said little on this important event that has had lasting implications for the historical development of Somalia. For that reason, this paper will reopen the Family Law case and investigate this event substantively. Moreover, because of the paucity of written sources, as will be seen in the literature survey, it will also make use of oral sources. The paper makes two main arguments on the implications of the law. First, although the law placed women on the national agenda, in reality it caused enormous hardships for them. Second, the law pushed the emergent Islamic movement towards fragmentation and extremism.

Islamists and the issue of the Family Law

Contrary to the narrow definition of the term 'Islamist(s)', signifying politically motivated Muslim individuals and groups, here it stands for various Islamic scholars engaged in a wide spectrum of Islamic activism. The rationale behind this lumping together is that all Islamic scholars were unanimous in opposing the Law, either overtly or covertly. Moreover, those scholars who were executed or imprisoned represented the whole spectrum of Islamic activists, including traditional Islamic scholars and modern Islamic activists such as jurists *(fuqaha)*, teachers of the Qur'an *(macalimiin)*, members of various Sufi Orders and modern educated activists. These Islamists were in agreement in opposing any law that contravened the mainstream interpretation of Islam, and in particular whatever touched family affairs.

Family Law is a major component of Islamic jurisprudence, defined as the body of practical rules of the religion. The method that Islamic jurists use to derive rulings is known as *Usul-al-Fiqh* ('principles of jurisprudence'). According to Islamic legal theory, law has four fundamental roots, given precedence in this order: the Qur'an, the Sunna, *Ijma* (consensus) and *Qiyas* (analogy). It is important to note that Islamic jurisprudence is flexible within its broader paradigm. That is why early Islamic scholars, in developing jurisprudence in accordance with a framework and methodologies, produced different schools like Hanafi, Maliki, Shafi'i and Hambali.[11] The developed methodology also allows modern scholars to derive new laws on contemporary issues using the same process. Hence Family Law in various Sunni Muslim countries was derived differently in following one of the four schools of jurisprudence and reflecting different cultural norms.[12]

In Somalia, traditional Family Law is based on Shafi'i jurisprudence, coupled in some respects with the traditional clan laws (known as *xeer*) that vary from place to place. Indeed, Islamic jurisprudence has the capacity to absorb some elements of *xeer* as long as this does not go against the general principles of Islam. Moreover, it is permissible for the various Islamic schools to borrow rules from one another. These two areas, the viewpoints of the various jurisprudence schools and local customs, could have been used as a guide in any reform of the Family Law. Following such a road map, any new legislation could have been adopted as long as it did not contravene the explicit rules of the Qur'an and the authenticated Sunna of the Prophet. The new Family Law under investigation here, however, directly contravenes the Quranic verses in some of its articles, and thus deviates from the accepted methodologies of Islamic societies (Abubakar 1992: 127–30).[13]

The Family Law affair in the literature

There is a general paucity of research and analysis on Islam and women in Somalia, and the new Family Law did not provoke many research initiatives. A brief survey of the literature on Somalia since 1975 shows this shortage clearly. For instance, I.M. Lewis' general history *A Modern History of Somalia* treats the Family Law event in a few lines: 'The public execution of ten local religious Sheikhs in January 1975 had wider and more serious repercussions, touching a deeper nerve. [...] By this action, taken in International Women's Year, the government demonstrated its secular, reformist intensions—but at the cost of raising in an acute form the whole question of Islamic identity of the Somali people' (Lewis 1980: 213). Ahmed Samatar in his work

Socialist Somalia: Rhetoric and Reality focused on evaluating the socialist programmes of the military regime. He treated the Family Law under the topic of women's rights, arguing that the Family Law of 1975 was 'another important progressive step' (Samatar 1988: 107). However, he did not take account of the execution of the Islamic scholars and its implications for the history of Somalia. Another important work, *Somalia: Nation in Search of a State*, by Said Samatar and David Laitin, stated that 'Siyaad Barre's celebration of international women's year, in which he promulgated a new law giving women equal inheritance rights, brought many sheikhs into vocal opposition to Siyaad's secularism. In response to their opposition, in January 1975, the regime executed 10 of these sheikhs in public' (Laitin and Samatar 1987: 95). Finally, Ali Sheikh Ahmed Abubakar wrote a book, *Al-Da'wa al-Islamaliyah al-Mu'asira fi al-Qarni Al-Ifriqi*, that focused on the regime's instrumentalisation of women to further socialist ideology. The book also provided a detailed narrative of the execution of the Islamic scholars in 1975 and its implications. It also mentioned the anguish and anger of the Islamic scholars worldwide (Abubakar 1985: 154–76). His second work *Al-Somaal wa Judur al-Ma'asat al-Raahina*, written in 1992, presented a more nuanced and in-depth analysis of the events and developed an Islamist critique of the law (Abubakar 1992). These two works regarded the Family Law affair as a defining moment in the history of the struggle between Islamism and secularism in Somalia (Abdullahi 2007b: 44).

After the collapse of the Somali state in 1991, academic interest in the Family Law incident remained low. For example, in her book *Society, Security and Sovereignty and the State in Somalia* Maria Brons, while hailing the reformist policies of the regime regarding women's rights, criticised it for its violation of civil rights. She wrote, 'All civil rights were increasingly curtailed. Women's option for voice remained also very restricted,' and 'progressive opinions were suppressed and conservative critique was brutally silenced' (Brons 2001: 198). Further, Lidwien Kapteijns questioned the entire matter of Siyad Barre's state feminism, suggesting that it was 'clan-based—and class-based—clientage extended to a set group of women' (Kapteijns 1994: 229). Though Kapteijns did not highlight the Family Law and its implications, she did articulate the superficiality of the regime's policies regarding women, refuting the claim that it was improving the equality of men and women. She claimed that women climbed to higher positions within the government simply because of their being a 'relative of a loyal male client of the regime' or 'relatives of men needed to be kept out of power' or as a 'compromise [for] their sexuality' (ibid.). Catherine Besteman in her book *Unravelling Somalia: Race, Violence and the Legacy of Slavery* provided a chapter on 'violence and the state'; nonetheless, she did not mention the violence committed by the state in the name of gender equality in 1975 (Besteman 1999). Christine Ahmed's paper on the *Invention of Somali Women* criticised the Orientalist invention of Somali women, yet did not include any reference to the Family Law reform (Ahmed 1995).

More recent accounts of the Islamic movement in Somalia after the 9/11 attacks were no better regarding the issue examined here. Roland Marchal's paper entitled *Islamic Political Dynamics in the Somali Civil War* outlined the general developments of the ongoing Islamic revival in Somalia. However, he mentioned only briefly the adoption of the secular Family Law and the concerns of Islamic scholars that the country was drifting towards atheism (Marchal 2006: 118). He remains similar to other available authors in his lack of interest in the Family Law and the prosecution of the Islamic scholars. Mark Bradbury in his book *Becoming Somaliland* devoted a brief section to 'Islamic revivalism' (Bradbury 2008: 179–83). He also disregarded the Family Law factor in the development of the Islamic revivalism and persecution of the members of Al-Waxda, the early Islamic movement in 'Somaliland'. It would have been particularly relevant to mention the Family Law episode since the leader of the persecuted Islamic scholars was from the territory currently known as 'Somaliland'.[14] Andre Le Sage, in his PhD thesis on 'Political Islamic Movements and US Counter-Terrorism Efforts', repeated a short account of the Family Law episode without linking it to the development of the current extremism in Somalia (Le Sage 2004: 54). Finally, Hamdi's *Multiple Challenges, Multiple Struggles*, which focused on women's challenges in the diaspora, provides a good historical background to the position of Somali women, analysing the implications of the Family Law (Hamdi 2003). As she lucidly wrote:

> The law was contested by many groups from various perspectives. Feminists who drafted it and pushed for its announcement were shocked about the final contents of [the] law because they did not want to challenge Islam in such a way. Because it touched the most sacred and protected realm of the society—family—local religious leaders condemned it and advised women against

using it. [Also], average women [contested the law,] afraid of the implications of such [an] 'anti–Islamic' approach in resolving domestic matters (Hamdi 2003: 132–3).

This brief literature review shows that the most relevant works published on socialist Somalia and the Somali Islamic revival mention the Family Law affair either only briefly or not at all. There is no substantial analysis of the episode in terms of its implications for women and Islamic revivalism. In addition, there is no considered historical analysis linking current Islamic extremism in Somalia to the state repression that occurred in 1975. Conversely, the few works in the Arabic language published from an Islamist perspective provide a detailed description and consider the event as a national disaster and a confrontation between Islamism and secularism that is still intensifying in Somalia.

Historical background

Traditional power configurations in Somalia bind together two main groups of community leaders with complementary functions in society. The first group are traditional authorities. They are responsible for the worldly function of the clan, following a diversity of clan laws (Lewis 1961).[15] The primary *diya*-paying unit stems from the concept of common defence of its people and territory. Decision-making processes in the affairs of the clan exclude women while using a participatory model for all men. The second group of leaders are the Islamic scholars who undertake various religious functions in the community such as Islamic education, dispensing edicts and directing religious events.[16] Women, however, are not part of the religious enterprise, and their involvement in traditional Islamic education is peripheral. Therefore, in the traditional patriarchal power praxis in general, described by Lewis with reference to the terms of *waranleh* ('warrior', 'spear-bearer') and *wadaad* (religious man), women are excluded from participating in the decision making of the community (Lewis 1963: 109–16).

The colonial administration altered the traditional power praxis by absorbing traditional leaders into its institutions and marginalising the role of the Islamic scholars. Although the colonial rulers imposed their own legal systems on Somalia, they nevertheless respected the local Family Law based on Islam. The British administration undertook the first codification of the traditional Family Law in 1928, by promulgating the Natives Betrothal and Marriage Ordinance followed by the

Qadis' Courts Ordinance in 1937. The latter was repealed in 1944 by the Subordinate Courts Ordinance, which retained the jurisdiction of the Islamic jurists only in matters of personal law (Tahir 1987: 253). In Italian Somalia, Family Law remained local in accordance with selected Shafi'i Jurisprudence (Hess 1966: 43, 74 and 107).

Following modernisation theory, the post-colonial state of Somalia continued to adopt further policies and laws that curbed the role of the traditional institutions, introducing a framework founded on state hegemony. As a result, Somali women gained more power and benefits, including equality in citizenship, voting rights, equal opportunities in the social services and jobs and paid maternity leave (Abdullahi 2007a: 34–54). However, the Family Law remained unchanged, consistent with constitutional provisions; Article 50 of the Somali Constitution of 1960 clearly stated, 'The doctrine of Islam shall be the main source of the laws of the State'; Article 98, Paragraph 1, prescribed that 'Laws and provisions having the force of law shall conform to the Constitution and to the general principles of Islam' (Contini 1969: 58). Family and property laws remained in the realm of the Shari'a (ibid.: 35). Beyond this, the main feminist issues hotly debated in the Muslim World—such as the veil, seclusion, work and education—were not an issue of public concern and debate in Somalia until the era of military rule (1969–91). Overall, Somali women enjoyed enormous freedom in comparison with many Muslim societies in the Arab world.

When the military regime took Somalia over in a bloodless coup on 21 October 1969, few tears were shed for the corrupt civilian government, and the people of Somalia supported the new regime with the hope of relief from their economic, political and social hardships. On the first anniversary of the military coup, in 1970, 'scientific socialism' was adopted as the guiding ideology of the regime (Tuuryare 2009).[17] From that moment, the regime undertook policies designed to curb clanism overtly—and the Islamic ethos covertly—and embarked on the road towards dictatorship. The repressive course of the regime clearly began with the enactment of the notorious 'law of 26 articles', proclaimed on 10 September 1970. This law listed a number of serious crimes against the state as warranting the death penalty and life imprisonment, including 'exploiting religion to create national disunity or to undermine and weaken the powers of the state' (Pestalozza 1973: 318). The regime's initial policy on Islam was to emphasise that it and socialism were complementary in notions of social justice (Lewis 1980: 219).

Occasionally, Islam was even used as an instrument for furthering socialist goals, as evidenced by the declaration that 'Anyone opposing socialism should at the same time be considered acting against the principles of Islam and against its very system of life' (Pestalozza 1973: 138). But it was frequently considered that opposition to the regime had an Islamic colouring. In this way, the first explicit form of opposition came during an internal rift within the ruling junta, when two prominent generals of the Revolutionary Council (Generals Gabeyre and Caynaanshe) and a former colonel (Colonel Dheel) were accused of organising a counter-coup designed to introduce 'Islamic socialism'; all three were publicly executed on July 1972 (Pestalozza 1973: 150). In fact, these officers had belonged to influential clans during civilian rule and their execution was part of curbing the power of these clans.

After consolidating power over the first five years, by 1974 the military regime had realised a number of important achievements. For instance, in July 1974 Somalia signed a friendship agreement with the Soviet Union during the official visit of the Soviet President to Mogadishu. It also joined the Arab League in the same year, securing important political and economic support from the Arab world. Moreover, the Organisation of African Unity (OAU) held its annual summit in Mogadishu in 1974, with the president becoming Chairman of the OAU, boosting the image of the regime on the world stage (Lewis 1980: 227). The cultural revolution initiated in 1972 which adopted the Latin Script for the alphabet of the Somali language was showing great success. The literacy campaign that began in July 1974 allowed more than 30,000 high school students and teachers, both male and female, to travel to rural areas to teach the rural population writing and reading in their own language (ibid.: 216). On the other hand, Somalis increased their connection with the Arab world as Somali migrant labour flocked to the Gulf States during the oil price boom of the 1970s. These migrant workers and students in the universities spread the new revivalist Islam that was gaining momentum in Somalia. This Islamic movement alarmed the regime, which was poised to implement Marxist ideology. Moreover, a new challenge emerged in neighbouring Ethiopia, where the Marxist revolution had triumphed in 1974. Ethiopia, during this period, did not pose a military threat to Somalia, having been weakened during the revolution; however, it was competing with the Somali regime in soliciting socialist countries' patronage in the Horn of Africa. This competition pushed the Somali regime to undertake more programmes and reforms geared towards Marxism.

The idea of the new Family Law began when the UN General Assembly adopted resolution 3010 of 18 December 1972, proclaiming 1975 as International Women's Year, and calling on all member states to promote equality between men and women. The military regime offered new opportunities for Somali women to become more vocal and to participate in the grassroots revolutionary programmes. They became more visible in public, particularly in the socialist orientation centres. They participated more actively in education programmes and took higher positions in the public services. There were women in high ranks among the officers in the army and the air force, and they took up positions as general managers, ambassadors, and directors general. The military regime issued a number of laws designed to advantage women, such as ensuring equal salary for equal jobs and providing for paid maternity leave. Moreover, by the abolition of the *diya*-payment system, the penalty for killing a woman became the same as that for killing a man.[18] Furthermore, the military regime even established a women's mosque, as they did not have prayer space in the traditional mosques in Somalia (Sheikh Ciise 2009).[19] It was in the context of the socialist programme of the military regime, which had matured and strengthened over the previous five years and did not confine itself within Islamic boundaries, that the Family Law was introduced.

The passing of the Family Law

The codification of the Family Law was initiated in 1972 by the Ministry of Justice and Religious Affairs, following closely the United Nations' proclamation promoting gender equality. The available literature does not say much about the process of codification of the Family Law. Therefore, we must depend on an available oral source. Nuurta Xaaji Xassan, a drafting commission member, gave the following account of the history of the codification:

> Sheikh Cabdulqani, the Minister of Justice and Religious Affairs in 1971–73, was attempting to introduce codified Islamic Family Law in the light of the Egyptian Family Code.[20] Perhaps, that was the reaction of the Minister to the increased awareness of women's issues in the United Nations General Assembly. The Minister provided me copies of the Egyptian Family Law that comply with Islamic law to share with the Somali women employed in the different

ministries and to solicit their support. During this time, many of these women were stationed in the Xalane Military Training Camp.[21] We selected a committee of five women and I was one of them.[22] The selected women had graduated from the Italian sponsored Somali National University and were closely connected with the Italian Communist Party.[23] These women received strong support and encouragement from Dr. Maxamed Aadan Sheikh, Dr. Maxamed Weyrax and Dr. Cadisalaam Sheikh Xuseen—known leftists and cabinet members who were close to the President. Later, the President nominated a seven-member commission in 1974 to draft the Family Law, directing them that it should be 'progressive'. The commission submitted the draft to the President in December 1974.[24] Following this, the Family Law was publicly proclaimed by the President (Nuurta 2007).

The President publicly announced, 'As of today, Somali men and women are equal. They have the same equality, the same rights and the same share of whatever is inherited from their parents' (Siyad Barre 1979: 3). He openly stated—in a provocative manner—that the era of 'one half, one third, one quarter' was gone for ever (Abubakar 1992: 125). Moreover, the President stressed that the new law would change the 'unjust law of inheritance' ordained by the Qur'an that assigns different shares of the inherited wealth to the rightful heirs of men and women. The Family Law consisted of 173 articles and, according to Tahir Mahmood, reflected

> the character of the dominant Shafi'i Jurisprudence and adherence to the general principles of the Islamic law, however, on marriage, divorce and filiations, had many commonalities with the amended Syrian Personal Code of 1975. According to the article 13 of law, polygamous practices are restricted by putting preconditions of the authorization of the Courts. On the issue of inheritance, the Somali Family Law had no similarities to laws in the Muslim world except Turkey' (Tahir 1987: 225).

Although the Law contained a number of articles that went against accepted Islamic Shari'a law, the most provocative were the articles on inheritance. It offered 'equal rights of men and women under the rules of inheritance; and drastic curtailment of the list of heirs and application of new rules for the division of estate of a deceased person' (ibid.: 256).

According to its usual procedure, the regime mobilised public support for the new Family Law by organising demonstrations, in which state employees and students were forced to participate and listen to Vice-President Xuseen Kulmiye Afrax's speech at the Unknown Soldier's Square near the old parliament building in Mogadishu.[25] Even so, after five days, public anger was expressed in the Cabdulqadir Mosque in Mogadishu. Sheikh Maxamed Axmed Nuur Geryare, who was present that Friday, narrated the event as follows:

After the Friday prayer in the famous Mosque of Cabdulqadir about 1:00 pm, Sheikh Axmed Maxamed stood and began to deliver his critical speech against the Family Law considering it as "arrogance and transgression of the borders of the Law of Allah that is unacceptable to the Somali Muslims". Successive speeches by the other Islamic scholars continued until the afternoon prayer about 3:30 pm where as many as nine other Islamic scholars criticized the Law. Most of the people [who had] prayed in the mosque also remained listening enthusiastically. Moreover, many people gathered in the surrounding areas of the mosque in a show of support for the scholars. However, the event was perceived by the regime as anti–state protestation and a threat for the revolution. After the afternoon prayer (*salat al-Asr*), security forces encircled the mosque from all the corners, cut the electricity to silence the scholars and arrested hundreds of people in the mosque. There were no any violent confrontation with the security forces inside the mosque and the people have angrily dispersed (Geryare 2007).[26]

Indeed, the protest of the Islamic scholars was a spontaneous expression of anger and frustration. The Friday sermon was delivered by Sheikh Cabdulasis from the al-Azhar Mission in Somalia who explained the 'rights and fallacies' concerning Islam (Sheikh Ciise 2009).[27] Analysis of their affiliations demonstrates that most of these scholars belonged to the traditional jurists and *Sufi* Orders. The initiator of the protest was Sheikh Axmed Sheikh Maxamed, a prominent jurist for the town of Caynabo in northern Somalia who came to Mogadishu on the invitation of Ismaaciil Cali Abokor, a prominent member of the Revolutionary Council (Abubakar 1985: 165). Other scholars came to the Cabdulqadir Mosque for the Friday prayers. Sheikh Axmed considered the law 'a transgression of Allah's law' and requested others to speak up in defence of the Shari'a. Other scholars followed the same line in denouncing the law. Most of them were not part of what is termed 'political Islam', which was then in its early development. Moreover, prominent scholars of the modern Islamic revival, such as Sheikh Maxamed Macallin, Sheikh Maxamed Axmed Geryare, Sheikh Cabdulqani, and student activists belonging to 'Al-Ahli' were not among the executed scholars (Sheikh Maxamed 1985).[28] On Saturday, the second day, after the noon prayers, other scholars delivered supporting speeches and the demonstration moved up to the Municipality Headquarters in which many others were imprisoned (Sheikh Ciise 2009).[29]

In a hysterical reaction the regime detained most of these scholars, although some of them succeeded in escaping. For instance, Sheikh Maxamed Macallin, director of Islamic affairs at the Ministry of Justice and Religious Affairs and famous commentator on the Qur'an, was arrested a few months after the event. Sheikh Cabdulqani, the former Minister of Justice and Religious Affairs, was also arrested. Sheikh Maxamed Geryare, the former Director of Religious Affairs of the Ministry of Justice, succeeded in escaping after receiving a friendly warning of a warrant for his arrest (Jilacow 2004, Geryare 2004).[30] The military regime's use of the strong hand demonstrates that it perceived the peaceful protests as a threat and challenge to its authority and to socialist ideology. Certainly all forms of public protest were completely prohibited, according to the law enacted in 1970.

Why the Family Law and execution of the scholars?

There are three main theses for explaining why the regime adopted the Family Law and executed some of the protesting scholars. The first thesis claims that these actions were driven by foreign assistance; it denies any ideological motivation; in this perspective, the adoption of the law was simply a theatrical show of the regime's strength and its commitment to secular socialist ideology, competing with the new Marxist Ethiopia for assistance from socialist countries (Qaasim 2007; Casharo 2009).[31] Indeed, by the mid-1970s Ethiopia had adopted socialist programmes and attracted huge assistance from the socialist bloc in competition with Somalia. Siyad Barre, who had been playing the role of the key friend of the socialist bloc in the Horn of Africa, was losing that monopoly. Therefore, he strove to prove that he was the more committed socialist in the Horn of Africa, deserving to be considered as such and provided with generous support from the socialist countries (Casharo 2009; Shuuke 2009).[32] The second thesis refers to the dictatorial ambitions of President Siyad Barre. Some observers consider the Family Law event was purely a pre-emptive strike on the emerging Islamic movement, perceived by the regime as one of the two 'enemies of the revolution'—clanism and Islam. The early execution of General Caynaanshe, General Gabeyre and Colonel Dheel in 1972 was considered a blow to the centres of clan power in Somalia. Thus, now (in 1975) the Islamists had to be suppressed in order to remove all potential obstacles thwarting revolutionary programmes. The third thesis, finally, stresses that the motivation was ideological, assuming that the adoption of the Family Law and the crushing of the Islamists was 'part of the preparatory tasks to be accomplished before the formation of the Socialist Revolutionary Party in Somalia' (Shuuke 2009).[33] This party, established in 1976 at the beginning of the second phase of the revolution, was considered a pioneer and vanguard for socialist transformation of society. In conclusion, the adoption of the Family Law and crushing of its opponents aimed at accomplishing two objectives: recognition by the socialist countries, as well as the removal of potential local threats to power and obstacles on the way to a socialist Somalia.

The implications of the Family Law for women

The new Family Law was one of the most Westernised legal reforms in the Muslim world, comparable only to the reforms seen in Turkey. It created a crack in the fabric of society, culminating in the brutal execution of the Islamic scholars, violating human rights in the name of defending women's rights. The Family Law placed women onto the national agenda to a point where all groups debated it among themselves. The law had three principal results for women: increases in polygamy, divorce and domestic violence.[34]

These practices are directly linked to one another and are well entrenched in Somali society. However, most interviewees agreed that the situation worsened after the adoption of the new law, opening provocative debates on the status and role of women within every household. In these discussions many women who thought that the state was on their side began to challenge their husbands. Some of these women were educated and employed. As they contributed to the family income they became more assertive in family affairs. Others were recruited into low-paid jobs in Orientation Centres as militia of the revolutionary *Guul-wade* ('revolutionary guards'). This militia, combined with the general population, had to participate in vigilante and 'self-help' programmes. These activities generated mistrust between wives and husbands since women were forced to accompany the opposite sex, particularly at night (Abubakar 1992: 85–6; Diiriye 2009; Aamir 2009). Many women were also employed by the intelligence service to watch for 'enemies of the Revolution'—particularly the wives of individuals suspected of opposing the regime. Therefore new suspicions between men and women developed, greatly eroding intimate relations of love and affection. Because of this, conflict developed in many households, expressed in the form of violence, polygamy and divorce (Abubakar 1992: 83–4; Saynab Barako 2009).

In any case, polygamous and patriarchal Somali society—accustomed to investing men with absolute power within the family—could not easily swallow the concepts of the new Family Law. These included restraint of polygamous practices, equality between men and women in family affairs and equal shares in inheritance. To examine the level of family conflict as result of the new law one would require statistical data showing discrepancies between the practices before and after the law. However, since such data are not available, the only available method is to make use of oral sources that can provide qualitative answers. Many interviewees mentioned that polygamy, divorce and family violence had greatly increased after the adoption of the new Family Law. One such case is that of an employee in the Ministry of Planning. His wife used to frequent one of the Orientation Centres in Mogadishu. He tried to advise her to stop going to the centre, but she denounced him to the revolutionary authorities there. The husband was requested to come to the centre. After long and heated discussions with the authorities, he angrily divorced his wife on the spot.[35]

Nuurta Xaaji mentioned that some religious individuals aimed to derail the Family Law and married many wives as a sign of protest. Moreover, even a minister challenged the law openly. Cabdiraxmaan Jaamac Barre was the Foreign Minister and patrilineal cousin of President Maxamed Siyad Barre. He married his second wife after the promulgation of the Family Law. A court had to authorise the second marriage, which required the fulfilment of certain conditions according to the new law. However, when the President questioned his brother, he replied: 'Marriage is a personal matter and is in agreement with the Islamic law that permits men to marry up to four wives.'[36]

Thus traditional relations based on the complementary role of women and men were shaken up, the harassment of women increased, and some women were even killed (Hamdi 2003: 136).[37] Moreover, after the enactment of the law, some women started to offer more support to the regime, while their husbands moved towards the opposition. Yet, even so, the regime abused women in order to attack opposition movements, using relatives and wives of suspected supporters of these movements (Qaasim 2007; Aamir 2009). Some of these women were imprisoned or recruited as collaborators. In either case, women suffered greatly and, as a result, families broke up, and some women had to become breadwinners for their families because their husbands, fathers, brothers and sons had been imprisoned or had fled the country.

Finally, few cases were reported of the Family Law being implemented. Judges in the courts advised people against the law, warning them of its consequences for their faith. Security organs were reluctant to deal with breakers of the law. Many women disregarded it because of its negative effect on their relations with their husbands. Because of all the cumulative internal and external opposition and the growing weakness of the regime in the 1980s, the Family Law was finally revised to comply with the general principles of Islam.

The implications of the Family Law for the Islamic movement

Despite the later revisions, the Somali Family Law of 1975 had long-term implications. In particular, its impact within the wider context of Islamic revival in Somalia would prove crucial. The Islamic awakening in Somalia gradually began in the 1960s with the foundation of the renaissance organisations al-Nahda and al-Ahli in Mogadishu and Al-Wahda in Hargeysa. Their members were actively preaching the new ideas of the Islamic revivalist movement, in line with the Muslim Brotherhood's methodology. Ansar al-Sunna was an early Salafi organization led by Sheikh Nuur Cali Colow.[38] The famous Quranic commentary of Sheikh Maxamed Macallin in the 1970s, in the Cabdulqadir Mosque, was based on the Muslim Brotherhood's vision and understanding of Islam. Young devotees were spreading the same understanding of Islam in the other mosques and in homes underground. The works of Hassan al-Banna, Sayyid Qutb and Al-Mawdudi, with other educational literature of the Muslim brotherhood and Jamaat al-Islamiyah in Pakistan, were widespread and widely read in Islamist circles. These books were available in the libraries of the Renaissance Organisation and the Ministry of Justice and Religious Affairs (Geryare 2004).[39]

However, with the crackdown on Islamists after the Family Law episode, most of the leading scholars either were imprisoned or fled the country. Those imprisoned include Sheikh Maxamed Macallin and

Sheikh Cabdulqani, while Sheikh Maxamed Geryare succeeded in escaping and reaching Saudi Arabia. Moreover, many high school students fled the country to Sudan, Egypt, Saudi Arabia and the Gulf countries. Some of them obtained employment and many attended universities, in particular Islamic universities in Saudi Arabia. It is important to note that this occurred during a time of booming economies and Islamic revivalism throughout the Arab Muslim world. This economic wellbeing and education offered the emerging Islamic movement an impetus to reorganise and spread its message back in Somalia. Meanwhile, many of the students encountered different brands of revivalist movements, and brought these ideologies and approaches back with them. As a result, varieties of Islamism, ranging from the evolutionist Muslim Brotherhood to organised Salafism and extreme *takfir* ideologies, began to spread throughout Somalia. Because of the exodus of young Somali Islamic activists to the Gulf, the Islamic movement, hitherto united in its ideology and leadership, was fragmented and the ideology of extremism emerged strongly (Abdullahi 2008). The Salafi movement challenged the moderate view of Islam of the Muslim Brotherhood. The escapees educated in the Arab universities established the current organisations of the Islamic movements, such as Al-Islaax, Al-Itixaad and Takfiir. By 1980s, the conflict between the Sufi Orders and the Salafia movement was evident everywhere and religious conflicts were set in motion. There was gradually a drift towards an extreme version of Islamism. Thus the roots of the current Islamic armed groups fighting in Somalia can be traced to the proclamation of the Family Law and its implications.

How the various Islamic movements affected women requires separate examination and is beyond the scope of this paper. However, the impact of the conservative Gulf culture on Somalia, carried by migrant workers and students, was evident in the narrowing scope for women in the households of many Islamists. In particular, ultra-conservative clothing for women was introduced, such as face coverings, which were portrayed as the symbol of piety and faithfulness.[40] Moreover, many women were forced into seclusion, silenced, and denied jobs and education. On the other hand, moderate Islamists offered more space for women and advocated their empowerment through education and freedom from the rigid interpretation of Islamic texts. As a result, some women became more active and better educated and participated more in public affairs.

Conclusions

This paper has attempted to reconstruct the history of the Family Law in Somalia and its implications for women and the Islamic movement. It illustrated that available literature on this topic remains scarce, even though new studies of Islamism and feminism are emerging. Hence the use of oral recollections was necessary to fill the lacunae in the sources. Surprisingly, both proponents and opponents of the Law represented the patriarchal traditional society and shared the same mindset and attitudes towards women. This suggested that the issue of the role and status of women was used simply as a pretext for staging socio-political conflict and ideological antagonism between the Islamists and the repressive socialist-oriented regime. All interviewees agreed that although the Family Law placed women squarely at the centre of the national agenda, women suffered more after its adoption in a variety of ways. In particular, polygamy, divorce and family violence drastically increased, and social problems were augmented. The law did not take off; the public did not accept it and the law enforcement agencies undermined it in various ways. Because of cumulative internal and external opposition and the ideological and economic weakness of the regime in the 1980s, the Family Law was revised to comply with the general principles of Islam.

Regarding the implications of the Family Law for the Islamic movement, the harshness of the regime in dealing with the Islamic scholars, the encouragement and support of the Islamists by the conservative Arab regimes, and their contact with the varieties of Islamic ideologies and activism, changed the Islamic landscape in Somalia. As a result, students and scholars who migrated to the Arab world in 1970s created the current Islamic organisations. In fact, present day extremism in Somalia is rooted in those early years of fragmentation and migration. Finally, it appears that both the military regime and the Islamic scholars miscalculated the implications of their actions.

Notes

1. The new Family Law was criticised in many mosques all over Somalia and about ten mosques in Mogadishu alone.
2. Sheikh Maxamed Macallin completed his postgraduate studies in al-Azhar University and returned to Somalia in 1967. He was employed in the Ministry of Justice and Islamic Affairs. He is famous for his Qur'anic commen-

tary in the Cabdulqadir Mosque in the 1970s where most young Islamic activists of that time were educated. He was imprisoned for many years by the regime and died in Rome in 2000.

3. The National Security Court was established by the military regime to deal with those matters considered to endanger national security. Its rulings were final. Its long-standing chairman was Colonel Maxamuud Geelle Yuusuf.
4. Institutions that asked for forgiveness included al-Azhar and the Islamic University in Jeddah. Some individuals also appealed for leniency, including ministers like Cabdisalaam Sheikh Xuseen and Cabdisalaam Sheikh Xuseen and Islamic scholars like Sheikh Aadan Sheikh Cabdullahi and others, according to Maxamed Xaaji, the former vice-minister of the regime (interview, 5 July 2009, Nairobi).
5. The ten executed scholars were: Sheikh Axmed Sheikh Maxamed, Cali Xassan Warsame, Xassan Ciise Iley, Sheikh Axmed Imam, Sheikh Muuse Yuusuf, Maxamed Siyad Xirsi, Cali Jaamac Xirsi, Aadan Cali Xirsi, Saleymaan Jaamac Maxamed, and Yasin Cilmi Cawl.
6. Modernism departs from secularism in that it recognises the importance of faith in public life, and from Salafism in that it does accept most of the modern European institutions, social processes and values. Sometimes, its adherents stretch the meaning of the Qur'an and Sunna beyond their traditional limits. They draw conclusions and adopt laws that have no precedent in the Islamic Shari'a and are considered to be anti–Islamic by the majority of scholars. Such phenomena are evident in the speech of the President at the Stadium in which he concluded: 'I hope that those who are listening to me now through the radio will guide those who do not understand anything or those who are ignorant about these principles. And, to those who did not understand anything about the meaning of the glorious Qur'an and those who are demeaning Islam in their wrong understanding' (translated from Arabic by the author).
7. There are ten verses in the Qur'an that deal with inheritance. These are 2:180, 2: 240, 4:7–9, 4:19, 4:33, and 5:16–18.
8. Examples are the abolition of the *diya*-payment system by the military regime and many other laws.
9. The Islamic methodology in correcting wrongs takes three steps: correction by action, by tongue and by heart. Most of the Somalis opted to deny the Family Law by heart, while these scholars chose the second option of expressing their views by tongue. See Prophetic Hadith No. 34, Al-Nawawi, *The Book of Forty Hadith*.
10. The evidence is the continuation of many practices in the society that violate the rights of women offered by Islam, such as forced marriages and denial of women of their share of inheritance. Gender relations in Somalia are derived mostly from the pastoral culture based on the division of labour in that harsh environment. Most of the new élites and Islamic scholars are recent immigrants from the pastoral areas.

11. The four main Sunni Schools of Jurisprudence were developed in following order. (1) The Hanafi School was first established under the jurist Imam Abu Hanifa, born in Iraq in 689 AD (2) The Maliki School was established by the disciples of Imam Malik, born in Medina in 715 AD (3) Mohamed ibn Idris al-Shafi'i (767–820) is the founder of Shafi'i school of Jurisprudence; he is the first scholar who developed principles of jurisprudence in his famous work '*al-Risala*' (treatise). (4) The Hanbali School was developed by the students of Imam Ahmed ibn Hanbal (d. 855) and it is popular in the Gulf States.
12. A few Muslim countries, such as Turkey and Tunisia, developed more secular Family Laws.
13. Articles that contravene the Quranic verses, as analysed by Abubakar (1992) are: 4, 13, 31, 36, 158, 159, and 161.
14. Sheikh Axmed Sheikh Maxamed, the initiator of the Islamic scholars' protest in the Cabdulqadir Mosque, was born in Caynabo in contemporary Somaliland.
15. In the pastoral areas the system is based on descent, while in the agricultural areas it is founded on territorial attachments; and accordingly, various legal systems have developed to respond to the needs of the communities. Moreover, hierarchies of the clan system begin from the *diya*-paying sub-clan.
16. These functions include Qur'an memorisation, Islamic studies like jurisprudence concerning marriage and inheritance, prayers, fasting, celebrations of religious festivities and so on.
17. As narrated by the Professor of International Law, Maxamed Cali Tuuryare, a high ranking delegation from the Soviet Union paid a visit to Mogadishu before the promulgation of socialism in 1970. He and Colonel Yusuuf Dheeg were assigned to accompany them on the secret mission aimed at discouraging the Somali military regime from adopting socialism so early. However, President Siyad ignored their advice. The argument of the delegation was that the socio-economic environment in Somalia was not yet ripe for socialist transformation (Tuuryara, interview, Nairobi, 11 July 2009).
18. In the Somali traditional *xeer* and according to Islamic jurisprudence, the *diya* of women is half of that of men. However, there are minority voices that adhere to the equality of *diya* (compensation) for both genders.
19. This mosque was located near the Italian Club and National University City Centre in Mogadishu. Sheikh Aadan Sheikh Cabdullahi, a well-known scholar, delivered a commentary on the Qur'an on Radio Mogadishu and used to run a women's Islamic teaching circle in the Mosque.
20. Sheikh Cabdulqani (1935–2007) graduated from al-Azhar in 1957 and became a lecturer in the University and worked in the High Court. In 1967 when the Renaissance Islamic Organisation was formed, he became its chairman. During the military regime he became Minister of Justice and Islamic Affairs; nonetheless, he was imprisoned in 1973 for opposing

the regime's policies. Since 1982 he has become a researcher for the Islamic Encyclopaedia in Kuwait. http://www.islaax.org/arabic/Sheikh Abdulqani.htm

21. Xalane Camp was a military training school in Mogadishu used to indoctrinate civil servants with socialist ideology.
22. Nuurta was a member of the commission assigned to draft the Family Law and was a legal adviser to President Maxamed Siyad Barre.
23. Italy recovered its influence in Somalia after the establishment of the National University funded by an Italian cooperation programme, by adopting the Italian language as the language of instruction and Italian lecturers as the main faculty members. Most of the younger generation of Somalia were educated there.
24. The designated commission included Maxamed Sheikh Cismaan (High Court), Cabdisalaam Sheikh Xuseen (Minister of Justice), Maxamed Aadan Sheikh (Minister of Information) and four women: Nuurta Xaaji Xassan, Marxam Xaaji Cilmi, Faduumo Cumar Xaashii and Raaqiya Xaaji Ducaale.
25. The Vice-President's speech in the state sponsored demonstration is remembered for his use of the following expression: '*Yeere yerre yam. Yaxaas qaade Yam*' (Whoever speaks up will be eaten. The crocodile will take him and eat.) This expression is used in children's play and means that any attempt to confront the family will meet the strong hand of the revolution.
26. Sheikh Geryare was the director of Religious Affairs of the Ministry of Justice (1969–75) and a prominent scholar. When some people attempted to fight against the security forces, Sheikh Axmed requested them not to.
27. Islamic scholars from al-Azhar University were engaged in Islamic activities in Somalia and taught in many schools. Sheikh Cabdulasis was ordered to leave Somalia within 24 hours. The first speaker after the prayers was Xaaji Cilmi (Xaaji Dhagax) who shortly expressed how the words of Sheikh Cabdulasis were relevant to the Somali situation, and most likely provoked the subsequent Islamic scholars' speeches.
28. For example, Sheikh Maxamed Macallin did not attend Friday prayers in the Mosque. He revealed to me on 20 June 1985 that 'his students working seemingly with the National Intelligence, Xassan Qamaan, did not allow him to go out from his house'. On the other hand, Sheikh Maxamed Geryare prayed in the mosque and he did not participate in delivering speeches. Moreover, none of the leaders of the student activists were evident there. All this shows that the protest was not pre-planned.
29. Sheikh Ciise Sheikh Axmed narrated that he personally participated in the demonstration and was only saved from imprisonment by his Egyptian teacher Ibrahim al-Dusuqi who met him accidentally and recommended him to go away.
30. General Jilacow, head of National Security Service in Mogadishu, warned Sheikh Geryare and recommended him to escape. Interview with General

Jilacow in Nairobi, 5 February 2004, and Sheikh Maxamed Geryare in Toronto, 12 April 2004.

31. Maryam Cariif Qaasim, a prolific writer and a politician, interviewed in Djibouti on 12 November 2007.
32. Cawad Axmed Casharo, a member of parliament and former director of the Ministry of Trade during the Siyad Barre regime, interviewed in Nairobi, 30 June 2009.
33. Cabdiraxmaan Cabdulle Shuuke, former Minister of Education during the Siyad Barre regime, interviewed in Nairobi, 30 June 2009.
34. Because of the destruction of archives in Somalia, I did not succeed in finding any primary or secondary sources to refer to. My approach was limited to questioning the few personalities who claimed they knew something of the event and its implications. Consequently I have interviewed Professor Cali Sheikh Axmed, Saynab Xaaji Barako, Maxamed Xaaji, Nuura Xaaji Xassan, Cabdi Daahir Diiriye, Yaxye Sheikh Aamir and many others.
35. The narrator was interviewed in Nairobi, 10 July 2009. He requested anonymity.
36. This story was narrated by a fellow minister who requested anonymity; interviewed in Nairobi, 8 July 2009.
37. At least two such incidents happened in Wardhigley and Bondhere districts of Mogadishu. However, interviewees could not recollect the names of those involved.
38. Sheikh Nuur Cali Colow (1918–95) was a pioneer and prominent scholar who preached the thought of Salafism in Somalia for more than 60 years (1935–95). He graduated from al-Azhar University in 1963 and returned to Somalia establishing 'Ihya al-Sunna al-Muhamadiyah' (the Revivification of the Sunna of Mohammedans) in 1967. He became the Director of Religious Affairs in the Ministry of Justice and Religious Affairs. He was imprisoned twice, in 1969–70 and 1973–76.
39. The Islamic library was sent from Kuwait to Somalia and was shelved in the library of the Ministry of Justice and Religious Affairs. It incorporated specialised books of the Muslim Brotherhood, including the works of Hassan al-Banna, Sayyid Qutb, Al-Mawdudi, Abduqadir Audah, Al-Nadawi and others. Students of the Arabic schools such as the Institute of Islamic Solidarity (Ma'had al-tadamun al-Islami) and Egyptian high schools frequented the library and were influenced by these ideas.
40. All four schools of Sunni Jurisprudence (Hanafi, Shafi'i, Maliki, and Hambali) agree that entire body of the woman, except her face and hands, should be covered in the presence of someone of the opposite sex, other than close relatives. However, some Salafia scholars not only encourage covering the face, but also consider it obligatory. This understanding takes an extreme form and considers women who do not cover their face as loose in their faith.

References

Aamir, Yahye S. 2009. Interviewed 18 July, Nairobi.

Abdullahi, Abdurahman 2007a. 'Penetrating Cultural Frontiers in Somalia: History of Women's Political Participation during Four Decades (1959–2000).' *African Renaissance*, 4 (1), 34–54.

——— 2007b. 'Perspectives on the State Collapse in Somalia.' In A.A. Osman and I.K. Soure (eds), *Somalia at the Crossroads: Challenges and Perspectives in Reconstituting a Failed State*. London: Adonis & Abbey Publishers Ltd., pp. 34–54.

——— 2008. 'The Islah Movement in Somalia: Islamic Moderation in War-torn Somalia.' Paper presented at the Second Nordic Horn of Africa Conference held 31 October-1 November, Oslo.

Abubakar, Ali S.A. 1985. *Al-Da'wa al-Islamiyah al-Mu'āsira fi Al-Qarni al-Ifriqī*. Riyadh: Umayya Publishing House.

——— 1992. *Al-Somāl: Judūr al-Ma'āsāt al-Rāhina*. Beirut: Dar Ibn al-Hazm.

——— 2007. Interviewed 30 November.

Ahmed, Christine C. 1995. 'Finely Etched Chattel: The Invention of Somali Women.' In A.J. Ahmed (ed.), *The Invention of Somalia*. Lawrenceville, NJ: The Red Sea Press, pp. 157–90.

Sheikh Isse, Sheikh A. 2009. Interviewed 20 July.

Asharo, Awad A. 2009. Interviewed 30 June, Nairobi.

Baracco, Zainab H. 2009. Interviewed 10 July, Nairobi.

Besteman, Catherine 1999. *Unravelling Somalia: Race, Violence, and the Legacy of Slavery*. Philadelphia: University of Pennsylvania Press.

Bradbury, Mark 2008. *Becoming Somaliland*. London: Progressio.

Contini, Paolo 1969. *The Somali Republic: an Experiment in Legal Integration*. London: Frank Cass & Company.

Diriye, Abdi D. 2009. Interviewed 14 July, Nairobi.

Geryare, Sheikh M.A. 2007, 2009. Interviewed 5 November 2007 and 12 June 2009, Toronto and Hargeysa, respectively.

Hamdi S. Mohamed 2003. *Multiple Challenges, Multiple Struggles: A History of Women's Activism in Canada*. (unpublished PhD Thesis, University of Ottawa).

Hess, Robert 1966. *Italian Colonialism in Somalia*. London: University of Chicago Press.

Jilaow, General 2004. Interviewed 5 February, Nairobi.

Kapteijns, Lidwien 1994. 'Women and the Crisis of Communal Identity: The Cultural Construction of Gender in Somali History.' In A. I. Samatar (ed.) *The Somali Challenge. From Catastrophe to Renewal*. Boulder: Lynne Rienner, pp. 211–32.

Laitin, David D. and Said Samatar 1987. *Somalia: Nation in Search of a State*. Boulder: Westview Press.

Le Sage, Andre 2004. 'Somalia and the War on Terrorism: Political Islamic Movements and US Counter-Terrorism Efforts.' (unpublished PhD thesis, Cambridge University).

Lewis, Ioan M. 1980. *A Modern History of Somalia: Nation and State in the Horn of Africa*. London: Longmans.
——— 1961. *Pastoral Democracy*. London: Oxford University Press.
——— 1963. 'Dualism in Somali Notions of Power.' *The Journal of the Anthropological Institute of Great Britain and Ireland*, 93 (I), 109–16.
Marchal, Roland 2006. 'Islamic Political Dynamics in the Somali Civil War.' In A. De Waal, *Islamism and its Enemies in the Horn of Africa*. Bloomington: Indiana University Press, pp. 114–45.
Nuurta Xassan, H. 2007. Interviewed 15 October, Toronto.
Pestalozza, Luigi 1973. *The Somali Revolution*. Bari: Édition Afrique Asie Amérique Latine.
Qassim, Marian A. 2007. Interviewed 12 November, Djibouti.
Samatar, Ahmed 1988. *Socialist Somalia: Rhetoric and Reality*. London: Zed Press.
Shuke, Abdurahman A. 2009. Interviewed 30 June, Nairobi.
Siyad Barre, Mohamed 1979. *My Country and my People: Selected Speeches of Jaalle Siyaad*. Ministry of Information and National Guidance.
Tahir, Mahmood 1987. *Personal Law in Islamic Countries*. New Delhi: Academy of Law and Religion.
Turyare, Mohamud A. 2009. Interviewed 11 July, Nairobi, Kenya.

PART V

SPIRIT POSSESSION

10

SPIRITS AND THE HUMAN WORLD IN NORTHERN SOMALIA

Marja Tiilikainen

Introduction

Naasa Hablood is a landmark of Hargeysa, the capital of northern Somalia. The two rocky mountain tops at the outskirts of the city resemble a girl's breasts, giving inspiration for its Somali name. Naasa Hablood is recognised as a beautiful, but also strange and mysterious place. Local people know it as the mountain of *jinn* spirits. As described by I.M. Lewis (e.g. 1956, 1966, 1998), spirits have historically belonged to the life of Somali Muslims and played an important role in the cultural understanding of health, illness and misfortune in Somalia. Even today, spirits are part of everyday life in Hargeysa. It is commonplace to hear about unexpected and unexplainable events that are connected to spirits. Indeed, the existence of spirits and their influence have become even more visible following the civil war. According to my interlocutors, an increasing number of people suffer from problems caused by *jinn*. Moreover, the increased number of *jinn*-related problems is reflected by the emergence of *cilaaj*, Islamic healing clinics. There is a long tradition of healing with the help of the Koran in Somalia as in other Muslim countries, but professional Koranic healers in Somaliland are a new development. In addition, the methods in *cilaaj* differ from the previous Somali ways of dealing with spirits.

This article will address the changing religious and cultural understandings regarding spirits and healing in northern Somalia. I approach illness and healing as socially, culturally and religiously constructed experiences, concepts and practices that are interconnected with larger societal, political and economic processes (e.g. Kleinman 1995: 123–5). I suggest that the emergence of Koranic healing clinics does not primarily tell about the increased number of possession cases *per se*, but indicates a change in how the relationship between human beings and spirits is seen, and what is regarded as proper treatment. Moreover, changed explanations for and relations to spirits reflect the social, political, economic and religious changes in Somali society as a consequence of a devastating civil war and strong politicisation of Islam during the past twenty years. Owing to the push for more puritanical forms of Islam, *saar* spirit possession as well as Sufi healing practices are being marginalised.

Islam has provided a central source for illness explanations and healing for Somalis from ancient times, but the new Islamic presence in the society at large can be expected to have an influence on illness-related experiences, conceptions and practices. For example, in Egypt religious symptoms among patients with psychotic illness were found to correspond with the changing patterns of religious emphasis in Egyptian society (Atallah *et al.* 2001). According to Morsy (1988: 358–60), the spread of Islamic clinics in Egypt can be seen as part of the overall Islamic orientation supported by the state and as an opportunity to gain legitimacy within existing power structures. Finally, Sengers (2003: 123) highlights that Koranic healing in Egypt is also a source of income; the healers fill a gap in the market.

This article is based on data gathered by ethnographic methods in northwestern Somalia, often referred to as Somaliland, where I spent four months in total in the summers of 2005 and 2006 and the winter of 2007 as part of my post-doctoral research.[1] The data consist of interviews and participant observations of local healers and their patients. Moreover, I attended healing and religious rituals mainly organised by women. The fieldwork was concentrated in Hargeysa, but some data were also gathered in the cities of Gabiley, Borama, Burco and Berbera. As my Somali language skills are rudimentary, I worked with male and female assistants who also helped to obtain access to the field. All names in this article are pseudonyms.

After a brief historical introduction I will describe spirits in my field context. Next I will outline the main differences in ideas regarding spirits and their treatment by focusing both on healers who have contracts with spirits and on healers who aim at exorcising spirits. Finally, I will discuss the changing relations to spirits in Somaliland.

Islam, spirits and healing—a brief historical outline

Most Somalis are Sunni Muslims belonging to the Shafi'ite school of Islamic jurisprudence. Islam reached the Somali coast in the early 7th century. The new religion gradually started to spread to Somali hinterlands from trading ports such as Mogadishu and Seylac (Lewis 1998: 7–8). In this context, pre-Islamic Cushitic religious beliefs were syncretised with mystical Sufism. The Qadriyya, Ahmediyya and Salihiyya became the most important Sufi orders among Somalis (Cassanelli 1982: 24–5; Laitin and Samatar 1987: 44–6; Lewis 1998). Until recently, Sufi orders have had great influence and Somalis have been moderate in their religious views.

The rise of Islamist movements in Somalia began in the 1970s, their influence being strongest in the cities. Under President Maxamed Siyad Barre, Islamic reform in Somalia was violently oppressed.[2] Islamism gained freedom and room for manoeuvre in the course of the state collapse. According to Le Sage (2001), in the 1990s Islamists were divided into different groups such as the moderate Al Islaax and the politically radical Al Itixaad al Islaami. In its interpretations of Islam, the latter was close to the puritanical Wahhabi and Salafiyya movements of the Arabian Peninsula. Islamic political activity in Somalia increased significantly (Menkhaus 2002: 110). Islamist groups have gained wide support, particularly in southern Somalia where no effective government has been established so far. They provide schools, orphanages, aid agencies and services to poor people who have suffered tremendously during the prolonged war and instability (ibid.: 114). Because of these influences, Sufi practices such as annual commemorations of popular Sufi sheikhs have declined. For example, in the summer of 2006 the annual pilgrimage, *siyaaro*, to the shrine of Aw Barkhadle outside Hargeysa attracted only some 500–600 people and the event was hardly noticed in Hargeysa. This observation is in stark contrast with the description of Lewis. During his fieldwork in the 1950s and 1960s, several thousand pilgrims from all over the northern regions attended the same *siyaaro* and large numbers of livestock were slaughtered for the feasting (Lewis 1998: 89–98). Moreover, only a few of Hargeysa's 300 or so reconstructed and new mosques are Sufi mosques.

Islamisation is visible also in ways of dressing, as an increasing number of women cover themselves by large *jilbaab*s and face veils, *niqab*s, which is a new dress code in Somalia.

Islamic medicine, in particular the Prophet's medicine (Perho 1995) which included spirits, witchcraft and the evil eye among the causes of illnesses, entered the Horn of Africa as part of the expansion of Islam. In addition to Islamic texts and sources, there have been other discourses aiming to understand and deal with the universe of spirits among Somalis. The spirit possession cult of *saar* is one of them. Sufi sheikhs are often believed to master divination and magic and be acquainted with spirits (Luling 2002: 227), for instance, to be able to call the assistant spirits, *rooxaan* (Helander 1989: 90).

Somali *saar* belongs to a wider spirit possession phenomenon, which Lewis calls the *zar-bori* cult. According to Lewis, the complex of cults originates from western Africa and from Ethiopia, with both Islamic and Christian elements (Lewis 1991). Spirit possession is widely known on the East African coast and its hinterland. Despite different cultural and historical characteristics, the basic structures in the different areas are usually quite similar (e.g. Boddy 1989; Lewis *et al.* 1991; Lambek 1993; Nisula 1999).

Spirit possession in *saar* is a state where a spirit has entered a person. A spirit can be inherited from a near relative, in particular one's mother. Alternatively, it may enter a person through strong emotions like anger or love. Possessions of a person who has a spirit, such as clothes or shoes, may also transmit spirits. Spirits can cause various illnesses and other problems. Common symptoms connected to spirits include, among others: fear, anxiety, general malaise, unhappiness, sleeplessness, tiredness, feebleness, lassitude, mental confusion, nausea, fainting, persistent headache, unwillingness to eat or talk, loss of weight, vomiting, sadness, 'madness', feeling of pressure in the chest, unspecified aches in muscles and bones, infertility, violent bodily agitation, blindness, paralysis without apparent organic cause, and epilepsy (Boddy 1989: 145; Lewis 1998: 109; Tiilikainen 2003: 248).

Saar among Somalis includes many different cults and spirits, for instance *mingis*, *boorane*, *sharax*, *wadaado* and *numbi*. Different spirits have specific ritual practices, which may also vary in different areas and groups. Healing rituals often include special incense types, dance styles, music and animal sacrifices (Antoniotto 1984: 164; Ahmed

1988: 241–2; Pelizzari 1997). According to Lewis' early study in Somaliland (1966: 314), Somali men alleged *saar* possession to be more common among the wives of the wealthy men, whereas women stated that there were spirits which attacked the wealthy, and others which possessed the poor.

Lewis (1998: 28–9) has pointed out the similarities between *saar* and the Sufi *dhikri*, even though the aims and the performances of the two rituals are different. *Saar* can be seen as part of the religious, spiritual and moral order of the Horn, although today, many Somali Muslims reject any connection between *saar* and Islam (Boddy 1989: 278; Lewis 1991: 3). In many East African Muslim communities the existence of spirits is a cultural fact. Furthermore, many researches have shown that women in particular seem to be prone to spirit possession (Boddy 1989; Lewis *et al.* 1991; Nisula 1999). Lewis (1966, 1998) regards *saar* as a deprivation cult, through which marginalised Somali women try to enhance their position. But *saar* has also been approached as a complementary cultural practice in relation to men's public role in Islamic rituals (Nisula 1999: 160–3), and as an inseparable part of women's cultural values and moral principles in their everyday life as Muslims (Boddy 1989: 276).

In the Islamic world a specific species of spirits is referred to as *jinn*.[3] According to Islamic theology, Allah created *jinn* from smokeless fire. Like humans, *jinn* are able to choose between right and wrong. *Jinn* are invisible, but they can take any form of animals or humans. There are *jinn* everywhere, but in particular, they like to reside in impure places such as toilets and rubbish dumps. *Jinn* have powers by which they can affect humans and cause them various kinds of problems. Possession may result if a *jinni* has been hurt or made angry. But possession may also occur because of jest, or even love. A *jinni* can even marry a human being and get children with her/him (Ashour 1989; Philips 1997). As Islam spread to the Horn, *saar* spirits were often classified as a kind of *jinn* so that they could fit better into Islamic categories (Boddy 1989: 27, 278; Lewis 1998: 28). It is often difficult to distinguish if a person is referring particularly to *jinn*, or if '*jinn*' is used as a general category for spirits, after which she or he may categorise the spirit in a more exact manner (Tiilikainen 2003: 236). Those who are involved with spirit cults may distinguish different spirit categories, symptoms caused by different spirits and appropriate treatments for particular spirits.

At various times and places there have been attempts to outlaw *saar* cults (on the Swahili coast, see Giles 1995: 92, 102; for colonial Aden, see Kapteijns and Spaulding 1996). In 1955, the British Somaliland Protectorate Advisory Council agreed that legislation was needed to make the practice of *saar* illegal (Lewis 1956: 147). Spirit possession rituals as well as other dances were also banned in Somalia during the rule of Maxamed Siyad Barre (Declich 1995: 208). More recently, the Union of Islamic Courts which held power in Mogadishu between June and December 2006 banned *mingis* rituals (Hiiraan 2006). Despite attempts to stop the *saar* cult, it has been practiced in Somalia and Somaliland until today.

The landscape of spirits in Somaliland

The political situations in northern and southern Somalia are remarkably different. The civil war started in the North in 1988, when the anti–government Somali National Movement (SNM) attacked the national army in Hargeysa and Burco. The army struck back, destroying northern villages and towns by, for example, aerial bombardments. Hundreds of thousands of people escaped to Ethiopia. In the South, the still ongoing civil war broke out in January 1991 after President Maxamed Siyad Barre had left the country. The same year, in May, the independence of Somaliland was declared by the SNM. Despite some local fighting, especially in the first half of the 1990s, people in Somaliland have managed to rebuild the country peacefully (Bradbury 2008).

The population of the secessionist Republic of Somaliland is estimated to be somewhere between less than two million and 3.5 million.[4] After the war, urban centres have grown quickly (ibid.: 161). Somaliland—which does not enjoy international recognition—is among the poorest countries of the world. Health indicators are extremely bad and the health sector suffers from lack of professional staff, financial resources and good governance (Leather *et al.* 2006: 1120). Unemployment is common and many households in Hargeysa are dependent on remittances sent from the diaspora. Hargeysa is a vibrant capital of about half a million inhabitants, where the parliament, the seat of the Somaliland president, ministries and other national institutions are situated. Hargeysa streets are full of cars, goats, donkey drivers with water-tanks, pedestrians and beggars mingling with each other. The tarmac roads have potholes and cars zigzag to avoid them. Afternoons are quiet as the majority of men concentrate on chewing *qaad*, but when the shops open after the siesta, the town turns busy again.[5]

The city is growing quickly as new houses and neighbourhoods are built on the outskirts. According to my interlocutors, after the war, uneducated people from the countryside moved into the city, while many of the original inhabitants of Hargeysa had died or left the country to seek asylum abroad. Nowadays, the Somalis in the diaspora invest in the country, and build houses for possible future repatriation or business purposes. In the city there are also large areas where internally displaced persons and returnees from Ethiopia live in makeshift huts.

Spirits also inhabit this urban environment. According to one man, 'in every house in Hargeysa there is somebody who has a *jinni*'. *Jinn* are particularly prevalent in Hargeysa because the empire of *jinn* is believed to be located close to Naasa Hablood. During my stay in Hargeysa, several people told me peculiar stories and experiences about Naasa Hablood. For example, hikers on the mountain have found unusual objects that have not been produced by humans, but by *jinn*. A family that lives in a new house near Naasa Hablood told me that when the sun goes down and darkness falls, they see small lights around the mountain and on hill slopes, even though nobody is living there. People are not willing to go to the mountain, unless *jinn* possess them, in which case they are attracted to it. For instance, I heard about a young woman possessed by *jinn* who suddenly disappeared from her home, and was found on her way to Naasa Hablood.

The world of spirits is a shadow world, another reality not far from everyday routines: locked doors may open by themselves. If a person is possessed by a *jinni*, another person cannot always be sure with whom she/he is talking—a *jinni* or a human being. One should not pick money or other things from the street, because they may belong to a *jinni* and cause problems later. A person's behaviour can change abruptly because of *jinn*. A man told about his housemaid:

> Once before the girl had tried to burn herself and she had ugly marks on her neck and face. She always covered herself with a *jilbaab*, so I did not know about it before. Yesterday evening, when I was at home, she suddenly was enraged, she was extremely strong although she is very small, she threw a heavy decorated table into the air and broke it. Four men used all their force

to keep her still. The father of the girl was asked to come as well as some religious men from a mosque. The father hit the girl and tried to exorcise the *jinn*. The girl, or a *jinni*, said that this time she would really kill herself. The girl was maybe 25 years old and unmarried. She used to work hard. She normally wakes up at five o'clock in the morning, and already at six, the whole house is cleaned up. I did not think about it before, but she never goes out of the house. We had to fire her. We told the father that we could not take the responsibility for what will happen to the girl. Had we not been in the house, the girl could have broken things or killed herself. I was shocked. Before this incident I did not believe in *jinn*, but now I do (Field notes, Hargeysa, 10.08.2005).

Night time is particularly risky. At sunset, the doors and windows should be closed, and *foox* (frankincense) burned to protect oneself from wandering *jinn* and keep them away from one's home. A young woman explained, 'for *jinn*, night is like day for humans'. She said that in the centre of Hargeysa there are many cars at night. These cars and the drivers, however, are different from those that can be seen at daytime. 'The drivers are *jinn*. They give women a ride, and when women return, they are not normal.'[6]

Not only Naasa Hablood, but also mountains in general are known to be places where spirits reside. Hence the mountainous northeastern part of Somalia along the coast of Somaliland and Puntland is believed to be particularly rich in spirits. According to legends, the origin of *mingis* is connected to that specific area and the best masters or *calaqad*s, of the *mingis* cult, are believed to be found there (Pelizzari 1997: 153–4). Outside Hargeysa, towards the cities of Berbera and Borama, there are places on the road that are known for frequent accidents because they are inhabited by *jinn* that cause drivers to suddenly see shadows or lights on the road. *Jinn* are also said to live inside high, sculpture-like hives built by termites frequently observed outside cities. Other natural phenomena connected to *jinn* include the sea and wind. Especially Somalis who live on the coast may tell how *jinn* tempt people into the sea. One type of *jinn* is known as *dabeyl*, which literally means wind. *Dabeyl jinn* refer in particular to 'dust devils' which can easily be detected in the countryside, where wind spirals raise dust from land in a treeless horizon. When a *dabeyl jinni* touches a person, she/he may be paralysed in the face or the body. A woman told how she as a young girl had been close to a tree and *dabeyl jinn* passed her, resulting in facial paralysis. At that time she was in Mogadishu, and acupuncture given by a Chinese doctor had healed her. According to Helander (1995: 85–6), *dabeyl* is often seen as the cause for polio.

After the civil war the number of *jinn* reportedly has increased and, moreover, possession by *jinn*, which used to be quite rare, has spread like an epidemic. Different explanations for the increasing number of *jinn* cases were given: when the war started in Hargeysa and everybody fled, Hargeysa became a ghost city. *Jinn* who like living in ruins then moved into the city's empty houses. Moreover, *jinn* fed upon bloodshed resulting from the war, and their number increased.[7] A healer in Burco mentioned that 'according to Islam, where blood of human beings runs, *jinn* pour down like rain. Then the merciful angels go away.' Nowadays, as the cities in Somaliland expand, people move into the outskirts where *jinn* used to live. Hence, according to common explanations, first the number of *jinn* has actually increased and second, people fight with *jinn* over the possession of land.[8] These frequent encounters with possibly evil and aggressive *jinn* increase the chances for possession, illness and suffering. According to other explanations, however, spirits cause problems and illness because Somalis do not follow the former cultural rules and have broken the previous agreements between humans and spirits. Sheekhad Habiba explained:[9]

> People fall ill now after the war more often than before, because they are mentally, spiritually and physically destroyed and handicapped. *Rooxaan* [spirits] also fight when there is war and people fight, and that is why people are not feeling well. People also fall ill, because they have denied our culture. They do not slaughter animals; they do not use perfumes [...] This is because people are poor, they have not enough money to slaughter and buy good clothes, and also people have become modern, they do not believe any more in those things that we used to believe. Somalis have abandoned their culture, and they do not make, for example, *siyaaro*, any more (Field notes, Hargeysa, 07.07.2006).

Hence the neglect of the former cultural rituals and the lack of respect for spirits, which used to be shown in ritual slaughter of animals and offerings of food, clothes and perfumes, makes spirits hungry and angry, and therefore Somalis get sick. *Rooxaan* spirits mentioned by Sheekhad Habiba and a few other Sufi healers are understood to be different from *saar* spirits; Sufi healers connect *rooxaan* to a Sufist world view, whereas they regard *saar* as being outside the realm of religion. However, both groups of healers develop a contract with the spirits with whom they work.

A contract with spirits

Rooxaan spirits. Sheekhad Habiba is a 45-year-old woman who is close to the Qadriyya order. People know her as *awliyo Allah*, a holy person or saint of Allah. She has been healing since she was a young girl, but in particular after the civil war when the suffering and illnesses of people increased. She told how she became a healer:

I was eight years old, when *rooxaan* [spirits] started to teach me. It was like I had attended a medical faculty. They first choose you, and then they start teaching. The learning is difficult. First you have to try all the medicines yourself, like electricity was in your body, and you must heal. Gradually a student becomes a teacher. When I was an eight-year-old girl, I saw something, like people, and I thought they were *jinn*. They said don't be afraid, we want to show you something. I saw a lion that nobody else could see. These creatures wanted to teach me first everything about *jinn*, how many children they have and so forth. It was the first lesson. I prayed and fasted, I believed I was getting crazy. I could not sleep at night, I saw more things. I decided to escape to a mosque, but they followed me even there. They were *rooxaan*. I understood that I could not refuse. They said that I saw the lion of Jilani.[10] You have to accept it, otherwise it eats you. First, when I was small, they told me to forecast the future to other children. Often I knew and had it right. *Rooxaan* also told me the right herbs, if somebody had a wound. If I refused to heal, I became unconscious and ill. In the beginning a student is like a person who cannot swim and who has been thrown in the middle of the sea. *Rooxaan* show you something that you have never seen. You have to suffer for a long time. But if you survive, you will be healed. In the end I got the final certificate from the *rooxaan* and a permission to heal (Sheekhad Habiba, Hargeysa, 07.07.2006).

Skeekhad Habiba explains the process of gaining embodied knowledge through spirit possession (compare Lambek 1993). The way she describes her initiation into the role as a healer is typical: a person first experiences strange visions and feelings, falls ill and suffers, before she/he gradually learns how to heal. Becoming a healer is a painful learning process which a chosen person cannot avoid without risking her/his own health. Once when I visited Sheekhad Habiba's home, I met a woman sitting close to her. She smoked cigarettes and sipped tea, every now and then her eyeballs turned around and she seemed to talk to herself. My first impression was that she was mentally disturbed, but Sheekhad Habiba explained that the woman suffered because *rooxaan* were teaching her. She was sure that one day the woman would become a healer. Sheekhad Habiba explained what *rooxaan* spirits are like:

I work with *rooxaan*. They have to be either good Muslims or good Christians. There are different kinds of *rooxaan* spirits: they have different powers, some of them belong to upper social class, some of them to lower social class, some are doctors, some are soldiers. *Rooxaan* are similar to people in the sense that they have alliances, like we have Russians, Europeans, and there are also racists who tease people. But *rooxaan* are also fair—if a person causes her/his own problems, they do not help. *Rooxaan* are mediators between humans and *jinn*. And a sheikh/sheekhad is a mediator between *rooxaan* and humans. A sheikh is able to communicate with *rooxaan* and to ask stronger *rooxaan* to come and help. Only a person who can do miracles can give orders to *rooxaan*. If you do not know how to deal with the relationship to *rooxaan*, you go mad. And if people are not good to *rooxaan* and do not treat them well, *rooxaan* start giving orders to people. If Allah wants, *jinn* and *rooxaan* discuss and negotiate peacefully. Sometimes force is needed, and the other party may be hurt. Sometimes *jinn* say that they go away, but they come back anyway. Then we can put *jinn* into a prison. *Jinn* also are powerful. There are two kinds of *rooxaan*, those who work like a camera and show everything, and those who can heal. *Rooxaan* teach and show something new all the time. But they are unpredictable in what they teach and also in when they come. When we slaughter animals, it means that we have an appointment with *rooxaan*. Slaughtering opens a door for them, but they only come if they want to and they also decide the time. It is possible to study culture and religion, but the knowledge of *rooxaan* is hidden. When you make a contract with *rooxaan*, you never get rid of them (Sheekhad Habiba, Hargeysa, 07.07.2006).

According to Calverley (1993) and Chodkiewicz (1995), the Arabic word *rūh* has several meanings, for example, breath of life, wind, a special angel messenger or a divine quality. *Rūh* has also been applied to human spirit, soul and all spirits, both good and evil. *Rūh* is closely connected to the concept of *nafs* ('self, soul'). *Rūhāniyya* is another Arabic word that may help in understanding the etymology of *rooxaan*. In the ancient texts its usual meaning has been spiritual beings and it has also been used to refer to *jinn*.[11] Moreover, among Sufis *rūhāniyya* denotes the angel who rules each of the celestial spheres (Calverley 1993: 880–3; Chodkiewicz 1995: 593–4). According to a sheikh in Burco, the Somali word *ruuxi* also refers to illnesses that belong to the mental or psychic area, in particular those caused by *jinn*, *isha* (evil eye) and *sixir* (witchcraft/sorcery), in contrast to physical illnesses, *cudurka jismiga*.

Sheekhad Habiba stressed that *rooxaan* were different from *jinn*. *Rooxaan* help healers in the healing process. *Rooxaan* may assist to find lost objects or people, bring medication, resolve witchcraft by finding 'packages' done by a witch, and tell the future. *Rooxaan*, like other spirits, are able to work in global context. For example, I was frequently told that spirits would bring items from abroad. But *rooxaan* may also cause suffering and illness if they are not dealt with properly. The actual healing and divination include different practices and rituals, depending on the healer. Sheekhad Habiba related:

When an ill person comes to me, I ask permission from God to heal. *Rooxaan* first examine the patient and tell me if I can and am allowed to treat her/him or not. Sometimes there may be more powerful *jinn* behind the problems, which cannot be treated. A healer must not be weak, but strong, because she/he attacks another power. Sometimes it takes one day, sometimes longer, to get an answer. *Rooxaan* tell me the answer in different ways: I can hear it like I listened to a radio, I can see it like I watched a television or I get an answer while I sleep (Sheekhad Habiba, Hargeysa, 07.07.2006).

A healing ritual arranged by Sheekhad Habiba and her companions often includes slaughtering animals, smoking cigarettes or a water pipe (*shisha*), using perfume and frankincense (*foox*), praying and doing *dhikri*. Healers, who work with spirits, commonly use *qaad* as part of making contact with the spiritual world; I observed also female healers and patients using it.

Saar spirits. The problems caused by s*aar* spirits are treated by a possession cult. The aim of the treatment is to pay respect to the spirit, to please it by slaughtering animals and offering special foods, beautiful clothes, incense (such as *jaawe*, *cuud*), perfumes, and by drumming, dancing and singing special songs. During a ritual, the patient usually falls into trance. The leaders of *saar* cults and their spirits are able to communicate with the spirits of the patients. For instance, in the *mingis* cult the leader, *calaqad*, may ask a spirit why she/he disturbs a patient, and what she/he wants. Afterwards the wishes of a spirit should be fulfilled. The recovery and well-being rely on the possession ritual and the continuous remembrance and respectful behaviour towards the spirit.[12]

Taking part in the ritual is a learning process. Gradually patients learn to deal with spirits, and finally become teachers and leaders of the cult themselves. At this stage, I have been told, spirits do not disturb any more, but the teacher her/himself has power to control the spirits. *Saar* ceremonies often last several days and demand costly preparations. Halimo, a *calaqad* in Hargeysa told about *saar Maama*, which is, according to her, another name for *mingis* ritual:

We slaughter a black and white male sheep, and blood is spread onto the hands and soles of a patient. The patient goes around the animal three times, before we slaughter it. Then *saar Maama* will come. We dance, sing and drum.

And we tell *saar Maama*, 'do not disturb [the patient] any more'. *Saar* may tell what she or he wants: red clothes, gold, perfumes. The patient must buy these, and then she will be healthy again. The patient stays seven nights with the *calaqad*. The ritual has to be repeated in the coming years, for total three times (Halimo, Hargeysa, 29.07.2006).

Halimo also treats people who have *wadaado*.[13] *Wadaado* spirits do not cause serious illness, nor are they very 'demanding', and they therefore only require one healing session. In *wadaado* there is no dancing or drumming, but it is important to offer the spirit popcorn (*salool*), a sweet jelly-like delicacy called *halwa*, dates (*timir*), coffee (*bun*) and red sauce (*maraq cas*) with meat. An elderly woman confirmed,

After the patient has tasted the food, *furcadde* or *cadar* [perfumes] is sprinkled on her, and applied to her ear, nose, head, forehead and neck. The teacher takes the *girgire* [incense burner] and goes around the patient. We beat the patient on the upper part of the back and tell *wadaado*, 'go to another Somali city'. If a small girl is ill, we say, 'when she gets married, she pays you'. You have to make the ceremony once a year, altogether three times. Then it is time to say good-bye to *wadaado*, we slaughter a sheep and say, 'do not come back any more'. Then the patient becomes a healer of *wadaado* (Field notes, Hargeysa, 16.08.2005).

Wadaado is more like an everyday practice that can be done at home alone or with a few friends. A middle-aged woman told that when she lived in the United Arab Emirates, she used to arrange *wadaado* once a week with her friend. They put on red clothes, drank coffee, and had all the necessary food. If she had a headache or was feeling down, after the ritual she became well again. According to my interlocutors in Somaliland, nowadays large *saar* rituals such as *mingis* are arranged very rarely by comparison with the past. During my ten-week stay in Hargeysa in summer 2006, a *calaqad* whom I knew arranged a *mingis* ritual only once. To arrange a full *mingis* ritual that lasts several days may cost from 200 to 1,000 US dollars, but simpler rituals such as *wadaado* are less costly. Even so, many patients and their families cannot afford healing rituals that require buying animals to be slaughtered or other expensive items, but search for cheaper treatments. In addition to economic problems, *saar* rituals are diminishing for religious reasons. As a result of the increasingly rigid interpretations by Wahhabi and Salafiyya-oriented Muslims in Somaliland and elsewhere, *saar* is seen as forbidden (compare Drieskens 2008: 225). Accordingly, spirits are reconfigured to more *jinn*-like creatures and are increasingly treated in Islamic clinics where healing is part of a wider agenda of promoting Islamic values and life-style.

Exorcising the spirits

'Somalis used to slaughter animals and give food to *jinn*. But if you give food to *jinn*, they will never go away. Now we just drive *jinn* away, they have no right to cause us diseases,' explained a female patient at an Islamic clinic in Hargeysa. Since 1991, an increasing number of Islamic healers in Somaliland have established clinics, *cilaaj*, where they claim to heal by 'purely' Islamic methods, derived from the Koran and the Prophet's *sunna*. One of the Koranic healers I met had a medical background as a veterinary doctor and another as a nurse, but the others had entered the field of healing through Islamic studies. All of the healers said that they had first studied Islam and gradually started to study Koranic healing as well. Many of them had studied under the guidance of other Koranic healers, and learned the use of herbs and other techniques. In contrast to healers who had been chosen by spirits, Koranic healers usually stressed the importance of personal inclination (compare Al-Krenawi and Graham 1999: 57). Moreover, they highlighted that after the war there was a great demand for people who could help, and they wanted to protect people from 'charlatans'.

Depending on the popularity of the sheikh, the waiting time may vary from some hours to several days, and a patient or her/his relative receives a queuing number. The diagnosis is based on questioning the symptoms and doing diagnostic tests that include reciting certain *sura*s of the Koran, sprinkling *tahlil* (water over which the sheikh has recited verses of the Koran), and certain ingredients which the patient has to inhale. Sheikhs mainly treat patients who suffer from *jinn*, evil eye or witchcraft, but natural/physical illnesses may also be treated. The treatment consists of listening to the Koranic recitation, receiving herbal medication and possibly cupping. To be a good Muslim is important for successful treatment and as protection from the *jinn*. A sheikh in Hargeysa explained: 'A person gets *jinn*, if she/he is afraid or angry, or she/he thinks a lot, does not pray or follow religion, if she/he uses *qaad*, indulges in free sex, or hurts a child of a *jinni*.'

In the clinics, in addition to a waiting hall and the sheikh's consulting room, there are often rooms for in-patients—violent patients whom the family cannot take care of or who require intensive care. There are separate rooms for women and men where patients listen to the daily Koranic recitation played loudly through microphones. Sheikhs give patients individual consultation, treatment and follow-up. Furthermore, they prescribe herbal and other medication, which usually can be obtained from the sheikh's own pharmacy: medicine that a person has to drink or eat, or a mixture of herbs and oils that is spread on the skin. Many of the sheikhs I observed also had an electric appliance, originally a muscle stimulator, which was used to hurt and exorcise the *jinn*. Moreover, *jinn* could be beaten with a stick, an electric wire or a rope.

A few times I was allowed to sit inside the room, where women listened to the recitation of the Koran. Certain *sura*s of the Koran are known to be effective in exorcising *jinn*, some others in healing witchcraft and so forth. Depending on the cause of the problem, women reacted to the recited text differently. During the recitation *jinn* may scream because the recitation of the Koran burns them. Affected women (or actually *jinn*) may also talk and shout, cry, stand up and bend their bodies in different directions, shiver, rotate their heads violently, hurt other women by hitting them or throwing objects at them, or they may faint on the floor.[14] The women attendants try to make sure that nobody gets hurt during trance and every now and then a male guard from outside may come in, a stick in his hand, and check the situation.

The whole setting and general feeling in *cilaaj*, compared to *saar* or *rooxaan*-related healing rituals, is very different: in Koranic healing no animal sacrifice is used and men and women are strictly separated during treatment. Koranic healers criticise *saar* rituals for being non-Islamic, because in *saar* women and men are mixed, blood and alcohol may be used, and *jinn* are persuaded to come and be celebrated, although they should be avoided. In *saar*, women wear beautiful, colourful clothes and decorations, and use perfume, but in Koranic clinics they mostly wear *jilbaab* and often also *niqab*. If they are not properly covered, a sheikh usually points that out. Moreover, a sheikh may complain if a woman has hair dye or nail polish; one sheikh explained that a *jinni* may hide under chemical colour (whereas natural henna is acceptable) and the colour must be removed before it is possible to exorcise *jinn*.[15] An important part of the healing is that a person starts reading the Koran, and follows Islamic rules in her/his life.[16] Treatment usually lasts weeks, even months, and during that period patients come daily to the clinic.

Compared to *saar* or *rooxaan* rituals, Koranic healing is much cheaper. Many sheikhs mentioned that if needed, a patient may pay what she/he can, even nothing. Normally, patients pay both for the appointment with a sheikh and for the medicines he prescribes. For example, in the summer of 2006 one of the sheikhs said that one appointment cost about 1.5 US dollars (10,000 Somaliland shillings). A one-month treatment cost about 22.5 US dollars (150,000 shillings), in addition to which a patient needed to pay 20 US dollars for herbal medication. At the same time, a visit to a private doctor cost some 6 US dollars (40,000 shillings) and to a doctor in public health care some 2 US dollars. The most popular Islamic healers have spacious clinics and they seem to do well economically. Some of the 'traditional' Sufi healers claimed with some bitterness that Koranic clinics also received funding from Arabic countries, and hence could afford to buy houses and cars.

Changing relations between humans and spirits

Spirits continue to be part of Somali society. In particular, spirits are significant in the process of making suffering and illness culturally meaningful. However, ideas concerning different categories of spirits as well as how to deal with them are changing as part of the religious, cultural, social and political changes in Somalia. The world of spirits is a kind of mirror world of the life of humans. An increased number of aggressive *jinn* can be interpreted as reflecting the mistrust and tensions in the human world—the damaged social relationships within and between families and clans. Furthermore, evil *jinn* are nourished by the impurity and blood of the civil war. As the relations between humans have changed because of the war, so have the relations between humans and spirits: mutual respect and tolerance no longer exist, and previous contracts are broken. A man in Hargeysa recalled that 'previously we discussed with *jinn*, today we beat them'. Furthermore, a sheikh in Borama explained, 'We treat *jinn* in the same way as they treat us'. If *jinn* treat one well, the *jinn* are treated well. However, if they cause problems and disease, they will be exiled, jailed or killed. Force, violence and revenge have overtaken traditional ideals of negotiation, compensation and collective responsibility. Images of *jinn* are malleable and draw on contemporary life and politics—*jinn* may be compared to electricity or the internet, and even Jewish *jinn* sometimes appear. They are usually perceived as the 'worst of all': unreliable and difficult to treat.[17]

New Islamic awareness and knowledge have resulted in redefining of healing practices. From the point of view of the healers, spirits may be divided into different categories such as *saar*, *rooxaan* and *jinn*. Most healers deny the practice of *saar*, but at the same time may use assistant spirits in healing. For instance, a female healer who relies on *rooxaan* spirits in her practice loudly berated a patient for arranging a *saar* ritual. Indeed, most healers discourage the continuation of *saar* whereas *jinn* cannot be ignored as they are mentioned in the Koran. By publicly condemning *saar* as non-Islamic, healers legitimise their other healing practices as Islamic.

Most Koranic healers included all spirits in the category of *jinn* and rejected any co-operation with them. One of the healers revealed that he earlier used to have a connection with *rooxaan*; he slaughtered animals for them and so forth. After the war in 1991, however, he realised that religiously his way of healing was not correct, and he left the *rooxaan* and started to study Koranic healing. Thus, some sheikhs are obviously adopting new religious healing methods, and moving from Sufi mysticism towards more puritanical interpretations of Islam. The ultimate power is given solely to Allah, and not to mediators such as spirits or saints. This is in accordance with the process of religious 'rigidification' that can be observed in the Somali context in recent decades. Hence, a basic difference between healers lies in how the relationship between a human and a spirit is seen: Koranic healers regard *jinn* as something one should get rid of, but according to more 'traditional' healers, a relationship with a spirit ideally develops into a lifelong, mutually beneficial acceptance and agreement. In this sense, spirits may be understood as enemies whom a person cannot trust, or as friends, assistants or neighbours whom one has to tolerate and respect.

Gender plays a role in the healing practice. Most patients in Somaliland who suffer from spirits are women, and all *saar* healers whom I met were women. Healers who work with *rooxaan* may be either male or female, but the Koranic healers are always men. Even though Islamic clinics are dominated by men, they also provide an interesting female space that should be studied further. As a result of daily gatherings—or 'seminars' as one woman called them—in a sheikh's clinic, women learn to know each other and each others' spirits. This contributes to a common sense of Muslim sisterhood.

Islamic clinics may be one gate through which more puritanical interpretations of Islam, even radical politicised views, get a stronger hold in Somaliland, whose government tries to maintain distance from radical Islamic groups in southern Somalia.[18] However, the increasing number of Koranic healing clinics is a sign not only of Islamisation, but of the crisis that continues on the individual, family and national levels following the civil war. Healing in general has become a way to earn a living in the midst of poverty. For example, some female healers narrated how they had been compelled to start a healing practice in order to maintain their families after the loss of a husband during the war. The most popular healers had managed to amass considerable property; for instance, one of the female healers who worked with *rooxaan* spirits owned several houses. Koranic and other healers also contribute to the overall healthcare system of Somaliland, which struggles with poor resources. Islamic healers in particular are trusted and appreciated, in many cases even more than medical doctors. Hence, clinics founded and run by Islamic and other traditional healers tell also about the appreciation and needs of the patients. Furthermore, the increasing provision of Islamic and Somali treatment through clinics which are organised in a similar way to medical clinics in general, can be seen as part of Somali modernity.

In conclusion, the civil war brought enormous suffering and illness to Somali people, on a hitherto unprecedented scale. Of course, Somalis had experienced hardship and war even before. Yet, the mass-violence during the all-encompassing civil war from 1988 onward distorted the previous equilibrium between everyday and spiritual life. The more blood was spilled, the more the number of *jinn* in Somaliland increased and created problems for humans. At the same time, the overall Islamisation of the region has affected how people evaluate *saar* and Sufi healing practices. Islamic clinics offer new powerful ways to deal with spirits, whereas *saar* and Sufism are being marginalised. Thus, even though the political situation in the North is different compared with the South, puritanical Islam is getting a foothold in Somaliland as well.

Notes

1. My research project 'Suffering, Healing and Health-care: The Transnational Lives of Somalis in Exile' has been funded by the Academy of Finland. I also want to acknowledge the Nordic Africa Institute and Ella and Georg Ehrnrooth Foundation for their grants. I am grateful to my assistant Jama Gabush, my driver Muxumed Maxamed Cabdi and other friends in Somaliland, and all the healers who so kindly allowed me to observe their healing practice. Janice Boddy, Francesca Declich, Karin Hjelde, Markus Hoehne and Michael Lambek provided highly insightful comments during the writing process.
2. Editors' note: see Abdullahi in this volume.
3. *Jinn* is the plural form; the singular form is *jinni*.
4. No reliable statistics are available and given numbers must be considered carefully because they have political significance.
5. The leaves of the *qaad* bush have a mildly stimulating effect.
6. I thank Markus Hoehne for his remark that these after-dark activities can be seen as hidden prostitution. Mohamed-Rashid Sheikh Hassan (2006) has also mentioned private cars as a site for sex work.
7. *Zar* spirits in Sudan require blood sacrifice and are thought to be drawn to human blood. They also 'follow the blood', i.e. the matrilineal line (Janice Boddy, personal communication, 9 July 2009).
8. Land disputes are the main source of conflict in today's Somaliland.
9. Sheekhad means a learned woman of religion.
10. 'Abd al-Qadir al-Jilani was the founder of the Qadiriya brotherhood.
11. In Sudan, *rowhān al-ahmar* (red spirits or red winds) is a synonym for *saar* (Boddy 1989: 187).
12. For a description of *saar* in Mogadishu in the 1980s, see A. Adam in this volume.
13. *Wadaado* is a plural form of *wadaad*, which means a man of religion, often an itinerant teacher of Islam.
14. Once I was also attacked when a *jinni* threw a water bottle at my face.
15. This is also required for prayer, as nail polish is regarded as impure (Boddy, personal communication, 9 July 2009).
16. According to Sengers (2003: 146), healers in the Koranic clinics in Egypt propagate an Islamic life-style and fundamentalist views stressing the role of women as wives and mothers.
17. According to Hoehne, anti–Semitic attitudes among Somalis are common; they are usually legitimated by reference to the suffering of the Palestinians caused by the Israeli state (Markus Hoehne, personal communication, 15 August 2009).
18. One of the most popular Koranic healers, Sheikh Muxumed Ismaaciil, was arrested in Hargeysa in September 2005 for alleged terrorist acts, and has since been jailed.

References

Ahmed, Abdullahi M. 1988. 'Somali Traditional Healers: Role and Status.' In A. Puglielli (ed.) *Proceedings of the Third International Congress of Somali Studies*, Rome: Il Pensiero Scientifico, pp. 240–7.

Al-Krenawi, Alean and John Graham 1999. 'Social Work and Koranic Mental Health Workers.' *International Social Work*, 42 (1), 53–65.

Antoniotto, Albert 1984. 'Traditional Medicine in Somalia: An Anthropological Approach to the Concepts Concerning Disease.' In T. Labahn (ed.) *Proceedings of the Second International Congress of Somali Studies*. Hamburg: Helmut Buske Verlag, pp. 155–69.

Ashour, Mustafa 1989. *The Jinn in the Qur'an and the Sunna*. London: Dar Al-Taqwa.

Atallah, S.F., A.R. El-Dosoky and E.M. Coker *et al.* 2001. 'A 22–Year Retrospective Analysis of the Changing Frequency and Patterns of Religious Symptoms among Inpatients with Psychotic Illness in Egypt.' *Social Psychiatry and Psychiatric Epidemiology*, 36, 407–15.

Boddy, Janice 1989. *Wombs and Alien Spirits: Women, Men, and the Zār Cult in Northern Sudan*. Madison: The University of Wisconsin Press.

Bradbury, Mark 2008. *Becoming Somaliland*. London: Progressio.

Calverley, Edwin E. 1993. 'Nafs.' In C.E. Bosworth, E. van Donzel, W.P. Heinrichs and Ch. Pellat (eds) *The Encyclopaedia of Islam*, 7. Brill: Leiden, pp. 880–3.

Cassanelli, Lee V. 1982. *The Shaping of Somali Society: Reconstructing the History of a Pastoral People, 1600–1900*. University of Philadelphia Press.

Chodkiewicz, Michel 1995. 'Rūhāniyya.' In C.E. Bosworth, E. van Donzel, W.P. Heinrichs and G. Lecomte (eds) *The Encyclopaedia of Islam*, 8. Brill: Leiden, pp. 593–4.

Declich, Francesca 1995. 'Identity, Dance and Islam among People with Bantu Origins in Riverine Areas of Somalia.' In A.J. Ahmed (ed.) *The Invention of Somalia*. Lawrenceville, NJ: Red Sea Press, pp. 191–222.

Drieskens, Barbara 2008. *Living with Djinns: Understanding and Dealing with the Invisible in Cairo*. London: Saqi.

Giles, Linda L. 1995. 'Sociocultural Change and Spirit Possession on the Swahili Coast of East Africa.' *Anthropological Quarterly*, 68 (2), 89–106.

Hassan, Mohamed-Rashid S. 2006. *A Situational Assessment on Vulnerable Population in Somaliland (Hargeisa, Berbera and Togwajale)*. Project plan March-April 2006 (unpublished report), UNAIDS.

Helander, Bernhard 1989. 'Incorporating the Unknown: The Power of Southern Somali Medicine.' In A. Jacobson-Widding and D. Westerlund (eds) *Culture, Experience and Pluralism: Essays on African Ideas of Illness and Healing*. University of Uppsala, pp. 86–99.

——— 1995. 'Disability as Incurable Illness: Health, Process, and Personhood in Southern Somalia.' In B. Ingstad and S. Reynolds Whyte (eds) *Disability and Culture*. Berkeley: University of California Press, pp. 73–93.

Hiiraan 21.8.2006. *Maxkamadda Islaamiga ah ee Ridwaan aa Albaabada u Laabtay Goob Mingiska Lagu Tumi Jiray* [Union of Islamic Courts Has Today Closed the Mingis Ceremony Houses]. Hiiraan online. Available at: http://www.hiiraan.com/news/2006/aug/wararka_maanta21.html [accessed 13.2.2007]

Kapteijns, Lidwien and Jay Spaulding 1996. 'Women of the Zar and Middle-Class Sensibilities in Colonial Aden, 1923–1932. Voice and Power: The Culture of Language in North-East Africa. Essays in Honour of B. W. Andrzejewski.' *African Languages and Cultures, Supplement*, 3, pp. 171–89.

Kleinman, Arthur 1995. *Writing at the Margin. Discourse between Anthropology and Medicine*. Berkeley: University of California Press.

Laitin, David D. and Said S. Samatar 1987. *Somalia: Nation in Search of a State*. Boulder: Westview Press.

Lambek, Michael 1993. *Knowledge and Practice in Mayotte: Local Discourses of Islam, Sorcery, and Spirit Possession*. University of Toronto Press.

Leather, Andrew, Edna A. Ismail and R. Ali *et al.* 2006. 'Working Together to Rebuild Health Care in Post-conflict Somaliland.' *The Lancet*, 368, 1119–25.

Le Sage, Andre 2001. 'Prospects for *Al Itihad* & Islamist Radicalism in Somalia.' *Review of African Political Economy*, 28 (89), 472–7.

Lewis, Ioan M. 1956. 'Sufism in Somaliland: A Study in Tribal Islam II.' *Bulletin of the School of Oriental and African Studies, University of London*, 18 (1), 145–60.

——— 1966. 'Spirit Possession and Deprivation Cults.' *Man*, New Series, 1 (3), 307–29.

——— 1991. 'Introduction: *Zar* in Context: The Past, the Present and Future of an African Healing Cult.' In I.M. Lewis, A. Al-Safi and S. Hurreiz (eds) *Women's Medicine: The Zar-Bori Cult in Africa and Beyond*. Edinburgh University Press for the International African Institute, pp. 1–16.

——— 1998. *Saints and Somalis: Popular Islam in a Clan-based Society*. London: Haan.

Lewis, Ioan M., Ahmed Al-Safi and Sayyid Hurreiz (eds) 1991. *Women's Medicine: The Zar-Bori Cult in Africa and Beyond*. Edinburgh University Press for the International African Institute.

Luling, Virginia 2002. *Somali Sultanate: The Geledi City-State over 150 Years*. London: Haan.

Menkhaus, Ken 2002. 'Political Islam in Somalia.' *Middle East Policy*, 9 (1), 109–23.

Morsy, Soheir A. 1988. 'Islamic Clinics in Egypt: The Cultural Elaboration of Biomedical Hegemony.' *Medical Anthropology Quarterly*, New Series, 2 (4), 355–69.

Nisula, Tapio 1999. *Everyday Spirits and Medical Interventions: Ethnographic and Historical Notes on Therapeutic Conventions in Zanzibar Town*. Helsinki: The Finnish Anthropological Society.

Pelizzari, Elisa 1997. *Possession et Thérapie dans la Corne de l'Afrique*. Paris: L'Harmattan.

Perho, Irmeli 1995. *The Prophet's Medicine: A Creation of the Muslim Traditionalist Scholars*. Helsinki: The Finnish Oriental Society.

Philips, Abu A.B. 1997. *Ibn Taymeeyah's Essay on the Jinn (Demons)*. Riyadh: International Islamic Publishing House.

Sengers, Gerda 2003. *Women and Demons: Cult Healing in Islamic Egypt*. Leiden: Brill.

Tiilikainen, Marja 2003. *Arjen islam: Somalinaisten elämää Suomessa* [Everyday Islam: Life of Somali Women in Finland]. Tampere: Vastapaino.

11

A *SAAR GAAMURI* IN SOMALIA

SPIRIT POSSESSION AS EXPRESSION OF WOMEN'S AUTONOMY?

Anita Adam

For those who believe in them, mystical powers are realities both of thought and experience (Lewis 1971: 24).

Introduction

The spirit-possession cult of *saar* is a familiar practice in Somalia, especially among women, and some of its most elaborate forms are found among women of the northern clans.The core material here is an account of a particular *saar* event called *saar gaamuri* that I attended in Mogadishu in 1988, taking place over seven days. This is not an account from an anthropologist's perspective, and my recollections are offered in the possibility that they will contribute to an appreciation of the many forms which *saar* take across northeast Africa. The material that precedes the account is to situate the story within the social and religious realities, which inform *saar* traditions. This background material is culled from my own conversations with women experienced in *saar*, parenthetically from living for many years in Somali society, and from some published academic literature on spirit possession—to which I.M. Lewis has been a major contributor.

Saar spirit possession among Somalis

The origins of *saar* in place and time are obscure. However, *saar* or *zar* (both spellings will be found in the literature), which is the belief in being possessed by harmful spirits, is commonly though not exclusively believed to have roots in Ethiopia; etymology is often cited in support of this. However, the cults are widespread throughout Somalia (Lewis 1969; Luling 1991), as well as among neighbouring peoples in northeast Africa, particularly in Ethiopia (Trimingham, 1949; Teshome-Bahire 2000) and Sudan (Boddy 1989; Constantinides 1978), and occur as far away as Egypt (Kahle 1912; see also Lewis, Hurreiz and Al-Safi 1991). In Saudi Arabia *zar* is reported to be practised by and to have originated with ex–slaves from Africa. It also affects Ethiopian Jews and other recent immigrants to Israel from the Horn of Africa.[1]

Mohamed Diriye Abdullahi (2001: 66), writing on Somali culture, suggests that *saar* belief in spirits is a religious relic of pre-Islamic deities. Pamela Constantinides (1978) on the other hand, writing on corresponding *zar* practices in Sudan, places their rise as a cult to as late as the 19th century, relating it to contemporary trends of urbanisation.

Spirit possession is known by a variety of names among Somalis, but these are little more than different names in different regions for broadly the same practice. Among Somalis from the northern clans the term *saar xabashi*—or Ethiopian *saar*—is used (*Xabashi* being used by Somalis for 'Abyssinian'), and *saar xabashi* is the genre to which the *saar gaamuri* of this paper belongs. *Mingis* is the most common term used in southern Somalia, especially in the urban centre of Mogadishu. Though Lewis says that *mingis* 'rigorously excludes ex–slaves' (Lewis 1971: 92), this was not my own experience; *mingis* was the name given to spirit possession practised by a wide range of groups in Mogadishu in the years that I lived there, including the ex–clients of some high status urban groups. *Mingis* is not a Somali word, but is said to derive from Amharic *mengist*, meaning 'government', 'power' (Lewis 1971: 92), which perhaps further supports the theory of an Ethiopian origin for the cult. Lewis and Luling are in agreement that some marginalised ex–slave groups in southern Somalia have their own 'possession club' known as *numbi* (ibid.; Luling 1991: 173; Luling 2002: 232). Among some clans from the southern interior, the names *wadaado* and *boorani* are frequently heard in reference to spirit possession.[2] *Wadaado* is the

Somali word for men of religion (sing. *wadaad*, pl. *wadaado*), but is also used to express a feeling of mental confusion caused by the ingress of evil spirits to the head. *Saar boorani* (Borana) is reported by Luling to be practised in Afgooye and the Shabelle regions; she notes that the name points to 'an origin in southern Ethiopia' (Luling 1991: 171).[3] Might such an etymological link also be applied to the Sudanese possession cult of Zar-Bori?[4]

During my earliest days in Somalia in the 1960s, *saar* was for me of peripheral interest and something of a curiosity of the culture in which I found myself living. The women with whom I was most closely associated comprised a small and educated elite who were sceptical and disdainful of *saar* and its superstitions—attitudes shared by their male partners and counterparts. They were disparaging of the practice and its efficacy, and indeed of its religious correctness. (Islam does not recognise the existence of *zar* spirits.) My circle of female friends, daughters of the political, business and religious elites, were trained in the professions, and intent on forging their own careers and taking control of their lives, and they had no need for *saar*. They were but a small sample of the female population, however. I occasionally came across others, some socially well-placed women, some from more humble circumstances, who resorted to *saar* possession ritual to cure ills. But it was many years later before I had my first serious encounter with possession practices. I was invited to attend a *saar* event that was being held for Amina, the mother of a close relative of my husband. It would include rituals to mark the culmination of her many years of involvement with the *saar* cult, and was to be the final step of her becoming a senior cult leader, referred to in Somali as *calaqad*,[5] with mastery over the mischievous and malevolent *saar* spirits.

Saar leaders in the Somali tradition usually acquire their status through apprenticeship, unlike in some other spirit possession traditions where the role may be inherited.[6] To become a leader, the person will have begun by having been herself afflicted at an earlier stage in her life. A sense of calling, vocation, or interest may be motivating factors to continue in the cult. To reach the status of *calaqad*, however, follows many years of apprenticeship

The *saar* cult is not an organised sect—though from empirical evidence it would seem that the ritual experts who lead the ceremonies have their own following, as I was to learn from my attendance at the event described below and from subsequent visits to related gatherings.

While the primary basis for recruitment into a *saar* cult group is illness, it is evident that the cults serve important social functions, providing opportunities for drama and entertainment and for women to widen their social contacts. One of my informants whose mother had, I knew, attended *saar* events frequently, emphasised to me that not all participants in *saar* events believe in the *saar* spirits; some women attend for social reasons or to support family and friends through a crisis. She recalled that her mother, who had been a drummer and hence significant to the ceremonies, had 'drummed to help the (sick) girls express themselves and climax in the *saar* dance', but had not believed in spirit possession (Conversation with Jawaahir Cabdalla Faarax, London, May 2009).

Saar spirits

The spirits are at the core of all possession rituals. They are believed to enter the head and cause mind changing behaviour and physical maladies, especially among women—though not only women. Lewis describes possession among young Somali camel herders, and from my own slim knowledge of *mingis* practices in southern Somalia male possession occurs, yet on the whole these often extravagant and expensive *saar* affairs are more the preserve of women than of men, and it is possession among women that is the focus of this discussion.

Regarding the spirits of the *saar xabashi*, there are many different spirits, both male and female, some Muslim, some Christian, and some of pagan or unidentified origin, each with its own character. These are a few examples, given to me by Cawraale Salax, herself a frequent participant in *saar* rituals: Maame (a male *jinn*; Muslim); Inaati (a female *jinn*; 'pagan'); Gaamuri (m.; Christian); Halange (m.; 'pagan'). Some, like Gaamuri, are considered to be particularly stubborn and difficult to appease, while others, like Halange, are weaker, and easier to handle—though all are unpredictable and capricious in varying degrees. So while less skilled leaders may be able to organise and manage a *saar* Halange, the veteran *calaqad* will be called upon to manage the more stubborn spirits. This tallies closely with the scenario found in the Sudanese version of the cults, the Zar-Bori, where there are among the spirit groups 'Muslim saints, early administrators (including General Gordon), and a diverse number of spirits associated with ethnic categories' (Constantinides in Morris 1998: 89).

The most frequently cited *saar* spirit amongst the northern Somali clans is Maame, whose name is even evoked in a commonly chanted rhyme by children and others whenever someone complains of a headache:

Saar Maama u weyne,	Big Saar Maame,
Saar Maama u weyn;	Big Saar Maame;
Saar-ow madaxa daa,	*Saar*, go from the head,
Saar-ow madaxa daa;	*Saar*, go from the head;
Maamow madaxa daa,	Maame leave the head alone,
Maamow madaxa daa!	Maame leave the head alone!

Some interpretations of saar/zar from the literature

For women at times of crisis there are ways out of the confined social 'space'. Bori is only one route of several (Last 1991: 58).

Anyone attempting research on any aspect of Somali society will find that I.M. Lewis has already been there, and the area of spirit possession is no exception. Lewis has written extensively on the social dynamics of spirit-possession cults, and his comparative studies of shamanism and spirit possession have been seminal—if also controversial—to the academic debate. In his work on spirit possession in Somalia, Lewis takes as his baseline model northern Somali pastoralist clans. He describes the 'stock epidemiology' as one where the situation of women is of 'a hard-pressed wife struggling to survive and feed her children in harsh circumstances, and liable to some degree of neglect, real or imagined, on the part of her husband [and of] prolonged absences by her husband [and] jealousies and tensions of polygyny [...] always menaced by the precariousness of marriage in a society where divorce is frequent and easily obtained by men' (Lewis 1971: 67). Lewis argues that the prevalence of women in spirit cults is essentially a reflection of the frustrations associated with their subordinate position in a male-dominated society as described (Lewis 1986: 96–103; Lewis 1999: 80–94). His presentation of the Somali men's perspective on *saar* is that it is a manipulative tool of women, viz.: 'Somali men see women's possession as a specialized strategy designed to forward feminine interests at their expense' (Lewis 1971: 69) reflects a view akin to one which I often found among educated Somali men. However, such expressions in Lewis' work as 'the use by women of *sar* [sic] spirit possession' (Lewis 1971: 70), with the implication of manipulation by women, have been criticised especially by other feminist writers on the subject, as presenting an ethnocentric and male-gendered perspective.

A type of women's *saar* found in Sudan is Zar-Bori, which has been documented by the anthropologists Janice Boddy and Pamela Constantinides. Boddy on Sudan, like Lewis on Somalia, emphasises the 'holistic social reality' as the context for understanding women's possession cults, and the social inequalities between male and female as key to understanding of these cults (Boddy 1989: 136–7). However, she criticises Lewis for presenting a male-centred view—what she terms an 'andro-centric' portrayal of women—which reacts to men's perspective rather than allowing for women being their own agents within a specific cultural context (Boddy 1989: 40). In spite of Boddy's protests at Lewis' 'instrumentality', she suggests an extreme cultural determinism within Sudanese society, and even that women are so culturally overdetermined that there is no such thing as individualism and free will (Boddy 1989: 252–3). Therefore, despite the protests, the absence of individualism that she suggests exists in Sudanese female society seems to be not such a different conclusion from the 'instrumentality' or lack of individual autonomy that she criticises Lewis for.

Constantinides, in contrast to the ambivalent male attitude towards spirit possession, which implies manipulation by and inadequacy on the part of the women who adopt what she terms the 'sick mode', offers a more sympathetic view on the range of causes, and from a female perspective: being unable to find a suitable, supportive husband; having an unsatisfactory marriage; failing to reproduce (she notes the high frequency of reproductive problems that are due to the practice of infibulation); or, more generally, failing to find any satisfaction in her life circumstances. For her, through the *zar* rituals a woman can indirectly and symbolically regain some control over conditions of her own existence (Constantinides 1985: 688–9). She proposes that the cults among women, rather than being traditional, are closely associated with the pressures of modern life and the move from traditional rural settings to an urban environment and the accompanying isolation from kin and restrictions on socialising and Islamic cultural demands on women to seclude themselves from unrelated males. Accordingly, she traces the rise of the cults in Sudan to the early decades of the 19th century when such social changes were taking place (Constantinides

1978: 192). In what might be seen as another feminist strike she notes that women who are cult leaders generally do not conform to the surrounding norms and ideals of womanhood (citing divorce, widowhood, and childlessness), and that in her experience such leaders often engineered their own divorces, refusing to be submissive to men, affirmed their own freedom of movement and action, and, as a medium for the spirits, suggested they had no real need for men (ibid.: 690).

Although women do not generally attend the formal group rituals of Islam, Constantinides see women's participation in the *zar* cults as corresponding to men's participation in the religious brotherhoods (Constantinides 1977: 64), and as she and Lewis both note, there are many parallels between the *zar* cults practices and those of the Islamic Sufi brotherhoods.[7]

An account of a saar gaamuri—1988

The zar ritual [...] is a theatrical event (Sellers 1991:162).

Against the backdrop of the above notes and perspectives on *saar/zar* cults in Somalia and northeast Africa, I now provide an account of a *saar* occasion at which I was a participant observer. It is my own interpretation of happenings of an event now twenty years ago. Footnotes are a later addition, some seek to illuminate aspects of the rituals whose significance were a mystery to me at the time. For most of the additional information I am indebted to recent discussions with Cawraale Saalax, a veteran of the cult, who also happened to have been a participant in the *saar gaamuuri* that I describe.

Day 1. We are in the house of Amina. Three rooms and the kitchen have been decorated with carpets and coverings, wall to wall, and ceiling to floor. The inner chamber is the most luxuriously adorned, and contains two cushioned sofa-benches to seat the *Calaqad*, who has been called to preside over the occasion, and Amina, who is the focus of the assembly. The *Calaqad* will be Master of Ceremonies, Senior *Calaqad* and Leader. Amina in the next few days is herself to be initiated into full status as a *calaqad*.

The attendants—members of the *Calaqad*'s entourage—also gather in this room, with some of the more prestigious of Amina's female friends and relatives; they sit around on the floor, or flank the most important personages on the benches.

Comment should be made on the imposing figure of the *Calaqad* who is strikingly handsome, generously proportioned, and with a countenance that is both sensual and enigmatic. In the context of the ceremony, she seems able to communicate without much need for speech. She and Amina each have excessively large and beautiful hubble-bubble pipes that they smoke. Several other pipes are on the floor of the room and are smoked communally with clusters of women gathered around each, the mouthpiece of the pipe being shared around. Bowls of pink bougainvillea flowers are arranged on the floors and side tables. Several of the women smoke cigarettes. In this room most are middle aged or elderly. There is a profusion of gold jewellery—bangles, earrings, rings, and necklaces—and these are especially profuse on the persons of the *Calaqad* and Amina. Both the latter are dressed predominantly in green—the colour for this first evening, the colour symbolic of *saar* possession, the colour which conveys the readiness or need for *saar* rites to be performed. Other personages important to the occasion can also be recognised by the green that they wear.[8]

Two ropes stretch from wall to wall across one end of this chamber. On these are hung an impressive array of fabrics—many coloured silks, fine cottons, and chiffons—the kinds which women drape around their bodies and wear as head and shoulder coverings. The quality and quantity of these cloths, along with the rest of the decor, are indicators of Amina's standing and substance.

In the second room women are seated on floor cushions. There are young and old women here. They are relatives and friends of the house. A third room is similarly occupied, though this room has fibre mats rather than carpets, and no cushions—later it will be used for dancing.

Some of the *Calaqad*'s retinue are assigned to cooking and serving duties, while at the same time they are an integral part of the ceremonies. Thus the kitchen, leading off from the centre chamber, is also carpeted and decorated in like manner to the rest, to be functional for sitting, smoking, etc., and to allow for the participation of those who have other tasks to perform. To add to this exotic affluence, the smell of perfumes and burning frankincense pervades the air.

At the start of this first evening the atmosphere is relaxed, and there is a quiet murmur of conversation, and some movement to and fro as additional women arrive, come to the inner chamber to greet the primary personages, kiss hand to hand, then take their places here or there in one room or another.

Soon the *Calaqad* begins to recite a blessing, and with palms raised, all join in chanting verses of the Qur'an. This lasts for several minutes. After this, *bun*/coffee is served. Large trays each containing a dozen or so small glasses are brought into the room and placed in the centre of the floor. From huge kettles the servers pour the coffee infusion into the glasses which are then passed around to the seated assembly, in order of precedence. This is done under the watchful eye of the *Calaqad*. A short time elapses in a relaxed manner while the coffee is drunk and the pipes are tasted.

But before long Amina, for whom the initiation has been called, becomes the focus of attention. More bangles, silver with bells on, are brought and placed on her arms, and she collects in her hands her regalia: a leather whip, a feathered fly whisk, and—the *pièce de résistance*—a sceptre; the cane is ornately decorated on the handle and shaft with silver.[9] Drumming is heard and the piercing ululations of the women as Amina comes forward from her couch to the centre of the floor and begins a very determined and rhythmic stamping dance of a dozen or so steps and a pause, more stamps and a pause... The ornamentation on her body creates its own music in unison. Women gather and crowd around her, ululating and clapping in rhythm, but leaving free the floor space between Amina and the *Calaqad*—who remains seated. At a certain point in her dance, a white cloth is draped over Amina's shoulders.

From the kitchen area two goats, one of which is reddish brown and one white, and a kid are led into the forum and presented to Amina. She takes charge of them and anoints their foreheads with a butter ointment. After these are led away four chickens are brought for anointing. But before smearing their heads with the butter, Amina grasps each by their legs, two by two in each hand, slings them over her shoulders, and continues her stomping, staccato dance to the clapping and swaying accompaniment of the gathering. (The animals are for ritual slaughter, and will eventually be fed to the party.) She all the while signals with a gesture of her head and the cessation of her rhythm when each round of clapping should end, and when the ceremonials should move on. Under the supervision of the *Calaqad*, Amina has performed her rituals with authority.

By the time the chickens are carried out there has occurred a distinct rise in tension of the occasion, and three drummers repair to the third room where women are gathering in anticipation of a dance. Meanwhile the senior authorities, including Amina, relax in the chamber with soft drinks, refreshments and companionship as the dancing and festivity gains momentum in the neighbouring room.

The dancing is traditional Somali, with a circle of women clapping and stamping and swaying to the beat of the drums; several women take up positions in the centre of the circle and weave patterns around each other. There is a change of pace for a while as one of the older women struts and trips jauntily in the circle singing the praises of Amina to the continuing rhythmic clapping. Each line of her set-pattern composition is punctuated by the chanted agreement of her surrounding coterie. The accolades for her performance come in the form of money, as several women step forward and push banknotes into her headscarf. The tone has now been set for continued dancing and merriment for several hours to come.

Day 2. On the morning of the second day an ox has been brought and tethered to a tree in the courtyard at the back of the house. The ox is draped with embroidered and brocaded cloths and made ready for Amina to mount. Most of the women from the evening before have reassembled, and some, including the *Calaqad* and her contingent, have been at the house throughout the night. Today the *Calaqad*, Amina, and primary personages are dressed predominantly in black. Today Amina and the *Calaqad* are wearing gold crown-like headbands, and are even more profusely jewelled than yesterday. I notice that two or three other women, who yesterday seemed merely part of the general throng, today emerge as also having *calaqad* status—as indicated by their wearing gold headbands. The crowns are symbols of their rank as *boqortooye* (female sultans or 'priestesses'), versed in *saar* spirit possession and practitioners of the exorcism rites. The *Calaqad*'s headband is noticeably broader than the rest and signifies a more senior status. A significant other addition to Amina's accessories is a very large silver *hersi*, a '*porte qur'an*', around her neck which hangs almost to the waist, and is studded with a ruby-like stone, and has silver bells suspended from the lower edge of the pendant. Special foods and sweetmeats—*shuuro*, honey, soup, *subag*—have been prepared and laid on the ground amidst bowls of bougainvillea flowers.

The ox is ready. Amina must anoint the ox's head with *subag* and with *malmal* before mounting.[10] Then she steps up to a low table placed beside the ox, and then she mounts it. The *Calaqad*, ever present, does not speak, but seems to be in silent communion with Amina throughout the business. The cane, the feather whisk, and the leather whip have been delivered to Amina by the *Calaqad*'s officiators, and she now performs some shaking movements for the several minutes she remains mounted. This ritual has been built as one of the most important of the series of rites associated with the preparation of a trainee to graduation as a practitioner of *saar* exorcism rites.

Once this is over, and with Amina back on terra firma, the *Calaqad*, in the manner of the priest at communion, feeds samples of each of the prepared foods into Amina's mouth. These foods have been prepared by the *Calaqad*'s cooks and need Amina's agreement that they will satisfy the spirits.

There is now a lull in the general proceedings as Amina repairs to a small bedroom off the main chamber with the *Calaqad* and a few chosen from the inner circle. The ox is taken off for slaughter (ritual sacrifice). Soon a bowl of the ox's blood is taken to the anteroom. There Amina will be bathed in the blood, after which she will be washed and bathed many times with soap, shampoo, sweet-smelling ointments, and perfumes.[11] When this is well underway, away from the eyes of the crowd, the rest of the women, who have meanwhile been reclining and chatting in groups, respond to the beating of drums, and the serious dancing of *saar* begins.

Unlike the familiar traditional dancing of the night before, ecstatic rhythms are built up by the three drummers. The monotonous chants which accompany these are sung by two chanteuses and are sung in the Qoti language.[12] The keening lines of the chanteuses are interspersed with short responses in unison from those who have congregated. Clapping, with palms and fingers aligned—not in diagonal pattern—that gives the clapping its distinctive and deliberate message, reinforces the rhythms of voice and drum. There is an inherent eroticism as bodies begin to move to the rhythms, and individuals respond by breaking from the crowd to enter the circle, first in a state of fainting, then by violent shaking and dancing towards ecstasy. These individuals are believed to be in a state of spirit possession, and their actions are involuntary. The *saar* dance is both the effect of the possession and the means of release from it. Only a few of those present, and from among the younger women, affect this state. But the rhythms are compelling, and the environment is a closed and supportive one.

As the spirit enters the subject the body becomes limp and goes into a light faint. Some women may fall completely to the ground, for others it is enough that the limp body is prevented from falling by outstretched hands from the surrounding crowd. The faint is momentary, and the body quickly changes to a more rigid state to resume the ecstatic dance—thrashing movements, which are concentrated in the upper body—spurred on by the pervading and irresistible crescendo rhythm of the drums, handclaps, foot stomping, swaying and chanting. The state usually lasts for several minutes, with some women taking more time, some less, to reach release; there may be one or more women going through the process at the same time, though it is unlikely that they will start and finish in unison. All eyes of the surrounding group are on the performers, and the group rhythms are synchronised to those of the possessed, creating a bond between the two, with each part following the natural progression of the dance, responding to the needs of each dancer through to the point of ebb of her energies. When she has finished the *saar* dance she leaves the circle to sit quietly on the periphery in the care of a friend.

After the *saar* dances, sweet tea spiced with cinnamon, cardamom and cloves, and small confections are served as a welcome repast. The rest of today sees more social activities and more traditional dancing and singing as mood dictates.

Day 3. On the evening of the third day all the women are wearing red. This is in honour of female spirits. Today is women's day and the female spirits will receive homage and be satisfied.

Before sunset a further round of *saar* dancing occurs. Periodically the Senior *Calaqad*, the newly initiated *calaqad* Amina, and several minor *calaqaas* (this is an anglicised plural of *calaqad*) come to check the dancing and by their presence exert authority over the proceedings. There seem to be more *calaqaas* present than on previous occasions. Whether they were here earlier and part of the crowd, or whether word went out that an important initiation was in progress, I cannot say. But they are recognisable by the gold cords around their head, and by much gold embroidery on their headscarves and robes. Whenever the Senior *Calaqad* appears she is the recipient of much touching and light embraces by those women who over the past few days have found themselves compelled, by whatever force, to break ranks and move to the centre of the circle to perform the *saar* dance. The Senior *Calaqad* and Amina do not stay long. The other *calaqaas* remain, to bolster and guide the proceedings—much as a conductor will manage the interplay and harmonies of his orchestra in a finely tuned performance.

The inner chamber meanwhile is being made ready for the culminating rituals. The two sofas are suitably draped with plush fabrics. Benches have been put in place either side of the sofas to accommodate the senior women among Amina's guests and the resulting rectangle of floor space is made clear. One pipe only remains—placed in front of the *Calaqad's* sofa. A low curtain divide has been slung across the room at shoulder height, sectioning off a rectangular area containing the two sofas and some adjacent benches that have been put in place. For the moment the curtain is rolled up, but eventually it will be lowered to create an inner sanctum within which the important rites will be enacted.

But first comes the money-giving ceremony. The Senior *Calaqad* and Amina are in their places. They are joined by the minor *calaqaas* and by two or three women experienced in *saar* rituals. An order is given to halt the drumming and dancing in the other rooms, and there is much to-ing and fro-ing as the assembly is called. In the inner section of the divide, the drummers and chanteuses sit on the floor against the wall. This company is joined by those few women who have been most manifestly affected by the *saar*; they squat on the floor beside Amina.

As many persons as can be accommodated crowd into this room, seating themselves cross-legged beyond the curtain. The rest find space in adjoining rooms. Two senior women of Amina's entourage officiate in the process of receiving gifts of money which are collected from the assembly and passed into their care. As each token is received they announce the name of the donor and the sum of the donation. The announcements are met with the noise of jubilation and ululation from the throng.[13] This excited hubbub is in contrast to Amina's studied watchfulness as the pile of money mounts—for it is being given by her friends, destined as a gift to the *Calaqad*, and the extent of its richness will reflect the high regard in which Amina is held and the wealth and substance of her close friends and relatives. The *Calaqad* is at this moment seemingly removed in contented smoking of her pipe.

This over, the curtain is lowered and the serious business of appeasing the demons and *jinn* begins its course. Now that the actions of the inner sanctum are veiled from view, the main body of the assembly must take its cues for participation from auditory signals, from accumulated experience of past occasions, and from the actions of the two standing attendants of the inner circle whose head and shoulders may be perceived above the cloth screen. I am accorded a place in this inner space.

The Senior *Calaqad* has joined Amina on her sofa and, in guttural voice, leads the singing which will call the spirits that are abroad to come and join the gathering. The accompanying hand claps take on a compelling and changing double syncopated rhythm. After it seems that the invitation has been accepted and the spirits are in our midst, a further one and a half hours are passed in intense concentration as move follows move and mood follows mood, as the pageant moves superbly forward from rite to rite.

All the while the Senior *Calaqad* is in charge. She is the medium of communication with the spirits. Frequently she speaks strange utterances, often she trembles, sometimes she laughs; her voice takes on unexpected tones; Amina's swaying body as she sits beside her seems to add support. The inner group add further support with appropriate voicings and clapping rhythms, which are in turn supported from beyond the screen. (My own efforts to follow the rhythms proved discordant and I was instructed to cease clapping.)

The *Calaqad* is the means by which Amina will receive final induction, having perfected her skills in dealing with the unpredictable ways of spirits. Beneath canopies held over them, first a red then a white, Amina and the *Calaqad* together engage in tremors and utterances. The parched dry leg and thighbone of the ox once ridden, since sacrificed, are brought to Amina and placed momentarily across her shoulders. Spirits are called on by name and sung to. They are offered a splendid feast of meat, grains, butterfat, honey and sweetmeats, to be washed down with specially prepared mead.[14] Samples of each item are fed into the mouths of the *Calaqad* and Amina by the hand of a serving woman, for the approval of the sprites. It is found to be acceptable and is then similarly fed to each of the inner circle, followed by the bowl of fermented drink being passed around.

Two further offerings are called for the insatiable spirits—hot roasted coffee beans and pots of burning incense. These most pleasant aromas appear to provide the final satiation, as we learn from the ecstatic motions of Amina and the *Calaqad* that the spirits are now taking their leave of this place, for who knows where, until the next occasion of their mischief.

There remains the business of receiving the blessing of the Senior *Calaqad*. The *Calaqad* washes a draught of mead around her mouth, then through pursed lips sprays it on the face of Amina. Then she does the same for each member of the gathering in turn,[15] more generally directed, first to those of us in the close group of the sanctum, then, as the dividing curtain is raised, to the throng who clamour and come forward.

Soon, calm descends on the gathering. Bodies take on reclining postures in informal groups. A quiet murmur of conversation ensues, and warm milky tea is served around. Much later, and before midnight, the red goat which we encountered on the first evening is led out of the compound to be taken to some designated remote place as a final sacrifice to the female spirits. But those who are sent to follow, and report on the execution of the order, soon return to say that the goat and the man who was leading it seem to have vanished into thin air. This news is received at Amina's house with great satisfaction, as one might welcome a good omen, and as if it is what those who know these things had hoped and expected would happen.

Days 4–6. The next few days, until the completion of a seven day cycle, Amina's house continues to extend hospitality, and is a place where her friends can continue to enjoy the intimate society of women, and where time may be passed in pleasant and relaxing mood with Amina clearly contented in her new status. The *Calaqad* and her party stay on at Amina's house throughout. Others come and go as we attend to matters of work and daily duty—the time spent in this community being a deserved respite from routine.

In a more public space at the front of the house is where Amina, surrounded by the many fine fabrics and perfumes that display her wealth, goes to receive visitors—male and female—who come to pay their respects. From now on the numbers of women friends and relatives present at any given time grows less, though evening times ensures a goodly crowd. Food seems always to be available; it is served on large enamel trays set down on the floor, each tray to be shared by three of four persons. Utensils are dispensed with and as is the custom, the right hand is used for eating. A bowl of water always accompanies food to wash the hand before eating; water and soap to wash hands and mouth afterwards are followed by a liberal sprinkling of cologne to rub into the palms and fingers, masking any remaining odours. The activities and functions of these last few days are not integral to the *saar*, and happen according to whim or desire. They are enjoyments to pass the time and extend the period of pleasurable companionship and the intimate community of women.

Day 7. The get-together of the final evening is to be an all-night affair. The bond that has developed among the women as a result of their having spent this period together is perceptible. There is an easy atmosphere and unselfconscious movement of people through the interior spaces of the house, sometimes to engage in light-hearted dancing, sometimes to sit with this group or that to engage in desultory chatter.

Those who opt to stay through the night can be comfortably accommodated in the inner chamber, which is now bedecked with opulent cushions, new flowers, hubble-bubbles, and very large incense burners. (Certain types of Somali incense have the reputation of being the best in the world, and were traded for use in the temples of Ancient Egypt.) But first, it is necessary to symbolically leave behind the world of the sprits and return to the good grace of Islam. Very late in the evening everyone gathers in the second chamber for recitations of verses from the Qur'an; the rhythmic chanting in unison brings a sense of comfort. Then one further indulgence, as a sister brings around perfume—the oil-based musky Arab type—that she rubs into one's brow, hair, and the back of hands.

Those who are to depart now take their leave. For the rest, the night will be passed in conversation and reciting poetry, pipes will be smoked, and trays of coffee beans roasted in *subag* will be brought sizzling hot and set around strategically to be chewed. *Qaad* may also be available for those who wish it. (*Qaad* is a plant whose succulent purple-green leaves when chewed have a mild narcotic effect, and are said to heighten the senses and make speech more erudite and thinking more lucid.) The early light will bring to an end Amina's *saar gaamuri*.[16]

Conclusion

In reflection on the *saar gaamuri* described, and on a much longer period of association with the surrounding social dynamic, one or two things emerge clearly. The companionship and trust that develop among participants through the days of shared experiences are palpable and underline the notion of a social solidarity that *saar* spirit possession cults have been observed to engender. The sense of drama as the rituals climax is seductive, affording excitement beyond life's routine. Vulnerable 'patients' receive the unconditional support of friends and relatives as manifest in donated time, gifts and affection. Overall, the women-only 'safe space' that *saar* provides allows for expression of pent-up emotions, or a sharing of personal insecurities, sexual feelings, frustrations and desires that would be impossible to articulate within prevailing conservative social norms. These few propositions are not of course original, and will find echoes in the extensive discussions of *saar/zar* cults in the academic literature.

The syncretism existing between *saar* possession cult rituals and Islamic Sufi traditions has been well documented by anthropologists, and certainly the parallels are many. Compare the role of the sheikh with the *Calaqad* (in Sudanese Zar Bori cults, the leader is actually called *sheikha*), the *weli* as 'friend of God' and worker of miracles with the *Calaqad* as medium and agent for the spirit world, the exclusion of women from one arena and men from the other, ceremonial and rituals that feature states of ecstasy, either from the chanted *dhikri* of the Sufi brotherhoods or from the frenzied rhythms of the *saar* dance.

Before leaving the subject of syncretism and the possible assimilation of pre-Islamic practices to the Muslim religious formulae, mention is made of a little-cited practice among Somali women known as *sitaat*,[17] where women gather for the purpose of devotional poetry recitals. These sessions are an acceptable way for women to congregate and commune together, but are surely not far from the *saar* clubs (and may even be comparable to poetic performance and oral erudition that often accompanies male *qaad*-chewing sessions).

Finally, Lewis notes that complex economic and political factors and other conditions of change and dislocation may influence the development of religious movements (Lewis 1989: 29–30). This accords with my own experience of the ebbs and flows of *saar* spirit possession activity, and the observation that resurgences coincide with social and environmental volatility in the wider society. The *saar gaamuri* of this paper occurred during one such period of extreme social unrest and uncertainty, in the dying days of the widely unpopular Siyad Barre dictatorship, when high-ranking men not closely linked to Siyad's own clan were preoccupied with their political survival, and their women were left to manage the family's affairs.[18] The *saar* gathering in such circumstances may be a fundamentally important meeting place, and the cult rituals with their predetermined formulae provide a framework for dealing both individually and collectively with personal issues and with changing contemporary circumstances.

Notes

1. Most studies on *zar* in Israel, such as by Teshome-Bahire, are from a medical perspective and post-date the migration of the Beit Israel or Beta Yisrael (commonly referred to, derogatorily, as 'Falasha') from Ethiopia in the late 20th century.
2. Field Notes: Saynab Cali Ibraahim 09/12/08; Interview: Cawraale Saalax, Newham, London,18/05/08.
3. Borana: the name of the southern branch of the Oromo people of Ethiopia.
4. It is noted, however, that Bori is also the name of a Hausa possession cult.
5. One explanation I have been given for *calaqad*, meaning 'leader', is that it is a derivative of *caqil* = chief (Cawrale Saalax: Interview, Newham, London, 18/05/08).
6. However, if 'inherited' is taken to mean following on a family tradition, then this does occur (Conversations with Jawahir Abdalla Farah, London, May 2009).
7. For a more thorough comparative analysis of the work of these leading scholars on *saar/zar* possession cults in eastern Africa the reader is referred to chapter 3 of Brian Morris' *Religion and Anthropology*.
8. Constantinides also notes the colour symbolism involved in Sudanese Zar possession ritual.
9. Regalia: Leather horse-whip made from cowhide (Som.: *shaabuug*); highly decorated cane (Somali: *ul*); fly whisk made from horse's tail hair (Somali: *bal*); gold headband/tiara—sign of kingship/queenship.
10. *Subag*—clarified butter; *malmal*—a medicinal paste made from the sap of a native aloe plant and used widely in Somalia for its antiseptic properties.
11. 'After being washed in ox's blood, she is cleansed many times with henna and *qasil* (shampoo) and drenched with colognes.' (Cawrale Saalax interview, Newham, London, 18/05/08)
12. The spirits have their own language, and among the women I have interviewed, this is said to be Qoti, a dialect of Oromo; the special *saar* chants as recited by the *Calaqad* and chanteuses in this argot are not generally understood by the rest.
13. Guided by my friend Nuuriin Mariano, and my position as one of close family, and knowing that as the wife of a high ranking government member it was expected of me at this juncture to be an early and generous contributor, so as to set the bar high for later donations. My contribution was announced and I was a little taken aback by the enthusiastic applause.
14. The drink is called *tif-tif*, and is made from lime, honey and wheat flour, fermented for seven days.
15. Spraying or spitting on someone is a standard way of blessing in much of the Horn of Africa.
16. Graduation to *calaqad* is at the end of the seven days. But the previous apprenticeship will have lasted for many years.

17. For an account of a *sitaat* among Somali women in Djibouti, see Kapteijns (2007).
18. In the weeks and months which followed, I was frequently invited to or informed of Amina's '*saar* club' meetings, and became aware of a network of such clubs.

References

Boddy, Jane 1989. *Wombs and Alien Spirits*. Madison, WI: University of Wisconsin Press.

——— 1994. 'Spirit Possession Revisited: beyond Instrumentality.' *Annual Review of Anthropology*, 23, 407–434.

Constantinides, Pamela 1978. 'Women's Spirit Possession and Urban Adaptations.' In P. Caplan and J. Bujra (eds), *Women United, Women Divided*. London: Tavistock, pp. 185–205.

——— 1991. 'The History of Zar in Sudan.' In I.M. Lewis, A. Al-Safi and S. Hurreiz (eds) *Women's Medicine: the Zar-Bori Cult in Africa and Beyond*. Edinburgh University Press, pp. 83–99.

——— 1985. 'Women Heal Women: Spirit Possession and Sexual Segregation in a Muslim Society.' *Social Science and Medicine*, 21, 685–92.

Diriye Abdullahi, Mohamed 2001. *Culture and Customs of Somalia*. Westpoint, CT: Greenwood Press.

Kahle, Paul 1912. 'Zar-Beschwörungen in Egypten.' *Der Islam*, 3, 1–41.

Kapteijns, Lidwien and Maryan (Ariette) Omar 2007. '*Sittaat*: Women's Religious Songs in Djibouti.' *Halabuur* 2/1&2, 38–48.

Last, Murray 1991. 'Spirit Possession as Therapy: *Bori* among non-Muslims in Nigeria.' In I.M. Lewis, A. Al-Safi and S. Hurreiz (eds) *Women's Medicine: the Zar-Bori Cult in Africa and Beyond*. Edinburgh University Press, pp. 49–63.

Lewis, Ioan M. 1969. 'Spirit Possession in Northern Somaliland.' In J. Beattie and J. Middleton (eds) *Spirit Mediumship and Society in Africa*. London: Routledge, pp. 188–220.

——— 1971. *Ecstatic Religion: An Anthropological Study of Spirit Possession and Shamanism*. Harmondsworth: Penguin.

——— 1986. *Religion in Context: Cults and Charisma*. Cambridge University Press.

——— 1989. *Ecstatic Religion: A Study of Shamanism and Spirit Possession*. London: Routledge.

Lewis, Ioan M., Ahmed Al-Safi and Sayyid Hurreiz (eds) 1991. *Women's Medicine: the Zar-Bori Cult in Africa and Beyond*. Edinburgh University Press.

Luling, Virginia 1991. 'Some Possession Cults in Southern Somalia.' In I.M. Lewis, A. Al-Safi and S. Hurreiz (eds) *Women's Medicine: the Zar-Bori Cult in Africa and Beyond*. Edinburgh University Press/International African Institute, pp. 167–77.

——— 2002. *Somali Sultanate: the Geledi City-state over 150 years*. London: Haan.

Morris, Brian 2006. *Religion and Anthropology: a Critical Introduction*. Cambridge University Press.

Sellers, Barbara 1991. 'The *Zar*: Women's Theatre in the Southern Sudan.' In I.M. Lewis, A. Al-Safi and S. Hurreiz (eds) *Women's Medicine: the Zar-Bori Cult in Africa and Beyond*. Edinburgh University Press, pp. 156–64.

Teshome-Bahire, Wondwosen 2000. 'Initiation of Healers in Ethiopia.' *Collegium Antropologicum*, 24 (2), 555–563.

Trimingham, John S. 1949. *Islam in the Sudan*. Oxford University Press.

PART VI

POETRY

12

SOMALIA

A NATION'S LITERARY DEATH TOPS ITS POLITICAL DEMISE

Said S. Samatar

Introduction

Somalia has been falling apart for over two decades—and counting. However strenuously the international community—the African Union, the European Union, the United States, and the UN—have striven to put the African humpty-dumpty back together again, the Somali centre refuses to hold. Consequently, this demented nation seems only too happy to lurch heedlessly towards self-destruction. Can it be said that hope springs eternal where Somalia is concerned? Be that as it may, this essay aims to explore three inter-related themes: firstly, to revisit the ongoing story of the centrality and salience of oral (and subsequently written) poetry as Somalia's principal cultural achievement; secondly, to contend that years of random violence attendant upon the collapse of the state in 1991 have left the country collectively unhinged, and impoverished of soul in a manner that beggars description; and thirdly, to make a feeble attempt at charting a tentative course towards national redemption and renewal.

Once upon a time—a nation of poets

After 20 years of civil war and related social cataclysms, the international community knows only too well Somalia's demise as a nation-state. What the world doesn't know—a far greater calamity than the political collapse—relates to Somalia's other loss, the loss of her literary soul as a direct result of years of relentless violence and random anarchy. Once upon a time, Somalia was known as a nation of poets whose poetic heritage was intimately connected with the people's daily lives. In particular, foreign students of Somali language and culture used to remark, often in astonished tones, on the pervasive, sometimes sinister, influence of poetry and poetic arts on Somali life and lore. Typical of these observers of the Somali literary scene was the peripatetic romantic British traveler, Richard (later Sir Richard) Burton, who visited the Somali coast of Seylac and the city of Harar in 1854, disguised as a Muslim holy man named al-Xaaj Cabdalla. Burton wrought a number of subterfuges on the unsuspecting Somalis, one of which was to con them into appointing him as imam (Friday prayer leader), as well as their spiritual guide and all-purpose mentor. The eccentric Englishman distilled his Somali experiences into a book that, not without self-aggrandisement, he entitled *First Footsteps in East Africa*. (Someday when I grow up I should want to write a tome entitled *First Footsteps in America* as a payback to Burton and his spiritual offspring, the supercilious Americans!) Burton's condescending outlook notwithstanding, he expressed notable respect for Somali culture, especially the keen cultivation of the poetic arts by the 'natives'. He observed with a note of astonishment:

> The country teems with 'poets' [...]. Every man has his recognised position in literature as accurately defined as though he had been reviewed in a century of magazines–the fine ear of this people causing them to take the greatest pleasure in harmonious sounds and poetic expressions, whereas a false quantity or prosaic phrase excites their violent indignation [...]. Every chief in the country must have a panegyric to be sung by his clan, and the great patronize light literature by keeping a poet (Burton 1987 [1856]: 82).

Burton's judgment has been echoed over the years by other observers of the Somali cultural landscape—M. Maino, Margaret Laurence, B.W. Andrzejewski, I.M. Lewis, John Johnson. Nearly without exception, these expatriate scholars and unmentioned others emphasise the pervasive role that oral poetry plays (or at least played once upon a time) in the social fabric of Somali life. The foreign observers' assessment of the pre-eminent role of poetry in Somali life and lore has received unequivocal confirmation on numerous occasions from Somali pundits and public commentators, most remarkably the late president of the

Somali Republic, Dr Cabdirashid Cali Sharmaarke. Sharmaarke judged his country's pastoral verse as one of the two national assets of 'inestimable value' (Information Service of the Somali Government 1962: v). Islam was the other asset that Sharmaarke had in mind as being of equal merit, and in setting his nation's pastoral poetry on the same pedestal as the sacred Koran in the ranks of cherished national values, the president unmistakably meant to lavish the highest possible praise on his country's poetic heritage.

I recounted elsewhere the reasons for the enduring popularity of poetry and poetic arts in Somali life (Samatar 1982). Therefore, I should confine my remarks here only to a few snippets of an episodic kind. B.W. Andrzejewski, the late and lamented 'elder statesman of Somali literature', reported a revealing vignette about the supremely prestigious place that poetry occupies in Somali literary temper and tastes, to say nothing of its potent use in socio-political relations. In the late 1950s, while engaged in the study of Somali prosodic systems, he was accosted by a group of hoary elders who queried the foreign researcher somewhat provocatively, thus: 'You English [...] You make wondrous machines: lorries, airplanes, steamships, instruments that get water spewing out of the bowels of the earth. You are undoubtedly skillful as engineers. But as poets [...] Do you have poets!?' (Personal Conversation Andrzejewski, October 1976).

The reader should be alerted at this point that my use of the present tense notwithstanding, the poetically endowed Somalia described in the foregoing notes seems to have gone dormant, if it has not altogether disappeared. That Somalia seems to have been replaced by another, a barren Somalia—politically, socially, literarily—scraped to the bone from any aesthetic sensibility, to say nothing of its bucolic, lyrical verse that once stirred the imagination of foreign observers. The nation of poets has given way to a nation of victims and criminals where the Kalashnikov has expelled the poetic craft as the mediator of social relations and the arbiter of ultimate authority. Thus, today's Somalia is a nation adrift, having hit bottom, and hence collectively deranged and constricted in the soul—a wistful, surrendering, supine Somalia—except in the employment of guns.

Yet, in the life of nations as of individuals, hitting bottom entails the lingering hope of bouncing back upwards, of climbing up from the depths of the abyss to the dawning hope of a national revival. More than this, memory seduces the mind, believing as it does in the notion of the good old days, when in fact there never have been any such. This sobering realisation of the possibility of memory as an illusion should perhaps serve as a salutary check on my romantic clatter above about the once-poetic Somalia. Still, remembering Somalis (of whom there may not be many) surely must lament the loss of their nationhood and their literary heritage, along with their dignity and, consequently, their becoming the laughingstock of the world; for statelessness and anarchy have become the synonyms of the word Somali. On the other hand, even though the modern outlook ranks statelessness the most primitive state of human existence, may one not ask whether a human community must inhabit a territorial state in order to have happiness and dignity? Consider the bizarre fact, for example, that despite the absence in Somalia of a functioning centralised state for close to two decades now, no less an economic authority than the eminent *Economist* reports that stateless Somalia outperforms in GDP per person (and therefore presumably in standard of living) the neighbouring states of Ethiopia and Eritrea (*Economist* 2008).

It may be of interest here that of the five zones (Kismaayo and its neighbourhood, the capital Mogadishu and adjacent lands, the Hiiraan hinterlands, and the breakaway statelets of Puntland and Somaliland), it is only in troubled Mogadishu and its outskirts, contested as they are by successive clan and religious factions, that people face daily violence and starvation; and that it is cheaper, and involves less of a bureaucratic obstacle course, to make a phone call from Hargeysa (Somaliland) or Garoowe (Puntland) than from Nairobi or Addis Ababa (Personal Conversation with anonymous source, 28 March 2007). Somalia's economy without a state amazes the expatriate community, having become the ultimate in laissez faire economics.

Still, the urge to belong to a national community, to have a state, a flag, a passport and a corner of the earth, remains a universal longing, and those who lack these are invariably the object of universal scorn. Thus, it may be that the yearning for respect and for collective self-esteem could prompt members of the Somali elite to remember the past, the idyllic yesterday, when theirs was a nation counted among the community of nations. With their memory thus triggered, they may bestir themselves eventually into playing their historic role in binding the wounds of their fallen nation. One hopes so, but one doubts.

Purposive violence and poetic creativity

The view has been expressed in the preceding notes that the 1991 Somali collapse and the violent upheavals that ensued did much to stifle Somali poetic creativity. This does not follow as cause and effect. Violence of itself does not explain the seeming current collective sterility in the Somali poetic imagination. To the contrary, experience shows that the period of the worst violence in recorded Somali history (1900–20) also stands out as the era of the greatest outpouring of the finest poetry in the annals of the nation's verbal/artistic productivity. Thus, the key to understanding the current desiccation of the Somali imagination is rooted in the kind of violence, as opposed to violence *per se*, that has overtaken the Somalis in recent years. To which we shall return shortly. For the time being it could be said that in the acephalous, schismatic segmentary lineage system that characterises the Somali polity, where feuds and vendettas are the order of the day, purposive violence in fact serves as the midwife and mother of the Somali pastoralists' poetic sensibility.

Take, for example, the three decades that followed the turn of the 20th century, during which the Somali Dervish anti–colonial movement led by the poet, mystic and warrior Sayid Maxamed Cabdille Xassan the 'Mad Mullah' of British colonial literature and 'il Mullah Pazzo' of the Italians, fought off the combined powers of Britain, Italy and Ethiopia, almost bringing them to a standstill. As a result, the Dervish resistance struggle and the colonial campaigns to put it down engulfed the Somali peninsula in an orgy of killings in which an estimated one-third of the population of northern Somalia perished. Yet, in Somali eyes, this was an age of heroic struggle that saw the composition and dissemination of massive amounts of high-minded oral poetry, by both the Dervish warriors and their opponents, the colonial-collaborating clans. Despite the cataclysmic social upheavals, the period brought to the fore an unparalleled concentration of poetic talent, resulting in the blooming and maturing of such notable bards as Raage Ugaas, Qamaan Bulhan, Cali Jaamac Haabiil, Salaan Carraby, Ismaaciil Mire and Cali Dhuux, to mention but a few. These gifted poets waged literary war on one another, and their pro- and anti–Dervish poetic duellings and diatribes reverberated throughout the Somali peninsula.

The first political poem on record involving the Dervish struggle seems, on the basis of internal evidence, to have been composed in

1900, shortly after the Dervish attack on the Ethiopian fortification at Jigjiga (Samatar 1979b: 151). It was not composed by the Dervishes but by their enemies. When the poet, Cali Jaamac Haabiil (whom we will come across quite frequently in these pages as the chief poetic antagonist of the Sayid), learned of Dervish reverses at Jigjiga, he composed his poem 'Maxamed the Mad or the Lunatic' (Maxamed Waal), thereby immortalising in prosodic formula the Sayid's enduring and unflattering epithet. (Samatar 1979b: 181).

With a measure of malice and withering sarcasm, Haabiil gloated over Dervish losses and scoffed at the 'vaunted martial prowess' of the Dervishes who bragged, he charged, of their bid to vanquish the Abyssinians:

The uncontrollable man—he who'd seek Minilik in battle,
Who says: 'with my sword I'll smite the Abyssinians,'
Who says: 'I will give you the Habar herds as booty,'
Who'd weave lies around us,
Who'd take away our minds as if we were brainless camels.

The implication of these lines, obvious in the Somali version, is that the Sayid promised more than he could deliver: over-inflamed with a false sense of his military might, he sought out Menelik (the wily sovereign of the Ethiopian Empire at the turn of the 20th century) in battle and lost miserably (historically, this is not completely accurate, of course). He further promised his followers the possession in booty of the fabulous Habr Yonis herds, and failed to do so equally miserably; so that the Sayid was a liar 'who'd take away our minds as if we were brainless camels.' Having thus scoffed at Dervish military capability, he turned to ridicule the notion of the Sayid as a miraculous man of God:

He who says: 'I'll spear the heavens and fill the earth with fine pastures,'
Who says: 'like a ship, my prayer-mat can take you across the seas,'
Oh, how hollow is our imagination when we deem the Lunatic Maxamed our apostle!

Curiously, the poetic response defending the Dervishes did not come from their camp but from an outsider, one Al-Xaaj Axmed Samatar (no relation), a poet who was a resident of Aden at this time. He dispatched an epistle which he sent with a dhow returning from Aden, saying:

Is Minilik of your kindred that you should sing praises to him?
As for the cruising ships of the infidels:

Know ye not they are but Allah's brief providence to the misguided?
If glorious were the infidels, they'd not be destined to perdition,
The things they invent, and the wealth they amass are but their damnation,
And the ingenious artifacts their abominable foretaste of ultimate perdition.
This revelling in material things brought the mighty Pharaoh down.
If the meaning of the prayer-mat moving you across the sea escapes your unbelieving mind.
Consider: your origin, the very first day when you were created,
In the darkness of the womb, the Lord protected you.
Miraculous was your place of origin!
You came into the world by the will of Allah,
O mindless one, make a reflection on this,
Speak not ill of the Sayid, O brainless one, lest this leads you to Hell,
The ways of the saints, you fool, are dark to you,
And do not take him (the Sayid) lightly,
For unattainable is his likeness!

(Samatar 1979a: 159).

By pastoral standards, Al-Xaaji Axmed Samatar does not pass muster in making a successful defence. Although his poem, with its heavy metaphysical focus, may appeal to the pious and the other-worldly, it falls far short of the first poet's assault, especially in its failure to address the issues raised by the attack-poem: Dervish reverses at Jigjiga, the Sayid's promises which proved hollow, and the charge of insanity in the Sayid. Nevertheless, the Sayid was sufficiently pleased with Samatar's repartee on behalf of the Dervishes that he was reported to have rewarded Samatar with the payment of 150 camels, quite a lavish gift even by today's standards (a fit stallion from Somalia fetches as much as $2,000 in the bazaars of the Gulf countries, Somali livestock being keenly sought after by the Arabs). Dervish sympathisers are quick to cite this incident of an outsider coming to their defence as showing the appeal that their cause had for the Somalis. Opponents of the movement, however, counter that the poet was motivated not so much by an alleged attraction which the Dervishes had for the Somalis as by sycophantic greed, claiming that he hoped to obtain material gain by toadying to the Sayid (Samatar 1979a: 161).

During this period, the Sayid does not seem to have joined the war of words. Other men, like the Khusuusi (council of advisers) member Afqarshe and Ismaaciil Mire, both of whom were poets of note, acted, so to speak, as ministers of propaganda. Space and thematic coherence do not permit a detailed description of how the Sayid, throughout the early days of the struggle, employed other men to conduct the war of propaganda for him. The intriguing question, though, in a study of the Dervish resistance struggle is to speculate about the Sayid's motives in suddenly taking to the composition of vast quantities of political verse from 1904 onwards, thereby becoming his own poet-in-residence, instead of delegating others to perform that task as he had before. When confronted with such a question, indigenous sources would argue that he did not compose political poetry before this date because he did not know how to, with the inference that he received 'an abrupt inspiration' to versify without foresight or premeditation (Samatar 1979a: 165). This view we may take note of, but would do well to treat with scepticism. Given the strenuous demands which the poetic craft imposes on its practitioners among Somalis, men/women simply do not become celebrated bards overnight.

Political poetry is a potent tool in socio-political control among the pastoral Somalis and the possession and use of this asset make for honour and influence in society. The Sayid knew this and he was likely to capitalise on the prestige of his talent in this respect and make sure that it was used to enhance his own authority within the Dervish leadership structure. Consequently, the composition and use of political verse became, later on, a jealously guarded affair with access to it limited to a select few. In order not to lose their privileged status, these few had to sing praise-songs to the 'Father' (Samatar 1979a: 165). They had to do a good deal of self-effacing, dwelling *ad nauseum* on the inferiority of their verse to that of the all-wise Sayid and their indebtedness to the master for inspiration. A case in point is Ismaaciil Mire, a capable military commander and an established poet. When he, together with the Sayid's brother Aw Yuusuf Cabdille, successfully mounted a raid against Colonel Richard Corfield's Somaliland Camel Corps, the general, in the great euphoria of the moment, inadvertently dashed off a narrative epistle 'Residing at Taleex' (*'Annagoo Taleex Naal'*) on the history of the expedition, apparently without prior clearance with the Sayid. Although Mire duly gave credit for the victory to his master—'Cartridges of bullets he distributed among us. Lord bless him. He prayed to God for us'—he was nevertheless asked upon return to Taleex, the Dervish capital, to 'explain the circumstances of his poem' (Samatar 1979a: 187). The remark hinted darkly at the Sayid's displeasure at the liberties which his lieutenant had taken. The Sayid is said to have added further that Mire's poem left something to be desired in that it failed to give a detailed description of Corfield's death. This gave Mire a chance to get off the hook. 'Master,' he is reported to have said ingratiatingly, 'I reserved that opportunity for you to put forth a poem that would make history for the Somali people' (Samatar 1979a: 166). For the occasion the Sayid did compose the history-making poem 'O Corfield, Now That Thou Hast Departed' (*Adaa Koofilow Jiitayaan, Dunida Joogayne*) (Andrzejeweski and Lewis 1964: 73–4).

To put the Sayid's poetic combat in wider perspective, it may be useful to discuss it in relation to that of the legion of poetic antagonists who did literary battle with him. The most notable among these are the two poets Cali Dhuux and Cali J. Haabiil. Throughout the long struggle, these two maintained virulent literary duels with him, managing, on occasion, to more than hold their own. Ali J. Haabiil was a resident of the colonial city of Berbera. Urbane, pious and of an unusually handsome physique, Cali Jaama utterly lacked those traits that would be vulnerable to slander by the Sayid. He pilloried the Sayid:

And a thousand devout worshipers he butchered as one would a he-goat,
And caravans are given the safety of Allah,
But he wantonly cuts the tendons of weary travellers and hogs their dates,
He's battened on the weak and the orphan,
Call ye this infidel a Mahdi? How puzzling the thought!

(Samatar 1982: 164).

The accusation here is that anyone guilty of such atrocities as those that Cali Jaama claims were regularly committed in the name of Dervishism could not be a genuine Muslim but rather a vicious charlatan. Further, the Sayid, by all accounts, had his share of the poet's weakness for pleasures of the flesh, and the 'beauty of women' received persistent attention both in his poetry and lifetime pursuits. He is said to have contracted at least a dozen nuptials, some of them, no doubt, political marriages while others followed his 'keen eye for the fair maiden' (*bikrad bilic leh*) (Samatar 1979a: 176). Cali Jaama further accuses the Sayid of being a libertine and an adulterer: 'Of free women, he cohabits with seven.' Cali Dhuux for his part went further and charged the Sayid with incest:

And the women you consort with are fifteen.
Like a fattened ram among sheep in heat,
He tires not of lust, the lecherous devil,
In a crimson shawl and a silken veil,
Many an innocent lass night-visited him,

And lo, Rooxa, his sister, has come to the office,
Testifying to partnership of lust.

(Samatar 1979a: 177).

In the end, it becomes clear that the combined weight of his legion of attackers was having a corrosive effect on the Sheikh and, on occasion, he betrayed the extent of his bitterness against his accusers. In 1908, he wrote to the British Commissioner of Somaliland that one of the prime causes of the disturbance of the peace stemmed from the insults, intrigue and envy directed at him by poets of the colonial government clans: 'Being cursed is harder for us to bear than having our necks cut off [...]. I am considered by opponents and called a bad man, such as "old singer", "looter", "disturber of the peace"' (Jardine 1923: 163).

The foregoing poetic exchanges—at once lyrical and playful, polemical and acrimonious—that played so vital and fateful a role in the national struggle against colonialism constitute what the Somalis call the Dervish *silsilad* (an Arabic loan word which means 'Chain'), a series of political or social debates traded through the medium of oral verse. It forms an intimate part of a vast corpus of Somali traditional systems of prosody that have alarmingly declined if not died with the demise of Somalia as a nation. Their animated style of charge and rejoinder, jab and counter-jab along with sharply deployed witticisms embodies a dramatic illustration of the traditional centrality of vibrant poetic discourse that was intimately linked with the vicissitudes of the people's daily lives. Other *silsilad*s that in the course of time got seared into the collective Somali consciousness include the *Guba* ('Burner'), so named on account of the exceptionally bitter tone of the exchange, a *silsilad* par excellence considered by Somalis to be the crowning achievement of the genre. This was recorded and analysed for English readers as *A Somali Poetic Combat* by B.W. Andrzejewski and Muuse Galaal (1963: 15–28, 93–100, 190–205).

Then there is the *Hillaac Dheere* Series, a scorching composition that branded an Ogaadeen clan chieftain with shame, gleefully stigmatising him as an archetypal embodiment of greed and other ignominious character traits. This poisoned relations between the Ogaadeen and Majeerteen clans for a generation. Also the Nafti Hafar, or 'Self-Delusions' Series (1950s), so named because the poets in this contest ran amok with effusions of grandiloquent boasting that bore no relation to the actual merits of their respective clans; and finally the Hurgumo

(1970s through the 1980s), a series that foresaw, with stunning prescience and foresight, the impending collapse of the Somali state.

Random violence, wrecked souls

The above Dervish episode has shown that violence *per se* need not asphyxiate poetic creativity and that, to the contrary, purposive violence—that is, the kind of violence occasioned by the clash of high causes such as honour versus dishonour, group interest against group interest, freedom versus bondage, colonialism as opposed to the nationalist anti–colonial struggle—served to inspire, rather than stifle, the creative muse of the Somali clan world. What is unprecedented in the new catastrophic cataclysm of Somalia's continuing civil strife concerns a universal explosion of purposeless violence, a colossal mass hysteria which led to a wholesale unravelling of traditional normative values that mediated the rules of violence through time-tested sanctions of checks and balances. The consequence of this breakdown of the traditional regulators of inter-clan discourse is patently a traumatised deranged society, in which men and women have taken to blindly falling on one another, flailing amorphously, hacking away at one another, or rather indiscriminately machine-gunning everything that moves in a dazed hysteria reminiscent of a kind of mad dance that could only have been drawn from the pages of a Dostoevsky novel. Not only the state, the very Somali *Weltanschauung* has heedlessly reverted into a feral state. As I write, on the average, in the capital city of Mogadishu, thirty to forty people are killed daily with no one knowing who targeted them or why. The killing is all! If today a stranger with a loudspeaker descended from the sky and inquired of the denizens of Mogadishu: 'Why are you shooting?' the answer would undoubtedly resound back: 'Because this is our way of life.' No wonder Somalia is said to represent for African states a cautionary tale of where not to go.

To judge by this continuous random violence, the Somalis have created for themselves a hellish domain of indiscriminate generalised destruction. Fear, abject fear, has paralysed the Somali poetic sensibility. That is, the poetic muse is on the verge of vanishing from the collective Somali psyche.

There was one notable exception: in the late 1990s a group of Somali professors and professionals (including me) under the working name of Ergo, or the Peace Advocates, commissioned a number of poets inside the country to address the ills of the nation. The response was the composition—and dissemination on cassette tapes—of a sizeable corpus of modest-quality poems for which we lacked the needed resources to undertake the necessary follow-through. Additionally, the late satirist Axmed Ismaaciil Diiriye, a talented poet who wrote under the name of Qaasim, and the two urban poets Maxamed Ibraahim Warsame 'Hadraawi' and Maxamed Xaashi Dhamac 'Gaarriye', have addressed in poetry the ongoing Somali calamity. Qaasim's biting burlesques are—though of enormous interest and needing to be collected, studied and analysed in a monograph of their own—too passé to be of use here. With respect to Hadraawi and Gaarriye, I have yet to receive enough of their recent materials to undertake a worthwhile analysis. It would be desirable to inquire formally into the works of the latter two to examine how substantive their contributions are to Somali poetry in general, and to the national issue in particular. (Someday I should want to do this when their recent verse, I hope, becomes available to me.)

Other than these, to my knowledge, not a single line of poetry addressing the great issues of the day, as of olden days, has come out of Somalia in two decades (since 1991) of murderous upheavals. Instead, teenagers brandishing Kalashnikovs, high on the narcotic *qaad*, with sunken cheeks, popping eyes and haunted countenances, wildly shooting—to borrow a colloquialism—'every which way', roam the streets of the Somali capital. Further, the Kalashnikov has taken over from the pastoral bard as the ruling king of the roost. The result is that in the post-civil war Somalia of random violence and wanton destruction, there remain only wrecked, stunted souls. The nation of poets is no more, eclipsed as it is by a nation of dazed zombies, barren of the literary imagination and inventiveness of their forebears; *qaad* and the Kalashnikov nowadays define the new degraded Somali patrimony, especially in Mogadishu and its outskirts.

Cry, the Beloved Bard

In pre-collapse Somalia, poetry served as an all-purpose pervasive force, an aesthetically precious asset that at once betokened the pride of the nation and the boon of every Somali bosom. And yet so thoroughgoing is the current desiccation of the Somali poetic scene that I can scarcely believe that I wrote the following some 28 years ago:

> What makes poetry such a pervasive force in Somali society? To the Somalis the question is not so difficult to answer: poetry is the medium whereby an individual or a group can present a case most persuasively. The pastoral poet is [...] the public relations man of the clan, and through his craft he exercises a powerful influence in clan affairs. For unlike Western poetry, which appears to be primarily the concern of a group of professionals dealing with, more often than not, an esoteric subject matter intended for the members of a secret society, Somali pastoral verse is a living art affecting almost every aspect of life. Its functions are versatile, concerned not only with matters of art and aesthetics but also with questions of social significance. It illuminates culture, society and history. In addition to its value as the literary and aesthetic embodiment of the community, Somali poetry is a principal medium of mass communication, playing a role similar to that of the press and television in Western societies. Somali poets, like Western journalists and newspapermen, thus have a great deal to say about politics and the acquisition of political power. Because it is the language and the vehicle of politics, the verse which Somali poets produce is an important source of Somali history, just as the printed and televised word performs a similar function in the West. It is the duty, for example, of the pastoral poet to compose verse on all important clan events and to express and formalize the dominant issues of the age—in short, to record and immortalize the history of his people. And since the poet's talents are employed not only to give expression to a private emotion but also to address vital community concerns, his verse reflects the feelings, thoughts and actions of his age (Samatar 1982: 3).

The new cultural desert of today's Somali landscape must prompt us to intone despairingly: 'Cry, the Beloved Bard, bereft of your erstwhile place as prophet and seer of thy people, and banished now into an uninhabited wilderness by the AK-47.' For the grim fact is that Somalia's literary death tops its political demise. Will there ever be a light at the end of the Somali tunnel? Hope—as in Barack Obama's *Audacity of Hope*—may be abiding. Maybe this prophetic book should be made mandatory reading for all Somalis. Still, there are possible glimpses of recovery here and there, including the launching in Djibouti of a new literary journal in triplet tongues—English, French, Somali—entitled *Hal-Abuur*, or the Literary Inventor, under the able editorship of Maxamed Daahir Afrax, Professor Lidwien Kapteijns, Maxamed A. Riiraash and others. I have rummaged through a volume of this, and it shows promise in format, style and content. It surely deserves to be supported—financially, authorially, and morally—by all of good will. Moreover, if Nuruddin Farah finally manages to clinch the ultimate Nobel Prize, this could turn out to signal a major turning point. But will we, being Somalis, once again refuse to turn?

References

The Economist 17 April 2008. 'A Hint of Hope for a Broken Country.'

Andrzejewski, Bogumil W. and Muuse Galaal 1963. 'A Somali Poetic Combat.' *Journal of African Languages*, 2 (1), 15–28; 93–100; 190–205.

Andrzejewski, Bogumil and Ioan M. Lewis 1964. *Somali Poetry: An Introduction*. Oxford: The Clarendon Press.

Burton, Richard 1894. *First Footsteps in East Africa*. London: Tylston and Edwards.

Information Service of the Somali Government 1962. *The Somali Peninsula. A New Light on Imperial Motives*. Mogadishu.

Jardine, Douglas 1923. *The Mad Mullah of Somaliland*. London: Herbert & Jenkins.

Johnson, John 1974. *Heelloy Heelleellooy: the Development of the Genre Heello in Modern Somali Poetry*. Bloomington: Indiana University Press.

Laurence, Margaret 1954. *A Tree for Poverty*. Nairobi: Eagle Press.

Samatar, Said S. 1979a. 'Literary War in the Somalia of the Sayyid Mahammed Abdille Hassan: The Dervish Poetic Duels.' In H.M. Adam (ed.) *Somalia and the World: Proceedings of the International Symposium, held in Mogadishu, on the Tenth Anniversary of the Somali Revolution*. Mogadishu: Halgan, Vol. 1, pp. 154–90.

——— 1979b. 'Poetry in Somali Politics: the Case of Sayyid Mahammed Abdille Hassan.' (unpublished dissertation, Northwestern University).

——— 1982. *Oral Poetry and Somali Nationalism, the Case of Sayyid Mahammed Abdille Hassan*. Cambridge University Press.

13

THE POLITICS OF POETRY IN THE HORN OF AFRICA

A CASE STUDY IN MACRO-LEVEL AND MICRO-LEVEL TRADITION

John William Johnson

Introduction

Any traveller to the Somali Democratic Republic in the last days of the regime of Maxamed Siyad Barre might have been intrigued by the particular items that customs officials looked for in the luggage they checked through at the ports of entry. Among the items which one might not expect the authorities to search for were cassette tapes. Why should a cassette tape be considered potentially subversive to these officials?

The answer is that Somalis support a tradition of rendering to verse their most profound feelings and opinions in the political and social arenas of their lives. In those parts of the world where Somalis could be found at the time, there was a dramatic manifestation of this poetic tradition in the form of what Somalis call *silsilad*. This term comes into Somali from Arabic and means 'chain', and in its use here, it means 'chain of poems'. Verse which supported the government and that which criticised it could be found in this *silsilad*, which was commonly called *Diinley*. I was told that there were over 150 individual poems in this chain. I suspect that new chains are in progress today with the collapse of the Somali government and the resulting political upheaval.

A tradition in which the government was so sensitive to the uses of oral literature in politics is the stuff of which folklorists' research dreams are made. Somalis are obsessed with the notion that their poetry must employ a strenuous set of rules of prosody and that when a specific poem is recited or sung in public, it must be reproduced verbatim, or at least what the audience perceives as verbatim.[1] When a poem on a political topic does not scan properly, or when it is thought to have been manipulated or changed from its original form by its current reciter, he or she is chastised or ridiculed and his or her message is not taken seriously. And there are always people in a crowd to 'correct' any lines considered inaccurate by expert memorisers.

Important theoretical questions in the sociology of orature can potentially be answered by research into Somali verbal art. What is the relationship between form and social behaviour? Why is this obsession with form so important to Somalis, and what is its relationship to their social behaviour? Do these genres in fact produce once-created, often-repeated texts, or do they produce texts recreated each time they are recited? Can a once-created poem be utilised in more than one political context, or is it restricted to its original circumstances? These questions are especially important because they have implications in the area of politics, where poetry plays such an important role. In this essay I wish to offer results of field research into these theoretical questions, using a provocative theory concerning the dynamics of tradition as a process. Moreover, I hope to offer a solution to these questions, which may well contribute to broader theoretical issues in the discipline of folkloristics and in the humanities and social sciences in general.

Somali poetic tradition

Somali poetic tradition is something of an enigma in relation to at least two current theories concerning orature. One of the most prominent theories concerning the composition and performance of oral poetry is the Oral-Formulaic or Parry/Lord Thesis (see Lord 1960). Milman Parry and later Albert Lord, both professors at Harvard University and both scholars specialising in the printed epic poetry of Homer and the living South Slavic epic, have argued that at least one form of oral poetry, namely epic, is indeed recreated each time it is recited. Lord has tended to rule out any alternative creative method that does not conform to the Oral-Formulaic method. In light of long-time Somali claims of verbatim memorisation, therefore, an important theoretical question arises: whether Somali oral poetry represents a once-created and oft-repeated text, or whether it, too, is recreated each time it is recited.

Obviously, each time a Somali poem is recited, it is recreated in the contextual sense, but the crucial question here is, is it recreated *textually*? In other words, it is recomposed? Such a question has important social implications contextually, particularly in the area of politics. The collaborative research between me and two Somali colleagues, Cabdullaahi Diiriye Guuleed 'Carraale' and Axmed Cali Abokor, has led us to the conclusion that Somalis do indeed attempt to memorise their poetry verbatim. All our data point to the 'once-created'view, which is unpopular with scholars embracing the Oral-Formulaic Theory.[2]

Our studies of numerous poems, such as *Baabuulle* ('The Lion's Mane'), composed by Samatar Baxnaan, and *Kibir* ('Arrogance'), composed by Ismaaciil Mire, as well as many others, indicate that only minor portions of that poem differ in comparison of separate variants recited by different people even at different times.[3] Our analysis reveals a number of variation possibilities within the strict rules of Somali prosody. For example, dialect differences exist, but have no influence on memorisation. Some variations do play a role in memorisation, such as slight changes in grammatical use and minor morphological differences.[4] There are also line and stanza interpolations, and omissions in some variants. But a significant majority of contrasting lines scan properly within the extremely tight rules of Somali metrics. While perfect memorisation is not evident, the goal of verbatim memorisation is observable.[5]

Somalis possess a poetic tradition which can be of great interest to theoreticians of orature, as some of their genres represent an enigmatic creative process not yet fully exposed to the academy. What students of orature like Andrzejewski and myself, as well as a number of Somali and other European scholars, have claimed about Somali poetry over the years is the subject of a theoretical controversy in the school of folkloristics, which embraces the Oral-Formulaic Thesis mentioned earlier. A bit of the background to this controversy will illustrate how the composition and performance of Somali poetry are different from those traditions covered by the Oral-Formulaic Thesis. Moreover, a related theoretical problem in folkloristics, the long-standing debate on the nature of the concept of tradition, will also shed some light on Somali poetic composition and performance.[6]

The theoretical problem: tradition in folkloristics

In order to understand the process of tradition in the societies they have studied, many folklorists have been oriented towards the study of oral texts as one of the main conduits through which tradition is manifested, and over the years they have changed their minds about the nature of the texts and the variations they have found in different performances of them. Older views in the Historical-Geographical School of folkloristics considered change to be a negative and corrupting influence on tradition, a deterioration of older, purer forms. Change was described in such negative terms as forgetfulness and/or misunderstanding during diffusion. The dominant view of composition at the time held that oral performers were not very creative. They were only capable of 'carrying on' tradition. The text was seen as a once-created, often-repeated, and above all old form. Ironically, folkloristics began with a theory of memorisation, which turned out to be inaccurate in many cases, and, as we shall see, later rejected memorisation altogether.

From ballad scholarship came an idea first proposed by Gordon Gerould (1932) and Phillips Barry (1933). They proposed a theory of *communal recreation*, stating that a ballad text did indeed have a single origin but was recomposed, and thereby possibly changed, even if only slightly, by each singer who became involved in its diffusion. Barry, Gerould, and later folklorists had a very specific meaning for the idea of recomposition. Collected at any point in the life of its diffusion as a composite text of communal recreation, the text was considered the collective product of the folk. Change was not negative; it was the result of this collective recomposition.

Another challenge to the view that change was negative came from Carl von Sydow (1948: 11–43, 44–59), whose theory of the *oikotyping* of folktales argued that change was a reconstruction for local cultural consumption. Germans might tell the story of Cinderella in a way more meaningful to a German audience, and the French and others would do likewise. A readily available example is the fact that the French, who apparently had great difficulties in the Middle Ages feeding themselves, might reward the heroes and heroines at the end of a tale with a great feast, while the German variant of the same *Märchen*, or fairy tale, might end in a wedding, where the lowly peasant marries the royal prince or princess as a reward for valour (see Darnton 1984). Von Sydow's view of change involved a cultural reinterpretation.

The Oral-Formulaic Thesis was next on the academic scene. Milman Parry and Albert Lord postulated that change was due to individual, not communal reconstruction. They held that each time the text was performed, even by the same raconteur, it was completely recreated. Texts were never merely passed on; they were always reshaped. Using a methodology of morpheme-by-morpheme and line-by-line comparison of variants of the same poem composed by the same bard at different times and by different bards singing the 'same' poem, these scholars argued that epic poetry is recreated each time it is recited.

The most recent theory to which the Somali tradition also appears baffling on the surface is the performance-centred focus of the school of folklore called contextualism. Performance theory argues that folklore forms are deliberately manipulated and changed to fit new social contexts in which they are used. The crucial question of whether a Somali poem with a specific political and historical content can be changed to fit the new political situation is very relevant to this theoretical approach. While the oral-formulaic thesis appears to work well with longer poetic compositions like epics, it does not describe the Somali tradition very well. Performance theory carries the sociology of literature beyond mere formal analysis, and the work of several scholars including Richard Handler, Jocelyn Linnekin and Roger Janelli is very helpful in understanding issues surrounding the enigmas of Somali poetry

To get to the next phase in this progression of ideas, we must turn to a parallel progression of ideas concerned with the study of tradition as a concept. Again, views of the nature of change are important. For a long time in folkloristics, tradition was defined as *a body of knowledge passed down from generation to generation by word of mouth or by imitation*. This definition came under fire from a number of scholars, perhaps most articulately represented by Richard Handler and Jocelyn Linnekin (1984). Handler and Linnekin argued that tradition must be understood as a set of wholly symbolic constructs, and that there was nothing natural about it. They also postulated that, as an interpretive construct, tradition is composed of elements of both continuity and change. They argued that tradition was passed to individuals in both a formalistic and a symbolic state, each of which underwent change over time. Although they attacked another scholar who published what some considered the classic study of tradition, Edward Shils (1981), they agreed with him in stating that tradition may come from the past, but is of the present. Tradition, they argued, is a contemporary set of constructs, which influences the behaviour of its practitioners and is inherited from the past, but the constructs are not reconstructed perfectly when they are used in the present. The illusion that tradition is a flawless memory of the past is just that, an illusion. In reality, it is a contextually bound interpretation of the past for use in the present, and change is an integral part of it.

In a seminal article published earlier, anticipating the conclusions in Handler and Linnekin, Roger Janelli (1976) attempted to reconcile the older definition of tradition as a body of handed-down knowledge with some of the newer arguments from the contextualist school in folkloristics. If tradition is not an inherited body of knowledge in the real world, Janelli asked, 'how is it [...] that we can recognise textual or plot stability over centuries if each folkloric performance is unique to the immediate context in which it occurs?' (ibid. 61). On the surface, this question almost appears to challenge Handler and Linnekin's views, but it is in fact an attempt at reconciling opposing, extreme views. Janelli suggests two levels of causality, which produce the products of tradition. He calls these levels the macro-level and micro-level of tradition.

It is common for members of a folk group[7] to believe that they possess a 'collective memory' of past tradition. But in the real world, groups cannot have memories; only individuals can have memories. The actual process of tradition thus results when each member, relying upon his or her own individual memory, discusses and debates, indeed renegotiates, each given situation as it arises. This process results in end products which Shils names *tradita* (plural of *traditum*) in an attempt to differentiate the process of tradition from its products. In the real world, then, tradition represents not so much an actual body of knowledge as a form of group interaction of all participating members, relying on their own individual memories in an attempt to reconstruct what they think happened in the past and including not only their agreements but also their disagreements and resulting compromises. This process may be profoundly tempered by the needs of the present context, and it is during the performance of these forms that change occurs, invariably leading to unstandardised multiple variations in the *tradita* and in the resulting behaviour associated with it. The 'collective memory' of the folk and the older definition of tradition is thus an illusion, and it is this illusion that Janelli calls the macro-level of tradition. Because there may be a great deal of agreement about how to perform a *traditum*, the illusion is fairly strong and *tradita* may change so slowly that the members of the folk group do not notice the changes, or they may not consider them significant. But over a great deal of time, and after many performances, change may be so great that the earlier form may not even be recognisable.

Janelli called the performance level of tradition, where the renegotiated *traditum* is actually conducted and debated using the individual memories of its practitioners, the micro-level. Put another way, macro-level tradition is really a reification, believed by individual members of a group to be a real inherited body of lore, which has been passed down from generation to generation by word of mouth or by imitation. Micro-level tradition is the symbolic social interaction of tradition at the performance level, in which memories of past performances of tradition are reconstructed and renegotiated among the active bearers of tradition and their audiences. Working within a remembered set of literary conventions, the individual recreates a tradition and—because change occurs—influences the various ways it will be remembered in the future. As soon as a *traditum* is performed, it becomes a part of the memories of those present, thus again becoming a part of macro-level tradition. To summarise, macro-level tradition is a memory; micro-level tradition is a performance.

The potential for change thus occurs in every single performance of a *traditum*. I would like to add my own view of tradition to these theories. Tradition is a form of learned behaviour. It is not information deduced from reason or logic. It is not information that one learns by oneself. And it is not a part of instinctive behaviour inherited genetically, although it is bound by human limitations and possibilities. But it does not encompass all of what people learn. This learned behaviour contributes to group identity by verbalising the group's beliefs and worldview through the conduit of the lore. If one has learned most of what one knows from members of one's group, it only stands to reason that what one has learned may reflect the majority opinion of the individual concerns and worldview of those members. In turn, as a member of the group, one's own views influence the macro-level of the tradition that the group members negotiate together prior to performance. This idea of groupness is important to the practice of tradition because, through normative behaviour, it facilitates the recognition of form that Janelli postulates in his theory.

One more point needs to be made before continuing. While change was first viewed as a negative force in the process of tradition, it is now seen as a deliberate way of making the text more relevant to the context and to the audience for which it is intended, although the group practicing the tradition may not notice innovation as change at all. The illusion of changelessness in tradition is viewed as a macro-level of causality, while the actual performance of tradition is viewed as a micro-level of causality. And it is at this point that we might ask, if Somali poetry is recited in a near verbatim form, how can the same poem be employed over and over again in different contexts?

Macro-level and micro-level dynamics in Somali poetry and folklore

It is clear that the macro-level of Somali verbal art represents sets of complex expectations dealing with literary and social conventions concerning the performance of oral art. Somali poets, memoriser/reciters, and audience members alike share these overlapping individual sets of expectations, indeed this sense of what is proper and fitting for artistic verbal creativity. The heated debates on literary matters one hears in the tea shops and at other social gathering places in Somalia make it clear that there is both agreement and disagreement as to the specifics of these conventions at the macro-level of Somali poetic tradition. To approach an answer to the question of the relationship between form and social behaviour, I should like to explore both the formal and the social expectations at the macro-level of the Somali poetic tradition, and demonstrate with examples how they are realised at the micro-level.

An overwhelmingly prevalent macro-level expectation concerns Somali notions of accuracy. One of the ways this expectation is manifested is in the custom of citing the poet by name before the recitation of any poem. In his study of the Somali national hero Sayid Maxamed Cabdille Xassan,[8] Said Sheikh Samatar (1982: 64) refers to this expectation as an 'unwritten copyright law', and he cites an interesting example of its violation and the resulting social reaction. One of the major contexts for poetry recitation in Somalia is during a session of *qaad* chewing. *Qaad* is a mildly intoxicating leaf chewed in East Africa and the Yemen (and now in the diaspora) for its stimulating effects. During one such session in which Samatar was present, a young poet was reciting with such skill that the audience was enthralled, but in the midst of his performance, an elder Somali in one corner of the room shouted out: 'Liar—thou art a liar and a charlatan.' An uneasy silence ensued among the company of all-male chewers.

At long last the poet inquired, 'Who?'
'Thou,' the elder responded.
'Why do you insult, uncle?'
'Because thou claimest what thou hast not laboured for.'
'I only claimed what is mine.'

After the elder repeated some of the lines of the poem, the young would-be poet left the room, and the men later inquired of other town elders as to the veracity of the first elder's claim. Because they were able to recite the debated lines verbatim, it was easily determined that the poem belonged to Ugaas Nuur, a mid-19th-century ruler in northwestern Somalia. Samatar concluded the episode as follows (ibid: 65–7): 'So the amiable [elder] was vindicated; as for the poet, rumor had it that, far from attempting to take legal action [against the elder, as he had threatened], he left town in a hurry rather than linger around to face the laughter and ridicule which were certain to greet him upon discovery of his unsuccessful antics.'

Verbatim reproduction of a poet's work, like stated authorship, is an important manifestation of Somali notions of accuracy. Verbal messages are often sent in Somalia in poetic form and sometimes have to be given to a stranger to deliver. The message is recited to the carrier until he or she has it memorised, and the messenger is often asked to repeat the poem until the person wanting to send the message is satisfied. In order to maintain secrecy, the poet will employ veiled speech with which to deliver his or her message, a system Andrzejewski (1981: 5–10) called the 'oral envelope'. The combination of tight prosodic rules with veiled speech is often an important technique when politics is the topic of a poem, as I shall illustrate below.

Verbatim and near-verbatim memorisation of poetry is made possible by the incredibly complex rules of prosody in Somali verse, one rule of which involves the rhyme scheme. Somali classical poetry alliterates with only one sound per poem, a sound here defined as a single consonant or all the vowels collectively. Another example from Samatar's study will illustrate the relationship between form and social behaviour (ibid: 149). In his twenty-year struggle against the colonial powers which occupied his country, Sayid Maxamed Cabdille Xassan often sent messages to his enemies, both foreign and Somali, in verse. His Somali enemies sometimes answered in *silsilad* fashion described at the beginning of this chapter. In a poetic diatribe against the poet Cali Jaamac Haabiil, with whom he frequently debated, Sayid Maxamed composed a line, which Samatar translates: 'Call you this Italian-infidel a Mahdi? How puzzling the thought.' This passage was first translated in the early part of this century by an Italian Roman Catholic priest, who was offended by the snide remark about his countryman. His substitution of the word Jew (*Yuhuudi* in Somali) for the word Italian (*Talyaani* in Somali), was however easily detected by Somalis, because the poem alliterated in 'T'.

Another set of literary expectations at the micro-level of this tradition is the imagery employed in pastoralist poetry. Groups tend to employ their environment and its folklife as symbols in their folklore. I propose to call this phenomenon the *premise of environmental semiotics*. This premise attempts to codify what folklorists mean when they say that a group's worldview or culture is reflected in its folklore or by its tradition. This is not to say that environment causes oral literature to take the shape it does; it merely provides potential symbolism for use by its creative raconteurs. The public expects specific pastoralist symbols to be maintained with a certain semantic continuity. The late great Somali scholar Xaaji Muuse Xaaji Ismaaciil Galaal divided Somali poetic images into two main groups: the 'wet' images and the 'dry' images.[9] With a few exceptions, most of the images used in Somali poetry that derive from the rainy season are positive, while drought provides many negative symbols.[10] At the micro-level of this tradition, however, it is the poet's skilful use of this imagery in composition that constitutes creativity. A poem will illustrate this point (see Johnson 1996a: 120–23).[11]

The social background to this poem is very interesting. It was composed in late 1960 or early 1961 and is really a shining example of veiled speech. The poet claimed that his verse concerned a bad match for marriage. The literal meaning of the first stanza argues this point, and the poet claimed that stanzas two through five were metaphors supporting the first stanza. Government officials, however, saw the entire poem as a metaphor criticising the 1960 political unification ('marriage') of the British Somaliland Protectorate and the United Nations Trust Territory of Somalia Under Italian Administration as the new Somali Republic. The poem goes as follows:

Haweeyoo geyaanoo, gacal igula taliyaa,
Garbo ii hillaacdoon, sii daayay gacantee,
  Anigaysu geystoo, galabsaday xumaantee,
  Wixii ila garaadow, gobannimo ha tuurina.
Adoo guri barwaaqo ah, geel dhalay ku haysta,
Geeddi lama lallaboo, abaar looma guuree,
  Anigaysu geystoo, galabsaday xumaantee,
  Wixii ila garaadow, gobannimo ha tuurina.
Adigoo golmoonoo, gaajo ay ku hayso,
Gorogkaaga xoorka leh, layskama gembiyo,
  Anigaysu geystoo, galabsaday xumaantee,
  Wixii ila garaadow, gobannimo ha tuurina.
Intaan gudin afaystaan, laabatada is gooyoo,
Caqligayga guuroo, garab maray waanaaggee,
  Anigaysu geystoo, galabsaday xumaantee,
  Wixii ila garaadow, gobannimo ha tuurina.
Nabsigaan guntaday baa, goobtaa i joojoo,
Ninna garawsan maayoo way goonni xaajadu,
  Anigaysu geystoo, galabsaday xumaantee,
  Wixii ila garaadow, gobannimo ha tuurina.

When my kinsmen advised me to wed Haweeyo, who is marriageable to me,
Lightning flashed for me by a precipice and I stretched out my hand towards it.
'Tis I who brought this evil upon myself;
  All ye who think as I do, do not cast aside your freedom.
While you keep camels, which have just given birth in a prosperous camp,
You should not arrange a move and travel into a drought.
  'Tis I who brought this evil upon myself;
  All ye who think as I do, do not cast aside your freedom.
You who are lean and whom hunger grips
Should not o'erturn your frothing milk vessel.
  'Tis I who brought this evil upon myself;
  All ye who think as I do, do not cast aside your freedom.
When I sharpened the axe, I cut my own joint;
My senses left me—I have missed the good things of life.
  'Tis I who brought this evil upon myself;
  All ye who think as I do, do not cast aside your freedom.
The Fate, which I sealed for myself, halted me in that place;
I will take counsel from no one, for the matter is special to me.
  'Tis I who brought this evil upon myself;
  All ye who think as I do, do not cast aside your freedom.

Here we see at the micro-level the individual poet's genius at manipulating macro-level images to fit a social context of political controversy. At the micro-level of tradition, creativity is measured by how far the poet can manipulate or even deviate from the expected literary conventions. Thus, it is the aspiration of a poet to introduce innovation at the micro-level within the constraints of the literary conventions at the macro-level.

It must be the ultimate aspiration for a poet to become known as the innovator of a completely new genre of poetry. I know several ways this can be accomplished by formal manipulation. One of the traits in the prosody of Somali classical poetry involves long and short vowels and their syntax on a line (called *semic structure*). To cite an example, the foot pattern of a *gabay*, one of the classical genres, must be *long, long, short*. Long and short refer to the *semes*, which make up the recurrent pattern in a foot. A *monoseme* (short) may be filled only with a short vowel, while a *diseme* (long) may be filled either with two short vowels or one long one. The rearrangement of the syntax of these semic patterns into new combinations is one way new genres may be created. There are other formal ways to accomplish innovation, but that is the subject of another essay. Much more common is the manipulation of one of the conventions within an existing genre. Sayid Maxamed Cabdille Xassan, for example, introduced the innovation of composing *gabayo* in triplet lines.

There are many other ways the structure of poetry may be changed within macro-level expectations, but let us now explore some of the macro-level *social* expectations of the Somali poetic tradition, which also involve creative innovation within conventions. Notions concerning the proper role of poetry in Somali society are especially strong. Somalis expect certain genres to deal with certain designated topics. And there is even an expectation that certain genres are reserved for one or the other of the sexes. The genre called *buraambur*, for example, is reserved at the macro-level for women, and there are scores of *buraambur* composed by and for women each year. But at the micro-level one again finds deviation. There is a large body of Sufi poetry composed in this *buraambur* metre by and for men.[12] In another case, I was told by Xaaji Muuse Galaal that Sayid Maxamed Cabdille Xassan once composed a poem in the rhythm of a women's churning poem as a joke on his 'secretary of state', Xuseen Diqleh. Although women more commonly compose these poems and the expectation is that they will, at the micro-level of performance many things are possible.

Although there are many social expectations concerning the role of poetry in Somali society, one of the strongest, and the one relevant here, concerns its place in the political arena. No political movement in the period from 1960 to 1972 was possible without the aid of a skilled poet, and scholars like Said Samatar have pointed out that one of the keys to Sayid Maxamed Cabdille Xassan's many successes was his ability to carry on political debates in verse. The expectation of political content, especially through 'veiled speech', is so strong that a piece of oral literature is sometimes suspected of political content when none was intended.

In 1968 when I was working in the Ministry of Education with Xaaji Muuse Galaal, Yuusuf Dhuxul, a local lawyer and publisher of the bimonthly political journal *Dalka*, asked Muuse to give him a folktale or legend transcribed in the Latin script that Muuse, together with other scholars including B.W. Andrzejewski, had prepared for the Somali language. Yuusuf did not care what we gave him; his intent was to show the public what Somali would look like using the proposed script. Somali was not officially written at that time, and there was a great national debate in progress over which of some 25 or more proposed scripts to adopt.[13] Muuse and I had just finished transcribing and translating a folktale that he called *Basho iyo Jiir*, 'The Cats and the Rats', which we decided to give to Yuusuf, who subsequently published it. A résumé of the plot follows:[14]

> The Cat Clan held a meeting to discuss the total elimination of the Rat Clan, and they proposed a meeting with the latter ostensibly to discuss peace between their two clans. The Rats smelled the ruse however, and agreed to the meeting only after they had made preparations to defend themselves by digging trenches in which to hide very close to where they would stand when the official meeting took place. These trenches were carefully concealed so the Cats would not see them. Sure enough, when the meeting was held, the Cats attempted to kill the Rats, but to their dismay, the Rats were prepared for them and were able to jump to safety into their trenches and escape.

An innocent folktale? The public did not think so. For about two weeks after *Dalka* was released, our daily work was often disturbed by people coming into Xaaji Muuse's office at the Ministry wanting to know the identity of the person or persons represented by the Rats and the Cats. They inquired about the situation that the story represented. Muuse did his best to explain that the entire exercise of transcribing and publishing the folktale had merely been an experiment in rendering the Somali language to written form, but few believed him. The macro-level expectation called for a veiled political message in the story.

Another rather remarkable case involving two micro-level uses of the same poem is relevant here. The first incident happened in the Somali Parliament when I lived in Somalia in 1967. Early in the year, Axmed Suleebaan Bidde composed a poem, which Somalis call *Leexo*. The text of the poem deals with unrequited love on the surface level, but the expectation of veiled political content was strong with this poem. In those days, the president of the Somali Republic was elected in the parliament and not by the public. The president then appointed a prime minister who would form a government, much as in Italy today. The incumbent president, Aadan Cabdille Cismaan, was again running for the office, and he was being challenged by Cabdirashiid Cali Sharmaarke and others. No clear majority was gained by anyone for two ballots. The whole process was being carried live by Radio Mogadishu, and between ballots, music and poetry were played and also broadcast onto the floor of Parliament. During the caucus between the second and third ballots, the poem *Leexo* was broadcast, and on the third ballot the new president Sharmaarke was elected, and the old president was defeated. Soon after this incident, the radio announcer who played the poem on the air was arrested and hauled off to court. Because of veiled speech in the poem, however, nothing could be proved against him, and he was released. The poem goes as follows:[15]

Innakoo lammaane ah,
Iyo laba naf-qaybsile,
Talo geed ku laashee,
Adigaa is lumiyo,
Isu loogay cadowgoo,
Libintaadii siiyee,
Waadiganse liitee,
Leexaadu ku sidatee,
Hadba laan cuskanayee,
Liibaanteed adduunyada,
Ruuxna laasan maayee,
Maxaa luray naftaadii.
Waa laac adduunyadu,
Labadii walaalo ah,
Midba maalin ladanyoo,
Ruuxii u lill-galay,
Lama loolo dhereggoo,
Luggooyada ma haystee,
Waadiganse laabtiyo,
Lugaha is la waayaye,
Meel sare lalanayee,

Liibaanteed adduunyada
Ruuxna laasan maayee,
Maxaa luray naftaadii.
Anigaba lafiyo jiidh,
Waa kii i laastaan,
Liqi waayay oontee,
Adigaa lis caanood,
Iyo laad xareediyo,
Laydhiyo hadh diiddee,
Waadigan sidii liig,
Laasimay ugaadhee,
Waaclada u leexdee,
Liibaanteed adduunyada,
Ruuxna laasan maayee,
Maxaa luray naftaadii.
Dhaaxaad ladnaan rays,
Sidaad aar libaax tay,
Tallaabada ladhaaysoo
Anna lahashadaadii,
Ledi waayay ciil oo,
Liidnimo i raacdee,
Lallabaa habeenkiyo,
Ma libdhaan jacayl oo,
Waa labalegdoodaan,
Liibaanteed adduunyada,
Ruuxna laasan maayee,
Maxaa luray naftaadii.
Innakoo lammaane ah,
Iyo laba naf-qaybsile,
Talo geed ku laashee,
Adigaa is lumiyo,
Isu loogay cadowgoo,
Libintaadii siiyee,
Waadiganse liitee,
Leexaadu ku sidatee,
Hadba laan cuskanayee,
Liibaanteed adduunyada,
Ruuxna laasan maayee,
Maxaa luray naftaadii.

While we were yet together,
Helping each other in every way,
You cast good council away to the top of a high tree;
You caused yourself distress,
And slaughtered yourself for your enemy,
Giving your victory to him.
Now you are so weakened

That the light breezes bear you up,
And from time to time you grasp at a branch.
For all the pleasures of this earth
One cannot fully enjoy;
Tell me: what causes you this distress?
The world is but a mirage.
And for every two brothers,
Only one being happy each day,
The one who is fortunate
Should not abuse his prosperity—
Should not maltreat his neighbour.
And in your case, however,
Your breast and feet were out of accord.
For you are drifting up, up into the air.
For all the pleasures of this earth
One cannot fully enjoy;
Tell me: what causes you this distress?
Look at me: my flesh and all my bones
Were completely consumed by him.
I cannot even swallow food!
The abundance of milk,
Pure rainwater,
Fresh air, and rest in the cool shade, you have rejected.
It is you, who like the male garanuug,
Left the other game, and
Turned to a desolate place.
For all the pleasures of this earth
One cannot fully enjoy;
Tell me: what causes you this distress?
So often in the prosperity of the rains
As though you were a proud lion
You walked about majestically,
Whilst I, because of your carousing,
Had sleepless nights from impotent anger,
And sometimes behaved like a fool.
The beacon fire in the dark night
And love, never disappear;
They roll on after you, unrestrained.
For all the pleasures of this earth
One cannot fully enjoy;
Tell me: what causes you this distress?
While we were yet together,
Helping each other in every way,
You cast good council away, to the top of a high tree;
You caused yourself distress,
And slaughtered yourself for your enemy,

Giving your victory to him.
  Now you are so weakened
  That the light breezes bear you up,
  And from time to time you grasp at a branch.
    For all the pleasures of this earth
    One cannot fully enjoy;
    Tell me: what causes you this distress?

This incident clearly illustrates how a poem, once created, recorded on magnetic tape, and often broadcast over the radio, and thus already a part of the macro-level of tradition, came to be used in a new way at the micro-level in a specific political context. But did the disc jockey have a political motive, or was he just playing a popular love poem with a good musical tune for the sake of entertainment? It is interesting that this disc jockey went on to become the director of the Somali national radio station after the change of government under Maxamed Siyad Barre. The macro-level expectation of both the audience and the government rejected the latter explanation, and two consequences followed. The first was the arrest of the disc jockey. The second was that, regardless of the man's real intentions, this poem became known as 'the poem that overthrew a president'.

A second incident involving the same poem strengthens our understanding of the micro-level use of once-created poetry. This incident was related to me in a letter, dated 25 February 1991, from Martin Orwin, reader in Somali language and literature at the School of Oriental and African Studies, University of London. In early 1991 forces of President Maxamed Siyad Barre, were under attack from the forces of General Maxamed Faarax Caydiid, who went on to overthrow the government after an armed struggle. During the fighting, a radio announcer at the Somali Section of the BBC in London asked for permission to play the poem *Leexo* over the air because he knew the poem had become politicised and wanted to check with his superiors before airing the piece, which would go over the airwaves to Somalia. Permission was granted, but ironically, the poem was broadcast on 26 January 1991, at about 5:30 pm East Africa Time. It was later reported that at 6:30 pm, the opposition forces overthrew the Siyad Barre regime in the capital city. Orwin went on to say in his letter that the reporter was aware of the increasingly weak position of Siyad Barre, and he did play the song deliberately knowing its history and associations. He was not, of course, aware of the details of Siyad Barre's immediate weakness or when he would finally be toppled. What a coincidence that it should be the very same evening as *Leexo* was broadcast! The poem has now become known as 'the poem that overthrew two governments'.

In summary, poetry created for specific contexts at the micro-level, having been performed, thus becomes a part of macro-level memory, but may be reused in other contexts again at the micro-level. Memory of the reuse becomes a part of the macro-level of this tradition yet again. The constant interplay of macro- and micro-level causalities in the Somali poetic tradition provides us with the answer to the problem of how verbatim texts can be employed in changing political and other social contexts.

Conclusion

Several theoretical questions have been asked in this essay concerning the relationship between form and social behaviour, particularly political behaviour, in poetry in the Horn of Africa. Why are Somalis obsessed with verbatim, or near verbatim, form in their poetic structures? Is the Somali poem in fact a once-created, often-repeated text, or is it recreated each time it is recited? Each time a Somali poem is recited, it is obviously physically recreated, but the crucial question is, is it recomposed? Can a Somali poem with political and perhaps historical content be changed to fit a new political situation, or, since the poem is expected to be delivered verbatim, can it only be used to argue its original point?

The key to the issues suggested by these questions lies in the nature of language and in the nature of politics. When I was a postgraduate student, I studied French as one of my required languages. French-for-postgraduate-students really is not designed to help a student learn to speak the language, but rather to help him or her to use it as a research tool. Therefore, the chief pedagogical method employed involved teaching enough of the grammar to help a student translate printed matter. I remember really struggling with the exercises in our textbook, which always involved translating French literature. I wondered if I would ever learn enough of the language to be able to read scholarly articles. One day, I put aside the daily assignment in creative literature and, on my own, attempted to read a nonfiction scholarly article in my field. I was astonished to find that I could do so with relative ease, as long as I kept my dictionary close. I think that this incident, more than any classroom discussions in linguistics on the concept of semantics in language, taught me the difference between technical language and literary language. Poetry is by its very nature ambiguous. It is not the kind of language intended to be semantically precise. It does not eliminate ideational possibilities in order to arrive at a clear point; it does just the opposite. It creates them. It deals in trope, metaphor, image, and symbol, and above all, the creative manipulation of language.

Using his or her memory and understanding of a complex set of images and cultural expectations at the macro-level of the poetic tradition, the creative Somali poet poses political arguments and viewpoints in verse. Creativity and the sheer manipulation of ideas and of language itself are often so impressive to an audience that the argument gets lost in the aesthetics of the poem. An argument may be won by a good poet regardless of the social implications or the political results the actual argument may have in the body politic. Veiled speech, which functions to avoid open political conflict and possibly a prison term for the poet, is language at its most ambiguous. The goal of verbatim memorisation in Somali poetry reinforces a macro-level *illusion* of truth, while in reality the memorised lines are arguing social and political opinion, which brings me to the nature of politics.

In a sense, politics is to social interaction as literature is to language. While it may not be ambiguous, it is opinionated. We say that lawyers *practice* the law and *argue* their cases before the bar. In Somalia, the poet serves some of the roles of the lawyer, because politics is argued most effectively in verse. People expect it to be done in this manner. While composed of certain formal expectations, macro-level tradition is also composed of certain social expectations. Poets create verse in order to argue political points of view. In the case of the poem *Leexo*, we can even see that a once-created poem can be used to relate to one or more political situations for which it was not originally composed. The reinterpretation of the lines in this poem after its composition leads to the conclusion that Somali poetry is not textually recomposed, but it is in a sense *contextually recomposed*. The interplay between form and social behaviour in the Somali poetic tradition, and the interplay between the macro- and micro-levels of causality in this tradition, thus helps us to understand how public expectations are both met and changed in the performance of Somali oral poetry.

Notes

1. My research has shown that verbatim memorisation becomes possible in proportion to the degree of complexity in the prosodic pattern of individual genres. Readers interested in the intricacies of Somali prosody may consult Abdillahi Derie Guled (1980), Antinucci (1980), Banti and Giannattasio (1996), Johnson (1979, 1980, 1985, 1988, 1993, 1996b, 1997, 2001, Orwin 1996, 2000, 2001), and Orwin and Maxamed (1997).
2. There is however a parallel tradition of extemporised poetry, using formulae, in southern Somalia; see e.g. Luling (1996).
3. For a detailed study on the question of verbatim memorisation of Somali poetry, see Johnson (2002).
4. Two main morphological differences are worth mentioning. One finds *quasi–synonymous* pairs of words in different texts, evident when two words or phrases have nearly the same or similar meanings, but sound differently. Compare the following pair of lines delivered by different reciters:

   Tuulada ninkii buul ka yiil, bacadlihii saar ye.
   Tuulada ninkii aqal ka yiil, bacadlihii saar ye.

   An *aqal* is a nomadic house, and a *buul* is a smaller version of the same. Both scan properly. The other morphological difference is a *quasi–homophonous* pair, evident when two words or phrases sound similarly, but have different meanings. In two variants of the same poem, one find *degay*, 'settled', contrasted in the second variant with *tegay*, 'went'.
5. This concept was first introduced by Andrzejewski (1981: 3). The first major work intended to introduce Somali poetry to non-Somali audiences was Andrzejewski and Lewis (1964).
6. For a survey of the various uses and meanings of the concept of tradition in American folkloristics, see Ben-Amos (1984). For a similar article on European uses and meanings of the same concept, see Hofer (1984). See also my description of the concept in Johnson (1998).
7. A folk group is defined as two or more people that practice at least one tradition together.
8. Sayid ('Lord') Maxamed Cabdille Xassan was a skilled Somali poet, a sheikh and a warrior, who did battle with colonial forces from 1900 to 1920 in the British Somaliland Protectorate. His poetry is some of the most often quoted and respected verse on the Horn of Africa.
9. For a discussion of the imagery employed in Somali poetry, especially in the modern poem *heelloy*, see Johnson (1996a: 166–75).
10. This also resonates in the title of this whole volume, *Nabad iyo caano, col iyo cabaar* (peace and milk, war and drought).
11. This poem was never sung on the radio, because the censors suppressed it. I never knew who composed it. As far as I know, I was the first to publish a complete text.

12. A doctoral dissertation on this topic has been written in the School of Oriental and African Studies, University of London (see Abdisalam Yassin Mohamed 1977).
13. On this issue, and a related controversy in the present, see Mukhtar in this volume.
14. This résumé of the plot is taken from my field notes and was transcribed and translated in 1968.
15. This poem is published in Johnson (1996a: 139–44).

References

Abdillahi, Derie G. 1980. 'The Scansion of Somali Poetry.' In H.M. Adam (ed.) *Somalia and the World: Proceedings of the International Symposium Held in Mogadishu, October 15–21, 1979*, Mogadishu: Halgan Editorial Board, pp. 132–40.

Abdisalam Yassin M. 1977. 'Sufi Poetry in Somalia: Its Themes and Imagery.' (PhD thesis), London: School of Oriental and African Studies, University of London.

Andrzejewski, Bogumil W. 1981. 'The Poem as Message: Verbatim Memorization in Somali Oral Poetry.' In *Memory and Poetic Structure: Papers of the Conference on Oral Literature and Literary Theory held at Middlesex Polytechnic, 1981*, London: Middlesex Polytechnic, pp. 1–25.

——— and Ioan M. Lewis 1964. *Somali Poetry: an Introduction*. London: Clarendon Press.

Antinucci, Francesco 1980. 'Notes on the Linguistic Structure of Somali Poetry.' In H.M. Adam (ed.) *Somalia and the World: Proceedings of the International Symposium Held in Mogadishu, October 15–21, 1979*. Mogadishu: Halgan Editorial Board, pp. 144–53.

Banti, Giorgio and Francesco Giannattasio 1996. 'Music and Meter in Somali Poetry.' In I.M. Lewis and R. Hayward (eds) *Language and Culture in the Horn of Africa: Essays in Honour of B.W. Andrzejewski*. London: School of Oriental and African Studies, University of London, pp. 83–127.

Barry, Phillips 1933. 'Communal Re-creation.' *Bulletin of the Folksong Society of the Northeast*, 5, 4–6.

Ben-Amos, Dan 1984. 'The Seven Strands of Tradition: Varieties in Its Meaning in American Folklore Studies.' *Journal of Folklore Research* 21 (2/3), 97–131.

Darnton, Robert 1984. *The Great Cat Massacre and other Episodes in French Cultural History*. New York: Basic Books.

Gerould, Gordon H. 1932. *The Ballad of Tradition*. London: Clarendon Press.

Handler, Richard and Jocelyn Linnekin 1984. 'Tradition: Genuine or Spurious.' *Journal of American Folklore*, 97, 273–90.

Hofer, Tamas 1984. 'The Perception of Tradition in European Ethnology.' *Journal of Folklore Research*, 21 (2/3), 133–47.

Janelli, Roger 1976. 'Toward a Reconciliation of Micro- and Macro-level Analyses of Folklore.' *Folklore Forum*, 9, 59–66.

Johnson, John W. 1979. 'Somali Prosodic Systems.' *Horn of Africa*, 2 (3), 46–54.

——— 1980. 'Recent Contributions by Somalis and Somalists to the Study of Oral Literature.' In H.M. Adam (ed.) *Somalia and the World: Proceedings of the International Symposium Held in Mogadishu, October 15–21, 1979*. Mogadishu: Halgan Editorial Board, pp. 117–31.

——— 1984. 'Recent Researches into the Scansion of Somali Oral Poetry.' In T. Labahn (ed.) *Proceedings of Second International Congress of Somali Studies*. Hamburg: Helmut Buske Verlag, pp. 313–31.

——— 1988. 'Set Theory in Somali Poetics: Structures and Implications.' In A. Puglielli (ed.) *Proceedings of the Third International Congress of Somali Studies*. (Rome: Il Pensiero Scientifico Editore), pp. 123–33.

——— 1993. 'Somali Poetry.' In A. Preminger and T. V. F. Brogan (eds) *The New Princeton Encyclopedia of Poetry and Poetics* [Third Edition]. Princeton University Press, pp. 1164–5.

——— 1996a. *Heelloy: Modern Poetry and Songs of the Somali*. [First published in 1974] London: Haan.

——— 1996b. 'Musico-Moro-Syllabic Relationships in the Scansion of Somali Oral Poetry.' In I. M. Lewis and R. Hayward (eds) *Language and Culture in the Horn of Africa: Essays in Honour of B.W. Andrzejewski*. London: School of Oriental and African Studies, University of London, pp. 73–82.

——— 1997. 'Music and Poetry in Somalia.' In *Garland Encyclopedia of World Music, Volume I Africa*. New York: Garland Publishing, pp. 610–21.

——— 1998. 'Tradition.' In M. E. Brown and B. Rosenberg (eds) *Encyclopedia of Folklore and Literature*. Denver: ABC/CLIO, pp. 658–9.

——— 2001. 'Somalia.' In *The New Grove Dictionary of Music and Musicians, Second Edition*, London: Macmillan, vol. 23, pp. 660–2.

——— 2002. 'A Contribution to the Theory of Oral Poetic Composition.' In L. Honko (ed) *The Kalevala and the World's Traditional Epics: Studia Fennica Folkloristica 12*. Helsinki: Finnish Literature Society, pp. 184–242.

Lord, Albert B. 1960. *The Singer of Tales*. Cambridge: Harvard University Press.

Loughran, Katheryne, John L. Loughran, John W. Johnson and Said S. Samatar 1986. *Somalia in Word and Image*. Washington, DC and Bloomington: Foundation for Cross Cultural Understanding in cooperation with Indiana University Press.

Luling, Virginia 1996. 'The Law Then was not this Law: Past and Present in Extemporised Verse at a Southern Somali Festival.' In I.M. Lewis and R. Hayward (eds) *Voice and Power; Essays in Honour of Professor B.W.Andrzejewski*. London: SOAS/ University of London, pp. 213–28.

Orwin, Martin 1996. 'A Moraic Model of the Prosodic Phonology of Somali.' In I.M. Lewis and R. Hayward (eds) *Language and Culture in the Horn of Africa: Essays in Honour of B.W. Andrzejewski*. London: School of Oriental and African Studies, University of London, pp. 51–71.

——— 2000. 'A Literary Stylistic Analysis of a Poem by the Somali Poet Axmed Ismaciil Diiriye "Qaasim".' *Bulletin of the School of Oriental and African Languages*, 62 (2), 194–214.

——— 2001. 'Language Use in Three Somali Religious Poems.' *Journal of African Cultural Studies*, 14 (1), 69–87.

——— and Maxamed C. Riiraash 1997. 'An Approach to Relationships Between Somali Metre Types.' *African Languages and Cultures*, 10 (1), 83–100.

Samatar, Said S. 1982. *Oral Poetry and Somali Nationalism: The Case of Sayyid Mahammad 'Abdille Hasan*. Cambridge University Press.

Shils, Edward 1981. *Tradition*. University of Chicago Press.

von Sydow, Carl W. 1948. (ed. Laurits Boedker) *C. W. v. Sydow: Selected Papers on Folklore*. Cøpenhagen: Rosenkilde and Bagger.

14

VIRTUAL GEMINATES IN THE METRE OF SOMALI POETRY

Martin Orwin and *Mohamed Hashi Dhama 'Gaarriye'*

Introduction

This article is the product of collaboration between the two authors which began in 2001 in Hargeysa, and a little background to that is appropriate here. In the late 1990s Orwin had begun working on the metre of Somali poetry using the literature available and examples of poems. As part of this research, some time about 1998, he read the original articles published in *Xiddigta Oktoobar* by Maxamed Xaashi Dhamac 'Gaarriye' and Cabdullaahi Diiriye Guuleed 'Carraale'[1] which were referred to in most of the works by Western scholars. The first of these articles was published in 1976 by Gaarriye (Maxamed Xaashi 1976), and when Orwin read this he was surprised to find details of metrical structure which had been neglected by all the subsequent literature, one such issue being the role of consonants. Johnson (1984: 314), for example, states, 'At this point, the reader is advised to think only of vowels in a stream of speech and not of consonants. Do not even think of word boundaries, as they do not apply when counting moras on a line of Somali poetry.' This neglect of consonants and word boundaries continued in all later work on Somali metre until Orwin (2001), in which the role of consonants, as originally presented by Gaarriye, was discussed in some detail. After writing this article Orwin felt it vital to discuss matters relating to Somali metre with Gaarriye, whose original insights had proved so illuminating, and it was with this in mind that he visited Hargeysa where Gaarriye lives. The two of us had never been in contact before this time, and when we met and discussed the interests we had in this field we began working together and continue to do so. In the present article it is later thinking by Gaarriye on the way certain consonants pattern in the metre that we shall discuss. This is a topic that has not been written on before.

Gaarriye's 1976 conditions

To begin at the beginning with Gaarriye's first article on metre, we present below the three conditions he gives for the *jiifto* line.[2] Condition 1 reads: *beyd kasta oo jiifto ihi, waa inuu noqdo sagaalley ama tobanleey ay xundhurtu isu dheelli tirto*, 'each *jiifto* line must be of nine or ten, balanced by the *xundhur*'.[3] Along with this condition he provides a diagram which shows the possible patterns of long and short vowels when the line is both 9 and 10 vowel units long which we reproduce below (retaining most of the original formatting).

B types (9 vowel units)	T types (10 vowel units)[4]
2,2 1 22	12,2 1 22
2,11 1 211	21,2 1 2 11
11,2 1 112	12, 11 1 11 2
11,11 1 1111	111,2 1 11 11

Although Gaarriye himself continues to use the 1 and 2 notation for long and short vowels, as do some other writers on Somali metrics,[5] here we shall use the annotation for these units better known in work in English on the metre of various languages which describes a short vowel position with the sign U and a long vowel position with the sign —. So the patterns for the *jiifto* line in Maxamed Xaashi (1976) may be restated as follows, where we keep the commas of the original.

B types (9 vowel units)	T types (10 vowel units)
— , — U — —	U — , — U — —
— , UU U — UU	— U , — U — UU
UU , — U UU —	U — , UU U UU —
UU , UU U UU UU	UUU , — U UU UU

We may go on to present this in a template form for the *jiifto* metre, something which has become well known in the literature, where UỤ is the symbol for a position which may be realised as a long vowel syllable or two short vowel syllables, and (U) indicates an optional anacrusis, although note that this is an exclusive disjunction, only one of these short vowel syllables may occur:

$$(\mathsf{U})\underline{\mathsf{UU}}(\mathsf{U})\underline{\mathsf{UU}}\ \mathsf{U}\ \underline{\mathsf{UU}}\ \underline{\mathsf{UU}}$$

The second of Gaarriye's conditions reads as follows: *shaqalladu iskama filiqsana. Waxay isu raacaan hab go'an* 'vowels are not just thrown together. They follow a specific system.' This condition needs to be read in conjunction with two example lines he gives: (a) *Waase lagu waayee* and (b) *Waa laguse waayee.*[6] Of these examples, he explains that the difference between the two relates to the structure of each: in (a) the first three vowel units go together in terms of pronunciation and the next two vowel units, of which one is the *xundhur*, go separately together, while in (b), on the other hand, the first four vowels go together as pairs whilst, from the point of view of pronunciation, the *xundhur* is separate. The principle behind this condition is that the position of word breaks and long vowels is constrained.

The third condition, which is of most concern to us here, reads as follows: *shibbanayaasha isxigsada ama labanlaabmaa meelo gaar ah ayey ku leeyihiin tusaha jiiftada—meel walba ma galaan* 'adjacent or geminate consonants have special places in the *jiifto* template—they do not go in every place'. This, again, is to be read with the example lines given, which illustrate some of the positions in which consonant clusters (or geminates) may or may not occur in a metrical line:

(1a) *Cabdi ma laha saaxiib* 'Cabdi has no friend'
(1b) *Saaxiib ma laha Cabdi* 'Cabdi has no friend'
(2a) *Lama oggola hadalloo* 'Speaking is not allowed'
(2b) *Hadal lama oggola oo* 'Speaking is not allowed'

Of these lines (1a) and (2b) are correct metrically whereas (1b) and (2a) are incorrect, despite being consistent with the patterning of vowels given in condition 1. This is because in the latter there is either a consonant cluster or a geminate consonant in a position in which these are not allowed. The rest of this article will look at this condition in greater detail and how it interacts with certain consonants which we, following Ségéral and Scheer (2001), shall call *virtual geminates*. As a first step we shall look at two important aspects of the condition, firstly its restatement in terms of syllable structure and secondly the positions in which it holds in the *jiifto* line.

Restatement of consonant cluster condition in terms of syllable structure.

The syllable structure of Somali may be summarised as follows: CV(V)(C), that is to say, syllables always comprise a vowel, whether long or short, and have an obligatory onset syllable. This latter feature of the syllable follows Orwin (1994) and (1996) as well as others, see for example Barillot (2002: 149). Although orthographically there are words which begin with vowels such as *af* 'mouth, language' and *ergo* 'delegate', these words underlyingly begin with a glottal stop. Arguments for this can be found in Orwin (1994) and (1996) relating both to the phonetics of these cases in isolation and to the pattern of reduplication, particularly in the plural of adjectives such as *ad'adag* which shows the repetition of the underlying initial glottal stop of the singular form *adag* 'hard, difficult' (see also Barillot 2002: 149). Given this structure of the syllable it is clear that any consonant cluster in Somali is necessarily heterosyllabic—that is, the first part (the *b* in the word *Cabdi* in the above example) is the final consonant (the coda) of a syllable and the second part (the *d* in *Cabdi*) is the first consonant (the onset) of the subsequent syllable. So, using '-' to divide a word into syllables, *Cabdi* is constituted as follows: *Cab-di*. This principle holds also for geminate consonants which, informally, we analyse as clusters of identical consonants, thus *oggola* in the examples above is structured as *og-go-la*.

Given this syllable structure we can make a more observationally adequate statement regarding consonant clusters and geminates by referring to the only difference when compared with simplex consonants, namely the syllable final consonant. We therefore restate Gaarriye's original condition as a constraint on syllable final consonants. Informally: 'syllable final consonants have special places in the *jiifto* template—they do not go in every place'. This constraint has serious implications in Somali metrical studies and indeed in the phonology of the language since it has always been assumed that Somali is a language in which CVC syllables are light.[7] Precisely how we deal with the notion of CVC as a heavy syllable in Somali in the cases in which this constraint holds when all points to CVC as light with regard to accent assignment, for example, is not something we shall look at here, merely noting it for future investigation.[8]

Where does the consonant cluster condition apply? Having now revised the condition, couching it in terms of syllable final consonants we shall look at where the constraint holds in the *jiifto* line. In order to show this we need to introduce some means of labelling parts of it which we do as shown in the diagram below.

UU	UU	U	UU	UU
MP1	MP2	MP3	MP4	MP5

In other words, leaving aside anacrusis for the time being, we label with MP1 (metrical position 1) the first part of the line in which either a long vowel syllable or two short vowel syllables may occur, with MP2 we label the second such position and so on. Note that MP3 is the position which must be realised with a short vowel syllable. Let us now turn to the positions within this line in which a syllable-final consonant could logically occur; these we shall label C with a single number for points within metrical positions and two numbers joined by a dash for positions between the numbered metrical positions; C6 indicates line-final position:

C1	C1–2	C2	C2–3	C3–4	C4	C4–5	C5	C6
UU		UU	U		UU		UU	
MP1		MP2	MP3		MP4		MP5	

We see there are nine positions in which a syllable-final consonant could logically occur. Of these positions, Gaarriye accounts for four in his original article, C1, C2, C3–4 and C5. Orwin (2001) ascertained the status of the other postions with relation to the constraint, and when we began working together in 2001 we found these findings coincided with Gaarriye's own conclusions regarding the postion of consonant clusters throughout the line which he had made when investigating these matters in the early 1970s. So, we can now state that syllable final consonants may occur in the following positions: C1, C1–2, C2–3, C3–4, C4–5; and they are not found in the following positions C2, C4 and C5. With regard to position C6, Orwin (2001) presents some preliminary findings on this, showing that in the poem *Hooyo* by Maxamed Ibraahim Warsame 'Hadraawi' (Maxamed Ibraahim 1993: 95–7) only the consonant *n* is found at the end of the line, and in the *masafo* poem *Dacwad baan ka leeyahay* by Sayid Maxamed Cabdille Xasan (Jaamac 1974: 78–82) *n* is to be found at the end of 18 first half-lines and 28 second half-lines. In this latter poem, however, other consonants are also present at the end of the first and second half-lines. Interestingly there are more at the end of the first half-line:

d is present six times, *g* once, *sh* once, *r* once and *l* twice. In the second half-lines on the other hand the only other consonants apart from *n* which appear are *d* once, *g* once and *c* once. Putting these findings into the template we give a revised version below in which a raised ^{c} indicates the positions in which a syllable final consonant may occur, in the final position the ^{c} is given in parentheses indicating its special status which requires further research. Syllable-final consonants are not allowed in any other position.[9]

$\underline{U^{c}U^{c}}$	$\underline{UU^{c}}$	U^{c}	$\underline{UU^{c}}$	$\underline{UU^{(c)}}$
MP1	MP2	MP3	MP4	MP5

Aside from being the only points in the line in which syllable final consonants may occur, it is important to note that these are the only positions where word breaks also may occur. We see here that the *jiifto* line displays an instance of the cross-linguistic generalisation that metrical patterning allows for greater flexibility at the beginning of the line and is stricter towards the end, the pattern of anacrusis also shows this. Since we see now that MP1 clearly differs from MPs 2, 4 and 5 we are led to consider this distinction in some more detail. It must be remembered that this template is nothing more than a convenient way of describing the line and the distributional asymmetry between the metrical positions with the labels $\underline{U^{c}U^{c}}$ and $\underline{UU^{c}}$; it is not a means of explaining this behaviour since that would be to assume these to be *a priori* metrical elements, some of the building blocks of the metre, which we do not wish to do here. However, when we look more closely, we find that the distributional asymmetry among the metrical positions correlates with a difference in frequency of long vowel syllable realisations and two short vowel syllable realisations across the metrical positions MPs 1, 2, 4 and 5. In an initial survey based on the texts of six poems by Maxamed Ibraahim Warsame 'Hadraawi'[10] which will be presented in more detail in Orwin (forthcoming a), the percentage of realisations of MPs 1, 4 and 5 as UU or as — shows definite preferences for one or the other, with MP2 seemingly without preference. The figures are given below and do not include details relating to anacrusis:

MP1: UU in 381 lines (81%), — in 90 lines (19%)
MP2: UU in 200 lines (42%), — in 271 lines (58%)
MP4: UU in 80 lines (17%), — in 391 lines (83%)
MP5: UU in 132 lines (28%), — in 339 lines (72%)

We see here a definite preference for MP1 to be realised as UU, for MPs 4 and 5 to be realised as — and for MP2 to be realised as either — or UU with a comparatively small preference for —. Without going into further details, we simply note here the correlation between the fact that MP1 is the position within which syllable final consonants may occur and the fact that this is the only metrical position with a preference for two short vowel syllables (at least in this corpus). Orwin (forthcoming a) will discuss the metrical implications of this patterning in greater detail; suffice it to say here that it gives a tantalising glimpse into some of the fundamental ways in which long and short vowel syllables relate to each other in the metrical line. Having now outlined the way in which syllable final consonants behave in the *jiifto* line, whether as part of a consonant cluster or a geminate consonant, let us turn to the virtual geminates.

The virtual geminates in Somali metre

The subject of virtual geminates in relation to the metre of Somali poetry has not been written about before, and the ideas were developed by Gaarriye, who discussed the matter with Orwin first in 2001. It was exciting for Orwin to hear of these ideas at the time, as expressed in his notebook (Orwin 2001b): 'I was ready for point 2 [on consonant clusters] but this point was a bolt from the blue! sh, s, t, f, j, k, w and y act like clusters. They are not found anywhere where clusters are not found.' In other words Gaarriye was stating that certain simplex consonants pattern in the *jiifto* line like consonant clusters. To state this informally as a further constraint on the metrical *jiifto* line we can say: where MP2, MP4 and MP5 are realised as two short vowel syllables, the consonants *sh*, *s*, *f*, *t*, *k*, *j*, *w* and *y* cannot occur *inside* these metrical positions, although they can occur on the margins of the whole metrical position (subject to general phonological constraints).

To give some examples, the lines below show these consonants present in the MP1 internal position where they are allowed

- *t* *Botorkiyo ciyaartoo* ('the *botor* and the dance', from *Uurkubbaale*, Maxamed Xaashi (2007: 22)).[11]
- *k* *Tuke Bari ka yimi baan* ('a crow which came from the east I…', from *Tog-dheer*, Maxamed Ibraahim (1993: 52))

sh *dusha kaa huwinayaa*, ('[I] cover you over with…', from *Hooyo*, Maxamed Ibraahim (1993: 97))
f *Afartaa dha'leydaa* ('those four in *dh*' from *Dhabtaa u Daran*, Aaden Diiriye Cali in Mohammed Sh. Hassan (1998: 135))
s *Asagoo dhawaadana* ('as he approaches', from *Dhabtaa u Daran*, Aaden Diiriye Cali in Mohammed Sh. Hassan (1998: 139))
w *hawo laguma gaadheen* ('one could have not reached the sky', from *Hooyo*, Maxamed Ibraahim (1993: 95))
y *biyo lulata guudkood* ('swinging above the water', from *Beled-Weyn*, Maxamed Ibraahim (1993: 89))

To show how the presence of one of these consonants makes the line unmetrical, we present a few artificially made lines of *jiifto* metre which are metrically correct in all respects except the presence of the constrained consonant.[12] The asterisk here marks unmetricality, not ungrammaticality.

* *barigu ka yimi tuke*: here the *k* in *tuke* is within MP5 ('a crow came from the east')
* *aan ciyaarno botorkiyo*: here the *t* in *botorkiyo* is within MP4 ('let us dance the *botor* and')
* *wax ka sheega afartaa*: here the *f* in *afartaa* is within MP4 ('say something about those four')
* *ii keena basal iyo*: here the *s* in *basal* is within MP4 ('bring me onions and')
* *ii keena dawadaa*: here the *w* in *dawadaa* is within MP5 ('bring me that medicine')

What was initially confusing for Orwin when he first learned of this constraint was that he assumed at the time that these consonants were phonetically and phonologically simplex, and yet they were behaving like geminate consonants. Gaarriye himself explained the phenomenon by stating that these consonants were somehow perceived like geminates, and so, at the time, we dealt with this matter initially by assuming these consonants to be what we called pseudo-geminates.

At the same time, however, Xavier Barillot in France was writing his PhD thesis on Somali as a language which displays templatic morphophonology (Barillot 2002). This work, some of which is referred to also in Ségéral & Scheer (2001) (from which we take the English term *virtual geminates*), looked precisely at the notion of phonetically simplex, but underlyingly geminate consonants in the phonology of

Somali. What is fascinating about this extensive and excellent thesis is the way in which all the consonants Gaarriye had determined as being constrained in the metre were precisely the consonants which Barillot presents as displaying geminate behaviour, despite being simplex phonetically. In other words Gaarriye and Barillot, working from different perspectives, came to conclusions which were mutually supportive.

As mentioned above, the set of consonants that are constrained in the metre are *s*, *sh*, *f*, *t*, *k*, *j*, *w* and *y*. We can see that these form natural classes: the oral fricatives[13] (*sh*, *s* and *f*), the two voiceless plosives (*t* and *k*) which are well known to form a natural class in Somali,[14] *j*, the only affricate in Somali, which is phonologically constrained in a similar manner to *t* and *k*, and finally the semi–vowels *w* and *y*. Here we shall be looking at these consonants from a synchronic perspective only, but the diachronic perspective also shows something of the nature of these consonants as underlying geminates. This is particularly the case with *t* and *k* for example, which Sasse (1979) sees as reflexes of Proto-East-Cushitic **tt* and **kk*, 'since intervocalic **t* and **k* yield Somali *d* and *g*' (ibid. 1979: 7, see also p. 9).

(1) t *and* k. The behaviour of these consonants as syllable-initial only is well known in Somali phonology. Where they occur underlyingly and surface in syllable final position they undergo voicing, hence the alternations *t~d* and *k~g* in the following examples: *wuu guntay, way gunudday* 'he tied a knot, she tied a knot' and *wuu bukay, way bugtay* 'he was ill, she was ill' in which underlying /t/ and /k/ surface as voiceless consonants when at the beginning of a syllable and as voiced consonants at the end of a syllable (in the first example triggering voicing of the initial /t-/ of the inflectional ending of the verb also).

One of the major arguments (presented in both Ségéral & Scheer 2001 and Barillot 2002) in favour of assuming intervocalic *t* as an underlying geminate is behaviour found in the 3rd conjugation verbs, the verbs generally referred to as autobenefactive or, following Saeed (1995), middle voice. In these verbs we find intervocalic *t* surfacing in 2nd person and 3rd person feminine singular forms (although we shall confine ourselves to 2nd person singular here), for example *waan dhigtaa* 'I learn it' and *waad dhigataa* 'you learn it'. Sometimes referred to as conjugation 3B verbs, these contrast with conjugation 3A verbs in which we find the following forms *waan doorsadaa* 'I change, heal' and *waad doorsataa* 'you change, heal'. Without going into full detail the *d* in the former form is the simplex /t/ of the derivational suffix /-at/ having undergone voicing intervocalically. The *t* in *dhigataa* on the other hand is the phonetic realisation of an underlying geminate, /tt/, resulting from the concatenation of the /t/ in the derivational suffix /-at/ and the /t-/ of the person marker. Note carefully that this recognition of the *t* being underlyingly geminate is only when it is found intervocalically, not when it is found at the beginning of a word. With regard to the constraint in the metre, however, this is not evident since, as mentioned above, the positions where syllable-final consonants may occur are also the only places in which word breaks may occur, and so any word initial *t* can only be found here also, essentially neutralising, in this context, the prosodic difference between *t* as an underlying geminate intervocalically and *t* as an underlying simplex consonant at the beginning of a word.[15]

Turning to *k*, Barillot presents an argument from middle voice verbs also, but the *k* in these verbs is part of the root, rather than any suffix. He points out that any verb of the pattern CV*ko*, such as *tuko* 'pray', always produces inflected forms as follows: *waan tukadaa* 'I pray' and *waad tukataa* 'you pray'. We never find the alternation *k~g* as we do in *waan bukay* and *waad bugtay* (</buk/, see above). So again the consonant in intervocalic position is assumed to be an underlyingly geminate, /kk/. With respect to the metrical constraint, therefore, its nature as an underlying geminate and the constraint on syllable final consonants explains its absence when intervocalic and the constraint on word breaks explains its absence when it occurs at the beginning of words.

(2) j, f, s, sh, w *and* y. An aspect of Somali phonological behaviour which Barillot looks at in relation to all of these consonants is vowel deletion in verbs of the pattern CVCVC, such as *dhereg* 'be full' where a vowel-initial suffix causes the second vowel to be deleted as in *waan dhergay* 'I was full', and a consonant-initial suffix causes the vowel to be retained, *waad dheregtay* 'you were full'.[16] Barillot looks at all verbs of this shape found in his sources and considers the role of the medial consonant in the process of vowel deletion. He concludes that where vowel deletion occurs it is due to the simplex nature of the medial consonant, and where it does not occur this is due to the underlying geminate nature of the medial consonant, despite that consonant being simplex on the surface. What is interesting from our perspective is that he classifies these consonants into three sets (Barillot 2002: 311), those

found in verbs in which vowel deletion is obligatory (*b*, *c*, *d*, *g*, *h*, *l*, *m*, *n*, *q*, *r* and *x*),[17] those in verbs in which vowel deletion never occurs (*j*, *k*, *sh*, *t*, *w* and *y*) and those in which vowel deletion occurs in some cases and not in others (*f* and *s*). The latter case can be exemplified by considering the behaviour of *qosol* 'laugh' which gives *waan qoslay* 'I laughed' where the vowel deletes, and the verb *fasax* 'let go' which gives *waan fasaxay* 'I let him/her/them go', in which the vowel does not delete. Looking at the set of consonants with which vowel deletion either never occurs or occurs sometimes owing to the virtual geminate nature of the medial consonant, we see that it is precisely the same set which Gaarriye ascertained to be constrained in the metre. In other words the behaviour analysed by Barillot in the phonology and the behaviour analysed by Gaarriye in the metrical system is mutually supportive of the assumption that these consonants are virtual geminates.

We have considered the semi–vowels implicitly with the other consonants above but some extra words on *y* are needed here, particularly with regard to the noun phrase coordinating conjunction *iyo*. We find many lines (see one of the examples above) in which this is found in one of the metrical positions where syllable final consonants are not allowed, and so if we are assuming *y* to be an underlying geminate this should break the metrical pattern, and yet it doesn't. We are unsure precisely how to handle this, but suggest that it may be due to a restriction on the pattern /yV/ as constituting a word on the surface, since there are no other words of this shape other than *iyo* and the independent pronouns *iyada* and *iyaga*. We suggest, therefore, that the initial *i* may be added to the underlying representation which in itself has /y/ at the beginning of the word, which since it is at the beginning makes it necessarily simplex. We acknowledge that this is a somewhat *ad hoc* argument and that further research on this matter is needed.

Conclusion

In this paper we have presented, for the first time, the way in which certain consonants are constrained with regard to where they may appear in a metrical *jiifto* line. This restriction is explained by analysing them as virtual geminates, a conclusion which is supported by Barillot's work on the templatic morpho-phonology of Somali in which he arrives at the same conclusion with regard to the underlying phonological nature of these consonants. The English term virtual geminates we use following Ségéral and Scheer (2001). We have also reaffirmed the fact that syllable final consonants do play a role in the metre of Somali poetry *contra* all the literature apart from Maxamed Xaashi (1976) (and subsequent articles by Gaarriye) and Orwin (2001). There is, of course, more work to be undertaken to come to a fuller understanding of the details of how this and other aspects of the metrical system work in detail, but we present this as a contribution to that task.

Notes

1. A list of references to these articles can be found in Johnson (1979: 53–4) and Lamberti (1986).
2. The whole text of this original article, along with others that were published by Gaarriye in *Xiddigta Oktoobar*, can be found in Cabdiraxmaan 2007.
3. The word *xundhur* means 'navel'. All translations in this article are by Orwin.
4. B and T are used as labels here as they were in the original. They are the first letters of the Somali alphabet following the Arabic order.
5. See, for example, the recent publication Abdulfatah (2007).
6. These lines are synonymous, although they have two possible readings—'But one failed with it' or 'But you were missed' according to whether the *ku* in *lagu* is read as the pronoun or the preverbal preposition. They are not part of any particular poem, but were produced to make the point of the condition.
7. Languages in which syllable weight plays a phonological role have generally been divided into two groups, those in which CVC is considered a light syllable and those in which it is considered a heavy syllable. See Banti and Giannattasio (1996: 86) where comparison is made with Classical Arabic, in which CVC syllables are heavy.
8. Orwin (forthcoming a) will look at this in some more detail.
9. Again, we are not including the anacrusis in this template as there is still work to be done on this, although initial investigations in Orwin (2001) do show that syllable final consonants may appear after a short syllable anacrusis at the beginning of the line.
10. The poems are *Hooyo*, *Jacayl Dhiig ma lagu Qoray*, *Haatuf*, *Amal*, *Hudhud* and *Beledweyn*. Using the poems of just one poet is not enough to make any more general statements, but it does allow us to make a statement based on this corpus, which is a start.
11. The observant reader will notice that *y* is found here in a position in which we claim it is not allowed; we return to this matter below.
12. These lines were made up by Orwin with the help of Maxamed Xasan 'Alto', to whom we are grateful for his assistance. Note they are not lines

of any poem and are not 'poetical' in their own right, they are simply examples of lines unmetrical because of the presence of one of the constrained consonants where it is not allowed.

13. Oral as opposed to guttural, which form a natural class of their own, see Orwin 1994 for further details and a more theoretically informed assessment of these classes.
14. We use the features voiced and voiceless here, although in Orwin 1994 unary features close glottis and wide glottis were used to explain certain behaviours of these and the voiced consonants.
15. It is interesting to note a further corollary here, namely that, since these are the only positions in the line where word breaks may occur, they are necessarily the only points in the line where the alliterative consonant may appear. All, that is, except the line-final C6 position. See Orwin (forthcoming b) for more details on alliteration in Somali poetry.
16. Note that Barillot explains this behaviour not as vowel deletion but as spreading of the vowel melody to the second vocalic position according to the CVCV theoretical model he uses. He does nevertheless use the French word *syncopation* to describe the process informally when considering examples. We are using the term vowel deletion in a similarly informal manner and are not making any theoretical statement in so doing.
17. Note that *dh* does not appear in the list he provides since there are no verbs he lists with this as the medial consonant.

References

Abdulfatah Abdullahi 'Gacmadheere' 2007. *Asaaska Suugaanta Soomaaliyeed: Cadadka Kowaad*. Stockholm: Scansom Publishers.

Banti, Giorgio and Francesco Giannattasio 1996. 'Music and Metre in Somali Poetry.' In R.J. Hayward and I.M. Lewis (eds) *Voice and Power: The Culture of Language in North-East Africa, Essays in Honour of B.W. Andrzejewski (African Languages and Cultures Supplement 3)*. London: School of Oriental and African Studies, pp. 83–127.

Barillot, Xavier 2002 . 'Morphophonologie gabaritique et information consonantique latente en somali et dans les langues est-couchitiques.' (unpublished PhD thesis) Université Paris VII.

Cabdiraxmaan C. Faarax 'Barwaaqo' 2007. *Mahadhada iyo Waxqabadka Maxamed Xaashi Dhamac 'Gaarriye'*. Ottawa: Hal-aqoon Publishers.

Jaamac Cumar Ciise 1974. *Diiwaanka Gabayadii Sayid Maxamad Cabdulle Xasan*. Mogadishu: Wasaaradda Hiddaha iyo Tacliinta Sare & Wakaaladda Madbacadda Qaranka.

Johnson, John 1979. 'Somali Prosodic Systems.' *Horn of Africa*, 2 (3), 46–54.

——— 1984. 'Recent Researches into the Scansion of Somali Oral Poetry.' In T. Labahn (ed.), *Proceedings of the Second International Congress of Somali Studies, University of Hamburg August 1–6, 1983. Volume 1: Linguistics and Literature*. Hamburg: Helmut Buske Verlag, pp. 313–331.

Lamberti, Marcello 1986. *Somali Language and Literature: African Linguistic Bibliographies* 2. Hamburg: Helmut Buske Verlag.

Lowenstamm, Jean 1996. 'CV as the Only Syllable Type.' In J. Durand and B. Laks (eds) *Current Trends in Phonology: Models and Methods, Volume 2*. Salford: European Studies Research Institute, pp. 419–41.

Maxamed Ibraahim Warsama 'Hadraawi' 1993. *Hal-Karaan: Maansadii Maxamed Ibraahim Warsama (Hadraawi) 1970–1990*. Kleppe: Den Norske Somaliakomiteen.

Maxamed Xaashi Dhamac 'Gaarriye' 1976. 'Miisaanka maansada.' *Xiddigta Oktoobar*, January 17, 3.

——— 2007. *Hagarlaawe: Diiwaanka Maansooyinka Abwaan Maxamed Xaashi Dhamac 'Gaarriye'*, ed. Maxamed Xasan 'Alto', Martin Orwin & Yaasiin Jaamac Nuux 'Suldaan'. London: Aftahan Publications.

Mohammed S. Hassan 1998. *Gurmad: Diiwaanka Gabayada Soomaaliyeed Caddadka Labaad*. Stockholm: Scansom Publishers.

Orwin, Martin 1994. 'Aspects of Somali Phonology.' (Unpublished PhD thesis) London: School of Oriental and African Studies.

——— 1996. 'A Moraic Model of the Prosodic Phonology of Somali.' In R.J. Hayward and I.M. Lewis (eds) *Voice and Power: The Culture of Language in North-East Africa, Essays in Honour of B.W. Andrzejewski (African Languages and Cultures Supplement 3)*. London: School of Oriental and African Studies, pp. 51–71.

——— 2001a. 'On Consonants in Somali Metrics.' *Afrikanistische Arbeitspapiere*, 65, 103–27.

——— 2001b. 'Personal notes on a research trip to the Horn of Africa in late 2001.' (Unpublished)

——— forthcoming a. *Metre in Somali Poetry*.

——— forthcoming b. 'Alliteration in Somali Poetry.' In J. Roper (ed) *Alliteration in Culture*. Basingstoke: Palgrave Macmillan.

Sasse, Hans-Jürgen 1979. 'The Consonant Phonemes of Proto-East-Cushitic (PEC): A First Approximation.' *Afroasiatic Linguistics*, 7 (1), 1–67.

Ségéral, Philippe and Tobias Scheer 2001. 'Abstractness in Phonology: the Case of Virtual Geminates.' In K. Dziubalska-Kołaczyk (ed) *Abstractness in Phonology: The Case of Virtual Geminates. Constraints and Preferences*. Berlin & New York: Mouton de Gruyter, pp. 311–37.

15

CABDILLAHI SULDAAN MAXAMED TIMOCADDE (1920–1973)

THE MAN WITH THE ROARING VOICE, LOOKING LIKE A LION

Boobe Yusuf Duale

Introduction

Cabdillahi Suldaan Timocadde is one of Somalia's most famous poets and a national hero. Most Somalis in the world knows the beginning of his poem *Dugsi ma leh qabyaaladdi*. Yet, as this article shows, there is much more to Timocadde's poetry than only this famous phrase. Cabdillahi lived through dramatic times and witnessed the colonial as well as the first post-colonial decades, including the military coup of 1969. Throughout his poetic life, he felt the need to engage with the social and political issues of the day, to comment and give advice. His interests were by no means limited to Somali affairs alone. Cabdillahi critically observed African and world politics, was a staunch anti–colonialist, defender of liberties, and analyst of Cold War politics. Despite his brilliance, which earned him national fame, he never lost his roots, and for most of his life he remained a member of a rural farming community in northwestern Somalia. Reading his verses today shows, on the one hand, the proverbial curiosity of Somalis in all matters, local, national, and international. On the other, many of his political comments, particularly those pointing to the problems of clanism in politics, have lost none of their actuality in the early 21st century and can in fact be read as comments on contemporary politics in many parts of the Somali peninsula.

This article is based on the collection of poems of and biographical information on Cabdillahi Suldaan Maxamed Timocadde over many years. It is a brief extract from a much larger volume on the poet and his work published originally in Somali (Boobe 1983, second edition 2006).

Biographical background

Cabdillahi Suldaan Maxamed, known as 'Timocadde' (white-haired), was born in Galoolley.[1] His mother was Habiba Seed Guuleed. Cabdillahi died in 1973 at the age of 53 years. He was born into a farming family and was the only child of his mother. He grew up in Gabiley District, particularly in Galoolley community where his family owned a farm. There he attended the Qur'an School in his childhood. In his youth, he left for Ethiopia. He had received an invitation from his cousin Maxamed Dugsiye Maxamed who had a home in Harar and was a soldier in the Italian forces. Maxamed Dugsiye enrolled Cabdillahi in school to study Islamic sciences and the Qur'an in Harar. In those years the town was still a centre of religious learning in the region. Cabdillahi learned the Qur'an and the Arabic language. He composed his first Somali verses there in 1936, and he wrote some of his later poetry in Arabic. Maxamed Dugsiye then left Cabdillahi in the town and joined his Italian company on the move.

After a short period away from home and stationed in the town of Jimma, Maxamed sent a message to Cabdillahi through the returning troops to come and travel with them. Cabdillahi went and joined the Italian troops; he was assigned to the same battalion as his cousin Maxamed. By 1938, Cabdillahi left the Italian troops and settled in Dire Dawa town. He moved to Djibouti in 1940 and resided there until 1949. Before he left Djibouti, he already had become a poet admired at forums and social gatherings, particularly at wedding ceremonies where he frequently recited his poems. At first he composed poems dealing with matters of everyday life, morals, values, and so forth. Soon, however he started reciting political poems commenting on the affairs of the time. Cabdillahi used to recite his poems in Djibouti in Dar-Al Akhbar square, later known as Place Rimbaud.[2] At the same time Cabdillahi was employed at the electric power plant in Djibouti and was a domestic servant for one of the French technicians of the plant.

The late Daahir Cabdillahi, Timocadde's best and closest friend, explained that the poems, stories, sense of humour and jokes of the poet were highly admired. During those days 'Tilley lamps' (oil lamps) were widely used because electricity was limited and did not cover the whole city. Daahir said that when Cabdillahi was reciting poems in wedding ceremonies he used to sit nearby and cover Cabdillahi's face from the reflections of the lamp.[3]

In Djibouti, Cabdillahi Suldaan met Barni Jimcaale and soon fell in love with her. In praise of her, this verse was recorded:

Barni Ina Jimcaalaan helee
Sow bar dahab maaha

Barni, the daughter of Jimale, I won, isn't she a piece of gold?
isn't she a piece of gold?

Cabdillahi and Barni Jimcaale were betrothed, and their marriage ceremony was conducted at Galoolley in 1952. In 1954 their only child Maryam was born. The marriage of Cabdillahi and Barni did not last long and they divorced in Djibouti in 1957. Cabdillahi finally left Djibouti in 1957 and settled permanently in Galoolley. In 1959 Cabdillahi married Ardo Qalinle Cige who bore him four daughters and a son, named Halimo, Fadumo, Mako, Nimco and Maxamed. Ardo and Cabdillahi were cousins and both of them lived in Galoolley. In those days Cabdillahi's main concern was the nursing and treatment of his ageing mother who had no other children than him.

Soon, however he got involved with politics in British Somaliland. He joined the Somali nationalists and registered himself with the Somali National League (SNL), which was the most popular political party in the protectorate. Together with the United Somali Party (USP) and the National United Front (NUF) it took over from the British upon Somaliland's independence on 26 June 1960.[4] The SNL headquarters was in the centre of Hargeysa, in the place called Khayriya today. It served as the main forum where most of the political poems of Cabdillahi were recited first, though of course not the only one. The political parties of those days had established a tradition of touring the country periodically to raise awareness of the national struggle for independence. In such tours, poets and particularly Cabdillahi played an important role in politicising the people with patriotic poems. Such mobilisation tours were the main reason why Timocadde's verses gained recognition and popularity among the masses.

Upon independence, when the British and the Italian Somali regions joined to form the Somali Republic on 1 July 1960, Cabdillahi left the SNL and became a member of the Somali Democratic Union (SDU). This was an opposition party with a socialist tendency known as the 'Red Flags' because their flag was red with the hammer and sickle, like those of the socialist countries at that time. Cabdillahi's membership in this political party made an indelible imprint on his way of thinking and his poetry. In fact, it made him a critic of Somali politics as well as a great defender of liberty and the freedom of the colonised countries in general. In the late 1960s, Cabdillahi turned his back on the Somali political parties most of which, including the SDU, were tribal icons and not representatives of clear objective political ideologies.

Cabdillahi had never been a government employee except for a brief period at Radio Hargeysa. In 1967, the incumbent administration was interested in using the poet's influence to its advantage against the opposition political parties. Nevertheless, Cabdillahi rejected the offer and stayed out of politics. In 1969 when the military officers led by Maxamed Siyad Barre staged the coup d'état, Cabdillahi shared the euphoria with the cheering public. The people, fed up with the corrupt civilian administration, were longing for political change. Corruption, nepotism, maladministration and all the vices that retard the progress of a society were the order of the day and rampant in all government institutions. The country had been labelled the 'grave of foreign aid', because most donations had not been used for the public interest. When the military took over, many thought that progress and development would take the place of underdevelopment and regress.

In 1971, Cabdillahi married Ardo Tukale, his third wife. She gave birth to only one daughter, named Samsam.[5] In the same year Cabdillahi's health deteriorated. He had been a compulsive smoker and had developed a throat ailment that was progressing rapidly. The military government of Siyad Barre sent him to Nairobi for medical treatment in the Kenyatta Hospital. For various reasons Cabdillahi could not stay there for a long time and he was brought back to Somalia. He was taken to Gabiley and back to his village in Galoolley, where his wife Ardo Qalinle Cige took care of him. When his condition deteriorated further he was taken to Kalabayd, a small town west of Gabiley, where his eldest daughter Maryam lived with her family. On Tuesday 6 February 1973, Cabdillahi Suldaan Timocadde died in Kalabaydh. In Gabiley, all schools, offices and business centres were closed so that the people could take part in the funeral.

Poetry in Somali society

Richard Burton in the 19th century already observed that the Somali were a nation of poets. Poetry continues to hold a special place in Somali society. Before the advent of modern telecommunications, poetry and poets effectively constituted the most important 'media network' for the traditional Somali pastoralists. Poetry filled the role of newspapers and radios, spreading the news from one place to another. The poet could instigate war and spread peace. Poetic exchanges also put rural communities in contact and facilitated communication. The (potentially) dangerous power of the spoken word is highlighted in a verse of Salaan Carrabey,[6] *Afku wuxu la xoog yahay magliga, xawda kaa jara'e* (The spoken word has the force of a dagger).

Poetry and the poet were responsible for preservation of the historical facts of the day. Poetry was the most expressive means of description and eloquence. It also provided a form of aesthetic enjoyment and an expression of deep feelings about love (Andrzejewski and Lewis 1964; Johnson 1996). The poet also has the power to reform and to introduce new styles of speech. He/she may be able to speak out against misconduct and the abuse of power as well.[7] Poetry was effectively used in the struggle against the colonial powers. It was used for raising the public awareness of the people and gave orientation and guidance to the masses. It was used in setting the political strategies and objectives of the independence struggle, as many examples of Timocadde's own verses below will show, and it is of untold importance in all spheres of life up to this day. Among the many Somali poets Cabdillahi Suldaan Timocadde was certainly an outstanding figure. The poet Cali Ibraahim Iidle described him as *Ninkii sowdka aarkiyo lahaa, summadihiisiiba* (The man with the roaring voice, looking like a lion).

The poetry of Cabdillahi Suldaan Timocadde

Skills and style of Timocadde. How did Cabdillahi succeed in winning the hearts and ears of his listeners? What were the sources of his success and fame throughout the Somali inhabited regions? Although there are general rules and regulations that limit the poet in composing his verses with respect to the religious, cultural and moral values of society, Cabdillahi had his own personal rules for composing poetry that was both beautiful and patriotic. This is one of his well-kept standards in one of his verses:

Arar culus codkiyo luuqdu waa, cududaheediiye
Carrab laylyan laab culan haddii, la cuskisiin waayo,
Cayo iyo wuxu kaa noqdaa, caws kaliishadaye.

A balanced opening, the voice and the style of transmission,
Are the most essential limbs of a poem,
If not from a tempered tongue and a clean heart,
Verses turn into dry grass wiped out by the wind.

At times Cabdillahi used to visualise the verses as a smart person walking in the streets: *Sida loodh Maraykan ah markay, luuqdu tamashlayso* (When the verse smartly walks like an American Lord).

Cabdillahi stressed that he would tailor beautiful dresses for his verses before reciting them in the public forums: *Arartaan dharkaw toli ogaa, waanigaan tirine* (In these days I have not recited the verses, for which I used to tailor the fine dresses). Upon closely scrutinising his opening style one can notice that he envisaged poetry as something portable that could be lifted up:

Sidde la qabsaduu leeyihiyo, subucyo dhaadheere
Labada markuu seego way, kaa surgucantaaye.

Poetry has handles and firm positions to hold
If you miss both you miss getting the best of it.

In accordance with the Somali norms of poetry composition, the poet is permitted to boast and praise himself at the opening of the poem. Traditionally, one has to talk about the richness, beauty and artfulness of the compositions and one's own skills. This is quite opposed to the usual norms of speechwriting and talking, where those who like to speak highly of themselves are considered mean, and the following proverb applies: *nin is-faanshay waa ri' is-nuugtay* (a man who praises himself is like a goat that sucked its own milk).

Cabdillahi Timocadde's specialty was the composition of 'strong' introductions. Consider the following example. Talking to his competitors, he stated:

Markaan anigu hoonka u tumey, haadka bixiyaane
Hanqadhkayga fedhaha la mood, halablihii Aare
Hagaag uma tallaabsado ninkaan, hamagga saaraaye.

When I blow the horn the other poets let me pass
My roaring voice is taken for that of the fearful lion
Who ever I attack will never walk straight.

On another occasion Cabdullahi set out to frighten his competitors in poetry:

Shan kastuu nin dhaar-gal ah yahuu, ararta dhaabeeyo
Markaan dhinac fadhiistuu sidii, shamac dhalaalaaye
Dhashuu kaga tagaa gabay ninkaan, ugu dhawaaqaaye

No matter how skilful one is in the art of poetry writing
Once I sit next to him he melts like a burning candle
Once I recite my verses adversaries lose their talent and potency.

He implied that his adversaries did not have the capacity to compose in his way and with his power: *Daruurahaba qaar baa onkoda, mana darrooraane* (Some of the clouds rumble and roar with thunder without raining).

I have never yet found an example showing that Cabdillahi, once he had found his position as a poet, composed poetry in the interest of his clan. Of course, Cabdillahi was part of the community that he lived with. He was born into a clan. He married from a clan. His neighbours belonged to clans. In Gabiley district, members of various descent-group cooperated in working the land. They fought, reconciled, and made peace. Cabdillahi was one of these people and shared with them feelings and thoughts about clan and other issues. Yet an important aspect of Timocadde and his work is that he grew up with a national consciousness and a tendency to think independently. As he matured, he left the clan mentality behind and increasingly engaged on the national level. Arguably, the last time Cabdillahi composed poetry on clan lines was in 1947, but from then on he climbed the hill of national views and perspectives. That is what makes him different from the other poets of his time.

Categories and examples of Timocadde's poems. One can divide the poetry of Cabdillahi into three phases: first, coming of age and turning to politics in the time of the anti–colonial and national movements (1936–60); second, commenting on Somali and world affairs at independence and in the early post-colonial years (1960–69); and third, advising and criticising the military regime (1969–71). So far, the number of Cabdillahi Suldaan Timocadde's poems collected by the author is 150; roughly half of these fall into the first phase, while of the reminder, more than two thirds were composed in the second phase. Only just over a dozen poems can be attributed to the last phase, which ended with Timocadde's death.

Cabdillahi's contemporaries asserted that he started composing poetry in 1936 as soon as he reached Harar. He was only 16 years old and most of his relatives and contemporaries believe his first poem was a brief verse that he composed for an Oromo woman married to his cousin Maxamed Dugsiye Maxamed. Maxamed used to complain about the regular absence of his wife from the house, who consequently did not attend her duties. Whenever the woman was asked about her absence, she used to say: 'I went to buy some frankincense (*foox*).' Cabdillahi composed his first poem on this subject:

Foox–doon haddaad tahay dukaan, furan ma weydeene
Is-na wuu ku filayaa intaad, fooggan tahay meele
Maxaa faras-magaalahan ku dhigay, fiidki laga hoyday?

If your intention was to buy frankincense, you would have found many shops open
And he [your husband] waits for you to come home while aimlessly you roam the streets
Why stay late in the town while other folks have gone home?

When Cabdillahi was recruited to join the Italian troops fighting in Ethiopia in the late 1930s, he did not miss the chance to compose a few verses on that occasion. In one of their social gatherings in Djibouti, Cabdillahi was asked by his friends about the war experience when he was part of the invading Italian troops.

Idinku jaadka uun baad hablaha, jeer u fidisaane
Alleylkiina waxad jiifsataan, jiidhka waaberiye
Korneylkii jaleelada hadh galay, janannadii yaacay
Meydkii jubeerrada xidhnaa, ma idinkaa joogay

You just enjoy *qaad*-chewing with a bunch of ladies
And in the small hours of the morning you go to bed—
The colonels who dived into the shade of the bushes,
The generals who took to their heels
The corpse in uniform—these you have not witnessed.

He also commented on aspects of the Second World War, which had an impact on the Somali communities as some British and French contingents were recruited there. When Berlin fell to the Allied forces in 1945 he was 25 years old.

Fantasiyaha yaynaan ka qadin, furantay Baarliine
Funanado xariiriyo dhar baan, filiqsan doonnaaye
Forontiinna Soomaalidaay, ficil ku nooleeya

We should not miss the festivities for the fall of Berlin
We will be enriched with wealth and clothes made of silk
Oh! Somalis defend your fronts with vigour and courage

Until the mid-1940s Cabdillahi's themes were local society and youth, in poems mostly recited in gatherings like marriage ceremonies. Yet he was on the verge of the composition of his political verses when he commented, still from Djibouti, on the emerging nationalist movements in the protectorate in the early 1940s. In the mid-1950s he joined the political struggle for the liberation of the Somali territories, especially in British Somaliland where he lived at that time. He became an active SNL member and also advocated unification with Italian Somalia. The following verses belong to two poems that point to the ongoing struggle that was waged, partly underground, on the side of the Somali nationalists. The true thoughts were not overtly spoken but hidden in riddling speech. The first extract is from the famous *Gabay* (which is a particular category of poetry) called *Murugo*, which can be translated 'despair':

Naftu in ay macaan tahay, anaa kuu markhaatiya'e
Mar se haddanay meel iyo lahayn, mowdac lagu aaso
Iyadoo maqnaataa sidaa, igala muuq-roone
Hadduu muruqa bowdadu ku go'o, waad makalantaaye
Ninkii midigta laga taabayoow, bidixdu waa maafe
Markaba daarka waxa loogu tolay, meel ha joogsado'e

Waxa maraqa loo seesayaa, Maahir yay jiqine
Miiraalaha hortii baa guryaha, la iska moosaaye
Mareegtaaba loo sii guntaa, maqasha neyloode
Ayaan hadalka muur-muurrinine, waxan ku meydhaamay
Macnihiyo ujeeddada ninkii, maaxiyaa garan

I admit and confess that life is sweet
But if you do not have a place to live and a place for burial
Living is not worthy of any leisure and enjoyment
You suffer if the main artery of your body is cut
If your right hand is tied your left is useless
A milk container is made adaptable so as to stand by itself

The udder of a she-camel is tied so as to stop the calf from sucking
Somali portable huts are rounded with drainage ditches before the rains
Ropes are prepared for the lambs to be tied
Mincing words I must not conclude my discourse
Which can be only understood by the wise and the sage.

In another poem called *Qabyo* (Unfinished) Cabdillahi is urging people to be united in the fight against the British colonialism. On the other side he is depicting the evils of clanism:

Ingiriiskan laga qayliyee, qaaq wax kaga siiyay
Isaguba mar buu qaadan jiray, qaanso iyo leebe
Qarfo iyo mar buu seexan jiray, qalanqal hoosteede
Hayeeshe quluub wada jirtaa, qaniya sheekhoowe
Qalalaase meel lagu lumiyo, qaylo iyo oohin
Qorraxdii dhacdaba teennu way, kala qaxaysaaye

The British that colonised from sunrise to sunset
Once they were equipped with the bow and the arrow
They used to live and sleep in the wilderness and caves
But unified strategies and thought lead to progress
Chaos and restlessness lead to regress [weeping and mourning?]
Every day we [the Somalis] are falling apart and getting scattered.

Cabdillahi was fortunate that he started recording his poetry on tape as early as 1958. This was possible because he had nothing to hide from the public as his themes were very general and of interest to all. After 1960 when the independence was attained, Cabdillahi's poetry became more patriotic, critical, analytic and influential. It attracted greater numbers of Somali people. Cabdillahi continued recording his poetry and this is why almost all of his poetry has been preserved until today.

The second phase of his poetry starts with the famous *Geeraar* (a particular style of poetry) that he had composed for the Somali flag on 26 June 1960 when British Somaliland gained its independence. On that historic day the people were gathered in a stadium in Hargeysa where the ceremony was held. Among the dignitaries were the Prime Minister of Somaliland, Maxamed Xaaji Ibraahim Cigaal, and the representative of the British colonial administration, Mr Philip Carl. The flag poles for the two flags were erected on the ground. The British flag was lowered down while the Somali flag was hoisted. Cabdillahi's verses, at least the refrain, are generally known among Somalis: *Kaana siib kanna saar* (Lower the one and raise the other!). A part of the poem reads like this:

Soomaaloo is-cunaysa oo
Isa seeggan dhammaanoo
Saqda qaylo dhawaaqdiyo
Sulub la isu cabbaystiyo
Hadba soof la xabbaadhiyo
Saraayaa demi weyday

Kii laydhiisu na saaqday
Kii sadqeeyay Qabaa'ilee
Isu saaray gacmaayee
Saf walaala ka yeelayoow

Saaxirkii kala guurraye
Sarreeyow ma-nusqaamow
Aan siduu yahay eego'e
Kaana siib kanna saar

Somalis fighting one another
Fractious and irritated with one another
Victims of looting and pillaging
Gun fighting and endless wars
The One that brought the breeze of peace
The One that evicted clanism and its vices
The One that settled the disputes and conflicts
The One that made them brothers unifying their lines

We have split with the demon
O hoisted, never to fall!
Eagerly I see it
Lower the one and raise the other!

A few days later, on 1 July 1960 the state of Somaliland was unified with Italian Somalia to form the Somali Republic. Aadan Cabdille Cismaan was elected President of the republic and appointed Cabdirashid Cali Shermaarke as Prime Minister. Cabdirashid made his first visit to the northern regions (former British Somaliland) in early August 1960. Somalis from the former Italian South dominated the new administration of the Somali Republic. The capital city Mogadishu, too, was situated there. People in the north, despite their nationalist euphoria, noted this disequilibrium of power sharing with concern. Cabdillahi met the Somali Prime Minister during his visit in the village of Kalabaydh. The poet sat on a horse while reciting his opening verses to the dignitaries:

Midi waa dariftayda
Dadkuna wayla qabaa
Midina waa ducadeenna
Midina way dihineyd
Midina waa ta danteenna
Midina waa dacwaddayda oo
Iyada waan ku danbeyn

One is my view
Shared by the people

One is our blessing
One is what has been waiting for us,
One is our interest and our target
And one is my accusation
And with that I will conclude.

After this introduction the poem continues with over 200 verses. Cabdillahi Suldaan first talks about the country and the people to the newly appointed Prime Minister, and then mentions the objectives of the unification and criticises the way the government members were appointed, which seemed likely to derail the integration process. He concludes:

Maalintii dabku qiiqayeen
Isticmaarki is-diidnay
Nimankii danta sheegtayee
Dariiqooda ka leexanee
Dacwaddooda dhammaystayee
Dalkan caawa an joogno
Dulligii isticmaarkiyo
Dahaadhkiiba ka siibayee
Karal daaqad ka saarayee
Duddaanu ahayne

Dawlad soo gashay mayhine
Danteennaa laba diiddaye
Dabuub aanu maqlaynay
Dareen baan ka qabnaayoo
Dugsigii Barlamaankiyo
Dekeddii Xamar baa leh
Berbera daadku ha qaado
Doonniyi yaanay ku leexan
Duqeydii Barlamaankaay
Labadaa kala daaya oo
Yaan loo daymo la'aan

The day the spark of liberation
Against colonialism was ignited
We are those who expressed their wishes
We are those who have not lost their way
We are those who clearly presented their case
We are those who liberated this country
From the yoke of colonialism and its misery
We are the ones, who forced Carl[8] to quit
We are not late-comers.

Our interest is not to remain divided
We reject a statement we have been hearing

The parliament's seat in Mogadishu
The seaport in Mogadishu;
Berbera to be washed away by the sea waters
With no dhow to anchor at its port.
O you leaders in Parliament,
Divided we will never succeed
And this must be observed with diligence.

Cabdillahi visited Mogadishu for the first time in the second half of 1961. He was astonished by the prevailing conditions and the political state of affairs where clanism and nepotism ruled the state machinery and government institutions. To depict this situation he composed the poem *Buul-duqeed* (An old woman's hut). Taking a few verses as an example, he had this to say:

Shacbigii dagaalka u galaa, daadsan suuqyada'e
Danbarkeedi Maandeeq nimaan, doonin baa dhamaye
Ninnaan dawlad baa Xamar fadhida, haw dabbaal-degine
Hadduun baa sidii Buul-duqeed, daaha loo rogaye
Kol haddaan Talyaanigan dhex degay, cidi ka duubaynin
Iga daaya gabaygaygu wuu, iiga darayaaye

The masses that fought for it are suffering in the streets
Those who never grazed and watered Maandeeq[9] are drinking her milk
No one should be cheerful that a State is functioning in Mogadishu
It has been dismantled like the broken down hut of an old woman
If the corrupting Italians are not going to be expelled
Leave me in peace! my poetry would only increase my woes.

In the same time he composed an analysis of politics in the Somali Republic, expressing his disappointment with what has happened and directly attacking those in power:

Muskii Baarlammaannada markaan, meel isugu geynay
Madaxweynayaal iyo markii, Minister loo doortay
Maskaxdii wacnayd iyo dadkii, meel u wada jeeday
Nimankii melmelay waa kuwii, maalay keligoode
Hadday maalintii na hor kacaan, midho ma weyneene
Ma-naxaannadii baan arladan, meerisna u toline
Mar naba yaydinnaan dhicin kuwii, male ku soo goostay
Suntay nagu mudeen wiilashii, lays martiyi waayay
Nimankii mabda'a reer galbeed, nagu maddiideeyay
Muraadkoodu nimankuu ahaa, moodhadhkiyo daarta
Nimankuu muggooduba ahaa, maalin la casuumo

When we merged the two Parliaments
When they were elected as Presidents and Ministers

The lovely aspirations and the people with a unified strategy
Those who betrayed them had exploited the national wealth
If they had only guided us properly we would have been prosperous
The cruel leaders did nothing for the country
Those who planned not to vacate and abandon positions
Those whose misdeeds led to chaos and civil wars
Those who imposed the Western ideology on us
Those whose aspirations were only to own a car and a villa
Those who lived for their personal gains and deeds.

Timocadde's most famous composition against the evils of clanism starts with the following verses that have become 'household maxims' for all Somalis worldwide:

Dugsi ma leh Qabyaaladi waxay, dumiso mooyaane
Nin qabyaalad beetow wanaag, kuu ma soo baxo
Nin qabyaalad heensaynayaa, guul ma haybsado
Nin walaalkii geed ugu jiraa, geesi noqon waa

Clanism is no shelter—it is a falling wall
He who grows and breeds clanism, will never harvest anything good
He who saddles clanism will never be victorious
He who plans to kill his brother, will never be recognised as a hero.

The poetry of Cabdillahi was not confined to the Somali territories and issues. Instead he covered regional and international issues of wider concern. In 1960–61 outsiders intervening in the Congo—the country's Belgian colonisers, the US, white mercenaries—and their Congolese accomplices deposed and then murdered Patrice Lumumba, the first Prime Minister of Congo; to this day his grave has not yet been found. Cabdillahi composed one of his most famous and patriotic poems on the mournful event.

Geesiga madow uma oggola, guusha reer Yurube
Geerida Lamuummbaa wadnuhu, noo gig leeyahaye
Geyigiisii goortuu qabtee, gees isugu leexshay
Iga guura galabtuu yidhaa, geeddan loo xidhaye
Godka waxaw qoday Haamarshool, waa gedduu rabaye

Europeans never acknowledge victory achieved by a black man
We are mournful and bemoan the death of Lumumba
As he unified the ranks and took the leadership of his country
As he instructed the oppressors to leave
They imprisoned and hand-cuffed him
It was Hammarskjöld[10] who betrayed him
It was the plan they wanted to execute.

Cabdillahi also reflected on international relations and the position of Somalia in the global political economy. He encouraged his people to be self-sufficient and count on themselves. In the following lines he speaks out against the dependency on foreign aid which, in the long run (long after Cabdillahi's death) proved disastrous for Somalia:

Madhax ma laha aadmigu wuxuu, kuu mitamiyaaye
Macaluul wax kaaga ma taraan, maal laguu guraye
Midigtaadu waxay xoogsataa, meydha kaa jara'e
Marke aanad lahayn looma lulo, maanka weligaaye
Maggaabada hashaada ka roon, meydhanaan kale e'
Marka aanad hammoon noloshu waa, mooyi dabadeede

What has been given in austerity had no reserve
Aid and assistance cannot meet your needs
What you strive and toil for could do away with hunger and disease
You should never be attracted by what you do not own and possess
A mouthful of your she-camel's milk is sweeter than anything else
When you have no plans and aims, life becomes futile.

The third phase of Cabdillahi Suldaan's work comprises poems composed during the first years of the military regime that had come to power in October 1969. Cabdillahi lived for two brief years with that regime, and most of the time he was suffering from a throat cancer. Unlike those of other Somali poets of his age, Cabdillahi's first and last poems are known. We have seen his first poem written in 1936 in Harar in Ethiopia. His last poem was composed and recited on 21 October 1971. As the masses were still in a festive mood after the military takeover, he confessed that this was his last poem in the prelude and initial verses of that *Geeraar* which he composed for the October festivities:

Hadal waa iga caawiyo
Hanbalyaynta Oktoobar

Tonight in the celebration of October
I quit the habit of composing and reciting.

In the brief period between the autumn of 1969 and his death Cabdillahi succeeded in composing 16 poems on a wide variety of both national and international affairs. He tackled economic issues extensively, particularly animal husbandry which was, and still is today, the economic backbone of the country. In 1970 the poet highlighted how enclosures burden the pastoral-nomadic economy:

Duunyadaynuu dhaqaynayee
Calankeenna dugsiisayee
Shisheeyaa u diraynaye
Dahabkeenna ahayd
Halkii ay degi layd
Dalkii waa laga ootayoo
Ninba deyray lix meyloo
Nin diyaarad ku guuriyo
Siisow duulaya mooyiye
Reer is-daaddihiyaa
Dushaba u bixi maayo

The livestock we have been rearing
Which was our export to foreign countries
The assurance and guarantee of our sovereignty
Our gold and hard currency
Has been deprived of its grazing plains
Every one fencing miles of enclosures
Pastoralists to migrate
Have to resort to trucks and planes
It is impossible for a nomadic family
To move from one place to another.

Even in those days, Cabdillahi remained political. Sharing the people's high hopes that the new revolutionary government would develop Somalia, he let his hatred of the corrupt civilian leadership loose. In his poem he asked the military regime to take them to court and declared that otherwise they would not be a genuine alternative. This clearly shows that Cabdillahi was not afraid of the new regime, mostly led by military officers, since he dared to give them advice:

Dhexda nimanki noo joogsadee, dhaxanta noo saaray
Dhiigya-cabyadii lama qab-qaban, dhiirranaan jiraye
Jeeroo rag dheeraad cunoo, dhumucle loo yeedhoo
Nin waliba wuxuu dhimay ilaa, dhabarka loo saaro
Dhacadiidka jeeroo rag badan, dhawda laga saaro
Jeeroo maxkamad loo dhisoo, dhididku hoobaano
Jeeroo waxay naga dhaceen, lagaga dheemaalsho
Daarahan la dhiibsaday ilaa, laga dhawaateeyo
Dhafoorkooda jeeroo rasaas, dhuuban laga saaro
Jeeroo rag lagu dhoogtamooy, dhaaftay la arkaayo
Dhunkaal shilinku jeeruu noqdoo, dhuunta mari waayo
Dhacarsiga la deyn maayo iyo, dhiilkii lays baraye
Dhabbadaa an soo jilay haddii, laga dhabayn waayo
Dhutis xaalku kama baaqsadee, dhuuxa hadalkayga

Those who betrayed and left us in the dark and wilderness
The brave blood-suckers have not been caught and hand-cuffed
Unless those who took the surplus and the fat are arrested
Unless everyone is held to account for the crimes he committed
Unless many culprits are beaten and sentenced
Unless a court is established to reach a verdict on their faults
Unless they are dispossessed of the wealth they accumulated
Unless they are shot with living bullets
Unless we witness and see the traitors shot and dead
Unless the shilling becomes a venom hard to swallow
Corruption and fraud will never stop
If the measures I have listed are not respected
Failure and disillusion are certain—mark what I say!

In conclusion of this third phase of Cabdillahi's poetry, I will present a few verses on international and regional issues. He noticed the continued legacy of colonialism, and was worried about neo-colonial tendencies. He also took note of the Cold War between the West and the East, including the struggles between capitalist and socialist ideologies, and the arms race.

Isticmaarku meeshuu ka tago, arami baa taalle
Ragguu ababshay buu sii dhigtaa, kaalintii adage
Irbaddiisu waayada danbay, eelo kicisaaye
Waa waxaa Afriikaba kharribay, ugax dillaacdaaye

Colonialists leave behind mines and explosives
They plant their agents in vital posts and positions
The legacies unfold intrigues and machinations
Africa is wrecked by what was left by the invaders.

On another occasion he had this to say:

Isticmaarkii waagii sunsumay, soo socdaal-celiye
Ninkii seexday way jecel yihiin, inay sinbiidhaane
Wuxuu saaka baadh-baadhayaa, dar u samaystaaye
Siraad waxay ku doon-doonayaan, sees ay dumiyaane
Weli seetadii baa ku xidhan, Saan-madoobaha'e.

The colonialists who left long ago have returned
They like to destabilise those who drowse
They are looking for establishments to tear apart
Torch in hand they look for structures to dismantle
The black man still remains chained and hand-cuffed.

On world peace and the arms race Cabdillahi Suldaan composed this poem called *Qodaxdii Qarbiga* (the thorn of the West), of which I present the following extract:

Qarammada hardamay dawladahan, wada qamuunyaysan
Qalabkiyo sawaariikhda iyo, bahalka quusaaya
Hubka samada loo qaadayee, laysu qarinaayo
Qorraxdiyo dayaxa weerarkaa, qoobka loo geliyay
Qalcadaha Mariikh laga dhisaa, qaci ka joogtaaye
Is-qaniintay aakhirona way, wada qar-taallaaye
Is-qabsade qab-weyniyo ninkii, quudhsi–diid ihiye
Quraankaa tilmaamiyo warkuu, qoray Rasuulkiiye
Ninna dunida qoodh uma noqdoo, qalin horaa yaalle
Waa wixii Fircoon loo qarraqay, qoor la fidiyaaye

The struggling nations, the conflicting states
The war arsenal, the rockets and the submarines
The secret weapons taken to the skies, to space
The constant attack on the sun and the moon
The fortresses built on Mars, are points of contention
The argument is so fierce it imperils the fate of mankind
The arrogant invader and the oppressed rebel are battling.
The Qur'an and the Prophet had prophecies for the future
No one can become a sole ruler, history teaches;
It was pride and vanity that drowned the Pharaohs.

Conclusion

In his everyday life Cabdillahi Suldaan managed to combine being a devout Muslim with being a nationalist and a social person with a good sense of humour. His friends and contemporaries said that before reciting a poem he had the habit of introducing it with a brief story related to its theme. He spent much time at the *mefrishes*, the places where Somali men gathered to chew *qaad*. Yet, he was not a 'chewer'. He used to take one branch of *qaad* from his friends and he used to wave it, pretending that he was eating it with them.

Cabdillahi left a rich treasure of poetry for the coming generations. His legacy remains the biggest collection of Somali poetry written so far, and that is because, first, he used the modern recording technologies as early as possible, in order to spread his word, and second, he took on general themes that were of interest to all Somalis, wherever they lived. He never shied away from criticising his contemporaries' misconduct and from pointing out the misrule of those in power. From his first poem in Harar he travelled a long way to being a nationalist, patriot, socialist and pan-Africanist who struggled against injustice wherever he could see it.

Notes

1. Much of the biographical information presented in this section was acquired through interviews with friends, relatives and in-laws of Cabdillahi, such as his cousin Isaaq Cismaan Maxamed.
2. The square has since been renamed after the national hero Maxamuud Harbi Faarax.
3. In fact, I wrote most of the unrecorded poems of Cabdillahi from the dictation of his friend Daahir Cabdillahi who knew them by heart.
4. In the elections in February 1959 the alliance of the SNL and USP won 32 out of the 33 seats in the parliament and only one seat was won by the NUF.
5. Out of the seven children of Cabdillahi Suldaan only three daughters, Maryan, Nimco and Samsam, are alive at the time of writing this paper (February 2009). His second wife Ardo Qalinle died and was buried in Gabiley in 2002. It is also worthy mentioning here that Daahir Cabdillahi who knew most of Cabdillahi Suldaan's verses, also died in 2002 in Gabiley.
6. Salaan Maxamed, better known as Salaan Carrabey, was one of the most outspoken poets of his era and was one of the contestants in the poetic duel called Gubo. He originated from today's Togdheer Region of Somaliland and travelled much in the neighbouring countries. He lived in the last years of the 19th century and the first part of the 20th century.
7. Many of the famous Somalis poets have been men. But there are also cherished female poets, who traditionally composed their verses in the style of *burambuur*. More recently, young Somali women try out also other genres.
8. Philip Carl, the last British representative in Somaliland, mentioned above.
9. *Maandeeq* was a symbolic she-camel that had twin calves symbolic of the independence and the unification of the two Somali regions, as the poets depicted it.
10. The Swede Dag Hammarskjöld was the Secretary General of the UN at the time. He was involved in the Congo crisis, and died in a plane crash in 1961.

References

Andrzejewski, Bogumil W. and Ioan M. Lewis 1964. *Somali Poetry: an Introduction*. London: Clarendon Press.

Boobe Yusuf Duale 1983. *Maansadii Timacadde*. Mogadishu: National Printing Press.

Johnson, John W. 1996 [1974]. *Heelloy: Modern Poetry and Songs of the Somali*. London: Haan.

PART VII

CULTURAL VARIATIONS

16

LANGUAGE MARGINALISATION, ETHNIC NATIONALISM, AND CULTURAL CRISIS IN SOMALIA

Mohamed Haji Mukhtar

Introduction

Somali people speak a number of languages and dialects, *Maay*[1] and *Maxaa*[2] being those of the majority. None of the Somali languages and dialects was written until late 1972, owing to disagreements based on clan-related scripts such as *Ismaniyya* (Darood), *Kadariyya* (Hawiye), *Kontonbarkadliyya* (Reewin)[3], *Gadabuursiyya* (Dir)[4]or religious and political issues that dictated whether these Somali languages should be written in an Arabic or a Latin-based alphabet.[5]

In 1972, however, a Latin-based *Maxaa* script[6] was adopted and *Maxaa* became the only official national language of the country. This experiment alienated speakers of other Somali languages; in particular *Maay* speakers were enraged. In 1976, they formed a literary association called *Af-Yaal*, 'the language keepers', whose main concern was the protection and revival of *Maay* culture and language. By 1980, many of the members of *Af-Yaal* were jailed, harassed, and killed by the military administration led by Maxamed Siyad Barre. This forced many into exile. The expatriate members of *Af-Yaal* developed several new *Maay* scripts. Since 1994, one of those scripts called *Alif-Maay*, the Maay Alphabet, has been circulated in Somali academic circles and has gained considerable support among *Maay*-speakers (Abdullahi 1994).

This essay will discuss *Alif-Maay*, focusing on the historical background of languages and dialects of Somalia. Furthermore, it will explore and attempt to recover literature from the *Maay* heritage previously excluded for political reasons from the Somali literary canon.

Historical background

The Somali languages and dialects belong to the Eastern Cushitic subbranch of the Afroasiatic language family. They are related to languages such as the Saho-Afar spoken in the northeastern part of the Horn, Oromo-Sidamo in southwestern Ethiopia, and Omo-Tana in northeastern Kenya. Historical linguists have tentatively subdivided Somali languages and dialects into more than 20 groups (Ehret and Mohamed Nuh Ali 1984). The northern Somali people speak what is generally referred to as *Af-Maxaa* with dialectical variants. From the central regions to the south, *Af-Maay* is the dominant language, though there are other languages and dialects such as *Af-Jiddu, Af-Tunni, Af-Dabarre* and *Af-Barawaani* who use *Af-Maay* as a *lingua franca* (see maps 1 and 2 in the appendix of this chapter).[7] In the language referring to business and religion, there are a large number of Arabic loan words (Zaborski 1967). Since none of the Somali languages had a script before the colonial era, Arabic, English and Italian remained official languages in the former Somali Democratic Republic until 1972 when a modified Roman script was adopted for *Af-Maxaa*. The technical language is largely formed after Italian and English models.

Arabic models

In the 13th century, Barkadle Yuusuf[8] adapted the Arabic script for the transcription of Somali vowels to facilitate the teaching of the Qur'an in the *dugsi* (Quranic schools similar to the *madrasa* or *kutaab* schools in Islamic Arabia). In the late 19th century, Sheikh Ibdille Issak (1796–1869)[9] and Sheikh Axmed Gabyow (1844–1933)[10] made poetic and mnemonic translations from the Qur'an and the Hadith, but these translations were not written down until recently. Sheikh Uways Ibn Mohamed al-Barawi (1846–1907)[11] used the Arabic script for writing and printing his *Af-Barawaani, Af-Maay* and *Af-Tunni qasai'd* ('poems'). In 1938, Sheikh Maxamed Cabdi Makahiil published an essay in the Isaaq dialect using Arabic script. In the 1960s, both Ibraahim Xaashi Maxamuud (1929–71) and Saciid Cismaan Guuleed promoted the use of the Arabic script (Ibrahim Hashi Mohamud 1963; Sa'id Usman Guleed 1969; Sa'id Usman Guleed 1973). However, a wider group of Somali scholars did not consider Arabic models because Arabic vowels do not correspond to the vowels in Somali languages, and other Arabic characters had to be modified. Most importantly, Arabic lacked 'emotional' support, as it did not have the characteristics of an indigenous script.

Indigenous models

In the late 1920s Cismaan Yuusuf Keenadiid, a Majeerteen of the Darood clan, developed a unique script known as *Ismaniyya* which, however, could be used only for the *Af-Maxaa* spoken in the northeast and, largely, in the central region. It was technically sound with a script resembling the Amharic script of neighbouring Ethiopia and using closely similar diacritical signs. However, some letters were written from right to left and others from left to right. This was a great source of confusion and made the development of a cursive system difficult. Furthermore, *Ismaniyya* was not a truly 'national' script. Nearly all its advocates were from the Cismaan Maxamuud sub-clan of the Majeerteen clan. Thus, there was much opposition from other clans (Laitin 1977: 89–91).

In 1933, Sheikh Cabdiraxmaan Sheikh Nuur Cabdillahi of the Gadabuursi clan (1900–90) introduced another unique script known as the Gadabuursi script. Some researchers believed that the *Gadabuursiyya* was phonetically sound (Lewis 1958), but the UNESCO Technical Commission evaluating over nine proposed indigenous scripts in 1966 found this script unclear (Andrzejewski, Strelcyn and Tubiana 1966). In the late 1940s, Mustaf Sheikh Hassan (1927–83) of the Hariin subclan of the Reewin devised a script to be used by those who spoke *Af-Maay* and related dialects, known as the *Kontonbarkadliyya* ('Blessed Fifty'), referring to the early composition of *Reewin* people. *Kontonbarkadliyya* was probably one of the most promising indigenous scripts, but the *Reewin*, the clan to which Hassan belonged, had not much political influence in post-colonial Somalia; therefore *Kontonbarkadliyya* was marginalised. In 1952, Xuseen Sheikh Kadare of the Abgaal sub-clan of the Hawiye introduced the *Kadariyya* script, based on a modified Latin orthography. The UNESCO Technical Commission in

1966 mentioned *Kadariyya* as one of the most appropriate scripts for Somali (Laitin 1977: 87). However, it was again perceived as a script of a particular group (which lacked clout in at the time) and did not gain acceptance among most other Somalis.

Colonial models

Christian missionaries developed Latin-based scripts. In 1897, Evangeliste de Larajasse and Cyprien de Sampont wrote a *Practical Grammar of the Somali Language*, which used a Latin orthography for *Af-Maxaa*. J.W.C. Kirk, in the British protectorate (1902–4) recorded the Somali he heard and developed a system of teaching the language using a Latin script of his own invention. He also included some features of the Arabic script. For instance, he employed an apostrophe for the Arabic *'ayn* and *hh* for *ha* and *gh* for the *ghayn*. In 1905, Kirk published a grammar for the Yibir and Midgaan dialects. Some Latin-based orthographies were examined by the Italian Orientalist Enrico Cerulli and the linguists Martino Moreno and Mario Maino (Cerulli 1957; Cerulli 1959; Cerulli 1964; Moreno 1955; Maino 1953). During the *Amministrazione Fiduciaria Italiana della Somalia* (AFIS), the Italian trusteeship period in Somalia (1950–60), Italy brought the language issue to the first *Consiglio Territoriale* (CT) (Territorial Council),[12] which unanimously adopted Arabic as the official language of the country.[13] Yet Radio Mogadishu conducted broadcasts in both *Af-Maay* and *Af-Maxaa* until 1959 when the transitional government of the Trust Territory adopted a resolution limiting broadcasts to *Af-Maxaa* only. When Somalia gained independence on 1 July 1960 it lacked a unified script for its languages.

Post-independence efforts

The first civilian administration (1960–64) set up a national language commission in October 1960 to 'investigate the best way of writing Somali, considering all the aspects of the language[s], with special eye on the technical side, and submit a report to the government by March, 1961' (Language Commission Report 1961: 2). It also should agree on one script suitable for all Somali languages. The commission was composed of nine members, most of whom had linguistic credentials, and who had invented their own scripts.[14] Special consideration was given to the representation of the different Somali languages and dialects. The commission found that the Somali languages had 44 basic sounds; thus, the future orthography should be represented accordingly (ibid. 22). The commission clearly stipulated in its report that the Upper Jubba 'dialects', otherwise known as *Af-Maay*, had two or more phonemes unknown to other Somali languages and dialects to be incorporated in the final script (ibid.). For the commission the future national orthography had to satisfy a number of criteria. Some of the related questions were: Is it simple in its lettering? Is it uniquely Somali? Is it phonetic? Are any 'printing machines', i.e. typewriters and presses, available for it? Is it economically and technically viable? Has it any intrusive and anomalous diacritics? Has it any signs with more than one function (ibid. 11–12)? It is important to bear in mind that the commission's concern was to agree on a script or orthography (*far Soomaali*) suitable for all Somali languages and dialects, not a uniform national language (*Af-Soomaali*).

The commission reviewed eighteen scripts: eleven indigenous, devised in unique Somali forms, four based on Arabic characters, and three based on Latin characters. The *Af-Maay* script submitted by Mustaf Sheikh Hassan had 42 characters and was ranked the second of the eleven locally devised orthographies. The Arabic-based scripts thought acceptable for religious use did not meet the major requirements sketched out above. The Latin-based scripts did satisfy most of these requirements, but as the Latin scripts were associated with colonialism and Christianity, their adoption was unlikely: *Laatiin waa bilaa diin* ('Latin is without religion').

Political and religious factors complicated the deliberations and led three significant members, including Yasin Cismaan and Ibraahim Xaashi, to resign in protest because their scripts, *Ismaniyya* and Arabic respectively, did not meet the criteria. Another important member, Mustaf Sheikh Hasan, a district commissioner and the only *Af-Maay* speaker among the members, and an advocate of an *Af-Maay* script, was transferred from Mogadishu to Balcad and could not contribute to the work of the commission any more. The remaining commission members could not come to a consensus, and the government decreed that Arabic, English and Italian should remain the official languages in the country.

During the second civilian administration (1964–67), the government invited a committee of three foreign experts sponsored by UNESCO.

The experts were B.W. Andrzejewski, S. Strelcyn, and J. Tubiana who arrived in Mogadishu in March 1966, when the city was shaken by demonstrations hostile to the adoption of a Latin-based script. The UNESCO committee reviewed existing scripts and interviewed most of their devisers. Although they could not come up with a specific recommendation, they were critical of indigenous and Arabic scripts and had few objections to Latin-based scripts (Andrzejewski, Strelcyn and Tubiana 1966). Still, for political reasons, the government did not adopt a Latin-based script.

In October 1969, the coup d'état led by Maxamed Siyad Barre established a military administration, the Somali Revolutionary Council (SRC), which, in 1971, appointed the *Guddiga Af-Soomaliga*, the Somali Language Commission without, however, specific instructions regarding the adoption of a script. The choice of a script would be political, and, indeed, on 21 October 1972, on the third anniversary of the coup, a helicopter dropped multi–coloured leaflets in a new Latin script over the parade passing before the tribune of the leaders and dignitaries. From that day on, this script became official, though few could read it. *Af-Maay* speakers, and speakers of other Somali languages, soon discovered that the script was only suitable for *Af-Maxaa*, but the government repressed all criticism in the name of cultural homogeneity and monolingualism. Thus, it was through the adoption of this script that one form of Somali, *Af-Maxaa*, became the only officially acceptable national language, and it was called *Afka Hooyo*, 'the mother tongue', much offending those whose mothers did not speak it.

By 1974 a major literacy campaign was launched to teach nomadic Somalis, particularly the non-*Af-Maxaa* speakers, how to read and write in the now official form of Somali. The ensuing literacy drive involved a national mobilisation. Schools and colleges all over Somalia were closed and some 25,000 students were sent into the nomadic areas as teachers. To their astonishment, the *Af-Maay* speakers in the former Upper Jubba, Lower Jubba and Banadir regions (where the campaign was concentrated) were told that *Af-Maxaa* was their mother tongue. The motto of the campaign was: *Sidii caanaha qurquriya* ('Drink it; it is smooth like milk'); the *Af-Maay* speakers choked. Nevertheless, through political fiat *Af-Maxaa* became the language of instruction in all schools and the language of the media and press.

The *Af-Maay* speaking regions were filled with schools in which pupils were forbidden to speak *Af-Maay*. First graders were anxious to go to pretty schools with playgrounds full of kids but were disturbed when they were told not to speak their mother tongue. If they did, they were sent to the principal's office and spanked. Eventually, they dropped out of school or played truant. The result for the *Af-Maay* speaking community was illiteracy and, related to that, economic misery. A significant number of students tried to assimilate and adapted to *Af-Maxaa*. Still, they were called *Eelay wiiq*, 'the devil gang', every day. They pretended not to hear it and suppressed their feelings without fighting back. After they graduated and became 'mother tongued', they were still outcasts in the racialised social environment dominated by other Somali clans. Many young men accepted their imposed identity and even married non-Reewin wives, giving their children non-*Af-Maay* names. Many of them could no longer make sense in *Af-Maay*, not even to their relatives. They lowered themselves and humiliated their children when they forced them to speak *Af-Maxaa* only.

This was also true in meetings and public speeches. Speakers were reminded to always speak *Af-Soomaali* (meaning: *Af-Maxaa*): *Warya! Af-Soomaali ku hadal* ('Hey! Speak Somali'). Siyad Barre announced that civil servants had to learn the new script in three months. Before the coup, *Af-Maay* speakers had their own political parties and cultural associations. Their MPs in the National Assembly deliberated in *Af-Maay* which was then translated and transmitted through headphones as in the meetings of the United Nations. Indeed, debates and speeches in the parliament were in Arabic, Italian, English and local Somali languages. Before *Af-Maxaa* became *Af-Soomaali*, all students studied and were taught in Arabic, Italian and English. Ironically, learning and being taught in *Af-Maxaa* disadvantaged speakers of not only *Af-Maay* but all other Somali languages apart from *Af-Maxaa*. It is also evident that, before *Af-Maxaa* became the language of instruction, *Af-Maay* speakers excelled because of their knowledge of writing and reading Arabic from the Quranic schools, which were more prevalent in the regions inhabited by the sedentary Reewin than in the areas where mostly nomadic *Af-Maxaa* speakers resided.

At schools and universities after the language 'reform', *Af-Maay* students had to study *suugaanta Soomaalida*, Somali literature, which dealt with poetry, story telling and cultural matters, but which excluded their own literature that was not even translated. The *Af-Maxaa* children's stories were not like the familiar stories they had heard from their mothers called 'Once upon a time' (Gekogeko), nor were the riddles (*Diilleey*) the ones they knew by heart. They did not memorise the classical poetry of their own bards (*Reegay*). The suppression and effective eradication of *Af-Maay* culture and literature was a cause for disagreement and social disruption in Somalia under Siyad Barre's regime; yet disagreement could only be voiced 'underground' or outside the country.

When the military regime fell in January 1991, the assertion of cultural and social homogeneity of the Somali people came under attack. The Inter-Riverine Studies Association (ISA)[15] emerged in 1993, and, at its first congress at the University of Toronto in Canada on 4 November 1994, adopted a new Latin-based script for *Af-Maay* called *Alif-Maay*, 'Maay alphabet' (Mukhtar 1997: 5–6).

Alif-Maay (Maay Alphabet*)*[16]

There are letters for 34 vowels and consonants in the *Maay* alphabet. The consonants are called *shibly*. They are: B, P, T, J, JH, D, TH, R, S, SH, DH, G, GH, GN,Q, F, K, L, M, N, NG, W, H, and Y. The vowels are called *Shaghal*: A, E, I, O, U, AA, EE, II, OO, UU, and Y if preceded by a consonant, as in *dugsy* 'school' (in contrast to *dugsi* in *Af-Maxaa*).

Six consonants are exclusive to *Af-Maay* and not present in the officially recognised *Af-Maxaa*. They are: P, which always occurs in the middle of a word, a sound produced by the lips, somewhat similar to the English P, as in *heped* 'chest', *hopoog* 'scarf for women', *opy* 'placenta'; JH, a guttural sound close to the English J, as in *jheer* 'shyness', *jhiring* 'fracture', *jhiir* (name of a grazing land northeast of Baydhaba);[17] TH, pronounced as in the English article 'the', as in *mathal* 'appointment', *ething* 'permission', *mathy* 'head'; GH, pronounced like the Arabic *ghayn*, as in *haghar* 'deceive', *nagar* 'leash'; NG, similar to the end sounds of the English word 'helping', as in *angkaar* 'curse', *engjeg* 'dry', *oong* 'thirst'; and finally, GN like the sound in the Italian '*signora*', as in *gnaagnur* 'cat' and *maagny* 'ocean'.[18]

When *Af-Maxaa* was the official language, speaking with these sounds would identify the speakers as outsiders, and therefore objects of discrimination. If one's name held those 'non-standard' sounds, it would be transliterated into *Af-Maxaa*. Sometimes, one's birthname changed considerably. For example, Iddiraang Mad Emed in *Af-Maay* would become (officially) Cabdiraxman 'Maxamed Axmed in *Af-Maxaa*.

Cultural renaissance

So far, I have shown that throughout the era of Siyad Barre the agro-pastoral Reewin who spoke *Af-Maay* were excluded from official Somali politics and culture. Against this background, the collapse of the Somali state might well have been considered a blessing in disguise for the *Af-Maay* speaking communities—at least regarding cultural freedom.[19] In 1991, the *Fannaaniinta Arlaadi*, an alliance of artists to preserve the *Maay* heritage of music, drama and poetry, was founded in Baydhowa. Many of its members had been active since 1959 when Radio Mogadishu dropped *Af-Maay* programmes in favour of *Af-Maxaa*. Previously, they had worked as educators, civil servants, or soldiers. In 1991 and afterwards, some poets began to speak out against past and current violence. Despite enormous hardship and suffering under the conditions of civil war, the time was ripe for a cultural revival in which *Af-Maay* speakers could refer to some older gems of their poets, as well as to newly created poems, songs and plays. The music teacher Abdulkadir Ali Hassan, nicknamed Baarudey ('Gunpowder'), wrote the poem *Ay Tiringney Maghaagheng*, *Isly tiirineeng*, 'Let us save our name, and hold onto it proudly' to restore *Maay* pride. Radio Baydhowa adopted it as signature tune; it also became the 'national anthem' of the Riverine State founded in 1995.[20] In face of the harassment and attacks from other Somali groups, the soldier Issak Nuuroow Eeding, a Reewin known by the appropriated clan name Abgaalow, wrote *Mawqif Mujaahid*, 'The way of the warrior', and *Isla Goroneeng*, 'Let us agree', poems which mobilised young men and women to defend their culture.

Already in 1978, Mohamud Haji Mohamed Tarash ('Weaver'), a member of *Horseed* Vanguard, the band of the Somali national army, had written *Doobnymaathey*, 'Never too late'. He was dismissed and then imprisoned for four years for this controversial and subtle play. It was considered 'anti–revolutionary', like some others of his works which the public nonetheless admired, especially *Saba Sabaabu*, 'Deceit'. Abdullahi Abdirahman Daash ('Courtyard') wrote the popular plays *Felek*, 'Astrology' (1975), and *Sahan*, 'Exploration' (1978). Daash's most politically provocative poems are *Iska Diing*, 'Shame', (1992), and *Dhaar*, 'Vow' (1993). The newly established Radio Baydhowa broadcasted *Maay* folk music, poetry, plays, and stories and thus served as a catalyst for the *Maay* cultural revival. Indeed, Radio Baydhowa was the first ever to broadcast and produce programmes exclusively in *Af-Maay*.

Since 1992, the group *Fannaaniinta Arlaadi* has been producing a newsletter named *Arlaadi* ('Homeland'), irregularly published in Baydhowa. It also produce videos of songs and plays. Moreover, it revived the publication and study of Maay classical literature (*Gopy*), poetry (*Weeryr* or *Bayting*), war songs (*Dheel*), dances (*Adar*), and religious poetry (*Naby Ammaang* and *Dikri*). They revived *Gekogeko* stories, sometimes set to music, and *Diilleey* riddles. In this context, a particularly old poem in *Af-Maay* regained popularity. *Shoofin* is a poem chanted by Quranic school students at the closing of a day session—a school anthem, so to say. The poem was composed by the millenarian Sheikh Ibdille Issak (1796–1869) in *Af-Maay*. *Shoofin* (pronounced also *Shoofyng*) refers to keeping devils at bay; it is chanted to protect communities from all evils. The poem has an epic sweep from the day of creation to the day of judgment, and lays out fundamental spiritual and moral values:

Aadamow intii jerto
Allaga ku obsoy
Nabygha ku obsoy
Seer allow sumung my le
Saf yera na haysyte.

As long as you exist (son of Adam)
Fear your Allah and your Prophet
Allah's universe is great, not measured
Greater than weak Believers are numbered

The poem then moves to describe the divine attributes:

Maajey weelshey allow
Maddi wal maaghy miing taagwaaye
Maas my kii lihiiny maag wal niing siyeey

Allah's will is not limited
Whatever he intends, his command is 'be' and it is!
Who gives without conditions?

Then the poem warns those who fail to obey God and His Prophet and shows what happens to those who do not believe.

Allishey ing gefow
Nabishey ing gefow
Adaabtis Ebeda
Agadshey ruuhshey kasaas

Those who dishonour Allah
Those who dishonour the Prophet
Will suffer now
And burn in hell for ever.

The poem goes on to bless the line of teachers, parents, neighbours from ancient times and ends with the verse from the Qur'an: *Wa-mā ramayta idh ramayta wa-lākinna llāha ramā*, 'It was not you, but Allah, who slew them. It was not you who threw at them: Allah threw at them so that He might richly reward the faithful' (Qur'an 8: 17). The students imitate the Prophet Mohamed's action in a battle throwing a handful of dust into his enemies' eyes: they throw the *Shoofin* into the eyes of their and their peoples' enemies and hope for Allah's help.

New chances for cultural and linguistic diversity

Since the mid 1970s Maay intellectuals denounced the linguistic and cultural "ethnocide" of the Barre regime. The activities of the *Af-Yaal*, the language keepers, were celebrated in Sahal Ma'llin Isse's poems such as *Sheleedeya* 'Sidelined' (1973) and *Huburow* 'Beloved' (1974).[21]

Substantial changes occurred in Somali Studies after the collapse of the Siyad Barre regime. Scholarship of the period, though focusing on the causes of the collapse of the Somali state and possible solutions, reported the social injustices suffered by the *Af-Maay* speaking people. Ali Jimale's edited volume *The Invention of Somalia* demonstrated that the widely accepted history of Somalia was a political myth (Jimale 1995). Catherine Besteman and Lee Cassanelli's (1996) collection of essays on the socio-economic causes of the civil war provided ample evidence on what went wrong in Somalia and how *Af-Maay* speaking people were culturally humiliated and economically deprived. Further significant sociological studies on the diversity of Somali society include Virginia Luling's (2002) outstanding work on the Geledi Sultanate and the late Bernhard Helander's (1996, 2003) texts on the Hubeer clan. Also I.M. Lewis' earlier anthropological studies of the population and land use in inter-riverine regions appeared in the reprint of *Peoples of the Horn of Africa* (Lewis 1994).[22] Finally, Ioan Lewis and Mohamed Mukhtar (1996) stressed the need for a thorough study of *Maay* poetry and the oral tradition that so far was neglected by or simply unknown to *Maxaa* speakers and most non-Somali scholars.

Linguistic studies expose the myth of Somalia's monolingualism. In the 1980s Marcello Lamberti (1986) and John Saeed (1982) had already explored linguistic and dialectical variations in Somalia. In 1998 Salim Alio Ibro contributed a *Dictionary of the Jiddu language*, and in 2007 Mohamed H. Mukhtar and Omar M. Ahmed published the first *English-Maay Dictionary* exploring the roots of *Af-Maay* and its relationship to the other Somali languages and dialects (Mukhtar and Ahmed 2007).

The representatives of the agro-pastoral groups strove to address the plight and situation of their people at various Somali peace and reconciliation conferences staged since the collapse of the state. Many of these *Af-Maay* defenders were killed or were blackmailed to such an extent that their lives were hardly bearable.[23] Truth eventually prevailed when the Somali Peace and Reconciliation Conference in Kenya (October 2002 to January 2005) acknowledged that *Af-Maay* would be another official language of the Somali Republic. The Transitional Federal Charter of the Somali Republic of 2003 stated in Article 7: 'The official language of the Somali Republic shall be Somali (*Maay* and *Maxaatiri* [*Af-Maxaa*])'.

Conclusion

In many religious traditions, the spoken word has creative power, but that word need not be confined to one language; thus, a diversity of languages and cultures is valued. In the Qur'an, the variety of linguistic expression among groups and individuals was seen as one sign of Allah's creative omnipotence: *Wa-min āyātihī khalqu l-samawāti wa-l-ardi wa-khtilāfu alsinatikum wa-alwānikum inna fi dhālika la-āyatin li–l-'ālimīn*, 'And among his signs is the creation of heavens and the earth, and the variations in your languages and your colours; verily in that are indeed signs for those who know' (Qur'an 30: 22).

According to the Acoma Pueblo Indians of New Mexico, the mother goddess *Iatiku* causes people to speak different languages so that it will not be so easy for them to quarrel. As a token of security, Islam encourages multilingualism, *man ta'allama lughata qawmin amina min makrihim* 'He who learns other people's language is safe from their mischief' (Hadith). 'Knowing how to speak' was, and is, a sign of wisdom and high social status. Those in high places cultivate many forms of verbal and rhetorical art. Commonly, language and self-reflection—'I am what I say'—are seen as what makes people human, and identification with one's own native languages defines individual and group identity.

Somali society, like other oral societies, places heavy weight on speaking well. To tell a person to speak proper Somali, *Af-Soomaali ku hadal*—an expression used by *Af-Maxaa* speakers to humiliate and degrade speakers of other Somali languages—indicates the degree of exclusion of (for example) *Af-Maay* speakers, particularly after *Af-Maxaa* had been politically endorsed by the government under Siyad Barre. Somali scholarship has so far failed to note that the imposition of monolingualism on a multi–linguistic people was a form of cultural and social oppression that contributed to the disunity of Somalia, which again contributed to the continued collapse of the Somali state. Now that Somali society is in disarray with no central authority, it is necessary to re-evaluate the diversity of Somali culture. Perhaps, at last, the arrogance and single-mindedness of monolingual empire builders will be condemned and cast aside, making space for a new and truly egalitarian Somali polity.

Notes

1. Also known as *Af-Maay*, *Af-Reewin*, *Maaymaay* or *Maayteri* (from the phrase 'What did you say?'). This is the language of many Somalis south of the Shabeelle Valley in the Middle and Lower Shabeelle regions, Upper and Lower Jubba regions, northeastern Kenya and Southwestern Ethiopia and most of the Banaadir. The Maxaa speakers, except for the urbanised and itinerant populations, do not understand *Maay*.
2. Commonly known as *Af-Maxaa*, or *Af-Soomaali*; the official language of the former Somali Democratic Republic since 1972. It is spoken widely in the central and northeastern regions, and in pockets of the Riverine regions, the Ogaden and northeast Kenya.
3. The Reewin or Reewing, formerly transcribed as Rahanweyn or Rahanwiin, are one of the Somali clan-families. They occupy large parts of southern Somalia; they are found in southeast Ethiopia and northeast Kenya. They are divided into major clans, the Digil and the Mirifle, who claim to be brothers and descendant of Mat or Mad (for Mohamed), historically known by the eponym Mat/Mad Reewin. For further details see Mukhtar (2003: 188–9).
4. These scripts are discussed below.
5. In this chapter, Somali personal names are written in *Af-Maxaa* and *Af-Maay* spelling, as well as in English transliteration of Arabic, depending on the background of the person in question.

6. This script is composed of 21 consonants and 10 vowels. Almost all the letters represent sounds similar to those in English, with the exception of three: first, C, a voiced pharyngeal fricative comparable to the Arabic *'ayn* as in *cimri* ('age'). Second, X, a voiceless pharyngeal fricative or emphatic h, corresponding to the Arabic ha, as in *xukuuma* ('government'). Third, Q, an uvular voiceless stop as in *qaran* ('nation'). Three Latin sounds, P, V, and Z, are not found in this script (Keenadiid 1976: xi–xxx).
7. Editors' note: Certainly, variants of *Af-Maxaa* are also spoken in the south, particularly by the Darood and Hawiye groups inhabiting the region.
8. A saint remembered for his system rendering Arabic vowel sounds into *Maay* Somali vowel sounds, *Alifly Kordhwey*, a system which made the writing and the reading of the Qur'an much easier for students in the *dugsy* (Mukhtar 2003:54–55).
9. Sheikh Ibdille was a millenarian and catechismal poet. He was an erudite Islamic scholar proficient in the Arabic and *Maay* languages. Sheikh Ibdille developed a teaching technique to explain and translate the Shari'a laws from Arabic to Af-Maay. Unlike traditional Sheikhs who followed the *laqbo* 'rename or nickname' translation system, he used poetry to teach the Qur'an and the Hadith. His poems range from *Towhiid* 'the unity of god', *Arkaan al-Islam* 'the basic five pillars of Islam', and *Arkaan al-Iimaan* 'the basic pillars of faith' to *Shari'a* 'Islamic jurisprudence'. They also include poems on Islamic history and stories from the Qur'an. Children, women, the youth or the elderly chant the poems in chorus. The most venerable is *Shoofin* chanted in the *dugsy*, by the *kutaab* (Quranic students), even now (Mukhtar 2003: 136–7, 211–12, 2223).
10. A poet-Sheikh who composed many *Masaffo* 'catechism poems' ranging from the *hanuunin* 'inspirational' to *digniin* 'admonitory'. In the early days of Italian colonial rule, Sheikh Axmed Gabyow composed patriotic poems defending country and faith. *Dariiq* 'the right path' and *Rafaad* 'suffering' are some of his most venerated poems (Mukhtar 2003: 204–5).
11. He was the reviver of the Qadiriyya order and the founder of the Uwaysiyya branch. In addition to his Sufi mystic powers, Sheikh Uways was a multi–lingual poet. He composed religious poems and addressed congregations in Tunni, his mother tongue, Arabic, *Maay*, *Maxaa*, and the language of Brava, *Chimbalazi*. His hagiographers published only some of the Arabic texts, because the other languages were only spoken. His rich literary legacy is largely unexplored. For more details, see Sheikh Abdi Ili, *al-Jawhar al-Nafiis fi Khawaas al-Shaykh Uways* (The precious jewel: The life, acts and graces of Sheikh Uways) circulated in manuscript and only published in 1964. Sheikh Uways also introduced new forms of *Naby Ammang* 'in the praise of the prophet' using stories of the *Siirah* 'The Prophet Mohamed's deeds'. Along the lines of *Naby Ammang*, Sheikh Uways further contributed poems on the life stories of saints known as *Munaaqib* 'biographical literature'. Sheikh Uways is also remembered by

his poem *Abaay Sitithey* in the praise of Fatima, daughter of the Prophet Mohamed. For more details on Sheikh Uways' literary works, see Sheikh Abdi Ili (1954). Sheikh Uways wrote his poems in Arabic characters. For a copy of the first page of *Abaay Sitithey*, see Banti and Puglielli (1988).

12. An advisory body created by the Italian Trusteeship administration in 1950 to debate and advise the administration on all issues concerning the trust territory of Somalia with the exception of defence and foreign affairs. Councillors were selected from Somali political parties, representatives of economic sectors and foreign communities (Mukhtar 2003: 245).
13. The council adopted its resolution on 2 February 1951.
14. The nine members of the commission were: Muuse X. Ismaaciil Galaal, Yasin Cismaan, Maxamed Saalax (Ladaneh), Dr Ibraahim Xaashi Maxamuud, Khalif Suudi, Mustaf Sheikh Hassan, Shire Jamaac, Xuseen Sheikh Axmed (Kaddareh), and Yuusuf Meygag Samatar (Linguistic Commission Report 1961: 2).
15. This association was founded on 5 December 1993 in Worcester, Massachusetts. It is committed to the re-examination of basic assumptions about cultural and social homogeneity in Somali studies. In contrast to previous representation of the Somalis, the ISA advocated a pluralistic perspective, regarding Somali society as composed of diverse groups brought together by shared historical experience. It rejected monolithic and hegemonic cultural markers and the very notion of a homogeneous Somali culture. The ISA publishes *Demenedung*, a quarterly newsletter.
16. This section draws on Mukhtar (1997).
17. The name of the town is Baydhaba in *Af-Maxaa*; in *Af-Maay* it is Baydhowa. In the following I will use the *Af-Maay* version.
18. In the 1994 version of *Alif-Maay*, this phoneme was represented by YC (Abdullahi Haji Hassan et al. 1994). However, Mukhtar and Ahmed (2007) use GN since this is clearer and closer to the International Phonetic Alphabet (IPA). Some argue that NY could even be more appropriate.
19. Editors' note: The fall of Siyad Barre was followed by massive inter-clan fighting in southern and central Somalia. In particular the more sedentary groups, such as the Reewin, were victimised by the well armed militias from the traditionally nomadic Hawiye and Darood clans. The famine of 1991/92, caused by draught and war, cost very many lives among the Reewin. Professor Mukhtar has written on this 'darkest' period of recent Somali history (Mukhtar 1996).
20. This bicameral council known as the Digil-Mirifle Supreme Governing Council (DMSGC) was created in March 1995 as an interim legislative body of an autonomous Reewin state. It had two houses, the house of representatives presided first by Sharif Hassan Sheikh Aden, then by Dr Hassan Ibrahim known as Hassey, and the house of elders, called the Supreme Traditional Counsel of Chiefs (STCC) chaired by Malak Mukhtar Malak Hassan. However, the council's life was cut short on 17 Sept. 1995 after the invasion of Baydhowa by Maxamed Faarax Caydiid (Mukhtar, 2003: 190, 243).

21. Sahal Ma'allin Isse graduated from the '11 January High School' in Baidoa in 1974. Already during school years he started composing poetry in *Af-Maay*. He joined the Somali National Security Service (NSS) but later got into trouble with the military regime. He eventually fled to Yemen and then further. He died in London.
22. In contrast to the first edition of 1955, the new edition includes three appendices: 1. Population and Land Use in the Somali Inter-River Areas, 2. The Rahanweyn Clans, 3. Traditional Water Regulations Amongst the Rahanweyn. Lewis' research on the non-*Af Maxaa* speakers was conducted in 1957, 1962 and 1964, but was not brought to light until the end of the Darood (*Af-Maxaa* speaking) regimes, since both the civilian and military Somali governments discouraged foreign scholars from studying these people. Indeed, scholars who tried to work in the inter-riverine areas were harassed and denied visas.
23. One of the last victims of the struggle for cultural recognition was the late Dr Ahmed Rashid Sheikh Ahmed, known as *Qulqule*, 'the flawless'. He was murdered in 6 November 2003 at the conference in Mbagathi. Dr Ahmed had participated at the meeting in his own individual capacity, but spoke for the acknowledgement of marginalised languages and cultures in Somalia.

References

Abdullahi, Haji H. *et al.* 1994. 'Draft Outline of the Maay Alphabet: Alif-Maay.' Paper presented to the First Inter-Riverine Studies Association Congress (ISA), Toronto, 4–5 November 1994.

Ahmed, Ali J. (ed.) 1995. *The Invention of Somalia*. Lawrenceville, NJ: The Red Sea Press.

Andrzejewski, Bogumil W., Stefan Streleyn and Joseph Tubiana (eds) 1966. *Somalia: The Writing of Somalia*. Paris: UNESCO (Ws/0866.90).

Banti, Giorgio and Annarita Puglielli 1988. *Scrittura in Aspetti dell'Espressione Artistica in Somalia*. Rome: Pagatto Libri.

Besteman, Catherine and Cassanelli, Lee (eds) 1996. *The Struggle for Land in Southern Somalia: The War Behind the War*. Boulder: Westview Press.

Cerulli, Enrico 1957, 1959, 1964. *Somalia: Scritti Vari Editi ed Inediti*. 3 Volumes. Rome: Istituto Poligrafico dello Stato.

Ehret, Christopher and Mohamed Nuh Ali 1994. 'Somali Classification.' In T.I. Labahn (ed) *Proceedings of the Second International Congress of Somali Studies*, Hamburg: Helmut Buske, pp. 201–69.

Guleed, Sa'id Usman 1973. *Alfaz 'Arabiyyah fi al-Lughah al-Sumaliyyah: Bahth Maydani* (Arabic words in the Somali Language: A field study). Aden: Matabi' al-Thawri.

——— 1969. *Yaumiyyat Sumaliyyah*. (A Somali Diary) Aden: Dar al-Jamahir li al-Tiba'ah wa al-Nashr.

Helander, Bernhard 2003. *The Slaughtered Camel: Coping with Fictitious Descent Among the Hubeer of Southern Somalia*. Uppsala: Uppsala Studies in Cultural Anthropology.

——— 1996. 'The Hubeer in the Land of Plenty: Land, Labor, and Vulnerability among a Southern Somali Clan.' In C. Besteman and L.V. Cassanelli (eds) *The Struggle for Land in Southern Somalia: The War Behind the War*. London: Haan, pp. 47–69.

Ili, Sheikh A. 1954. *Jala' al-'Aynayn fi Manaqib al-Shaykhayn, al-Shaykh al-Waliyyi Haji Uways al-Qadiri, wa al-Shaykh al-Kamil 'Abd al-Rahman al-Zayla'i* (The biographies of Sheikh Uways and Sheikh abd al-Rahman al-Zaylai). Cairo: Matba'at al-Mash-had al-Husayni.

Keenadiid, Yaasiin C. 1976. *Qaamuuska Af-Soomaaliga*. (Somali Language Dictionary) Mogadishu: Akademiyaha Dhaqanka.

Kirk, John W.C. 1905. *A Grammar of the Somali Language with Examples of Prose and Verse and an Account of the Yibir and Midgan Dialects*. (Reprint) Cambridge University Press.

Laitin, David D. 1977. *Politics, Language, and Thought: The Somali Experience*. Chicago University Press.

Lamberti, Marcello 1986. *Map of Somali Dialects in the Somali Democratic Republic*. Hamburg: Helmut Baske.

Lewis, Ioan M. 1958. 'The Gadabursi Somali Script.' *Bulletin of the School of Oriental and African Studies, University of London*, 21 (1), 134–56.

——— 1994 [1955]. *Peoples of the Horn of Africa: Somali Afar and Saho, New Edition*, London: Haan.

Linguistic Commission Report 1961.

Lewis, Ioan M. and Mohamed H. Mukhtar 1996. 'Songs From The South.' In R.J. Hayward and I.M. Lewis (eds) *Voice and Power: The Culture of Language in North-East Africa, Essays in Honour of B.W. Andrzejewski*. London: School of Oriental and African Studies, pp. 205–212.

Luling, Virginia 2002. *Somali Sultanate: The Geledi City-State Over 150 Years*. London: Haan.

Maino, Marion 1953. *La Lingua Somala Strumento di Insegnamento Professionale*. Rome: Istituto Poligrafico dello Stato.

Moreno, Martino 1955. *Il Somalo della Somalia: Grammatica e Testi del Benadir, Darood e Dighil*. Rome: Istituto Poligrafico dello Stato.

Mohamud, Ibrahim H. 1963. *Al-Sumaliyyah bi Lughat al-Qur'an: Muhawalah Wataniyyah li Kitabat Lughat al-Um* (Somali in the language of the Qur'an: A patriotic attempt to write the mother tongue). Cairo: Dar al-Tiba'ah al-Hadithah.

Mukhtar, Mohamed H. 1996. 'The Plight of Agro-Pastoral Society of Somalia.' *Review of African Political Economy*, 70, 543–53.

——— 1997. 'Alif Maay: Ploy or Pragmatic?' *Demenedung, Newsletter of the Inter-Riverine Studies Association*, 1 (4), 5–6.

——— 2003. *Historical Dictionary of Somalia, New Edition*. Lanham, MD: Scarecrow Press.

——— and Omar Moalim Ahmed 2007. *English-Maay Dictionary*. London: Adonis & Abbey Publishers Ltd.

Saeed, John J. 1992. 'Dialectical Variation in Somali.' In H.M. Adam and C. Geshekter (eds) *Proceedings of the First International Congress of Somali Studies*. Atlanta: Scholars, pp. 464–91.

Zaborski, Andrzej 1967. 'Arabic Loan-Words in Somali: Preliminary Survey.' *Folia Orientalia, 8*, 125–175.

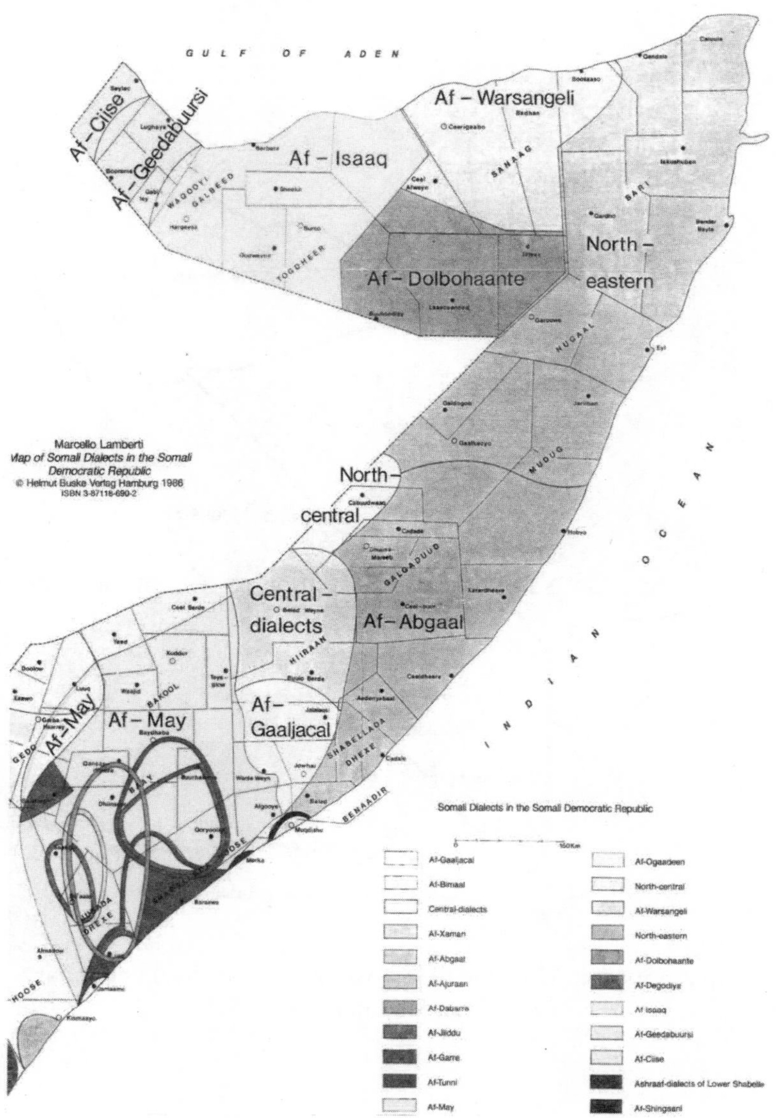

Map 1: Somali Dialects. (Source: Marcello Lamberti)

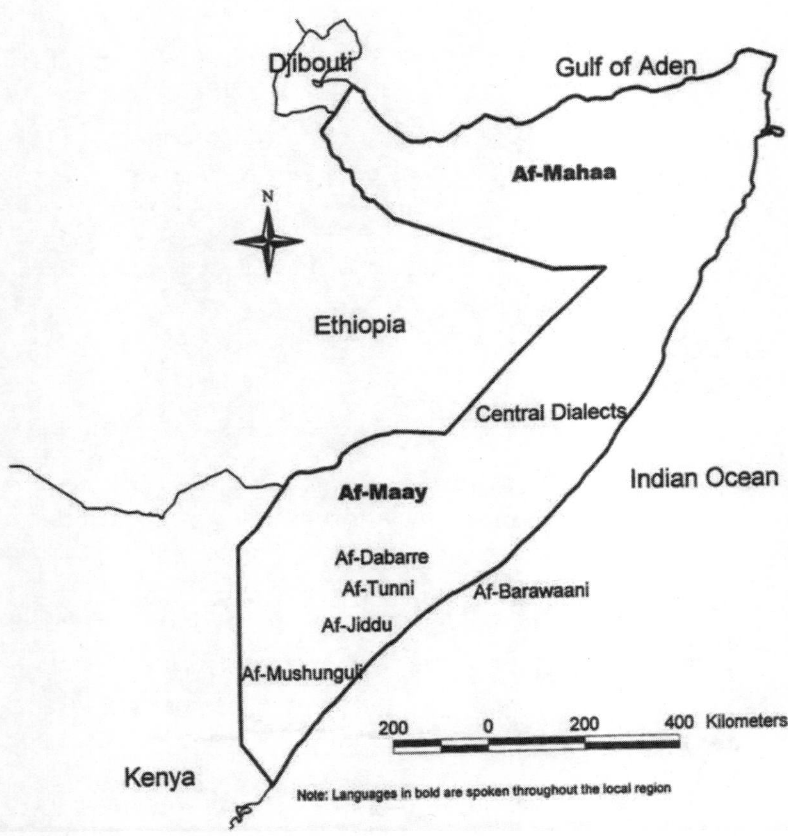

Map 2: (Source: Mohamed Haji Mukhtar, Historical Dictionary of Somalia).

17

FARMERS FROM ARABIA

THE ROLE OF GIBIL CAD GROUPS IN THE INTERIOR OF SOUTHERN SOMALIA

Virginia Luling

Introduction

Professor Lewis is chiefly known for his groundbreaking work on northern, pastoral Somali society. It is sometimes overlooked that he has also dealt with the more variegated society of the southern farming and agro-pastoral clans. His earliest piece of work, carried out even before he went to Somalia himself, was to undertake for the 'Ethnographic Survey of Africa' a summary of virtually all the information in European languages on Somalia, south as well as north, that was available at that time, a job which must have meant long and painstaking labour. It was published in 1955 as *Peoples of the Horn of Africa* and remains to this day an extremely useful resource. The second edition, published in 1994, contains as an appendix a study of the inter-river area that he had carried out in 1957, 1962 and 1964. His paper 'From Nomadism to Cultivation' (Lewis 1994) discusses the complexity of southern Somali society, which is also touched on in numbers of his shorter writings. The following paper deals with one thread in this complex pattern, the Gibil Cad or light-skinned lineages of the Shabeelle.

Gibil Cad and Gibil Madow

The distinction between Gibil Cad ('light skinned') and Gibil Madow ('dark skinned') is well recognised as existing between the lineages or sub-clans[1] of the communities that are now known as Benadiri, that is to say the Reer Hamar of Mogadishu, the 'twelve hats' (*koofi*) of Marka, the Sheikhaal of Jasira and and the Bravanese. The Gibil Cad lineages among them are those which trace their descent to immigrants who arrived from Arabia or Iran from the 10th or 12th centuries CE onward.[2]

This derivation is distinct from the claims of the majority Somali clans to descend ultimately from Arab sheikhs, which must be taken as symbolic rather than factual. (There were certainly Arab missionary preachers of Islam among the Somalis from early times, but though their cultural and spiritual impact was great, their genetic contribution was negligible.) The claim of the Gibil Cad to Arab descent on the other hand is certainly based in reality even if the details are open to question, and being generally endogamous, they have preserved their character. Their appearance witnesses to it, since most of them are noticeably, as their name declares, lighter skinned than Somalis generally. The Reer Faqi, for instance, were originally the Banu Qahtan, and the Shanshiya say that their ancestors migrated from southern Iran (Reese 2008: 65–6). On the other hand the Gibil Madow lineages of those same communities derive from offshoots of the surrounding Somali clans—the Moorshe for instance from the Ajuuran (ibid.)—and therefore look like them, since the term Gibil Madow can also refer to the general Somali population.

All these Benadiri communities live in the port cities or villages and have been from their beginning traders by profession. They are not farmers (though some have bought themselves farms or plantations inland to be worked by hired labour, or in the past by slaves).

What is less recognised is that Gibil Cad communities also exist inland, in the Shabeelle valley, where they form part by adoption of the the Geledi and Begedi clans of Afgooye district of the Lower Shabeelle Region (though they have some representation elsewhere). Like the Benadiri of the coast they trace their ancestry to Arabia or elsewhere in the Islamic world, but through a more recent immigration. Unlike the coastal communities they are farmers as well as traders, and seem to have been so from their first arrival. Like their counterparts on the coast they are generally endogamous, and while they share the language and general culture of their Gibil Madow neighbours, they have their own specific traditions.

Like those of the coastal cities, these people too have made an important contribution to the history of the region. The clans in which they are incorporated belong to the Digil family, and indeed they identify strongly with the Digil (as the later part of this paper makes clear). The result is that so far as they have been mentioned it is generally as part of the Digil, masking the other aspect of their identity. In singling them out my purpose is not to be divisive, but on the contrary to emphasise how they have been established for centuries, co-operating with their neighbours, as a working part of southern Somali society. This society is characterised by unity in diversity (see for instance Helander 1996 and 2003, and Lewis 1994) and this, as has been pointed out more than once, must be the basis of any future Somali state.[3]

Odaweyne and Begedi

I shall discuss two groups. Firstly, the Odaweyne (or Adawiin); these are the main Gibil Cad lineage of the Geledi clan, who live in and around Afgooye town. Secondly, the five Gibil Cad groups of the Begedi, who live about 30 kilometres downstream in the town of Awdheegle and the surrounding villages; these are the Aba Jibil, Aba Saad, Quriile, Quraabane (or Uraabane), and Reer Cumar (the last a very small group).[4]

There is some dispute as to whether the Quraabane are really Gibil Cad or not. They are often listed as one of the *Lix Aw Cadde*, the 'Six [sons] of Father [or Sir] White' among the Mirifle (*Aw* in the region is a term of respect for a senior man, especially but not necessarily a man of religion). The name might suggest that this grouping of clans are also Gibil Cad, but this does not appear to be the case; I have not found any suggestion that the other five—the Barbaari,Yantar, Heleda, Dawani and Awrlabe—have this sort of origin.[5]

The position of the Gibil Cad in these two clans is rather different. Among the Begedi they are dominant, and probably outnumber the Gibil Madow, who are said to be much reduced in population. They do not have any special collective religious status, though they have a tradition of religious learning, and there are important individual sheikhs among them. On the other hand the Odaweyne are in the minority among the Geledi and traditionally had little political power, but compensated for this by their important religious role. They are by ascription *mashaikh* or *culimmo*, men of religion.

The Odaweyne are divided into five sub-lineages. Two of these, Maxaad and Xuseen, have a close association with one of the main Gibil Madow lineages, the Abiikarow, for whose religious life they are especially responsible—they are their sheikhs. 'We were small in number and robbed by other tribes, till Abiikarow became our protector.' On the other hand it was the supernatural protection given by the Odaweyne that, according to legend, saved the Abiikarow from a mysterious curse that was killing all their young men, and has safeguarded them ever since. An Odaweyne should lead the prayers after a sacrifice or at a reconciliation ceremony. An Abiikarow marriage should be performed by an Odaweyne sheikh, or else, it is said, the bride will be barren or have no sons. The Odaweyne declare the right time to begin sowing, and are experts in astrology. When there is a sacrifice, they say what the animal should be, and of what colour. They are said to live around the edges of the town so that their sheikhs can keep vigil and guard the town against intruders by reading the Qur'an. For three centuries the Odaweyne, from father to son, have provided the muezzins for the mosque in their quarter of the Afgooye (interview with Axmed Baaxuur Axmed, Afgooye 22 October 1989; see also Luling 2002: 105).

While the principal religious leader among the Geledi is the Sheikh or Suldaan, who belongs to the Gibil Madow Gobroon lineage, he combines religious and political roles and the rest of the Gobroon are not *culimmo*. The Odaweyne on the other hand have their separate spiritual role.

In both Geledi and Begedi clans, the Gibil Cad and Gibil Madow live in close cooperation, but there is also a certain distrust as well as respect on the side of the Gibil Madow, and the two by tradition do not intermarry, though this rule is no longer always kept.

Origins and immigration

The representatives of these groups are clear that when they arrived in Somalia they joined the Gibil Madow lineage groups who were already there. In the case of the Begedi, these were the Hubsame, Hamaale, Jeedo and Maatiro. It is agreed that these groups, who say that they came from the Buur Hakaba area, were the original Begedi, and the earlier occupants of the site beside the Shabeelle, though they are now much reduced. They include members who are Jareer or 'Bantu' (Maxamed Xassanow Awale, telephone interview, February 2009). The Gibil Cad arrivals became incorporated with them by pact and alliance, in the way which is normal among the Digil-Mirifle clans. Moreover some of these Gibil Cad lineages are themselves composites, formed by the adoption of other lineages. The Aba Saad for instance contain the Dheegle, Arfaale, Reer Xaaji and Reer Sadiiq sublineages, and according to one account, the real Aba Saad were the Dheegle, and they adopted the other two: the Arfaale and Reer Xaaji are said to have originated from the Eelay, or else from the Ajuuraan (interview with Maxamed Abukar Cali, November 2004).

Among the Begedi lineages, the Aba Jibil and Aba Saad (with the now extinct Aba Abaa and Aba Hiya) are said to be the first to have arrived on their present site; the Quriile, Quraabane and Reer Cumar came later. According to one tradition, the original four were either sons or descendants of Sheikh Wahiib bin Imaam Cali Ba Sa'ad, from Arabia. They were sent in search of their father Wahiib's brother Ba Qaadi who had gone to the land of the Ethiopians, *Bilad al Habasha*—at that time the name would have included what is now Somalia. They came to Mogadishu, and in the end they found their uncle living in a village on the banks of the Shabeelle. As the soil there was fertile they eventually settled there, and the land was named after Ba Qaadi (Cabdulasis Muumin Mayow, interview, London 23 March 2008). Each lineage however has its own tradition of origin, which does not necessarily agree with the above.

Aba Jibil. The Aba Jibil trace their origin to Haji 'Abdirahman bin Mu'awiye bin Sufyan of the Quraysh. Many generations after his death, the descendants of Haji 'Abdirahman emigrated to Hadhramaut in Yemen where they settled in the town of Tarim.[6] Some of the the Aba Jibil, who have moved to Moyale on the Ethiopia-Kenya border as coffee traders, still keep contact with those of Tarim, but those who live by the Shabeelle have lost contact, and see themselves simply as Somali. From Tarim a man named Maxamed bin Sadiiq migrated to Mogadishu accompanied by his six sons, who were all traders and also preachers of Islam. The party landed in the quarter which is now known as Xamar Jabjab ('Broken Xamar') because it was later abandoned and became a ruin, but which at that time was flourishing. By one account this was in the fifth century AH (12th century CE); according to another, given to Maxamed Ibraahim Cumar by Aba Jibil elders in Somalia, it was in 800 AH, i.e. about 1400 CE. It is said that they had never intended to stop in Somalia; they were headed for Zanzibar, but their ship was wrecked on the coast near Xamar Jabjab. The people there asked them what they wanted to do, and were told, 'We know about farming and the Qur'an.' They told them that if they wanted land to farm, they need go no further as there was land available, and pointed in the direction of Afgooye.

As they moved inland, the Aba Jibil were approached by the Geledi and the Biimaal who, having seen them reading by their camp fire, wanted to know if they could teach them magical arts, but they replied that they could teach them the Qur'an, nothing else. But the religious learning of the Aba Jibil was—according to this account—rejected by the Geledi and the Biimaal. However, the news reached the Garre, who were at war with the Geledi and Biimaal, and the next day their representatives too arrived. They offered them a place to live, and asked them what knowledge they had. 'We know how to grow sesame and lemons.'[7] Thereupon the Garre and the Aba Jibil made a pact which continues to this day. The Garre said they would become their *amaan* (security), to defend them if they were attacked. In return, the Aba Jibil taught the Garre the Qur'an. In addition to their pact with the Garre, the Aba Jibil allied themselves with the Begedi Gibil Madow lineages, Hubsame and Hamaale, who were already living by the river. Their settlement at Bariire became a centre of learning, so much so that up to 70 or 80 years ago people came from Ethiopia and the Ogaden to study there (Maxamed Ibraahim Cumar, interview, Manchester November 2004).

Aba Saad, The name of the Aba Saad is said to be derived from their ancestor Sheikh Wahiib bin Imaam Cali Ba Sa'ad bin Saciid. Whereas the previous story tells how his sons set out in search of their uncle, another tradition asserts that it was he himself who who passed through the Bab al Mandab to the northern Somali coast where some say that his ship was wrecked. He went on to Harar, and then on to Waajid, and the kingdom of the Gasaara Gudda in Raxanweyn country (Hassan Mohamed 2003). Sheikh Wahiib married a daughter of the Gasaara Gudda Suldaan. His eldest son, Maxamed, got his nickname Awoow Dheegow or Dheegle from his mother, and the town of Awdheegle, where he is buried, is named after him. Some of the descendants of Aw Dheegle, the Axmed Maxaad, moved to Geledi where they were welcomed by the Reer Nuur and Reer Sharif of the Odaweyne, and the two groups intermarried (Cabdulasis Muumin Mayow, interview, London 9 February 2008).

Quriile. According to the elders of the Quriile, they first migrated from Medina to the cities of Mukalla and Tarim in Yemen, where they became rich and owned numerous properties. However, about AH 775 (CE 1373) a dispute arose between them and the rulers of Yemen. As a result of this a man named Aw Faqi Abiikar left the country, together with his three sons Maxamed Faqi, Sadiiq Faqi and Cumar Faqi, his daughter Caasho Faqi, his slaves, and as much of his wealth as they could carry. They arrived in Mogadishu and settled in Xamar Jabjab, where their descendants lived for about a century. Aw Faqi's daughter Caasha married their Qu'ranic teacher, Macalin Cumar Makaram, who was from the Mirifle. The Reer Cumar lineage are their descendants. Aw Faqi Abiikar and his three sons died and were buried in Xamar Jabjab. However, the country suffered from a succession of famines in which the family of Aw Faqi were reduced to begging and many of them died. Finally in about 875 AH (1470 CE) the survivors left the coast and migrated inland to the river, where they initially settled at Mareerey. There they lived until about 1175 AH, i.e. some time in the 18th century CE. They next migrated to Jowhar Awdheegle (not the Jowhar in Middle Shabeelle) and from there they moved out to found or occupy other villages (Suldaan Buube Suldaan Abdulle, 2008).

Odaweyne. The Odaweyne trace their origin to Iraq, where they say their tribe were the Bawazir (the ministerial tribe), responsible for religious affairs. Beyond this their genealogy goes back to the Prophet's grandfather, 'Abd al-Muttalib. Their ancestor Khadar is supposed to have emigrated from Iraq during the 'Abbasid period.[8] Khadar's son Cali is said to have joined the Geledi at a time when they were living in Gedo, long before they reached their present site. The Odaweyne therefore migrated with them.

The story tells how they discovered the river where they were to settle. There was a white she-camel which used regularly to escape, and they noticed that she was thriving when the other livestock were short of water. Her owner followed her tracks and so found the river. The Odaweyne say that it was their ancestor Cali, son of Khadar, who owned the camel, which he had brought from his home in Kufa near

Basra. (On the other hand the Gibil Madow Gaalabax lineage say that the owner was their ancestor.)[9]

I have no doubt that these accounts of origin in the Arab world are ultimately based in fact, however many legendary elements have become attached to them. I believe these traditions are not simply to be dismissed, but need further investigation.

Cutting the trees, bringing civilisation

An important element in all the stories of settlement is the cutting of the trees and clearing of the bush on the river bank to open it for farming. Before that, at least in the view of the settlers from Arabia, much it was a pathless wilderness full of dangerous wild animals: crocodiles, lions, snakes, hippopotami and elephants. In addition there were the *Jinn* who haunted it, and the sorcery (*sixir*) practised by the people who lived there. 'At that time,' at least according to some people, 'if you tried to cut a tree the axe would jump back and cut you—that was the *Jinni*' (Khadiija Baale, interview, Afgooye, August 1989). So the settlers in cutting down the trees believed that they were bringing—as well as agriculture—civilisation and true religion instead of dangerous occult forces and magical practices.

For instance, Maxamed al Sacadi 'Dheegle' was reported to have been the first to cut the trees and clear the land around Awdheegle, the town which is named after him and where he is buried, and also around other villages such as Jowhar, Malable and Mubaarak. Because of this he is called 'Aw Dheegle Geed-gooy', 'the tree cutter' (Cabdulasis Muumin Mayow, interview, London, 24 March 2008).

In the tradition of the Odaweyne, Cali Khadar, after following his camel and finding the site where the settlement of Baalgurey (part of Afgooye town) now stands, started to cut down the trees there. In one story, he made some great *Mukay* trees move from one side of the river to the other, hence his *nanays* (nickname) 'Aw Geedo-Guuris', Father Tree-Mover (Khadiija Baale, interview, Afgooye, August 1989). Others say he took his stick and drew a circle round Baalgurey to protect it from the *Jinn* and other dangers. Hence he is also called '*Cali Khadar carrada jiidow*', which means 'Cali Khadar who drew a line on the ground' (from a *shirib*[10] verse sung in 1989).

Having cleared the ground, these immigrants became important as farmers, for introducing new crops. The Aba Jibil are noted for cultivating sesame, maize and lemons; we have seen that they are said to have introduced themselves to the emissaries of the Garre by saying 'We know how to grow sesame and lemons' and a verse says: '*Aba Jibil liimo ku bartay*' ('The Aba Jibil were left with their lemons'). They traded sesame to Ethiopia, to Moyale, from where they brought coffee in return—some of them still live there (Maxamed Ibraahim Cumar, Manchester November 2004). The Odaweyne on their side say they were the first to introduce white sorghum, which their ancestor Khadar brought from Basra (Axmed Baaxuur Axmed, interview, 22 October 1989).

This view of themselves as a civilising force is an important part of their shared consciousness, and the same go-ahead attitude continues into modern times. There was for instance Xaaji Mayow Cumar Iikow of Bariire village (1888–1953) who under the British Administration had the first telephone line in the area installed. The same thing is strikingly expressed by Suldaan Buube Cabdulle (Quriile), in his description of development in the village of Dar es Salaam:[11]

> It seems to us that these people are more civilised than the other people who live with them. This can be seen from the progress that has been made by the village where they live, in that they have a Middle School and an Agricultural High School. They also have a Health Centre, with electricity and clean water. At present it is the only place in Lower Shabeelle Region with showers. In religion too they are far in advance and are famous. It is the only place where one can find 300–400 girls who know the Qur'aan and Tafsiir, and who all graduated together from the Middle and High Schools. They are also far in advance in agricultural production. The village has an NGO called Aw Faqi, named after Aw Faqi Abiikar. It is this that has brought the progress of the village, and at present it is taking steps to extend this progress to the whole of Awdheegle district. There are also offices of two of the largest telecommunications firms in the country (Buube 2008).

This is a remarkable though not unique example of how economic and cultural life has managed to flourish in Somalia in spite of the violence. It is also characteristic in its association of social progress and religious learning. It is noteworthy that the NGO is named after the ancestor of the lineage.

Notable men

The Odaweyne and the Begedi Gibil Cad have contributed their share of outstanding figures to the history of this part of Somalia; I shall deal with only four of them.

Sheikh Axmed Maxamed Aweys Baaxuur 'Darawushow'. Sheikh Axmed, born in 1878 (Cabdulasiis Muumin Mayow 2009) was one of a remarkable family, and his story really begins with that of his father Maxamed Aweys Baaxuur. Maxamed had, though not intentionally, killed a man from another branch of the Odaweyne, in a family dispute over land triggered by their wives, and he was ceremonially executed as Geledi law of that time permitted. The family of the dead man could have chosen to forgive him, but were implacable in demanding revenge.[12] His old father Aweys offered to take his place, but Maxamed refused; he said that he did not want the women singing as they pounded their maize to mock at his daughter Faduma. Bathed and dressed in his formal white cloth, he walked out to the cemetery of the Odaweyne, where he showed his slaves where to dig his grave. He had asked that only one particular friend, Aw Cadow, accompany him, and hold a cloth before his body in case he should be seen to flinch. He prayed and lay down on a *jimbaar*—a hide-covered bench—and was dispatched in the customary way by a blow to the back of his neck; Aw Cadow reported that he had not moved (Caasha Abukar Qaasim, 13/7/09). This was in 1890 (Mayow 2009), with the Italians already in Mogadishu; his son Axmed was 12 years old.

I owe the following account to Sheikh Axmed's grandson Axmed Baaxuur Axmed (interview, Afgooye, 22 October 1989) and to the document written by Cabdulasiis Muumin Mayow (Mayow 2009), drawing on the memories of his mother, Aisha Xaaji Axmed, who is Sheikh Axmed's daughter. After his father's death, and perhaps out of reaction to it, Axmed Maxamed at 16 went abroad. He had already been an exceptionally promising student; and he now went to learn in Egypt, Turkey, Iraq and other countries. His studies are said to have included science, mathematics, the religious sciences and astronomy. He brought back many books, and became famous as a teacher. But by this time the Italians were consolidating their power in Mogadishu and beginning to move inland. The Geledi Suldaan and most of the influential people in his community showed themselves ready to do a deal with the foreigners, but many among the Odaweyne were opposed to any compromise. They had heard of the great Sheikh in the north who was battling against the Europeans, and Axmed with five friends set out to join Sayid Maxamed Cabdille Xassan at Taleex.

Axmed and his friends fought as part of the Dervishes, and their group, it was reported, was always victorious. Axmed was the most learned among them and directed them to read appropriate verses of the Qur'an, which helped to account for their success. Later, because of his knowledge of the stars, he was appointed as astrologer to the Sayid (the Odaweyne generally are noted as astrologers).

When in 1908 the Dervishes came down the Shabeelle, attacked Balcad and got as far as Lafagaale, Axmed was with them. Because of this some of the Geledi—who were in general hostile to the Dervishes and saw them simply as northern invaders (Luling 2002: 31)—accused him and his companions of treachery; however, they maintained they never would have fought against their own clan.

Subsequently, the Sayid ordered Sheikh Axmed and his companions to leave and go south to continue the fight against Italy. They took 'rifles, ammunition and white horses' (few other Somalis at that time had guns) and became a guerrilla force. 'Meeting in various places, attacking at unpredictable times, the Dervishes sustained their resistance in the Benadir' (Cassanelli 1982: 214 and 245, drawing on information from Baaxuur Xaaji Axmed, 17 May 1971). In the end however they were forced to surrender: 'they rode into Mogadishu on their white horses' (Axmed Baaxuur Axmed) and gave themselves up. Thanks to the intercession of a friend, a Qadi, who had influence with the Italians, they were released after 90 days, but within a year were arrested again, because they had started inciting the people against the *Colonia*—forced labour on the Italian-owned plantations.

They were exiled to Kismaayo, which as his grandson pointed out was a completely foreign place to Axmed. However, he received support there, especially from the Bajuni, and became prosperous and opened a school. He returned in secret after seven years, when he heard his beloved son had died of smallpox. He came at night to his house, without reporting to the Governor, thus breaking the terms of his exile. Someone—not Odaweyne—reported this, and again he was arrested, but his relatives pleaded with the authorities, explaining the circumstances, and he was finally released. In his later years he remained an influential teacher.

Sheikh Axmed died at the age of 84 in 1962, having lived long enough to see the independence of Somalia. He had returned from his time with the Dervishes able to speak the northern dialect, and to recite the Sayid's poems, which he passed on to his family.

Axmed's resistance, like that of his leader, was justified in religious terms. But with independence, as the Sayid was made into a hero of nationalism, the authorities attempted to do the same with Axmed. Under Siyad Barre, his son Baaxuur was called to the Presidential Palace to tell his story. A street in Mogadishu was named after him, and the revolutionary government proposed to do the same in Afgooye, and to erect a monument to him—presumably one of those *taalooyin* that used to be a feature of Mogadishu. But Baaxuur refused to allow this, as being contrary to religion. To him, as no doubt to Axmed himself, such a thing would have been idolatrous—that was not what he had fought for. But Axmed's grandchildren, when they were taught the poems of the Sayid as part of their school curriculum, knew them better than their teacher did.

Sheikh Cabdullahi Begedi, Ustaad Cismaan and the HDMS. In the run-up to independence in 1960 two conceptions of the Somali state developed, which have been at odds ever since. One is the project of a unified, centralised state, which was associated with the Somali Youth League (SYL) and later with the 'revolutionary' regime of Siyad Barre. The other envisioned a federation, and is mainly associated with the Digil-Mirifle agricultural clans. In fact several prominent members of these clans were founder members of the SYL in its early days, but they came to feel that it was being taken over by representatives of the clans whose roots are pastoralist, principally the Darood. Hence they formed their own party, originally the HDM, 'Hizbia Digil Mirifle' ('the Digil Mirifle Party'). The original name did not include 'Somali', for the southern clans had not called themselves by that name (though foreigners did). Later 'Somali' was added, and in 1956 it was changed to 'Hizbia Dastur Mustaqil Somali' ('Somali Independent Constitutional Party'), abbreviated HDMS (or XDMS after the introduction of the new script) to avoid the imputation of 'tribalism'. However it remained 'Hizbia' to its supporters. Though accepting the nationalist project, the HDMS believed that the only way to protect the interests of its people was by a federal state.

While the memory of Sheikh Axmed, though not the man himself, was being co-opted into the nationalist, centralising project, his kinsmen and students were taking the lead in arguing for federalism. His student and son-in-law Sheikh Cabdullahi Sheikh Maxamed, known as 'Sheikh Begedi', became the Chairman of the HDMS. Sheikh Begedi (1908–81) is remembered with respect and affection by those who knew him. An eloquent politician, 'he used words that moved the heart'.

He was kind and courteous, full of humour, and 'would talk even to a small boy without patronising him' (Cabdulasis Muumin Mayow, interview, 2 January 2009).

In January 1948, Sheikh Begedi headed the HDM delegation to the Four Power Commission appointed by the United Nations to investigate before they decided on the future of Somalia. This was his testimony before the Commission:

We are called the Digil Mirifle. [...] We live in that part of Italian Somaliland which is more comfortable and fruitful than the rest, and we can produce all sorts of food in this place, maize and bananas. We always resist it when other people wish to make trouble or rob. Where we live there is no thieving or robbing.

I wish to request three things: (a) We wish to have peace and security. (b) Secondly we want the country in which we live to be always regarded as belonging to us, and if the government wishes anything from us, we want it to be discussed. (c) The other people who are not Digil Mirifle may live and stay with us, but we want them behind us, recognising the land as belonging to us and not to them (15th Hearing of the Four Power Commission, quoted in Salah Mohamed Ali 2005: 417–18).

Sheikh Begedi and his associates travelled the length and breadth of the Digil and Mirifle land, Baay. Bakool, Gedo, and Lower Jubba in order to unite the people under the banner of the Hizbia. Because of this political activity, he in his turn was exiled by the Italians from Afgooye to Kismaayo (where he married) but returned after independence.

One of his colleagues was Ustaad ('Teacher') Cismaan Maxamed Xuseen, who was Odaweyne (from the Nuur sublineage, whereas Axmed Darawushow was Xuseen). His father went on the *Xaaj* through Yemen, and decided to stay there. He married a Dhulbahante woman, and Cusmaan was one of their children, born in Aden. He studied in Aden, and learned French in Djibouti as well as Arabic and English, and was a schoolteacher. On his return to Somalia, be became one of the founding members of the HDMS. He became an MP in the National Assembly before independence, but in 1956 he was assassinated, the night before he was due to fly to New York to address the United Nations Trusteeship Council's meeting on Trust Territories. Nobody was ever arrested, but it was thought that elements in the SYL were responsible, and Cismaan's relatives and colleagues have no doubt of it. There are people who are said to know the names of the assassins (Cabdulasis Muumin Mayow, letter, April 2009; Dr Axmed Yuusuf Caliow, interview, 17 February 2008; Caasha Abukar Qaasim, interview, 13 July 2009). He too, like Axmed Darawushow, had a street in Mogadishu named after him.

Sheikh Begedi's son Maxamed Sheikh Cabdullahi became a general in the national army, and several other men of this background played a significant part in public life after independence, for instance Sheikh Cabdi Bariire (Aba Jibil) who was one of the first governors of the Central Bank and built the bridge at Bariire village.

The situation today

The Begedi Gibil Cad lineages and the Odaweyne have suffered like the rest of their communities from being under the control of the clan militia of the Habar Gidir. According to a Begedi (Aba Saad) man in London in 2004: 'We are a colony. People can't talk. All is controlled by the Habar Gidir, under the local warlord "Indha Cadde". Anyone who talks they kill. Even here in London, if they hear I talk, they could kill my brother out there. They confiscate what you grow—if you are taking tomatoes etc. to market they take more than half. They take the girls away by force. You have to pay to use the river water. We are like the Reer Hamar in Mogadishu—they say "You are foreigners".'

The situation is illustrated by an anecdote told (in English) by a young Odaweyne man (name withheld for his safety):

> One of the mornings in May, 2002 I was on my way to Mogadishu. There were a lot of checkpoints in between Afgooye and Mogadishu manned by Habar Gidir militia to extract money from passing vehicles. As we drove toward Mogadishu, the driver spent all the money on the checkpoints and unfortunately one checkpoint was ahead of us before reaching Mogadishu. There was notorious Habar Gidir Militia on that certain Checkpoint, the driver begged passengers to contribute some cash. After having reached the checkpoint, the conductor paid contributed money to the gunmen at checkpoint. To my surprise, they refused to accept it saying that the cash is not enough. Afterwards, they threatened to rob the passengers, but their commander said, 'We confiscate those three Gibil Cad men seated back there as a mortgage'. We were three boys, one Abaa Jibil, one Shariif Odaweyne and one Dheegle. But there were 20 passengers in the van.We were taken to a certain location nearby; our relatives heard the news about our abduction and paid a ransom of (less than $100 US) in the same day. The sole reason why we were targeted was only the colour of our skin. We were Gibil Cad!

This commander's action probably reflects the stereotype that the Gibil Cad are rich. But in spite of all this harassment, as we have seen, some of them have organised aid and educational projects.

Recently this control has passed to the Islamist groups Al Shabaab and Hiszbul Islam, who have to some extent absorbed the earlier militias. It is too early at the time of writing, and also too potentially dangerous, to comment on this complex situation as it affects the Begedi and the Geledi and the other peoples of the Shabeelle, including their Gibil Cad members. Some reports indicate that the oppression and targeting of the minority groups continue even under the so-called Islamic militias (US Department of State 2009).

Meanwhile many of the Begedi and Geledi Gibil Cad form part of the Somali diaspora, especially—building on their tradition of learning—its more educated portion. Among them are engineers, businessmen and doctors. This element in southern Somali society, who have so far received little attention from students of Somalia, have made a significant contribution to its history, and are likely to continue to do so.

Notes

1. For the sake of consistency I continue to used the terms 'lineage' and 'lineage group' as I did in my former work on the Geledi (Luling 2002), following the usage of anthropologists like Lewis and Helander. 'Sub-clan' is often used today by other writers to refer to the same groups.
2. On all these movements see Hersi (1977). Note that the genealogies of these groups *do not* link up with the Somali 'total genealogy'.
3. Editors' note: on this issue see also Mukhtar in this volume.
4. There are no population figures for these groups, but on the available evidence I am talking about not more than about 20,000 people. There are said to have been earlier Begedi Gibil Cad groups who have died out: the Aba Hiya (from Aba Yahya), Aba Abaa (=Aba Abakar), and Genden.
5. This is the list supplied to me by Abdi Mohedin of Somali Human Aid (email 10/7/2009). It differs from those given by Maxamed Abdi Maxamed (1984, IV: 964) and Colucci (1924: 103). These agree on the Barbaari, Yantar and Heleda, but the former then gives Qurbo Labow and Goohiyow, and the latter the Gibile and Goolkullaba (the last is probably the same word as Qurbo Labow).
6. Maxamed Ibraahim stated that he had travelled to Yemen, and confirmed this with informants belonging to a branch of the lineage who live near the town of Hodeida. According to them the emigration was 'in the time of Ibn Battuta', i.e. the 14th century CE. However, Hersi (1977: 236) says that the main migration to Somali from the Hadhramaut (before the 19th century) was in the 16th century CE.
7. The word *liimo* actually can refer to any citrus fruit.

8. This is the genealogy as it was dictated to me in 1989 by Axmed Baaxuur Axmed; the earlier part was written in the Qur'an inherited from his great-great-grandfather Aweys. 'Axmed–Baaxuur–Axmed 'Darawushow'—Maxamed–Aweys (the writer of the genealogy from this point)–Baaxuur–Maki–Jibriil–Xuseen–Odaweyne (ten generations)–Maxamed–Cali–Khadar (12 generations.)' The remainder of the genealogy goes back through a further 20 generations to 'Abd al-Muttalib.
9. A more detailed account is in Luling (2002: 104–5, 275).
10. *Shirib* is a type of extemporised verse chanted at certain festivals (Luling 2002: 243–8).
11. It used to be called Danyeerey, 'Monkey Place', which suggests the former wildness of the area. It is not surprising that its inhabitants prefer the new name. The change encapsulates the transition from 'jungle' to civilisation.
12. According to my informants Caasha Abukar Qaasim and Cabdulasiis Muumin Mayow, he chose death rather than pay a very heavy *diya* which would have ruined his family. This conflicts with my other information that *diya* was not exacted within the Geledi community—the choice was between free reconciliation and the exaction of the death penalty (Luling 2002: 187).

References

Cabdulasiis Muumin Mayow 2009. *The Biography of Haji Ahmed Mohamed Aweys Bahur*, WP document, August 2009.

Cassanelli, Lee V. 1982. *The Shaping of Somali Society; Reconstructing the History of a Pastoral People 1600–1900*. Philadelphia: University of Pennsylvania Press.

Colucci, Massimo 1924. *Principi di Diritto Consuetudinario della Somalia Italiana Meridionale*. Florence: Società Editrice 'La Voce'.

Hassan Mohamed Ahmed Turki, WP document 2003.

Hersi, Ali A. 1977. 'The Arab Factor in Somali History.' (unpublished doctoral dissertation, University of California, Los Angeles)

Lewis, Ioan M. 1994. 'From Nomadism to Cultivation: the Expansion of Political Solidarity in Southern Somalia.' In I.M. Lewis, *Blood and Bone, the Call of Kinship in Somali Society*. Lawrenceville, NJ: The Red Sea Press.

——— 1994 [1955]. *Peoples of the Horn of Africa*. London: Haan.

Luling, Virginia 2002. *Somali Sultanate; the Geledi City State over 150 years*. London/New Jersey: Haan/Transaction.

Mohamed, Mohamed A. 1990. 'La Somalie aux hautes périodes (De l'Antiquité à l'avènement de l'Islam) Vols I,II,III,IV.' (Unpublished dissertation, Université de Franche-Comté)

Reese, Scott 2008. *Renewers of the Age; Holy Men and Social Discourse in Colonial Benaadir*. Leiden/Boston: Brill.

Salah, Mohamed Ali 2005. *Huddur and the History of Southern Somalia*. Cairo: Nahda Bookshop Publisher.

Suldaan Buube Suldaan Abdulle of the Quriile, WP document, 9/09/08, with information from his father Suldaan Xaaji Abdulle Buube (90 years) and Xaaji Maxamed Mahday (86 years)

US Department of State 2009. *2008 Human Rights Reports: Somalia*. Online at http://www.state.gov/g/drl/rls/hrrpt/2008/af/119001.htm [accessed 25.08. 2009].

PART VIII

LANGUAGE

18

THE STRUCTURE OF COORDINATION IN SOMALI

Annarita Puglielli

Introduction

There are a number of different conjunctions in Somali, and this is striking since many languages show just one for each semantic type. This is the case for both English and Italian, where *and/e* are used for conjunction, *or/o* for disjunction and *but/ma* for adversative meanings. From a syntactic point of view *e* and *and* can join together any type of constituent:

1) a. John is going to London and Mary is going to Paris.
   b. I am going, and what about you?
   c. Jane will go to the meeting and speak to the students.
   d. John and Bill are good friends.
   e. Give back to John the grey book and the red one.
   f. The grass must be cut next to the well and under the olive tree.
   g. The book that you gave me and I have just finished reading is very interesting.

More examples could be given with other types of constituents. What is important for us to show is that independent of the type of element conjoined, the English conjunction is always *and*.

In Somali, on the contrary, we find a number of different conjunctions, that is, more than one for each semantic type:

conjunction	disjunction	adversative
-na 'and'	*ama* 'or'	*-se* 'but'

oo	'and'	*mise?*	'or'	*laakin*	'but'
ee	'and'				
iyo	'and'				

Assuming that economy is one of the basic principles of language organisation, it becomes an important issue to understand the possible differences between the various conjunctions and eventually to what extent these differences correlate with typological characteristics of this language. The present analysis is limited to conjunctions, and in order to understand the phenomena related to complex sentences, it is first necessary to examine rapidly some of the characteristics of sentence structure in Somali relevant to coordination.

Main properties of Somali

Simple sentences. The basic characteristic of the sentence (S) is the presence of a verbal complex (VC) that can be considered as a 'micro-structure of the whole sentence' (Puglielli 1981: 15). In the VC in fact all the predicative elements are present, as well as as the clitic resumptive pronouns related to the Noun Phrases (NP), selected by the verb that are 'dislocated' (that is, they do not occupy the argument position in the syntactic structure). All the elements present in the VC are disposed in a templatic structure shown in Table 1:

Table 1

impersonal SUBJ CL *la*	one Obj cl	Preps	Obj cl	deictics	some adverbials	Verb
		(2 at most)	(poss. pron.)	*soo/sii*	of place/ manner	

Consequently, NPs that are external to the VC, and occur in *extrasentential* position, have free order.[1] Here are some examples:

(2) *Axmed baa gurigii [nooga (= Ø+na+u+Ø+ka) soo qaadáy]*
Axmed FM house.AN OCL3SG-OCL1PL-for-OCL3SG-from take.PST.RED[2]
'Axmed took it from home for us'

(3) *Xaawo baa [igu (i+ku) kaa aamintáy]*
Xaawo FM OCL1SG-to you (lit.: your) entrust.PST.RED
'Xaawo entrusted me to you'.

Notice that third person object clitics have no phonetic realisation, but as they have a referential meaning they are always recoverable, no matter where the coindexed NPs occurs. In fact for a sentence like (2) we could also have these alternative orders of constituents:

(2) a. *Axmed baa nooga soo qaaday gurigii*
b. *Gurigii Axmed baa nooga soo qaaday.*

This means that NPs are realised in extrasentential position and associated with a specific discourse value, i.e. they have the value either of Topics (as *gurigii*) or Foci (as *Axmed*).[3] This leads us to say something about the discourse configurational characteristics of this language.

In a simple declarative sentence Somali must have either a focalised NP (4a-b) or a Declarative Marker (5).

(4) a. *Nimanku* *HILIBKA* *bay* *cunayaan*
men.DET.NOM meat.DET.NONNOM[4] FM.SCL3PL eat.PRES.PROG.3PL
'The men are eating the meat'.

b. *NIMANKA* *baa* *hilibka* *cunayá*
men.DET FM meat.DET.NONNOM eat.PRES.PROG.RED.
'The men are eating the meat'.

In (4a) *hilibka* is an NP marked by *baa*, and is therefore signalled as new information; note that the Focus Marker that marks the object is accompanied by the subject resumptive clitic *ay*. In (4b) it is the NP subject *nimanka* that is marked by *baa* as the Focus in the sentence. We thus have the so-called antiagreement effect: the NP, traditionally considered subject of the sentence, does not show Nominative Case, and there is no agreement between the subject and the verb (that shows the reduced paradigm). In a sentence like

(5) *Cali* *Maryan wuu/waa* *arkay*
Cali Maryan DECL.SCL3M/DECL see-PST.3SGM
'Cali saw Maryan'.

There is no focalised NP, but the marker *waa*—placed at the beginning of the VC—tells us that the sentence is a declarative one, and in absence of a focalised NP the informative part of the sentence is the VC (Frascarelli and Puglielli 2007).

The main constraint on Somali word order is imposed by the focused constituent; it must be left adjacent to the Focus Marker *baa/ayaa* and the two together must precede the VC. All other NPs—that are

Topics—can occur either to the right or to the left of the focused NP and the VC. The following sentences are all grammatical except (6d) where NP *baa* follows the VP:

(6) a. *Nimanku* *HILIBKA* *bay* *cunayaan*
men.DET.NOM meat.DET.NONNOM FM.SCL3PL eat.PRES.PROG.3PL
'The men are eating THE MEAT'

b. *HILIBKA* *bay* *cunayaan* *nimanku*
meat.DET.NONNOM FM.SCL3PL eat.PRES.PROG.3PL men.DET.NOM
'The men are eating THE MEAT'

c. *HILIBKA* bay nimanku cunayaan
meat.DET.NONNOM FM.SCL3PL men.DET.NOM eat.PRES.PROG.3PL
'The men are eating THE MEAT'

d.* Nimanku cunayaan HILIBKA bay.[5]

On the other hand, an NP Topic cannot occur in between *waa* and the VC as shown in (7), whereas *Soomali* can occur in all positions except the one just mentioned:

(7) *(Soomaali)* *Cali (Soomaali)* *waa (*Soomaali)* *ahaa (Soomaali)*.
Somali Cali DECL be.PST.3SG
'Cali was a Somali'

Word order with the aforementioned exceptions is free, but from a typological point of view, Somali has always been rightly considered an SOV language, that is, a verb final language with the subject-object order as the unmarked one.

One more structural fact of Somali, relevant for coordination, is the status of constituency at the syntactic level. The fact that more elements belong to a single syntactic constituent is explicitly shown, since several morphological markers occur only once and at the end of the given constituent. As a consequence these elements constitute a useful test for constituency. Here is some evidence:

I. The Nominative Case Marker occurs only once in an NP subject, independent of its internal structure, and is realised as the rightmost suffix:

(8) a. *Ninku* *waa* *yimid*
Man.DET.NOM DECL come.PST.3SGM
'The man arrived'

b. *Wiilkaaganu* *waa* *yimid*
boy.POSS2SG.DEM.NOM DECL come.PST.3SGM
'This boy of yours has come'

c. [*wiilka aan af Talyaaniga ku hadlini*] *waa*
boy.DET NEG language Italian.DET in talk.NEG.NOM DECL
walaal-kay
brother-POSS1SG
'The boy that cannot speak Italian is my brother'.

II. The FM *baa/ayaa* marks the NP to its left and can only occur at the end of it:

(9) a. *Cali* [*adiga*] *buu ku dilay*
Cali you FM.SCL3M OCL2SG hit.PST3SGM
'Cali hit YOU'

b. *Cali* [*Maryan (*buu) walaalkeed*] *buu dilay*
Cali Maryan brother-POSS3F FM.SCL3M hit.PST.3SGM
'Cali hit MARYAN'S BROTHER'

c. *Cali* [*nin ka (*buu) Xamar ka yimid*] *buu dilay*
Cali man-DET Xamar from come.PST.3SGM FM.OCL3M hit.PST.3SGM
'Cali hit THE MAN WHO CAME FROM XAMAR'.

Complex sentences.

Polysynthetic languages have fewer types of embedded clauses than other types of languages; in particular they lack non-finite clauses such as infinitivals, gerundives and participials (Mithun 1984).

The same is true of Somali which does not have non-finite clauses, and where finite subordinate clauses do not belong to the complement type introduced by a complementiser (such as *that* in English) . All subordinate clauses, including adverbial ones, have the syntactic structure of a relative clause; in other words they occur as modifiers of a head noun within an NP. Furthermore, the relative clause in Somali belongs to the head-deletion type, that is, it is not introduced by a complementiser, nor is the NP heading the clause resumed by any type of relative pronoun:

(10) a. *Wiilka* [*Maryan la hadlayaa*] *waa walaalkay*
Boy.DET.M Maryan with talk.PRES.PROG.RED.NOM DECL brother-POSS.1SG
'The boy (who is) speaking with Maryan is my brother'.

b. *Mooska* [*aad cunaysaa*] *waa ceerin*
banana.DET.M SCL2SG eat.PRES.PROG.2SG DECL unripe
'The banana that you are eating is unripe'.

The same is true in sentences like:

(11) a. [*Goorta qorraxdu dhacdó*] *imaw*
Moment-DET sun-DET.NOM set.DEP come.IMP
'When the sun is setting, come'.

b. [*Sida* *Axmed* *uu* *oonayó*] *ereyga* *u* *qor*
way-DET Axmed SCL3SGM want.DEP.PROG. word.DET to write.IMP
'Write the word *as* Axmed wants'.

The clauses in brackets interpreted as adverbial clauses have the noun + modifier structure; the nominal nature of *goor* and *si—the heads—is* in fact unquestionable, since they co-occur with determiners, demonstratives etc. This means that the relevant clauses are included within the NPs or, in other words, that sentential subordination is realised as *nominal subordination*. This property is also true for sentences like:

(12) *in* *lacag* *ah* *I* *sii*
part/thing money be.PRES.3SG OCL1SG give.IMP
'Give me some money'. [lit.: 'give me the thing that is money']

This means that completive clauses also have the structure of relative clauses. This has been proved true on the basis of morphosyntactic evidence (Antinucci 1981) as well as on the basis of intonational properties (Frascarelli and Puglielli in press and Frascarelli and Puglielli 2009b).

A final consideration should be made regarding the structure of relative clauses, which from a semantic point of view can be divided into *restrictive* and *appositive* according to their function in respect to the noun they modify. In particular restrictive relative clauses provide a reference value for the head noun and are therefore necessary for interpretation, while appositives only supply additional information and are therefore considered 'circumstantial elements'.

In Somali appositive relative clauses are introduced by a specific morpheme, namely *oo*; note the contrast in (13 a-b):

(13) a. *Wiil-kaas* [*Maryan* *la* *hadlayaa*] *waa walaal-kay*
Boy-DEM.M Maryan with talk.PRES.PROG.RED.NOM DECL brother-POSS.1SG
'That boy that is speaking with Maryan is my brother'

b. *Wiilkaas* [*oo Maryan la hadlayaa*] *waa walaal-kay*
'That boy, who is speaking with Maryan, is my brother'.

In (13a) the clause in brackets is necessary for the identification of the referent of the NP *wiilkaas*, while in (13b) *wilkaas* is independently identified within the context of discourse and the relative clause introduced by *oo* gives additional information (about that boy). The same is true in a sentence like:

(14) *Iyada* *(oo* *isbitaalka* *ku* *jirtá)* *ayuu* *dhintay*
She CNJ hospital.DET in stay.PRES.RED FM.SCL3M die.PST.3SGM

'He died while she was in hospital' (lit. he died she being that was in hospital).

This example shows that the appositive relative clause in brackets modifies the NP *iyada* and forms with it an NP with adverbial function within the main sentence. The NP is focalised by *ayaa* on which the resumptive subject pronoun is cliticised.

We shall now conclude this brief description by focusing on the relevant structural differences between main clauses and relative clauses. It is only in a main clause that a Sentence Marker like *waa* or a focalised NP can occur. According to generative linguistic theory, the syntactic structure of a sentence includes a 'left periphery' where functional categories related to the 'grammar of discourse' such as *Topic* and *Focus* are present (Rizzi 1997).

But there are differences in the 'left periphery' of main sentences and relative clauses. In a relative clause structure we cannot have a Focus category nor a Sentence Marker, but of course we can find NPs that are Topics,[6] and as we shall see this has an impact on other aspects of syntactic structure in Somali.

Given what we have said about subordination in Somali we reach the conclusion that coordination assumes a fundamental role in the production of complex sentences, and this becomes particularly evident in the written language.

Coordinate structures

Coordination has an extremely important role in the construction of complex sentences and paragraph organisation; here we will try to describe its main mechanisms, given that a detailed description of its syntactic and semantic aspects is beyond the aims of this work.

In fact there are many questions that a detailed description should answer:

- which type of constituent can be joined?
- are there restrictions on coordination between sentences given the specific typological characteristics of this language? For example the presence of a VC or the necessity of discourse markers such as Declarative or Interrogative Markers, Focus Markers and so on;
- given that there are specific characteristics with respect to the order of constituents (as a relatively free order for Topic NPs within a S),

are there restrictions in this respect when we join two sentences in a coordinate structure?

– what are the conditions that allow deletion of equivalent elements in coordinate sentences?

We could add more questions, but in this context we shall limit ourselves to some of these; we will then try to describe the basic mechanism of coordinate structures in Somali.

Given the basic structure described we expect coordination to be possible between Ss, NPs and VCs, but if we go back to our initial list of conjunctions we have three of them—*ee, oo,—na*—to coordinate Ss and one—*iyo*—for NPs (Gebert 1981b, Saeed 1999). There is no specific word to coordinate VPs, and in fact VP coordination implies S coordination; when we find two joined VPs (with finite verbs in them) there is always an underlying deleted subject, and this means that in fact there are two Ss joined together even if in the surface structure only the VP of the second sentence is present:

(15) a. *Cali baa cunáy, cabbáyna*
Cali FM eat.PST.RED drink.PST.RED.CNJ
'CALI ate it and drank it.'

b. *Cali wuu cunay wuuna cabbay.*[7]
Cali DECL.SCL3M eat.PST.RED DECL.SCL3M.CNJ drink.PST.3SGM
'Cali ate it and drank it.'

Let us start our description considering NP coordination.

Nominal coordination

Iyo is the conjunction used with Noun Phrases. Here are some examples where each NP has a different function within the sentence and a different internal structure:

(16) a. [*Maryan iyo Faadumo*] *way yimaadeen* (NPsubj+ NPsubj)
Maryan CNJ Faadumo DECL.SCL3PL arrive.PST.3PL
'Maryam and Faadumo arrived'

b. [*Geri iyo libaax*] *baan arkay* (NPobj.+NPobj)
Giraffe CNJ lion FM.SCL1SG see.PST.1SG
'I saw A GIRAFFE AND A LION'

(17) a. [*Waalashay iyo saaxiibkeed*] *baan la kulmay*
Sister.POSS1F CNJ friend.POSS3F FM.SCL1SG with meet.PST.1SG
'I met with my sister and her friend'

b. [*Maryan ninkeeda iyo Axmed walaalkiis*] *warshadda*
Maryan husband.POSS3F.DET CNJ Axmed brother.POSS3M factory.DET

sonkorta bay ka shaqeeyaan
sugar.DET FM.SCL3PL at work.PRES.3PL
'Maryam's husband and Axmed's brother work at the sugar factory'

c. *Gabadha yar iyo wiilka dheeri*] *way yimaadeen*
Girl.DET small.RED CNJ boy tall.RED.NOM DECL.SCL3PL come.PST.3PL
'The small girl and the tall boy came'

d. [*Wiilka jidka ordayá iyo wiilka wargeyska*
Boy.DET street.DET run.PRES.PROG.RED CNJ boy.DET newspaper.DET
iibinayá] *waa saaxiibbo*
sell.PRES.PROG.RED DECL friend.PL
'The boy who is running in the street and the boy who is selling newspapers are friends'.

In these examples the two joined NPs have the following structures: in (17a) there is a head noun plus a possessive, in (17b) the head noun is modified by another noun, while in (17c and d) the head nouns are modified by relative clauses (Antinucci 1981). It is therefore evident that NPs can be joined by *iyo* independent of their internal structure and syntactic function.

From a syntactic point of view the two joined NPs form one constituent. As we know, in Somali, Case Markers occur only at the end of the marked constituent. This is exactly what happens in (17c) where the Nominative Case Marker *-i* occurs on the last element—a relative clause modifier—of the marked NP, or in a sentence like

(18) a. *Buugagga iyo qalinku miiska way saaran yihiin*
Book.PL.DET CNJ pencil.DET.NOM table.DET DECL.SCL3PL stay.PRES.3PL
'The books and the pencil are on the table'

b. * *Buugaggu iyo qalinka.........*

c. * *Buugaggu iyo qalinku.........*

Here the NOM *-u* appears only on the second NP while the first shows the unmarked (Non-Nominative) Case. This morpho-syntactic property allows for a clear identification of the right boundary of NPs and gives us clear indications about the internal structure of coordination. In fact this kind of data shows that two joined NPs are included in a 'bigger NP' and that within this structure the rightmost NP is syntactically the most embedded one (Frascarelli and Puglielli 2009a: 40). It should be noted that this analysis applies even in a complex NP with a relative clause, a type of nominal modifier that is rarely marked for Case in the languages of the world.

One more fact demonstrates that the structure NP *iyo* NP is one constituent. When two joined NPs are focalised, the FM *baa/ayaa* can only occur once and at the end of it:

(19) a. *Naag iyo nin baan la kulmay*
woman CNJ man FM.SCL1SG with meet-PST.1SG
'I met a woman and a man'

b. * *Naag baan iyo nin ....*

Sentence Coordination. We will split our analysis into two parts; first we will examine the coordination between root clauses and then coordination of subordinate clauses, i.e. relative clauses, since as we have already said, all subordinate clauses in Somali are syntactically modifiers of a head noun. For simplicity we will use the term sentence coordination for the first case, and clause coordination for the second.

Coordinated sentences.

In Somali there are three different conjunctions used to coordinate sentences: *-na, ee*, and *oo*. Since from a semantic point of view there are no differences—they are all used with the same meaning ('and')—we expect to find differences at other levels of organisation of the language, for example at the syntactic and/or pragmatic level. And in fact we will show that the three conjunctions have a different distribution and therefore the Somali system is not as redundant as it may appear.

On the basis of what we know about the structure of Somali and the structure of coordination in general, there are a number of facts to be investigated:

- possible restrictions with respect to the co-occurrence of focalised constituents and Sentence Markers in the second S,
- restriction on the relative order of constituents in the two combined Ss,
- possibility of deletion of identical constituents in the two sentences and relative consequences on what can be left.[8]

Given the impossibility of a complete description in this context, we will try to provide the basic characteristics and differences in this system of conjunctions.

-Na is used to link two Ss of the same illocutionary type—two declaratives, two imperatives etc—cliticised on the first constituent in S2:

(20) a. *Xasan wuu dheer yahay, Calina wuu gaaban yahay*
Xasan DECL.SCL3M tall be.PRES.3SGM Cali.CNJ DECL.SCL3M small. be.PRES.3SGM
'Xassan is tall and Cali is small'

b. *Cali wuu cunay, wuuna cabbay*
Cali DECL.SCL3M eat.PST.3SGM DECL.SCL3M.CNJ drink.PST.3SGM
'Cali ate it and drank it'

c. *Faadumo baa caano cabtay, Maryan baana rooti cuntay*[9]
Faadumo FM milk drink-PST.3SGF Maryan FM.CNJ bread eat.ST.3SGF
'Faadumo drank milk and Maryan ate bread'

d. *Cali shineemada buu tegay, aniguna guriga*
Cali cinema.DET FM.SCL3M go.PST.3SGM I.NOM.CNJ home.DET
'Cali went to the cinema and I went home'.

In (20a) the two Ss are simply joined together, in (20b) the subject of the second S, *Cali*, has been deleted and therefore *-na* is cliticised on the constituent that has become the first (*wuu*) and in (20c) *-na* is on the focalised subject of S2 and as expected on *baa* (the last element of the first constituent). Finally in (20d) it is the verb that has been deleted in the second sentence and *-na* is on the NP subject; note that the FM that we would expect on the object of S2 is not present, nor can it be (**Cali shineemada buu tegay, aniguna guriga baan*). This shows that the FM even if structurally part of the NP, is linked to the VP (Svolacchia, et al. 1995).

There are no syntactic restrictions relative to the distribution of Sentence Markers and/or FM in the two sentences:

(21) a. *Aniga baa buug soo gatay Cali waalalkiis baanna siiyay*
I F book buy.PST.3SGM Cali brother.POSS3M FM.SCL1SG.CNJ give.PST.1SG
'I bought a book and gave it to Cali's brother'

b. *Wiilkaas baa yimid gabadha agtaada joogtayna way tagtay*
Boy.DEM FM arrive.PST.3SGM girl.DET near.POSS2SG stay.PST.3F.CNJ DECL.SCL3SGF go.away.PST.3SGF
'That boy arrived, and the girl that was near you went away'

c. *Cali wuu seexday, Xasanna Jamacadda buu aaday*
Cali DECL.SCL3M sleep.PST.3SGM Xasan.CNJ university.DET FM.SCL3M go.PST.3SGM
'Cali slept, and Xasan went to the University'

d. *Cali wuu yimid Xasanna arkin muusan*
Cali DECL.SCL3M arrive.PST.3SGM XASAN.CNJ SEE.PST.NEG NEG.SCL35GN.NEG
'Cali came and Xassan did not see him'.

In these sentences we have FMs on NPs with different functions (21a), the presence of FM in one sentence and a Sentence Marker in the other with inverted orders in the two Ss (21 b-c), and the presence of two Sentence Markers (21d). In conclusion we can join with *-na* any two declarative sentences and there are no syntactic restrictions in relation to the distribution of FMs and DECL Markers.

As we expect, however, there are differences in the semantic interpretation with regards to the connection between the two linked sentences. And in fact in a sentence like:

(22) *Dugsigii baa la xirayaa, fasaxiina wuu*
school.AN FM IMPERS close.PRES.PROG.3SGM holidays.AN.CNJ DECL.SCL3M
bilaabmayaa
start.PRES.PROG.3SGM
'The schools are closing and the holidays are starting'

the two events are interpreted as sequential. We do not have the same degree of acceptability for a sentence like:

(22) a.?? *Dugsigii baa la xirayaa, fasaxii baana bilabmayaa*

with the NP *fasaxii* marked by the FM *baa* that would produce a contrastive reading (less acceptable given the semantic content of each sentence). But a detailed semantic analysis is beyond our aim.

Deletion can take place if there are two identical constituents. This is exemplified by:

(23) a. *Cali baa albaabka xiray, Xasan baana furay*
Cali FM door.DET close.PST.3SGM Xasan FM.CNJ open.PST.3SGM
'Cali closed the door and Xasan opened it'

b. *Jidku waa fiican yahay, waana toosan yahay*
Street.DET DECL good be.PRES.3SGM DECL.CNJ straight be.PRES.3SGM
'The street is good and straight'

where we have two identical objects and two identical subjects respectively.

Let us now consider the following sentences:

(24) a. *Maryan baa timid, kuna aragtay*
Maryan FM come.PST.3SGF OCL2SG.CNJ see.PST.3SGF
'Maryan came and saw you'

b. *Cali albaabka buu xiray, Xasanna furay*[10]
Cali door-DET FM.SCL3M close.PST.3SGM Xassan.CNJ open.PST.3SGM
'Cali closed the door and Xasan opened it'

and compare them with the ungrammatical

(25) * *Cali baa albaabka xiray, Xasanna furay.*

We must conclude that a focalised NP in S2 can be deleted only if the coreferent NP in S1 is also focalised.

There are some restrictions regarding the relative order of the constituents in the two joined sentences, when the order of constituents is not the same. This complex topic, however, will not be explored here.

Summing up, *-na* is mainly used to coordinate two sentences of the same type, where deletion operates when two constituents referentially identical and with the same function are present. This conjunction must be cliticised on the first constituent of the second sentence.

The conjunction *Ee* is also used to join two independent sentences, but let us see what type of sentences:

(26) *Waan ducaysanayaa ee Ilaahow iga aqbal!*
DECL.SCL1SG pray.PRES.PROG.1SG CNJ God.VOC OCL1SG-from accept.IMP
'I am praying, and oh God accept it from me!

(27) *Boostadii waa tan ee warqaddan dir!*
Post-office.AN DECL DEM CNJ letter.DEM send
'This is the post office and (then) send this letter'

(28) *Cali keligiis ma ahayn ee Maryan ayaa la socotay*
Cali alone.POSS NEG be.PST.3SG.NEG CNJ Maryan FM with follow.PST.RED
'Cali was not alone, and Maryam followed him'

(29) *Xasan caanihii buu cabbay ee hilib ma cunin*
Xasan milk.AN FM.SCL3SGM drink.PST.3SGM CNJ meat NEG eat.PST.NEG
'Xassan drank the milk and didn't eat meat'.

In not one of the above sentences can *ee* be replaced by *-na*; if it is, we get ungrammatical sentences. The same ungrammatical result is obtained if we take away the Negation Marker from (28–29). In all these examples the complex sentence is formed of two sentences that belong to different types: in (26–27) a declarative and an imperative sentence are joined together, while in (28–29) one is an affirmative and the other is a negative sentence.

Ee is then used to join two sentences with a different illocutionary force: in fact a declarative sentence is used by the speaker to give information, while an imperative one is used to request an action from the listener. The difference between the two speech acts is evident; the case in (28–29) may appear less evident in that we usually consider both to be declarative sentences with different polarity. In an affirmative sentence the speaker informs the listener about a certain 'state of affairs', but in a negative one he has a different communicative intention. In fact he is either answering a previous affirmative statement or contradicting a presupposition (that is, an expectation shared by speaker and hearer). We must therefore come to the conclusion that even in this case we are dealing with two different speech acts.

There are other contexts where *ee* can be used:

(30) a. *Caasha baa seexatay ee Cali wuu shaqeeyay*
Caasha FM sleep.PST.3SGF CNJ Cali DECL.SCL3M work.PST.3SGM
'Caasha slept and Cali worked'

b. *Cali baa saaxiibkiis la hadlaya ee Maryan bariis*
Cali FM friend.POSS with talk.PRES.PROG.RED CNJ Maryan rice
way karinaysaa
DECL.SCL3F cook.PRES.PROG.3SGF
'Cali is talking to his friend and Maryan is cooking the rice'.

In both sentences we have a different distribution of the informative value in the two coordinated sentences; in the first the subject NP is focalised—hence it is the new information—while in the second we have a Declarative Marker that makes the predicate the relevant information.

Note that a change in this respect, such as a FM on the subject of the second sentence as well, would result in an ungrammatical sentence:

(31) * *Caasha baa seexatay ee Cali baa shaqeeyay.*

To join the two sentences in (31) we would have to use *-na*.

We could add more examples to show that when a different distribution of the elements that carry the informative value in the two sentences creates a semantic contrast between the two sentences, the use of *ee* is required. It thus becomes an interesting issue for linguistic theory to understand the relationships between different speech acts and a different distribution of the informative values ('given' vs 'new' information) in coordinate sentences.

The conjunction *Oo* is the last one that we find in Somali which can join two independent sentences:

(32) a. *Cali wuu cunay oo wuu cabbay*
Cali DECL.SCL3M eat.PST.3SGM CNJ DECL.SCL3M drink.PST.3SGM
'Cali ate it and drank it'

b. *Cali warqad waa qoray oo Xassan wuu akhriyay*
Cali letter DECL write.PST3SM CNJ Xassan DECL.SCL3SGM read.PST.3SGM
'Cali wrote a letter and Xassan read it'.

The presence of a Declarative Marker in each sentence shows that *oo* can join two independent sentences; notice, however, that both in (32a) and (32b) a deletion of an NP has taken place. Furthermore a sentence like the following would be ungrammatical:

(33) * *Cali wuu cunay oo Caasha way cabtay.*[11]

Therefore, in order to use *oo* there must have been a deletion of a coreferent NP in the second sentence. Why should this be so?

Our hypothesis is that the origin of this type of coordinate structure lies in the fact that relative appositive clauses in Somali are introduced by *oo* and can be extraposed, i.e. separated from their head noun and put at the end of the sentence after the VC of the main sentence. A sentence like:

(34) *Cali baabuurkii oo aad ka jebisay buu soo iibiyay*[12]
Cali car.AN CNJ SCL2SG break.PST.2SG FM.SCL3SGM buy.PST.3SGM
'Cali bought the car that you broke'

can alternatively have the form

(35) *Cali baabuurkii buu soo iibiyay oo aad ka jebisay*

Now let us examine the following sentence:

(36) *Aniga baa imanayá oo hadiyad keenayá*
I FM arrive.PRES.PROG.RED CNJ present bring.PRES.PROG.RED
'I am arriving and bringing a present'.

This could be interpreted as being formed by two coordinate independent sentences with FM on the subjects, the second being deleted. But (36) could also be the result of extraposition of a relative appositive clause on the head noun subject of a simple sentence:[13]

(37) *Aniga oo hadiyad keenayá baa imanayá*
I CNJ present bring.PRES.PROG.RED FM arrive.PRES.PROG.RED
'I, that I am bringing a present, am arriving'.

In fact the function of a modifier within an NP and the necessity of an NP coreferent with the head noun in the clause is enough evidence to consider '*oo hadiyad keenayá*' a relative clause, if we keep in mind the structural characteristics of relative clauses in Somali. On the other hand, an appositive relative clause is additional information with respect to the head noun and it does not have the same function as restrictive relatives that are used for referential identification of the noun; this is explicitly shown by the presence of *oo*.[14]

When *oo* is used to join two independent sentences, it maintains as one of its restrictions the need for deletion of an NP, and this demonstrates its correlation with relative clause structure. Therefore a structure of this type has probably started as an extraposed appositive relative clause and has been later reanalysed as an independent main clause. As a result the clause introduced by *oo* in the complex sentence has recovered all the necessary characteristics of an independent sentence, that is, the presence, in order to be grammatical, either of a Declarative Marker or of a Focus Marker. This is clearly shown in written texts, as illustrated by the following example:

(38) *(Xabbad) waa la necbaa oo [ceelasha lagu cabbo buu]*
Xabbad DECL IMPERS hate CNJ wells IMPERS.from drinks FM.SCL3SGM
[dhardhaar weyn oo isaga mooyee aan cid kale
stone big CNJ PRO3M.NONNOM except NEG person another
qaadi karin] ku gufeyn jirey
lift can.NEG up plug use.PST.3SGM
'(Xabbad) was hated and he used to block up the wells that one drinks from with a large stone that nobody but him could lift' (Xaange 1988: 42).

This is the structure of this sentence:

(38')

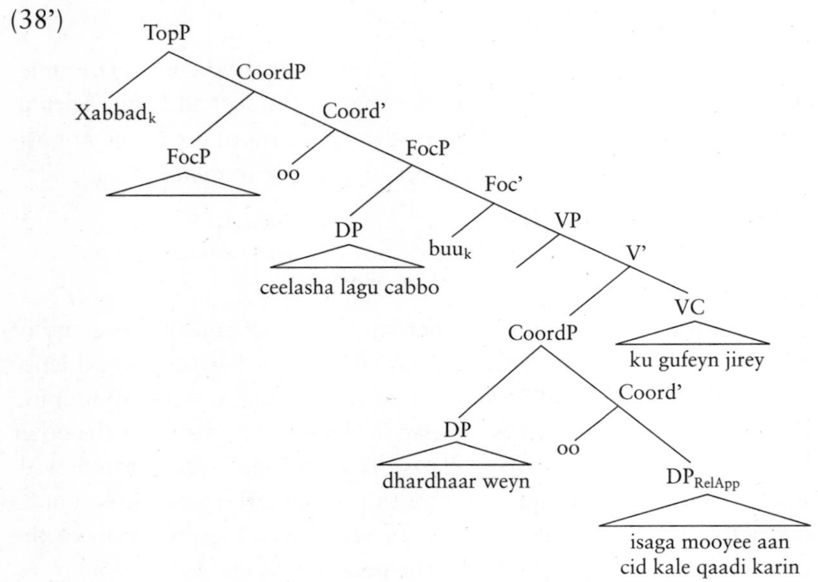

In conclusion, the three conjunctions used in Somali to coordinate sentences appear to be in complementary distribution, and therefore their use is differentiated.[15] The main features that characterise each of them are: *-na* is less restricted in occurrence and joins two sentences belonging to the same illocutionary act, *ee* can only join sentences with different illocutionary force (i.e. two different speech acts) or different information-structural values, and *oo* can join a second sentence to a main sentence provided that there has been the deletion of an NP (which therefore must be coreferent to an NP in the main sentence). We will comment further on the consequences that this has on syntactic structure at the end of this paper.

Clause coordination refers here to those structures where two sentences are joined and they both modify a noun; in other words they are constituents inside an NP. We are referring to NPs with a complex structure in which modifiers that can be nominal or clausal are present (Gebert 1981a). We will consider cases where we find two modifiers and therefore we can expect a possible coordinate structure depending on the internal structure of the NP.

In the following sentences:

(39) a. *Dhismaha ururka shaqaalaha waa fiican yahay*
Structure.DET union.DET workers.DET DECL good be.PRES.3SGM
'The organisation of the workers' union is good'.

b. *Shirweynaha xisbiga sanadkan bishay waa*
conference.DET party.DET year.DEM started.PST3SGM DECL
fiican yahay
goodbe.PRES.3SGM
'The conference of the party that started this year is good.'

we have an NP with the following nested structure:

$[_{NP} N \; [_{MOD} X \; [_{MOD} Y]]]$

where X is the first element that modifies the N that is the head of the whole NP, and Y is an element that in turn modifies X. In (39a) X and Y are both NPs, but in (39b) the first modifier is an NP which is modified by a restrictive relative clause.[16] In sentences like

(40) a. *Xasan baa dukaanka dharka ee Cali ka shaqeeyá*
Xasan FM shop.DET materials.DET CNJ Cali at work.PRES.PROG.RED
'Xasan is working at Cali's materials shop'

b. *Shirweynaha xisbiga ee xarunta Xamar ka dhacay*
conference.DET party.DET CNJ site.DET Xamar take.place.PST.RED
waa fiicnaa
DECL good be.PST.3SGM
'The conference of the party that took place in Xamar was good'

The NP object in (40a) and the NP subject in (40b) both have a complex structure with a head noun and two modifiers. The second of them is introduced by the conjunction *ee* and its function is to modify the head noun exactly like the first one. Therefore we have a structure where two joined constituents modify the same head: [N [X *ee* Y]]. Once again the two constituents may be either two NPs (as in (40a)), or an NP and a relative clause (as in (40b)).

Two more observations should be made. First, the NP with the above structure constitutes a single constituent as shown by Case marking:

(41) a. *Gabadha yar ee qurxooni waa Soomaali*
Girl.DET small.RED CNJ beautiful.RED.NOM DECL Soomaali
'The beautiful small girl is Somali'

b. * *Gabadha yari ee qurxoon waa Soomaali*

Note that, as usual, the Nominative Case must occur at the end of the complex NP.

The second modifier is introduced by *ee* independent of its structure (NP in (40a) and S in (40b)). From a semantic point of view the two joined modifiers are used together to identify the referent of the head noun; this means that the relative clause introduced by *ee* is a restrictive relative clause.

As we might expect there are NPs where the second modifier, a relative clause, has an appositive meaning. In this case the relative is introduced by *oo* as in (42):

(42) *Cali baabuur fiican oo duq ah buu soo gatay*
Cali car good.RED CNJ old be.PRES.RED FM.SCL3SGM buy.PST.3SGM
'Cali bought a beautiful and old car'(lit. a car that is beautiful and that is old).

The use of *ee* vs *oo* to introduce the second modifier within the NP structure is therefore determined by the restrictive *vs* appositive value of the relative clause they introduce.[17]

We could give further syntactic evidence in support of the proposed analysis: for example the different possibility of co-occurrence of elements used for identification of the referent of the noun and different articles (Ø, *ka*, *kii*), the role and position of NOM Case marking in the different contexts and the possibility of extraposition for appositive clauses, *vs* its impossibility for restrictive relatives. This however is beyond the scope of this paper.

Conclusion

We have attempted to show that the different conjunctions *-na, ee, oo*, and *iyo* have a distribution that is basically different, and are therefore used in different contexts with different syntactic restrictions. We would like to conclude with some remarks on what we can deduce from the Somali data on the syntactic structure of coordination in general and the implications for the linguistic theory on this matter. Finally, we will examine a very short Somali text to focus the role of coordination.

Given the facts that we have been observing, it seems feasible to state that coordination can operate at different levels of the syntactic structure. Coordination can put together two independent main sentences that at a syntactic level of description we generally call declarative, interrogative, imperative, exclamative. Each syntactic type, however, correlates with a different speech act that has a different pragmatic function or illocutionary force: assertion for declarative, request of information for interrogative and so on. This pragmatic information that relates to the communicative aim of the speaker has also recently been introduced in the syntactic formal representation of each sentence, and corresponds to the highest part of the structure of a sentence (Puglielli and Frascarelli 2008). Therefore if a conjunction joins two sentences with different pragmatic value, it means that that constituent joins two Illocutionary Force Phrases each of which dominates the respective sentence.[18] This is precisely what *ee* does.

Going down the structure we find that it is possible to coordinate two sentences that are governed by a single speech act and therefore the pragmatic value of the two sentences is one and the same. *-Na* is used in this part of the structure, as well as *oo*, but with the aforementioned syntactic restrictions.

We find the last possibility of coordination very low down, in that part of the structure of the sentence where the semantic propositional content is represented by the predicate and its arguments. The arguments, which are NPs, are the constituents that can be coordinated using *iyo*.

So far the general picture; let us now look at the other contexts where recursion allows the presence of coordinate structures, that is, within the NP structure where relative clauses are present. The previous observations about coordinate syntactic structures and their semantic and pragmatic values make it easy to understand why, given the typological characteristics of Somali, a relative clause with an appositive value is introduced by the conjunction *oo*, and it does not make any difference if the appositive relative is the only modifier or the second of two on the same head noun.

The use of *ee* to coordinate two modifiers on the same head noun—independent of their being two NPs or an NP and a restrictive relative clause—seems to be related to the fact that the two elements are structurally parallel and, even more important, have the same function (that is, the referential identification of the head noun).

We mentioned at the beginning that coordination is particularly important for text organisation. We will try to demonstrate this with a very short citation from an article by Axmed F. Cali 'Idaajaa', *Afsoomaaliga & Warfaafinta Maanta* (manuscript), where we will highlight conjunctions in bold and underline NPs with relative clauses:

(43) '*In kastoo*[19] *aanu maanta lahayn dawlad u xilqabata, isla markaas***na** *aanu jirin guddi* **iyo** *hay'ado* u gaar ah **oo** *dibudhacii kolba uu muto ka samatabbixiya* ***am****aba lagala xisaabtamo, haddana afsoomaligu wuxuu weli inaga mudan yahay inaynu sidan u dhaanno*!'

'Though today it [the Somali language] does not have a government/state that is responsible for it and though a commission or a particular institution that could save it from the decay that sometimes it encounters or could testify for it does not exist, now the Somali language deserves to be treated better than we are doing.'

We have purposely produced a literal translation that is as near as possible to the Somali text. Many interesting facts about these phenomena could emerge from an extensive analysis of written texts, and this is a topic that deserves further research.

Notes

1. Within a formal Generative approach, this property has led Svolacchia and Puglielli (1999) to consider Somali as a polysynthetic language (following

Baker 1988), that is, a language in which the assignment of θ-roles is possible only for clitics incorporated onto the verbal head. As a result NPs are never assigned θ-roles directly, and occur in dislocated position with a resulting free word order.

2. Abbreviations: AN = anaphoric article, CNJ = conjunction, DECL = Declarative Marker, DEM= demonstrative, DET = definite article, F = feminine, FM = Focus Marker, IMP = imperative, IMPERS = impersonal clitic, M = masculine, NEG = negation, NOM = Nominative Case, NONNOM = Non-Nominative Case, OCL = object clitic, PL = plural, POSS = possessive, PRES = present, PROG = progressive, PST = past tense, RED = reduced paradigm, SCL = subject clitic, SG = singular, VOC = Vocative Case.
3. The notions of Topic and Focus relate to the informative value that different elements in a sentence can have. As is well known, Topics relate to given information, while a focused constituent represents the new information.
4. Somali marks all objects with the same Case marking, which is distinct from NOM Case. This is why we prefer to indicate it as 'Non-Nominative'.
5. The asterisk is put in front of a sentence when it is not grammatical.
6. A detailed description of these aspects can be found in Frascarelli and Puglielli (2005a).
7. Note that in (15a) the subject *Cali* with *baa* has been deleted, and in (15b) the deletion of the Declarative Marker *waa* is not possible:* *Cali wuu cunáy, cabbáyna*. This is an interesting fact that can be explained.
8. This list is not intended to be exhaustive since there are more facts relevant to a full description of coordination.
9. Note that a preferred form for this sentence would be with the inversion of subject and object in the second sentence and *-na* enclitic on *rooti* rather than the focalised subject.
10. Sentences with this structure are not considered perfectly grammatical by some speakers who prefer: *Cali albaabka buu xiray, Xassanna wuu furay* with the presence of a DECL Marker in the second sentence.
11. In a S like (33) we can only use -na to join the two constituent sentences.
12. For a detailed description of relative clause construction see Antinucci (1981), Gebert (1981a), Frascarelli and Puglielli (2005a).
13. The possibility of extraposition is not possible in languages like English or Italian when the relative appositive is introduced by a complementiser rather than by a conjunction; a sentence like *John is arriving soon, that is late, becomes acceptable if we transform the subordinate clause into a coordinate: John is arriving soon, and he is late.
14. The different value of the two types of relative clauses is also shown by the different determiners with which they can co-occur: the anaphoric kii–tii can be followed only by a relative introduced by oo, i.e. appositive ones.
15. There is sometimes some overlapping, for example Saeed (1999) gives some examples of *-na* used to join an affirmative and a negative sentence.

A more detailed description should in fact be based on an extended analysis of texts.

16. The structure this time is [N [NP [S]]] where the relative clause—S—is needed to identify the referent of the NP xisbiga, and NP + relative clause, which are one constituent, modify the head noun and identify its referent.
17. Note that the use of *oo* is always linked to the presence of a clause (i.e. a sentential structure) and it can never occur when the second modifier is an NP.
18. The formal representation of these structures is normally given in terms of a tree structure where the different levels of the elements/constituents involved are made evident.
19. This expression is now lexicalised, but it clearly originates as an NP plus an appositive relative clause.

References

Antinucci, Francesco 1981. *Tipi di frase*. In A. Puglielli (ed.) *Sintassi della lingua somala* (Studi Somali 2). Rome: Ministero degli AA.EE, pp. 219–95.

Baker, Mark 1988. *Incorporation. A Theory of Grammatical Function Changing*. University of Chicago Press.

Frascarelli, Mara and Annarita Puglielli 2005. 'A Comparative Analysis of Restrictive and Appositive Relative Clauses in Cushitic Languages.' In L. Brugè, G. Giusti, N. Munaro, W. Schweikert and G. Turano (eds) *Contribution to the IGG XXX*. Venice: Cafoscarina, pp. 307–32.

——— 2007. 'Focus in the Force-Fin System. Information Structure in Cushitic Languages .' In E. O. Aboh, K. Hartmann and M. Zimmermann (eds) *Focus Strategies in African Languages. The Interaction of Focus and Grammar in Niger-Congo and Afro-Asiatic*. Berlin/New York: Mouton de Gruyter, pp. 161–84.

——— 2009a. 'Somali in a Typological-Comparative Perspective: from Data to Theory.' In A. Puglielli (ed.) *Lessons in Survival: the Language and Culture of Somalia. Thirty Years of Somali Studies*. Turin: Harmattan Italia, pp. 30–58.

——— 2009b. 'Information structure in Somali: Evidence from the Syntax–phonology Interface.' *Brill's Journal on Afroasiatic Language and Linguistics*, 1: 146–75.

Gebert, Lucyna 1981a. 'Il sintagma nominale.' In A. Puglielli (ed.) *Sintassi della lingua somala* (Studi Somali 2). Rome: Ministero degli AA.EE, pp. 47–132.

——— 1981b. 'La coordinazione.' In A. Puglielli (ed.) *Sintassi della lingua somala* (Studi Somali 2). Rome: Ministero degli AA.EE, pp. 141–213.

Mithun, Marianne 1984. 'How to avoid Subordination.' In *Proceedings of the 10th Annual Meeting of the Berkeley Linguistic Society*. Berkeley: University of California.

Puglielli, Annarita (ed.) 1981. *Sintassi della lingua somala* (Studi Somali 2). Rome: Ministero degli AA.EE.

Puglielli, Annarita and Mara Frascarelli 2008. *L'Analisi Linguistica. Dai dati alla teoria*. Rome/Cesena: Caissa Italia Editore.

Rizzi, Luigi 1997. 'The Fine Structure of the Left Periphery.' In L. Haegeman (ed.) *Elements of Grammar. Handbook in Generative Syntax*. Dordrecht: Kluwer Academic Publishers, pp. 281–337.

Saeed, John 1999. *Somali Syntax*. London: John Benjamins.

Svolacchia, Marco, Lunella Mereu and Annarita Puglielli 1995. 'Aspects of Discourse Configurationality in Somali.' In K.É. Kiss (ed.) *Discourse Configurational Languages*. Oxford University Press, pp. 65–98.

Svolacchia, Marco and Annarita Puglielli 1999. 'Somali as a Polysynthetic Language.' In L. Mereu (ed.) *Boundaries of Morphology and Syntax*. Amsterdam/Philadelphia: John Benjamins, pp. 97–120.

Xaange, Axmed C. 1988. *Sheekoxariirooyin Soomaaliyeed. Folktales from Somalia*. Uppsala: Somali Academy of Arts and Sciences in Collaboration with the Scandinavian Institute of African Studies.

19

SOMALI (NICK)NAMES AND THEIR MEANINGS

Markus Virgil Hoehne with *Muuse Cali Faruur* and *Axmed Cabdullahi Du'aale*

Introduction

In many societies, names have meanings derived from specific cultural, social, environmental or historical contexts. They relate to specifics of social organisation, belief systems, indigenous knowledge, local events, and so forth. Besides, names often express wishes and hopes of parents for their children, which again are related to social and/or cultural values (Antoun 1968; Sharma 1997–98; Yimam 2006). Nicknames, on the other hand, usually point to particular physical markers, personal traits, quirks or (historical) deeds of an individual (Antoun 1968). Some physical markers are congenital, while others date from events in later life, such as sickness, accidents or violence. Finally, nicknames may indicate the occupation or the place of origin of a person.

In Somali society, two basic categories of personal names can be distinguished: the names given to a person at birth by the father and/or mother (*magac*), and the names given to a person later in life by friends and/or others, which are added as nicknames (*naanays*) to the birth names, and sometimes even replace the latter (Mohamed Abdi Mohamed 1993: 181). Since contemporary Somali society is a Muslim society, many names belonging to the first category, which can be called 'proper names', are Muslim names such as Maxamed, Axmed, Fadumo, or Samsam. This has not always been so. There have been, and still are, Somali names which are of non-Islamic origin. Rather, they are Cushitic and can be understood as 'true' Somali names (ibid. 177). The Somali names, however, have been increasingly marginalised over centuries of Islamisation.[1] Only within the category of nicknames do Cushitic names prevail.[2]

As is well known, the Horn of Africa was the first place where Islam set foot outside the Arab peninsula (during the so called first Hijra of 615, when the Prophet directed some of his followers to seek refuge in the kingdom of Aksum). Urban centres of Islamic learning were established from the 7th century onwards (Trimingham 1952; Hussein Adam, this volume). Yet it took centuries before Islam gained a foothold in the hinterland of the Somali peninsula where pastoral nomads and agro-pastoralists resided. Even then, Sufism, which characterised Somali Islam until recently, was quite tolerant towards pre-Islamic Somali culture and traditions (Lewis 1955). In the late 19th and early 20th centuries, a first wave of 'modern' Islamic reform movements took hold of Somalis and other Muslims in the Horn of Africa. This was related to the advent of 'infidel' colonialists which triggered Islamic self-reflection and sometimes resistance (Cassanelli 1982; Cassanelli, in this volume) culminating, for instance, in the Dervish wars (in the Somali Peninsula) and the Mahdi uprising (in Sudan). These developments were supplemented by increasing urbanisation in the 20th century. Administrative urban centres were established and, at least from the 1940s onward, attracted politicians, businessmen, students and those who wanted to flee the burdensome life in the countryside. In this way Islam, which for centuries had been concentrated in the few centres of Islamic learning in the Horn, such as Harar, Seylac and Mogadishu, reached the masses.

Subsequent experiences of work migration to the Arab Peninsula, and the 'return' to Islam during the Somali civil war and under diaspora conditions (particularly in the West) as an anchor in a 'sea of madness', continued the process. In this context, Somali traditions and culture changed in many ways. Personal names are one aspect of the culture in which changes are clearly visible and traceable.[3] While some changes establish a historical pattern, others can be followed up in our lifetimes. Cabdiraxmaan Faarax Barwaaqo (2008: 113–17) recently pointed to 'new names for girls and the problems with them' (*Magacyada cusub ee hablaha iyo dhibatooyinkooda*). Such new names fancy famous cities such as 'Istaanbuul' or 'Daarasalaam', continents such as 'Afrika' or 'Yurub', currencies such as 'Doollaro','Istaralliin' or

'Ruubliana' or just huge amounts of money such as 'Million'. Some of them relate to migration experiences (or dreams about such experiences) of the parents, or can be read as blessing and expression of the wish to become rich. Certainly, such 'fancy' names may occasionally seem odd and somewhat ridiculous to other people. Barwaaqo has described this as a problem with these new names (ibid.).

This chapter follows a tradition of folklore studies and investigations into Somali society, to which I.M. Lewis (1959) contributed a short piece on the 'names of God in northern Somali', and which was taken up again by Mohamed Abdi Mohamed (1993). Also Cabdiraxmaan Faarax Barwaaqo (2008) has substantially contributed to the research into Somali (nick)names.[4] Yet, as this rather short list of relevant authors indicates, much remains to be done in this field of study. This chapter introduces a number of Somali names and nicknames, and briefly explains their meanings. These meanings testify to the ingenuity and creativity of Somalis and are part of the Somali folk heritage that is both a store of knowledge and an indicator for innovations. Past as well as recent events are integrated and remembered in names, as well as in folktales, poems and songs (Andrzejewski and Lewis 1964; Johnson 1996).

The names presented here are a selection out of a body of about 350 male and 150 female names that have been collected during several interview sessions with Muuse Cali Faruur in Hargeysa in Somaliland between December 2008 and May 2009. Axmed Cabdullahi Du'aale assisted me during the research and participated in all interview sessions. He also helped with the translation of the recorded material. Additionally, a few names were contributed by Cabdi Yere, an informant from Buuhoodle. Yuusuf Shacir, a poet from the Haud region (south of Burco), commented on the list of names we had compiled and suggested some corrections and/or additions. Our research certainly shows a northern Somali and urban (mostly Hargeysa) bias. Many more names and possibly additional or alternative meanings of the same names could have been found if the research had been extended to the countryside and to other regions of the Somali peninsula. Somali names are often related to particular local contexts. Typically for oral societies, the interpretation of their meanings depends on the richness of knowledge and the eloquence of the individual interpreter (in our case Muuse Cali Faruur, who certainly is a great cultural specialist).[5] Therefore, the list below could be expanded almost 'infinitely' in order to cover regional differences and other particularities of Somali names.

Categories of Somali (nick)names and examples

In everyday life, the distinction between Somali names and nicknames is not absolute. During a lecture on Somali poetry in the Maansoor Hotel in Hargeysa, on 9 April 2009, the famous poet Maxamed Ibraahim Warsame Hadraawi came to speak about Somali names. He mentioned that names are simply given by the parents at birth, while nicknames are given later, by the society (friends, others). However, in my view the distinction between the ways in which the names are acquired does not necessarily apply to the names themselves. First, some of the names which today appear exclusively as nicknames (since they are non-Islamic and therefore not acceptable to many Somalis as proper names) may very well have been proper names in the past.[6] Second, some names can clearly be either proper names or nicknames, depending on whether a particular physical marker has been congenital or acquired. The distinction between names and nicknames is clear only in cases where a nickname refers to a physical feature or a personal trait that can only have been acquired in later life, and never at birth. Things become more complicated, however, since Somalis can also inherit the nickname of a forefather. These then may be completely unrelated to any feature or trait of a newborn or adult, but still be used for him (rarely her).

The names and nicknames presented below belong to seven basic categories. They refer, first, to the environment (flora and fauna) and the pastoral-nomadic economy; second, to the time/day of the birth; third, to an event that happened around the time of birth; fourth, to the circumstances of pregnancy or birth; fifth, to the physical features of a person (newborn or grownup); sixth, to an important feature of an individual's character; and finally, to aspects of traditional social order in Somali society. (Nick)names indicating the occupation of a person are absent from the list. They seem to be generally very rare among Somalis and thus do not form a category on their own.[7]

Male (nick)names[8]

1. ***Biciid** waa bahal la qasho oo wayn oo geeso dhaadheer, waa bahalka libaaxuna uu ka baqo ee aanu la dagaalamin, kolkaa biciidow*

maxaa looga jeedaa, waa nin aad u adag oo sida biciidka aan loo dhawaan karin baa laga wadaa.

Biciid is a wild animal [male oryx] which can be slaughtered [and eaten]; it has long horns; the lion is afraid of this animal and does not like to fight with it. [If a man is called] Biciid, what does it mean? It is [the name] of a man who is tough/hard and one cannot come close to him; that is what it means.[9]

2. ***Baanji** ninka la leeyahay, laba siyood baa loo akhriyaa mar waxa la leeyahay reerka waa nin soo galeeti ah oo dhawaan la soo dagay, marna waxa la yidhaahdaa kolka hore ayaa buu ku yimi si aan haboonayn, waa baanji.*

[The name of] the man called Baanji can be understood in two ways: first, it is said somebody came to the family/village and settled there recently; second, it was used for somebody [a baby] who came in an unsuitable way [was born out of wedlock].

3. ***Bulaale** waa nin dheer, oo aad u dheer oo toosan ama dheer, ama xeerka kolka la eego dhaqanka somaliga reerka oo rag hore lahayn ayuu ku soo kordhay oo waa nin aad loogu baahnaa.*

Bulaale is a tall man, a very tall and straight man, and if you look at old Somali culture [Bulaale] was born in a family that did not have male children before; thus, he is a much needed baby [since he will inherit the family property and secure the lineage continuity].[10]

4. ***Barre** wuxuu leeyahay bar madow ama bar cambaar ah oo wajiga kaga taal oo si cad u muuqata ninka Barre la yidhaahdo ama luqunta ha ahaato ama wajiga ha ahaatee bartaasi waa inay meel muuqata ku taalaa.*

[The man called] Barre has a dark spot or some kind of skin infection (e.g. acne) in the face so that it clearly shows up/can be seen. The dark spot must either be in the face or on the neck, but it has to be visible.

5. ***Juujuule** waa nin hadalkiisu isku dhex jiro oo aan la fahmi karin ajajajaja hadalkaanu dadka maqashiin weeye.*

Juujuule is a man who talks with some incomprehensible sounds in-between, like '*ajajajaja*', which cannot be understood by other people (i.e. a stammerer).

6. ***Jinac*** *adduunyada waa ninka u camal xun, waa ninka u camal xun baa la yidhi, marka hore waxa magacaa la yidhaahdaa xayawaan yar oo jinac ah oo madow oo dhulka mara, si kasta ha ahaatee waa nin cadho badan oo cadho is mara.*

Jinac is [the name for] the most ill-tempered man. 'This man is very ill-tempered' is what people say. The name comes from a small and black animal called *jinac* that walks on the floor [a kind of ant]; be this as it may, [Jinac] is a man who is very angry and may even kill himself because of anger.[11]

7. ***Xadeed:*** *waa nin meel ban ah ku dhashay oo bakhaylna ah hadyo goor, waayo banka xadeed la yidhaahdo Laascaanood buu hoos ka xigaa, waa dhawr boqol oo kilo mitir oon biyo lahayn oo aan waxba lahayn, xadeed oo xaga Nugaasha ayuu xigaa.*

Xadeed is a man who was born in the desert and who is always stingy. The desert called Xadeed is south of Laascaanood; it stretches several hundred of kilometres without water or anything. This desert is connected to the Nugaal valley [north of Laascaanood].

8. ***Xoday:*** *waa geed la yidhaahdo xoday oo xooluhu aanay daaqin oo caleen wayn, hadyo goor caleentu way wanaagsan tahay. Xooluhuna ma daaqaan. Way ku dhimanayaan haday cunaan waxbay ku noqonayaan ma cunaan sun baa ku jirtaa, jiilaal kasta haday tahay cuni maayaan. Xoday waa nin dusha ka fiican oo hoostana ka xun.*

Xoday is a tree on which the animals do not graze. It has huge leaves; always its leaves are beautiful. [Yet,] the animals do not graze on it. They would die if they ate [from this tree]; they would get something from it; there is poison in [the leaves]. Even in the dry season they do not eat it. Thus, Xoday is a man who looks good from outside, but is bad inside.

9. ***Xeraad*** *wuxu dhashay iyadoo wax la cunayo. Habeenkii marka la soo hoyda cashada xeraad baa la yidhaahdaa waa xeradii tii lagu soo galay baa la cunayaa, xeriye ama xeraad iyadoo cashadii la cunaayo buu dhashay habeenkii.*

The man called Xeraad was born when [his family] ate something. In the night, when people come home to the camp/house the dinner is called '*xeraad*'. This is what you eat when you enter the camp [*xero* =

encampment/nomadic camp]. The guy called Xeriye or Xeraad was born when his family sat and had dinner at night.

10. ***Dibad*** *waa nin la tuuray oo la dayacay oo dibada la dhigay oo hooyadiiba waxay magaca ugu bixinaysaa isaga ayay ka xanaajinaysaa waa lagu nacay, cidi ilama kaa korin bay leedahay inanka inay gooni u goosato ayay doonaysaa, oo dadkiisa o dhan ku dirto.*

Dibad is a man who was abandoned [by his paternal family] and was put 'outside' [*dibad* = outside]. His mother named him accordingly. She wanted to make him angry [by reminding him]: 'you were hated; nobody helped me [to raise you].' Now she wants to cut him off [from his paternal family] and she positions him against his whole family.

11. ***Dacar*** *waa nin dagaal badan oo kulul oo deeqsi ah oo dadka wax siiya. Hadday dacar qadhaadhahay qof baa dani cabsisaa.*

Dacar is a hot blooded man who likes to fight, and he is generous and gives something to the people. [There is a proverb that says:] even if the *dacar* [the name of the aloe plant] is bitter circumstances compel one to drink from it.[12]

12. ***Dibjir*** *waa nin dhixid badan oo hadyo goor dibadaha iskaga hoyda, oo isaga reerkiisii oo halkeer jooga kayntaa inuu seexdo aan kala jeclayn. Waa nin aan baqanayn haduu baqanayo kaynta libaax muu seexdeen ee cidlada ah waa bilaa dareen.*

Dibjir is man who stays away from home a lot, who always sleeps outside, and even if his family is close to him, he does not care if he sleeps at home or in the forest. This is a man who is not afraid. If he had been afraid he would not have slept in the lion's forest where nobody stays. He is without feelings [does not feel fear or inconvenience].

13. ***Raage*** *waa ilmo quban jiray ilaa afar sano ama wax ka badan buu caloosha ku jiray wuu dhibay hooyadii oo aad u dhibay hooyadii.*

Raage is [the name of] a child that 'was late'. Four years or more he stayed in the mother's womb. He caused a lot of problems to his mother.[13]

14. ***Rooble*** *habeenkii uu dhashay ayuu roobkii da'ay ilaahay baa wax siiyay dadkiiba waxay u qaateen inuu isagu yahay kii roobka keenay.*

In the night when Rooble was born it rained. God gave his [Rooble's] people something. They thought that it was him [the newborn] who brought the rain [*roob* = rain].

15. ***Sigad*** *waa nin hooyadii libaax la tagay, oo laga riday libaaxii isna caloosha uu ku jiray markaa wuu sigtay.*

Sigad is a man whose mother was attacked by a lion [or any other wild animal], but the lion [wild animal] was shot [or forced to leave the mother], and he [Sigad] was in the [mother's] womb at that time; so he [the baby] barely escaped [death] [sig = to escape].

16. ***Suudi*** *waa nin geedi bacad ku dhashay iyadoo reerkuna geedi yahay cadceduna kulushahay buu dhashay oo haraad ay tahay oo suudi buu ku dhashay.*

Suudi is a man who was born during a journey through the sand [desert], while the family was on a journey, the sun was hot and the people were thirsty.

17. ***Sharmaarke*** *waa nin loo duceeyay oo inta reerkoodu u duceeyay ayaan ilaahay wax dhib ah aan tusin.*

Sharmaarke is a blessed man, and since his family has blessed him Allah did not show him any trouble [*shar* = malevolence; *ma* = negation; *arke* = see].

18. ***Shire*** *cirkoo daruur buuxa oo daruurtu jiq tahay oo roobna ilaahay laga doonaayo ayuu dhashay waa shire oo daruurtii baa shiraysay cirkaa shiraayay waa habeenka la yidhaahdo, ama dayaxa oo laxaha la jira, dayaxa wayn todoba xidigood yar yar oo isa saaran laxaha ayaa la yidhaahdaa iyo laxaha oo isa saaran buu dhashay.*

Shire was born when the sky was full of clouds and the clouds were dense, and rain was expected from Allah, the clouds were 'coming together' in the sky; it is the night when 'the moon was with the sheep'; the full moon together with seven small stars is called 'the sheep'; when the moon and the sheep were together, he [Shire] was born [*shir* = meeting].[14]

19. ***Dharaar*** *hadh cad buu dhashay markay duhurka cadceedu dhaafto ee salaada la tukunayo ayuu dhashay.*

[The man called] Dharaar was born at the time without shadow, when the sun has just passed noon and the [noon] prayer is prayed; he was born at that time.

20. ***Caydiid*** *waa nin halkaa ugu soo baxay deeq, dagaal, dood, qurux afartaas ayuu isku darsaday, waa caydiid wax ala wax lagu caayo ma laha xaga dagaalka, xaga deeqda, xaga dooda, xaga quruxda.*

Caydiid is a man who is well known for his generosity, [skills in] war, [skills in] debate, [and] beauty; he combines these four characteristics; Caydiid has nothing to be ashamed of regarding war, generosity, debate, and beauty [*cay* = insult; *diid* = refuse, abstain from].

21. ***Caateeye*** *waa nin dhibay uurkii hooyadii oo ay ku bukootay oo ay ku dhibaatootay oo ay aad ugu jilicday hooyadii way ku caatoowday.*

Caateeye is a man who made his mother suffer [when he was in her womb], she became sick, she suffered and she became very weak; his mother became very thin [*caato* = thin].

22. ***Colaad*** *iyo Colujoog iyo kuwii kale waa isku macno waa rag dhamaantood ku dhashay colaad.*

Colaad and Colujoog and some other names have all the same meaning. They denote men who were born during wartime [*colaad* = enmity].

23. ***Gurxan*** *waa nin hoos u hadla oo hadalkiisa aanu dadku aad u garan oo hadalka ayaanu cadayn, in yar baa af taqaan waa nin xan badan.*

Gurxan is a man who talks with a low voice and people do not know what he says, he does not make his speech clear, few understand him. He is a man who [supposedly] spreads rumours.

24. ***Galaydh*** *waa nin dhawaaq dheer ama kulul, qurux badan waayo bahalka galaydhaka la yidhaahdo waa shimbir cad oo aad u qurux badan oo dadku jecel yihiin lakkin markay qayliso dadku dhagaha is qabanayo; wuu kulul yahay.*

Galaydh is a man with a strong shouting voice; he is beautiful. The name comes from a white bird that is very beautiful and the people love this bird. But when it screams people hold their ears. [His voice] is loud [*galaydh* = eagle]

25. ***Filanwaa*** *waxa dhashay habar da' ah oo dadkeedii rag iyo dumar ba guryo leeyahay oo lagaba filayn caruur iyo inay uur qaado ayaa dhashay.*

Filanwaa was born to an old mother; all her male and female children already [are married and] have houses. Filanwaa was born when nobody expected [the mother] to have children and to be pregnant [*filanwaa* = unexpected].

26. ***Faruur*** *waa nin dibinta jeexan.*

Faruur is a man with a harelip.

27. ***Qaloon*** *waa bah gooni la fogeeyo cuqdad ciil buu qabaa hooyadii baa kaligii dhashay hadaad bah gooni maqasho bahdii kale inamaa jooga hadyo goor waa la riixayaa wuu qaloonayaa uun.*

Qaloon is the only child of his mother; he is isolated [from his brothers, born by the other wives of the father]; he feels anger; his mother has born only him; if you hear *bah gooni* then [it means that] there are boys from the other wife. [The man called Qaloon] is always pushed away, so he is feeling alone [*qalo* = feeling of being a stranger].

28. ***Qormeeye*** *waa nin talo wanaagsan oo hadyo goor dadka kula taliya wax wanaagsan, qormeeye hadyo goor wuxu leeyahay waar halkan baa wanaagsane aqal ka dhiso, halkaasaa wanaagsane xoolaha u foofi. Qormeeye waxa la yidhahdaa qormada waxa la yidhaadaa meesha la dago, ee reerku dago ayaa gurigii la dagayay ayaa qormo la yidhaahdaa, qormada reer hebel, qormada reer hebel, markaa qormooyinka wanaagsan buu yaqaanaa.*

Qormeeye is a man who gives good advice; he advises the people well. Qormeeye has information about good places to put up the nomadic hut and where to graze animals. [The word] *qormo* indicates the place for a camp—where the family puts up its hut. [In Somali one can say: this is] the *qormo* of family so and so. So, this man knows the good places for camps.

29. ***Koore*** *waa nin dhawaaqiisu meel aanu joogin laga maqlo oo fog oo, koor waxa la yidhaadaa bahal geela loo xidho sida taa dhawaaqeeda meel fog looga maqlayo ayaa koorena hadalkiisa looga maqlaa weeye.*

Koore is a man whose shouting can be heard in a far away place. *Koor* is the name of the bell bound around a camel's neck; just like the bell's sound, [the man called] Koore's voice is heard from afar.

30. ***Magan*** *wuu ku dhashay abtiyashii meeshoodii magan, reer abtigii ayuu ku dhex dhashay. Ilaahay buu magan u yahay oo dadkoodii lama noola.*

[The man called] Magan was born in a place where his maternal uncles and the mother's cousins reside. He was born under their protection. He is also under the protection of God, since he does not live among his people [his patrilineal relatives] [*magan* = protection].

31. ***Mooge*** *waa agoon uurku hadh ah isagoon dhalan baa aabihi dhintay.*

Mooge is the name of a man whose father died before his birth [*moog* = absent, lacking].

32. ***Waabari*** *waagoo baryay buu dhashay xiligaa aan cadceedu soo bixin.*

Wabeeri was born as dawn broke, just before sunrise.

33. ***Hillaac*** *waa nin lagu farxay oo cas oo dheer oo qurux badan.*

Hillaac is a tall and beautiful man, who is red [-coloured] and people are happy about him [*hillaac* = lightening].[15]

34. ***Yoome*** *waa raga lagu xanto cunto jacaylka oo hadyo goor cunto uun doonaya, wuu soo yoomayaa, cuntada markuu arko ayuu soo gariirayaa weeye.*

People gossip about [the man called] Yoome that he likes food, and he always looks for food; he mutters, and whenever he sees food he trembles.

35. ***Yogol*** *waa nin dheer oo toosan oo qurux badan sida geedka yogolka la yidhaahdo, yogolka geedka la yidhaahdaa waa geed dheer, intuu dheeryahay ayuu quruxbadan yahay oo tosan yahay oo an qallooc lahayn*

Yogol is a tall, straight and beautiful man like the tree called Yogol. This is a huge tree, which is as tall as it is beautiful, and which is straight and is not crooked.

36. ***Indhoyare*** *waa nin indho yar yar.*

Indhoyare is a man with very small eyes [*indho* = eyes; *yar* = small].

37. ***Abshir***—*tolkii oo dhan baa ku soo shiraaya oo halkaa ugu imanaya oo jecel, waa nin talo wanaagsan.*

Abshir—all his patrilineal relatives meet [in his house], they come to him and they love him; he is a man who has good advice. [*ab* = forefather; *shir* = meeting]

38. ***Obsiiye*** *hooyadii buu qalbiga u dajiyay wuu dajiyayba, hooyadii oo naag kale lala qabo, ayaa naagtii la guursaday oo aan waxba dhalin ayay iyadu inan dhashay markaa wuu obsiiyay oo wuu dajiyay habartii.*

Obsiiye calmed down the heart of his mother, whose husband [his father] has married another woman, and his mother has delivered him [Obsiiye] while the new wife has not yet become pregnant; so he calmed his mother down [and assured her the continued attention and care of her husband, since she bore him an heir].

Female (nick)names

1. ***Bookho*** *waxay dhalatay reerka oo shir jooga ama barwaaqo ah oo dadku barwaaqaysan yahay, waa tii cid waliba soo booqatay.*

Bookho was born to a family that held a meeting or that enjoyed plenty. She is the one whom everybody visited [*booqosho* = visit].

2. ***Bullo*** *waxay dhalatay waalidka oo is laayay, aabaheed iyo hooyadeed oo is diraray ayay dhalatay buuq iyo qaylo ayay ku dhalatay bullo.*

Bullo was born when her parents had a fight, when her father and mother were beating each other; she was born during screaming and shouting.

3. ***Bogsiiya*** *waa godob reeb, laba reer oo col ah ayaa kala guursaday way bogsiisay inantaasu labadii reer.*

Bogsiiya is a girl given as *godob reeb*;[16] she was married between two families that had been enemies, she heals [the wounds of] the two families [*bogso* = to heal].

4. ***Tooxyar*** *waa mid dhuuban waa mid dhex yar, tooxdu waa dhex oo xagan sare u buuran oo xagan hoosana u buuran lakin dhexda yar.*

Tooxyar is a girl with a slim waist; further up and further down she is plump, but in the middle she is slim.[17]

5. ***Xogla** waa tii iyadoo uurka ku jirta aabaheed dhintay.*

Xogla is a woman whose father died while she was still in the womb. [*xog* = information; *la'* = without]

6. ***Xareedo**—roobku markuu da'o biyaha ka soo dhaca ee u horeeya ayaa la yidhaahdaa xareed waa roobkaa soo da'ay markay dhulka yaaliin ee aan weel lagu shubin ee dhulka camuudi yaaliin baa xareed la yidhahdaa.*

Xareedo—when the rain falls, the first rainwater is called *xareed*; it is the water that is lying on the land and is not collected in a vessel by people; this is called *xareed*.

7. ***Deggan** way miyir badan tahay.*

Deggan is very calm [*deggan* = settled, calm].

8. ***Raaxo** waa furaashkii lagu raaxaysanayay ee aan midh xajiin ah lahayn ee lagu gamaayay.*

Raaxo is like the matress on which you can relax and that has nothing which can itch and where you can sleep well [*raaxo* = pleasure].

9. ***Sagal** waa daruurtii subaxii markuu waagu baryo halkaa ka soo baxda ee cas ee qurux badan oo waa sagal.*

Sagal are the morning clouds; these [clouds] are red and beautiful; this is Sagal [it is dawn]

10. ***Sado** waa ina boqor, waa sadadii boqorka ilaahay siiyay.*

Sado is the daughter of the 'king';[18] she is the 'present' that Allah gave to the 'king'.

11. ***Dhudi** waa dhudka geedka ee dheer, dhudi waa gabadh oo toosan.*

Dhudi is the branch of a tall tree; Dhudi is a straight girl.

12. ***Carfi** waa qolofta uduga, xalay roob ma da'ay saaka dhulka oo dhami waa wada carfi oo wuu udgoonyahay.*

Carfi is the bark of a fragrant tree; when the rain falls in the night it smells sweet everywhere in the morning [*carfi* = good smell, perfume].

13. ***Cosob*** *waa dooga xooluhu u jecel yihiin inay cunaan.*

Cosob is the young grass that the animals like best.

14. ***Cawrala*** *waa cawro malaha ceeb xun ma leh, lakin inagu waxaynu ka dhiganaynaa tii quruxda badnay ee wax ceeb ah lahayn.*

Cawrala is a girl without blemish or anything bad, but we also say [that Cawrala refers to] the beautiful girl who has nothing to be ashamed of.

15. ***Gacalo*** *waa gurigii abtigeed ayay ku dhalatay, dadku waa tol iyo gacal, gacal waa reer kaan ka qabo.*

Gacalo is born in the house of her maternal uncle [*abti* = mother's brother]; people are [of two kinds]: *tol* and *gacal*; *gacal* is the family to which one's wife belongs.

16. ***Qaafo*** *waa dumaal ba dhashay, habartii la dumaalay iyo ninkii ayaa iksu qayliyay oo isku qaylo batay wax dad ah inantaasay yeesheen kolkaa qaafo hadyo goor waa meel qaylo ka taagan tahay.*

Qaafo is born from [a relationship called] *dumaal*.[19] The woman [her mother] who was married in the context of *dumaal* and her husband always quarrel, and they have only that daughter. Qaafo indicates a place where there is always dispute.

17. ***Ladan*** *waa qoys aan wax baahi ah aan qabin baa dhalay.*

Ladan is [a girl] born to a family free from want [*ladan* = healthy, well].

18. ***Magool*** *waa geed abaarta baxa horta magoolku, marka ay abaarta tahay ayu geedkaasi caleen yeelanayaa oo qoyayaa markaa jiilaalka xoolaha oo dhan baa jecel oo dadkaa jecel.*

Magool is a tree that grows in the dry season/during a drought, and when it is drought season this tree gets leaves and in *jiilaal* [the long dry season] all animals and humans like this tree.

19. ***Hodan:*** *waxay hodan ku tahay qurux, laf, deganaan, caqli, qiimayn iyo qadarin mudan intaas oo dhan bay ku kulantay.*

Hodan is rich in beauty, body [physical appearance], calmness, wisdom and deserves respect, she has all those qualities.

Analysis and conclusion

The Somali names and nicknames presented in this chapter (with their northern Somali bias) are deeply embedded in the local environment and frequently refer to aspects of the pastoral-nomadic economy. Water and grazing are certainly the most important resources for Somali pastoral-nomads. References to rain and water, and the resulting plenty (*barwaaqo*), in names such as Rooble (for males) and Xareedo and Cosob (for females) indicate happiness or, possibly, can also be read as wishes of the parents for a good life (of the individual and the extended family). Other names (such as Dacar, for men) point to alternative sources for survival in times of drought, provided by the leaves and/or fruits of certain trees, the juice of some trunks or branches, roots, and so forth. On the other hand, the male (nick)name Xadeed either means that its carrier was born in the particular desert south of the town of Laascaanood called Xadeed, or (as a nickname), that somebody is stingy and greedy with his resources (like the desert). The nickname Xoday draws on the ambiguity of a tree that gives shelter, but whose leaves are poisonous, so that it is not really beneficial to men and animals. Here, the reference to the environment and the pastoral-nomadic economy connects with the society's judgement on a person's character. Of course, in addition the animal names like Biciid (male oryx) or Gaani (young male lion), fall into this category and, simultaneously, transcend it by pointing to the wish of the parents for their male child to be strong or by indicating a person's rather difficult character as somebody to whom one should not come too close.

The second category of names, such as Waabeeri and Xeraad (male) and Sagal (female), refer to the time when a baby was born. They are connected to social life (having supper in the camp) and the beauty of certain natural phenomena such as the dawn, or simply indicate a particularly remarkable moment such as the burning heat of noon, when people in northern Somalia prefer to take shelter and rest, after prayer.

Events that happened before or around the time of the child's birth (the third category) also influence the naming. Sigad, indicating that his mother was attacked by a lion (or any other wild animal) shortly before his birth, falls in this category, as do Mooge (male) and the corresponding Xogla (female), which both point to the father's death before the child was born. Names belonging to the fourth category, the circumstances of pregnancy and birth, include Caateeye, who made his mother sick, and Raage (as well as the female equivalent Raaga), who 'refused' to come out of the mother's womb. They testify to the harshness of life in an environment where people sometimes lack basic resources such as food and water, and medical care for pregnant women (and others) is scarce. Miscarriage and other complications of pregnancy and birth are common.

The physical markers (category five) feature prominently in many names and nicknames. While some certainly are only nicknames, such as Indhoyere (for men with small eyes) and the many other names constructed along similar lines (Sanweyne = Bignose, Agawyne = Bigfeet, and so on), others can be names *and* nicknames, since they refer to remarkable features already apparent in the newborn, for example Barre (the man with a dark spot in the face or on the neck), or Faruur (the one with the hare lip). Many female names refer to ideal physical features, highlighting (or wishing for) the beauty of those named Hodon, Tooxyar, or Dhudi.

The sixth category, pointing to personality traits, consists mostly if not exclusively of nicknames. The man who likes to eat (Yoome), the one whose voice is loud (Koore), or another one whose speech is not intelligible (Juujuule and Gurxaan) can be found here. All these examples point to rather negative traits of a person. Yet positive names can also be mentioned here, such as Caydiid, the 'perfect' man who is good looking, a fighter, knows how to talk, and has nothing to be ashamed of, and the corresponding Cawrala, the lady without blemish.

Finally, the last category consists of names referring to aspects of the traditional order of Somali society. Holding meetings and settling conflicts (Shire [male], and Bogsiiye and Bookho [both female]) is part of this order, as well as matters related to predominantly male inheritance (which is not in conformity with Shari'a regulations) pointed to by names such as Bulaale, Xiis, and Kahin. The relevance and complexities of patrilineal and affinal ties and association are expressed in names such as Abshir and Magan (both male) and Gacalo (female). Qaloon, Dibad and Obsiiye (male) refer to the problems involved with polygamy and divorce, whereas Qaafo reminds Somalis of the tradition of 'widow inheritance' and the associated tensions between the involuntary couple, who may be compelled to stay together for the sake of social security and lineage continuity in a social environment where one can, in case of escalating violence, only rely on one's close patrilineal relatives.

Somali (nick)names clearly provide a guide into the working, the values, and the living conditions of traditional Somali society. As in the Arabic world, male names often highlight generosity, braveness and physical strength, whereas female names stress the beauty and the good character of women (Sharma 1997–98: 155). On the other hand, some Somali names and particularly many nicknames are of a rather ambiguous or even clearly negative quality. One Somali commentator recently asked: 'Why do we have bad names unlike other nations? I abhor all nicknames' (Omar Ibrahim Hussein 2008). Isn't it astonishing that Somalis point directly to missing limbs (Langadhe, Gacame, Faroole), a missing eye (Indhoole), big buttocks (Dhabarweyne), a harelip (Faruur), as well as to negative personal traits such as being stingy (Xadeed), stammering (Juujuule), or even to illegitimate origin (Baanji)? On a meta-level, this may very well be an indicator for the Somali sense of humour, which, as Charles L. Geshekter and Said A. Warsama (1996: 144) observed, 'derived from the harshness and unexpectedness of nomadic pastoral life that required stoicism and an ability to laugh at oneself which, in turn, contributed to a self-confidence' that is sometimes hard to understand in the face of personal and collective plight endured by many Somalis (in the past and present). In this sense, Somali names may be an expression of resilience, which is much needed and certainly a part of the cultural heritage that must not be lost in the face of (Islamic) modernity.

Notes

1. This could certainly be shown through a systematic investigation in the Cushitic and Arabic 'layers' within the Somali genealogies. Mohamed Abdi Mohamed 'Ghandi' has done research on this topic in his voluminous PhD dissertation, which, unfortunately, is unpublished and thus difficult to access. It was therefore not possible to make use of it. Still, Markus Virgil Hoehne wishes to thank Virginia Luling for having brought Mohamed's work to his attention.
2. There are a few Arabic and other (e.g. English and Italian) nicknames as well. These are not considered in this text.
3. Sharma (1997–98: 157) showed that personal names may be used for the study of religious change. This, of course, implies also cultural change.
4. The first edition of Barwaaqo's *Magac Bilaash Uma Baxo* was published in 1998.
5. Despite the introduction of the Somali script in 1972 and the subsequent literacy campaign, Somali society is still 'semi oral'. The success of the lit-

eracy campaign in the 1970s was partly undone by the civil war and state collapse.

6. Barwaaqo (2008: 45) argued similarly when he mentioned that Somalis in the old days knew (or were able to guess) the future complexion of their children, when they named them at birth *Caddaani* or *Adar*.
7. I only could think of 'Geeljire' (Camel herder/Camelboy) as an occupational (nick)name. Yet, it may actually tell more about the perceived 'rudeness' and 'lack of civilisation' of its carrier than about his real occupation.
8. The order of the names follows the Somali alphabet. It starts with b and t and ends with the vowels. For reasons of space, each letter cannot be represented by a name. The names selected are illustrative examples of the categories mentioned above. For more names, presented according to a categorical system that differs from the one we propose, see Barwaaqo (2008).
9. This and the following explanations have been given by Muuse Cali Faruur. His Somali explanations were translated by Markus Hoehne and Axmed Cabdullahi Du'aale, who closely followed the Somali original.
10. Other names with basically the same meaning are Xiis, Buulle, Dayr, Kahin, Weerar.
11. The ant called *Jinac* has a painful bite. When it is under stress it produces a strange smell.
12. This small bush is part of the nomadic 'survival kit'. In times of severe drought, its trunk or branches are cut and the bitter juice is drunk.
13. The idea that a child can stay inside the mother's womb for years may be an indigenous way of dealing with the psychological and social problems related to miscarriage. For instance, in 2004 Markus Hoehne was told by a young Somali woman that her mother carried her for three years in her womb. In between her mother had bleedings, but she (the speaker) did not come out yet.
14. Another meaning is mentioned by Mohamed Abdi Mohamed (1993: 180) who places the name Shire among the 'social' names, which refer to peace making, conflict settlement, council, and so forth.
15. Somalis, like maybe most other people, have certain preferences of skin colour. Usually, a light, 'red' brown is preferred over a dark brown or black skin. However, there are kinds of black that are considered beautiful, as expressed by the nickname Beergeel (camel liver), which refers to a man who attracts attention by his very black and shining skin (that has the colour of camel liver).
16. Literally, *godob reeb* means 'extinction of bad feelings'. It refers to a traditional way of peace making among Somalis. If a settlement is sought for a particularly ugly murder or some exceptionally damaging fighting between two groups, the side of the killer not only pays the usual 'blood money' (Arabic: *diya*; Somali: *mag*), but also hands a young girl (or several of them) over to the side of the victim for marriage; thus, former enemies become in-laws/affines.

17. This obviously refers to a Somali beauty ideal.
18. Boqor is the title of a Somali traditional authority, similar to Ugaas or Suldaan. It is a common title among the Majeerteen.
19. *Dumaal* refers to the Somali tradition that a man is entitled to marry the widow of his deceased brother or close relative. This secures lineage continuity and protection for the widow and her children; yet it may also lead to tension between the involuntary couple.

References

Andrzejewski, Bogumil W. and Ioan M. Lewis 1964. *Somali Poetry: an Introduction*. London: Oxford at the Clarendon Press.

Antoun, Richard T. 1968. 'On the Significance of Names in an Arab Village.' *Ethnology*, 7 (2): 158–70.

Barwaaqo, Cabdiraxmaan Faarax 2008: *Magac Bilaash Uma Baxo: Ujeed-dooyinka magacyada iyo naanaysaha Soomaaliyeed*. Calgary: Hal-Aqoon Publishers.

Cassanelli, Lee V. 1982. *The Shaping of Somali Society. Reconstructing the History of a Pastoral People, 1600–1900*. Philadelphia: University of Pennsylvania Press.

Geshekter, Charles L. and Warsama, Said A. 1996. 'An Introduction to Humor and Jokes in Somali Culture. 'In J. Hayward and I.M. Lewis (eds) *Voice and Power. The Culture of Language in North-East Africa. Essays in Honour of B.W. Andrezejewski*, London: School of Oriental and African Studies, pp. 141–53.

Johnson, John W. 1996 [1974]. *Heelloy: Modern Poetry and Songs of the Somali*. London: Haan.

Lewis, Ioan M. 1955. 'Sufism in Somaliland: A Study of Tribal Islam I.' *Bulletin of the School of Oriental and African Studies*, 17 (3), 581–602.

——— 1959. 'The Names of God in Northern Somali.' *Bulletin of the School of Oriental and African Studies*, 22 (1/3), 134–40.

Mohamed Abdi Mohamed 1993. 'Les anthroponymes somalis.' In Mohamed Abdi Mohamed (ed.) *Anthropologie Somalienne (Actes du IIe colloque des études somaliennes, Besançon, 8–11 oct. 1990)*, Paris: Belles Lettres, pp. 177–83.

Omar Ibrahim Hussein 2008: What is in a name? published online at: http://harowo.com/2008/07/19/what-is-in-a-name-by-omar-ibrahim-hussein-phd/ [accessed 21.08.2009].

Sharma, K.M. 1997–98. 'What's in a Name?: Law, Religion, and Islamic Names.' *Denver Journal of International Law and Policy*, 26 (2): 151–207.

Trimingham, Spencer J. 1952. *Islam in Ethiopia*. London: Oxford University Press.

Yimam, Baye 2006. 'Personal Names and Identity Formation. A Cross-cultural Perspective.' In I. Strecker and J. Lydall (eds) *The Perils of Face: Essays in Cultural Contact, Respect and Self-esteem in Southern Ethiopia*. Berlin: Lit Verlag, pp. 37–69.

CONCLUSION

20

REFLECTIONS ON THE SOMALI STATE

WHAT WENT WRONG AND WHY IT MIGHT NOT MATTER

Sally Healy

Introduction

This essay offers an international relations perspective on what has come to be termed 'state failure' in Somalia. It examines the constraints surrounding the successful establishment of Somali statehood from two angles, first, those inherent in the Somali social fabric, secondly, those generated by the geopolitics of the Horn of Africa region and the international political system more widely. It seeks to evaluate the reasons for protracted state collapse in the Somali context. It also highlights the burgeoning of social capital that has occurred among Somalis to compensate for the absence of more usual political, economic and social institutions. The establishment of a global Somali Diaspora is a key feature of this.

The essay situates the Somali experience alongside the debate over the declining importance of the Westphalia model nation state in the context of globalisation. It offers some reflections on the weakness of the Somali state, on the strength of Somali identity, and notes that if globalisation is all about networks and connectivity, Somalis find themselves rather well equipped to operate in a global world, with or without a state. In a way, the factors that have made it difficult to engineer a nation state can be seen as assets rather than liabilities in the age of globalisation. Yet, as the current warring in much of the territory of the former Republic of Somalia shows, the vision of a Somali state remains both desired and deeply contested. Its realisation will have to contend with the attributes—not all of them negative—that contributed to the failure of the first model for a Somali state.

The two main problems of Somali statehood

The standard texts on African politics in the 1960s took the forging of a single nation to be the top challenge facing Africa's post-colonial states. The assumption was that African countries would come to resemble nation states elsewhere with new national identities forged from the diverse societies that were bundled so arbitrarily into separate European colonies at the end of the 19th century.

According to this logic, Somalia started out at a considerable advantage. It was one of just a handful of African countries that came equipped with the basics of (ethnic) nationhood in the shape of a common language and culture. Above all Somalis were bound by their religious traditions and a common faith, Islam. This Lewis (1980: 16) identified as 'one of the mainsprings of Somali culture', having also observed that 'one of the principal results of colonial rule has been to stimulate the growth of Somali sentiments of unity as Muslims opposed to rule by those whom they class indiscriminately as infidels' (Lewis 1961: 269). Lewis has represented the Somali quest for national self-determination as the story of the politicisation of Somali cultural nationalism (Lewis 1983: 9). He introduced his *Modern History* as 'a study of Somali Nationalism in the Horn of Africa [that] traces the unfolding of a process rare in the recent history of the continent—the transformation (albeit still incomplete) of a traditional African nation into a modern state' (Lewis 1980: iv).

There were two problems with this promise of Somali nationalism. The first was that the Somali nation spread far beyond the confines of the two Somali colonial territories—the British Somaliland Protectorate and the UN Trust Territory of Somalia under Italian administration—that formed the crucible of modern Somali nationalism. The latter was based on cultural nationalism and was therefore an inherently expansionist project with troublesome implications for Ethiopia, Kenya and Djibouti which had Somali–inhabited areas within their territorial boundaries. Immediately after the Second World War, as Britain prepared to return part of the Ogaden region to Ethiopian sovereignty, the British government (very) briefly espoused the concept of a Greater Somalia that would unite all Somali people in a single expanded state. The 1960 constitution of the Somali Republic pledged to 'promote by legal and peaceful means the union of the Somali territories' (1960 Constitution, Article 6[4]), an objective that Somalia's first post-independence governments tried to pursue, though not always peacefully. But the norms of African international politics soon crystallised in ways that made the notion of an all-embracing Somali state a political impossibility. The overwhelming consensus among African states was to settle for colonial boundaries (Mayall 1983). They had no time for special pleading from an unusually homogeneous and largely nomadic community spread across five territories in the Horn of Africa.

The other problem with Somali nationalism was the tenacity of the clan system. Much as Somalis had a long tradition of cultural unity, a vital component of that culture was embodied in the lineage genealogies through which Somalis distinguished themselves from one another. The early nationalists of the Somali Youth League (SYL) understood all too well the divisive nature of these clan attachments, and like African nationalists elsewhere sought to do away with divisions based on ethnicity (Egal 1968). All subsequent Somali governments have railed against the clan and Siyad Barre's government went so far as to ceremoniously bury it. But far from fading in the face of modernity, clannism has adapted and flourished and had proved to be more resilient than the Somali state itself.

This combination of a problematic Somali state and an unusually strong Somali cultural identity is still a defining feature of Somalia's political condition. In 2010, fifty years after the establishment of the first Somali Republic, the relationship between nationhood and statehood remains as problematic as ever.

Historical roots of the Somali state

As is well known, modern African states are a legacy of colonialism, structures that were roughly superimposed upon the huge variety of political arrangements that already existed in the continent. However ill fitting these structures were in relation to pre-colonial political formations, they were the only vestments in which Africans could recover their independence and divest themselves of colonial rule.

Despite its origin as a 'one size fits all' external construction, the modern African state has, for the most part, proved remarkably enduring (Jackson and Rosberg 1982; Clapham 1996; Herbst 2000). Why not in Somalia?

The colonial history of the Horn of Africa had a number of distinctive features that may have hampered the prospects for a Somali state to become well established. First of all, the Somali regions were claimed in piecemeal fashion over a period of some twenty years (1889 to 1908), ending up with administration by three different European powers, Britain, France and Italy. In addition, Ethiopia was involved as a fourth major power in the carve-up of the Somali territories. This profoundly affected the colonial experience in the Horn. The survival of Ethiopian independence coincided with and depended upon its expansion within the region and the incorporation of new territories. Ethiopia's defeat of the Italians and its accession to membership of the international community in 1896 empowered it to enter into recognised international agreements, including negotiations over its boundaries. This was especially galling for Somalis in the British Protectorate who saw the treaties of protection their elders had signed with the British authorities between 1884 and 1887 overturned in favour of a Treaty with Ethiopia in 1897 that transferred sovereignty over their traditional grazing grounds in the Haud to that country. Ethiopia was unique in being party to the creation of its borders, which therefore lacked the 'out of nowhere' character of other African boundaries drawn up remotely among European rivals. In short, the Somali experience of colonisation included colonisation by Ethiopia.

By comparison with other regions of Africa, the colonial period was characterised by an unusual degree of turbulence and transience. Boundary adjustments continued up to 1925 when the British authorities in Kenya transferred a large section of Jubaland to Italian Somalia. Ten years later the region entered a new period of turmoil as Mussolini set about realising his ambitions to conquer Ethiopia and establish an Italian empire, the short-lived *Africa Orientale Italiana*. For a five-year period between 1936 and 1941 most of the Somali territories—excluding Djibouti and Northern Kenya—came under a single Fascist Italian colonial administration. After the defeat of the Italians by the British in 1941 the Somalis experienced another short period of unification, this time under British administration. Only the French territory, today's Djibouti, was excluded. This changed bit by bit to the pre-war dispensation. Nonetheless, after the brief unity came renewed partition: the Ogaden was returned to Ethiopian rule in 1948; Italian Somalia reverted to Italian administration from 1950 to 1960 as a UN Trust Territory; finally Britain handed the Haud and Reserved Area over to Ethiopian administration in 1955.

Given the context of several decades of conquest and frequently shifting colonial administrations, it is less surprising that Somali nationalist leaders ventured to envisage new kinds of territorial arrangements at independence. The Somali experience of the colonial state had failed to convey the sense of permanence and solidity that had been achieved by colonial ventures elsewhere in the continent. By the same token Somalis experienced somewhat less of the social and economic transformation normally associated with colonisation. The Italian presence had a more lasting impact on the agricultural areas of southern Somalia, but for the pastoralists in the Northern regions the experience could perhaps be described as colonialism-lite.[1] Several factors accounted for this, among them the transience of different administrations, the limited resources at their disposal and the weak political and economic interests of the colonial powers themselves. They also encountered resistance to change from the Somali population, not only in the lengthy rebellion mounted by Sayid Maxamed Cabdille Xassan from 1900 to 1920 but subsequently in resistance to everything from taxation to education.[2] Through a combination of these various factors, Somali political culture had endured rather more successfully than in many other African colonies as the independence movement gathered momentum in the 1950s.

Lewis located the development of the new conception of Somali nationalism, a nationalism aimed at unifying the several Somali territories, as one of the many side effects of the Second World War (Lewis 1980: 116). Cultural nationalism still carried some weight in international discourse. As the Four Powers and then the United Nations argued over the future of the former Italian colonies (including Somalia), Ethiopia could plead for the return of Eritrea on the grounds that they were one and the same people, identical in race, language, culture and history. The SYL appealed for Somalia to be amalgamated in a union with the other Somalilands on essentially the same grounds, namely that Somalis share a common race, culture, language and religion. But in the course of the next decade new international norms were to evolve, particularly in the United Nations, which in galvanising support for decolonisation simultaneously closed the door on any territorial adjustments for ex–colonial territories.

Building the Somali state

Inspired by Pan-Somali nationalist ambitions, the unification of British Somaliland and Italian Somalia took place on 1 July 1960. British Somaliland had been formally granted independence five days earlier on 26 June but the leadership had the clear intention of joining with Somalia, the first two of the five Somali territories that would become united. The joining of two states, with the merging of their two different colonial traditions and associated systems of administration and bodies of law, was far from simple. The economic and political case for these two territories to be united was not self-evident. Yet the Somali regions, in their entirety, could readily be recognised as the basis for a single political and economic entity. It was the belief in pan-Somali nationalism and the expectation of establishing a large union of all the Somali territories in the longer term that held the union together. Without that larger prize, the effects of a partial union—particularly in administrative terms—probably only served to weaken the new Somali state.

Nonetheless, Somali egalitarian and democratic traditions seemed to be alive and well in the early years of independence, resting on seemingly strong foundations of cultural homogeneity. But what looked like a source of strength could also be viewed as a critical source of weakness for building a new state. The cultural and linguistic diversity that characterised most African postcolonial states has made a necessity of new kinds of accommodation among the political leaderships. These have proved difficult in the extreme and the results were very mixed, but the post-colonial state as a model provided a fulcrum for innovation and new forms of politics. *Ex post*, it may be possible to argue that a state based on cultural nationalism is harder to build than one that is not. For Somalia's relative lack of diversity, combined with the unsuccessful efforts of the colonial authorities to transform the Somali social order, meant that the clan divisions that were part and parcel of Somalia's pastoral traditions could be effortlessly transposed into the modern political institutions. Here they took root and flourished.

The lifespan of the first modern Somali state was just over thirty years. It can be divided into three distinct phases: the democratic period from 1960 to 1969, the military socialist period from 1969 to 1977 and the period of slow institutional collapse from 1978 to 1991. Throughout this time the authorities recognised and railed against the evils of clannism or 'tribalism' as it was also called. Siyad Barre memorably said: 'It is unfortunate that our nation is rather too clannish; if all Somalis are to go to Hell, tribalism will be their vehicle to reach there' (quoted in Lewis: 1980: 222).

Meanwhile Somali academics and intellectuals denied the prevalence and relevance of clan allegiances, offering alternative and innovative interpretations of Somali political divisions. The most spirited attempts to overcome these clan divisions occurred during the early part of Siyad Barre's military socialist rule when, for a brief period, democracy and civil liberties were traded for revolutionary zeal. In the midst of this the alphabetisation of the Somali language was adopted and a remarkable literacy campaign carried out. It would be difficult to overstate the importance of language and communication, including poetry, as an expression of Somali identity and culture. The adoption of written Somali facilitated its use as the language of government, ending any further use of English and Italian and marking a decisive break with the colonial past.

At first sight, the problem of clanism in Somali politics looked rather similar to the ethnic particularism that manifested itself in a great number of other African states. As time wore on and problems of what is now called governance multiplied, the liberal assumptions about the nation building that would follow decolonisation began to look rather facile. The mobilisation of ethnicity for political gain or for state capture continued to be a significant feature of African politics, but it has not for the most part resulted in the complete breakdown of the state as it has in Somalia. Two particular factors in the Somali situation may be relevant to explaining this difference. The first is that the entire population of the country already belonged to a single political community, albeit one that was built upon on the shifting sands of the segmentary lineage system. This highly fluid system has been aptly described by Said Samatar (1998: xi) as 'the humpty dumpty of Somali social relations [...] a social system that results in, and enshrines, structural precariousness as a norm.' Fractious and divided as the system was (and remains), it nonetheless provided a commonly understood system that belonged to all the citizens in the country, besides extending to communities outside its boundaries. Notwithstanding the manifest differences that exist within Somali society and the inequalities to which these have undoubtedly given rise, there were no explicitly 'non-Somali' communities to be accommodated within the modern state structures.[3] Correspondingly there was less obvious need for the kind of overarching institutional state framework that was the principal political legacy of colonialism elsewhere. This framework typically created multi–national African states that define themselves territorially and base their identity as political communities on juridical sovereignty. So while Somalia certainly shared the problem of managing tribal or clan differences, it clearly departed from the African norm in the relationship between the state and the political community it contained.

A second distinguishing feature of Somali statehood, related to the first, concerns the law. It is indisputably the prerogative of the state, however imperfectly this is executed, to define and enforce the laws of the land and punish those who break them. In the case of Somalia the newly independent state inherited not only two foreign legal systems (British and Italian) but also an extremely strong system of indigenous law, known as *xeer*, based on Somali cultural traditions and religious tenets and firmly rooted in the clan culture. For the pastoralist majority living far from the centres of power, customary law continued to be the main instrument for resolving disputes even when the Somali state was in existence (Osman 2003). A key component of *xeer*, and one that links it organically to clan culture, is the institution of *diya* which sanctions collective payment and receipt of blood compensation among close kinsmen. Traditional and customary law was eroded to some extent during the first phase of Somali statehood and more so during the Siyad Barre era when, in an effort to abolish clanism, *diya* payment was prohibited and efforts were made to enforce the concept of individual responsibility before the law. A Somali penal code, in the Somali language, was established for the first time. However the new criminal justice system that was supposed to replace the traditional system became increasingly arbitrary, so that by the end of the 1980s Somalis found themselves caught between two stools. They could depend neither on the collective accountability of the past nor on the state criminal justice system that was supposed to have replaced it (Alasow 2010). After the collapse of the state in 1991 Somalis' most readily available societal form of protection was to be found in clan solidarity.

Breaking point for the Somali state: the Ogaden war

Somalia went to war with Ethiopia in 1977. The Ogaden war, and Somalia's defeat, is a major watershed in the short history of the Somali state. It illustrated with peculiar clarity the entanglement that exists between the dynamics of modern Somali nationalism, the difficulties of Ethiopian state cohesion and the fickleness of international politics during the Cold War. Defeat and its repercussions inside and outside Somalia sent the Somali state into a steep decline from which it never recovered.

The context within which the Ogaden war occurred can be described at three separate levels, each providing the means, the motive and the opportunity for war. At the international level the Cold War had penetrated the Horn of Africa. The United States had a longstanding military and political relationship with Ethiopia dating from the 1950s. The Soviet Union developed links with Somalia in the 1960s that were significantly strengthened after the 'socialist revolution' initiated by Siyad Barre's military rule. Military co-operation was a key feature of this relationship in which Somalia provided access facilities to the Soviet Union in return for assistance in training and equipping a very sizeable army.

The overthrow of Emperor Haile Selassie in October 1974 marked the beginning of the Ethiopian Revolution that threw the country into serious political turmoil. Ethiopia's predicament was made worse by the distaste with which its longstanding American allies viewed the violence and the socialist orientation of the emerging military regime. With Eritrean rebels scoring major successes in the north and violent opposition in many other parts of the country, this was a perfect opportunity for Ethiopia's Somali population to flex their muscles. The Western Somali Liberation Front (WSLF) came into being to fight for self-determination. In such volatile times it quickly gained a sizeable following and the clandestine support of the Somali government. (Apart from the ideals of Pan Somali unity, Siyad Barre's maternal family ties to the Ogaden clans provided more parochial reasons for this support.)

The rhetoric of anti–imperialism lent itself quite well to explaining Somalia's renewed interest in the politics of the Ogaden region. On the somewhat inauspicious occasion of Major General Siyad Barre handing over the OAU chairmanship to Field Marshal Idi Amin in July 1975, Siyad Barre explained his government's position:

> We have affirmed that self-determination of our peoples in the occupied territories is a natural right that cannot be denied. We will continue our peaceful efforts to demand self-determination and unity for our people who have been divided by colonialism. We have already made it clear that Somalia abhors the use of force and will not resort to use it unless all other avenues have failed. [...] We sincerely hope the recent historical changes around us will permit our neighbours to see this colonial inherited problem from a fraternal and responsible standpoint (Somalia Ministry of Information: 1979:60).

The security situation in Ethiopia continued to deteriorate and in 1977 Somalia seized its chance and launched an invasion of Ethiopia, notionally in support of the WSLF, successfully capturing the Ogaden region. Although Siyad Barre insisted that Somalia had not invaded Ethiopia and it was the liberation movements that were scoring victories, the rest of Africa was not convinced and Somalia's actions were roundly condemned in the OAU as acts of aggression designed to alter colonial boundaries by force. The Somali invasion turned out to be a shot in the arm for Colonel Mengistu: the crisis enabled him to establish himself at the helm of the Ethiopian Revolution and to galvanise support for his embattled country.

The international consequences were dramatic and involved a wholesale reversal of Cold War alliances in the Horn. The Soviet Union stepped in with massive military assistance to Ethiopia, displacing the US from its favoured position. Somalia responded by expelling all its Soviet military advisers. The ramifications of this sudden switch, and the scale of Soviet military involvement in the region, were sufficient to upset delicate US-Soviet negotiations on arms limitation. It prompted President Carter's National Security Adviser Zbigniew Brzezinski's remarkable observation that 'SALT II lies buried in the sands of the Ogaden'.[4] Cuban forces were deployed in support of the Ethiopian army and Somali forces and their WSLF allies were driven out of the Ogaden in 1978.

The Somali state in terminal decline

Many of the factors that undermined and eventually destroyed the Somali state date from the failed Ogaden adventure. With the collapse of external support, the immediate effect of the war was to render an already poor country bankrupt. The political fallout was swift. A group of Majeerteen colonels staged an unsuccessful coup in 1978. One of their numbers, Colonel Cabdullahi Yuusuf, managed to flee the country to establish an armed rebel movement, the Democratic Somali Salvation Front, which operated in North East Somalia with Ethiopian support for several years. In the North West of the country, the huge influx of refugees from the Ogaden region received favourable treatment from the government, exacerbating the sense of marginalisation that already existed in this region. The war had a significant negative impact in parts of the former British Protectorate (particularly those inhabited by members of the Isaaq clan-family) whose union with the South has been based on a hope of Pan Somali unity that also lay buried in the sands of the Ogaden. Emigration to the Gulf States increased and in 1981 the Somali National Movement was formed among Isaaq in the diaspora. It later gained Ethiopian support for military operations. Both these rebel movements had localised clan support, setting the trend for all future opposition groups. Despite their common objectives—the overthrow of the Siyad Barre government—they demonstrated that they were unable to unite.

After 1980 Siyad Barre's government was able to attract economic aid from the United States on the back of a military access agreement that gave the US access to facilities in Berbera (Metz 1992). The US assistance amounted to about $100 million per year and was a key source of patronage in a political system that became increasingly moribund and corrupt. There were no more of the grand development programmes that had characterised the first phase of 'scientific socialism' and Siyad's Barre's rule, never liberal or benign, became increasingly harsh. Individuals belonging to sub-clans associated with the armed rebel groups were punished and mistreated on clan grounds alone. The government was increasingly maintained by a combination of force and clan manipulation, so that by the late 1980s Somalia showed all the symptoms of a 'hollowed out state' (Clapham 1996) in which public institutions served only the private interests of the office holders who were fortunate enough to acquire them. The moral collapse of the Somali state became clear in 1988 when government forces responded to an SNM assault on the towns of Hargeysa and Burco in the north by aerial bombardment and almost complete destruction, putting its inhabitants to flight (Africa Watch 1990).

Ethiopian support for internal rebellion had played its part in weakening the Somali state. But the People's Democratic Republic of Ethiopia was on a parallel trajectory of regime collapse (but not state collapse) by the end of the 1980s. Ethiopia made peace with Somalia in 1988 in order to concentrate its resources on fighting the rebellions in Eritrea and Tigray, and was not a factor in the denouement of 1991. Wider external support really started to fall away after the events in Hargeysa and Burco in 1988. The US had never been an enthusiastic supporter of Siyad Barre and had little interest in propping him up at a time when the Cold War was petering out. The US was more interested in the prospect of a post-Mengistu Ethiopia and began to prepare for a 'soft landing' in Addis Ababa for Ethiopia's rebel groups. No such preparations were in hand for Somalia. The ousting of Siyad Barre from Mogadishu in January 1991 was very much a Somali affair. It was achieved by opposition forces that were clearly mobilised along clan lines and had in most cases already started to carve out clan fiefdoms in different parts of the country. Almost immediately a fight broke out between rival Hawiye sub-clans for control of the capital city.

Somalia was not alone in being a weak African state. The phenomenon of state fragility and conflict in Africa attracted much scholarly and policy interest during the 1990s as a considerable number of states in Africa fell into disorder under the combined pressures of structural adjustment policies, democratisation and the loss of external state patronage. Changes in development orthodoxy required African governments to adjust the ways in which they had managed power and resources. The process produced a great deal of conflict and generated much gloom about the prospects for African states in general. In time, however, most African leaders rallied to the new situation. By 2000, conflicts in the continent had significantly reduced and the great majority of African states had returned to some sort of functionality, at least for the purpose of conducting international relations. This was not in prospect for the Somali state. In the 1990s Somalia seemed to be just one of a number of African states in serious crisis, and their symptoms were indeed similar. But as others in the 'collapsed state' category have gradually recovered some normality, it has become apparent that none had closed down quite so completely as Somalia. Any prospect of the Somali state contributing to development had been abandoned more than a decade earlier after the Ogaden debacle. By the time Siyad Barre departed most state institutions, including the security forces, had ceased to function. The administration was barely operating and public services had all but ceased. The Somali state was in a more advanced state of collapse than other African states that broke down during the 1990s. Clan competition to control whatever form of state was to emerge was to prove ruinous.

The strengthening of Somali social networks

What happened to the Somali sense of identity while the state in which it had sought to find political expression stumbled and fell? In many ways it became much stronger, not at the level of the nation—which had always been an aspirational community—but at the level of the clan. The weaker and more capricious the Somali state and government became the more Somali people placed their confidence in their clans, and more specifically their lineages, for their security and their social and economic well being. The stage was set for the revitalisation and politicisation of the clan during the dying years of the Siyad Barre government, when opposition to the regime developed along clan lines. It accelerated during the time of confusion and conflict in the immediate aftermath of Siyad Barre's flight from the capital in January 1991. In conditions of extraordinary hardship, Somali people found their way to the safety of their clan areas or else took refuge abroad. What occurred in Somalia showed the burgeoning growth of social capital in obverse relation to the collapse of the Somali state.

Much of the groundwork for survival without a state was already in place. The formal Somali economy was almost moribund but the informal economy, largely based on trade, was vibrant and ready to expand. Large-scale migration to the Gulf States had taken place during the 1970s and 1980s, particularly from Northern Somalia. Remittances became a major part of the local economy, sent through informal channels and distributed along kinship lines. With foreign currency reserves under the tight control of the government, the earnings of migrant workers in the Gulf were used for reciprocal trading arrangements. The trade networks that flourished in the North from the 1960s onwards were based on the segmentary lineage structure of Somali pastoral society. As Lewis (1994: 126) observed, 'Somali regard the extension of their corporate lineage interests into the spheres of trade and commerce as partly a natural continuation of the collective economic interests of agnates [...] a man's prosperity is counted a direct gain to his clansmen, a trader expects the protection as well as the patronage of his dia-paying kinsmen as matter of social right.'

With the continuing increase of the Somali diaspora since 1991 the geographically dispersed trading networks have strengthened and expanded. Little (2003: 164) noted that these networks have grown in significance with the implosion of the Somali state. He observed that 'the segmentary kinship principle is embedded in the regional and international trading diasporas that are so important for Somalia. It has abetted traders in gaining access to markets, finance and information [...] it has also aided the global trade and remittance networks that have helped to keep the Somali economy afloat.' (ibid) Much as these alternative economic networks sustain life inside Somalia and beyond it, they also share the attributes of what Duffield (2000: 81) called post-nation state war economies that empower violent non-state actors and furnish the means for warring parties to engage in protracted conflict outside the control of the international community.

From nation state failure to globalised nation

The size of the Somali diaspora is difficult to estimate with certainty because of the different ways in which host countries count their immigrant populations and the multitude of different nationalities that Somali people now possess. At least one million Somalis (out of an estimated 7.4 million inhabitants of Somalia and Somaliland) live outside the country (Menkhaus 2009). The oldest Somali communities in Europe were started a century ago by Somali seafarers. Today the diaspora ranges from large communities of dependent refugees in the Horn of Africa to settled and prosperous communities across the Gulf States, Western Europe and North America. Remittances from the diaspora continue to grow with recent estimates of transfers of $1.6 bn to Somalia and $700 million to Somaliland (Lindley 2007). The speed and efficiency of Somali money transfer operations, facilitated by rapid communications and networks of trust, demonstrate important strengths in Somali social organisation.

Recalling the foundations of the Somali state as an entity that excluded some parts of a wider Somali community, it can be said that Somalis have always maintained something of a 'transnational' edge to their social, political and economic order. Somalis inside the old republic were intimately connected with Somalis in the neighbouring states of Kenya, Ethiopia and Djibouti. Today Somali social relations based on kinship spread comfortably across the globe regardless of spatial constraints. Globalisation and the revolution in communications made such connectivity very much easier. Somalis instantly embraced mobile phones, the perfect accoutrement to an oral culture. Equipped with a mobile phone and a money transfer operation Somalis can easily fulfil the obligations of family and kinship from anywhere in the world. The very features of Somali society that made establishing statehood difficult—the clan solidarities, the orality, the mobility, the fluid organisational structures, transnational identity—all turned to assets in adapting to globalisation.

Meanwhile the future of the Somali state remains as problematic as ever. Despite the easy transnationalism of the Somali diaspora abroad, the territory of the Somali state has become one of the least susceptible to penetration by international agencies and NGOs—what Ferguson (2006: 93) has called 'the transnational apparatus of governmentality'—that tend to proliferate, especially in Africa, where the nation state cannot perform its traditional functions. Somalia was the laboratory for the most thoroughgoing attempt of the 1990s to recreate a state, but UNOSOM failed in its mission. International agencies and NGOs are very far from influencing what happens on the ground inside Somalia. What access and influence they had in the past has been significantly diminished in the face of the growing power of militant Islamist groups in the South. However, the situation is different in Somaliland where a weak state exists and NGOs have a sizeable presence and exert some influence.

The decline of the Westphalia model of sovereign statehood and the demise of the nation-building project are not confined to Somalia. Ferguson (ibid: 93) suggested that the broad trend is for globalisation to accelerate regionalism (and the decline of the nation state) in the advanced industrial economies. At the same time, pressure for reforms by the poorest have often resulted in a diminished role for the state, producing less order, less peace and less security. Somalia is certainly in this condition. But the unsuccessful Ethiopian intervention of 2006-8 demonstrated the capacity of Somalis to keep external forces at bay.

The concept of the state within Somalia remains bitterly contested, yet the international community can brook no prospect of the Somali state being allowed to disappear permanently. At least three different visions of a new form of Somali statehood are currently vying for recognition. The most firmly rooted is in Somaliland where government structures have been restored. These evolved slowly from local mediation among the clans. Somaliland declared its independence in 1991 seeking to re-establish the separate identity it had known as a British Protectorate before its union with Somalia. Although such colonial origins form the juridical basis for almost all other African states, the African Union has not agreed to recognise Somaliland and treats the case as one of attempted secession. Somalis in the rest of the country are opposed to such a separation (Bradbury 2008; Hoehne 2009).

The second vision, espoused by Somalia's African neighbours and endorsed by the international community, is a federal vision in which the country would be divided into several clan areas, each exercising considerable autonomy within its own region. This approximates to the *de facto* governance arrangements that have developed in much of the country, but the troublesome detail of territorial division has not been fully explored. Puntland represents a model for a future federal state in a federal republic of the future.

Opponents of this vision see federalism as divisive and hark back to a more unitary Somali nationalist project. Others articulate a radical new vision for an Islamic state in Somalia under Shari'a Law in which the clan divisions of the country would be overcome. Much of the most recent fighting in the country is ostensibly being carried out to achieve this objective. It is a vision that embraces the Somali communities in neighbouring countries and in this way provides a thread of continuity with the older pan-Somali vision (Marchal 2009). If any of these visions are to be attained they will have to contend with the many constraints surrounding the successful establishment of Somali statehood, not least those generated by the geo-politics of the Horn of Africa and the international system of which it forms a part.

Notes

1. Editors' note: On this issue see also the contribution of Prunier in this volume.
2. Editors' note: Boobe in this volume deals with with aspects of anti–colonial resistance in the Protectorate as reflected in the poetry of Cabdullahi Suldaan Timocadde, a northern Somali poet who came of age in the colony.
3. Of course, underneath the 'lineage idiom' other factors of inclusion and exclusion were also relevant. The most distinctive factor dividing Somali society, besides patrilineal descent, was the pseudo-racial distinction between 'noble' and other Somalis. The latter were mostly members of the agro-pastoralist clans in central and southern Somalia, the caste groups (e.g. Midgaan or Yibir), the so called 'African' groups (Jareer, or today: Bantu), and the urban communities with longstanding traditions pointing to their separate origin from Arabia, such as the Reer Xamar (see also Luling in this volume). While this distinction did not play a prominent role in post-colonial politics until 1991, it clearly informed the dynamics of violence escalating during the civil war (Besteman and Cassanelli 1996).

4. SALT II refers to 'Strategic Arms Limitation Treaty' and to the negotiations then in train between the United States and the Soviet Union to contain the proliferation of nuclear weapons. SALT I had secured an agreement between the two sides in 1972 not to increase the number of strategic ballistic missiles. SALT II was intended to reach mutual agreement on reducing the respective nuclear arsenals. It was eventually signed in July 1979. The Ogaden War was a factor in damaging confidence between the two sides.

References

Africa Watch 1990. *Somalia: A Government at War with its own People*. New York: Africa Watch Committee.

Alasow, Omar Abdulle (2010). *Violations of the Rules Applicable in Non-International Armed Conflicts and Their Possible Causes: the Case of Somalia*. Leiden: Martinus Nijhoff.

Bradbury, Mark 2008. *Becoming Somaliland*. Oxford: James Currey.

Clapham, Christopher 1996. *Africa and the International System: the Politics of State Survival*. New York: Cambridge University Press.

Duffield, Mark 2000. 'Globalization, Transborder Trade, and War Economies.' In M. Berdal and D. Malone (eds) *Greed and Grievance: Economic Agendas in Civil Wars*. London: Lynne Rienner, pp. 68–89.

Egal, Mohamed H.I. 1968. 'Somalia: Nomadic Individualism and the Rule of Law.' *African Affairs*, 67 (268), 219–26.

Ferguson, James 2006. *Global Shadows: Africa in the Neo-Liberal World Order*. London: Duke University Press.

Hoehne, Markus V. 2009. 'Mimicry and Mimesis in Dynamics of State and Identity Formation in Northern Somalia.' *Africa*, 79 (2), 252–81.

Jackson, Robert and Carl Rosberg 1982. 'Why Africa's Weak States Persist: the Empirical and the Juridical in Statehood.' *World Politics*, 35 (1), 1–24.

Herbst, Jeffrey 2000. *States and Power in Africa*. Princeton University Press.

Lewis, Ioan M. 1999. *A Pastoral Democracy: a Study of Pastoralism and Politics among the Northern Somali of the Horn of Africa*. (IAI, 1960, Reprinted). London: James Currey.

——— 1980. *A Modern History of Somalia: Nation and State in the Horn of Africa*. London: Longman.

——— 1983. 'Introduction.' In I.M. Lewis (ed.), *Nationalism and Self Determination in the Horn of Africa*. London: Ithaca.

——— 1994. *Blood and Bone: the Call of Kinship in Somali Society*. Lawrenceville, NJ: The Red Sea Press.

Lindley, Anna 2007. 'Remittances in Fragile Settings: A Somali Case Study Household.' *Conflict Network Working Paper no 27*.

Little, Peter 2003. *Somalia: Economy without a State*. Oxford: James Currey.

Ministry of Information and National Guidance 1979. *My Country and My People: Selected Speeches of Jaale Siyad 1969–1979*. Mogadishu: Ministry of Information and National Guidance.

——— 1979. *March of the Revolution 1969–1979*. Mogadishu: Ministry of Information and National Guidance.

Marchal, Roland 2009. 'A Tentative Assessment of the Somali Harakat Al-Shabaab.' *Journal of Eastern African Studies* 3 (3): 381–404.

Mayall, James 1983. 'Self Determination and the OAU.' In I.M. Lewis (ed.) *Nationalism and Self Determination in the Horn of Africa*. London: Ithaca, pp. 77–92.

Menkhaus, Ken 2009. 'The Role and Impact of Somalia Diaspora in Peace Building, Governance and Development.' In R. Bardouille, M. Ngulo and M. Grieco (eds) *Africa's Finances: the Contribution of the Diaspora*. Newcastle upon Tyne: Cambridge Scholars Publishing, pp. 187–202.

Metz, Helen C. 1992. 'Somalia: A Country Study.' Washington, DC: U.S. Government Printing Office.

Osman, Abdurahman A. 2003. *Somali Customary Law and Traditional Economy*. Garowe: PDRC.

Samatar, Said S. 1999. 'Introduction.' In I.M. Lewis *A Pastoral Democracy: a Study of Pastoralism and Politics among the Northern Somali of the Horn of Africa*. Hamburg: Lit Verlag, pp. ix–xiv.

21

THE SOCIAL ANTHROPOLOGIST AS HISTORIAN

IOAN LEWIS AS CHRONICLER OF SOMALIA

Charles Geshekter

History is a record of 'effects' the vast majority of which nobody intended to produce.

(Schumpeter 1939: 1045).

Introduction

For over fifty years, Ioan Lewis has explained how Somali kinship ties and domestic political alliances affected internal government policies and external engagements. He emphasised how Somalis used fluid clan and contractual links as critical survival mechanisms inside a unified central state (1960–91) and in the absence of one (1991–2009). From his fieldwork in the 1950s, Lewis as a social anthropologist extolled the dignity and strength of Somali traditions as he examined the clash of modern territorial nationalism with traditional local kinship as forces shaping his narrative of Somali history. As a historian, Lewis emphasised causal connections between important events, wrote in an accessible literary style and excoriated ahistorical post-modernists who imagined Somali clan and kinship relations were mysteriously 'constructed' by outsiders. As Somali kinship was slowly decoupled from its traditional moral order under the weight of political changes wrought by the demands and interventions of a post-colonial central state, indiscriminate violence and lawlessness eventually spread unchecked. Lewis argued that without smaller, democratic political units, such criminal and dysfunctional behaviour was likely to continue.

Maitland (1936) insisted that anthropology choose between being history and being nothing; Evans-Pritchard (1962), Lewis' mentor at Oxford, reversed the adage to suggest history must choose between social anthropology or being nothing. Evans-Pritchard taught anthropologists to 'reconstruct from historical records and verbal traditions the past of the people they have studied' (Evans-Pritchard 1962: 176). That way, history would be 'part of the thought of living men and hence part of the social life which the anthropologist can directly observe' (ibid.). His ideal researcher played three roles: recorder, historian, and anthropologist. What a document is to historians, fieldwork is to anthropologists. Tutored by Evans-Pritchard, Lewis' research explained the logic and dignity of Somali life. Perceiving Lewis as an interdisciplinary 'cross-breed', this essay argues that the historical writings on Somalia by the anthropologist Ioan Lewis provide compelling examples of how inseparable the two disciplines really are.

What Somalia has become and methods of assessment

Nowadays, the name Somalia conjures up negative clichés and associations—looted cities, kidnapped or killed relief workers, endless civil war, massive refugee problems, and even piracy. Somalia is a stereotypical basis for cartoons. A recent cartoon depicted a disgruntled American conservative in four panels; above each panel was a different question: Hate Taxes? Hate Government? Hate Regulations? Love Guns? The single answer to each one appeared in the bottom half of the cartoon where the man was smiling broadly, wearing a shirt that said 'Anarchy' and surrounded by masked, gun toting thugs under the caption, 'It's better in Somalia' (Matson 2009).

A commentary on the alarmist journalism often associated with global warming or looming epidemics concluded that 'the existential threat so many of us fear is that we might all end up in a kind of global Somalia characterised by failed states, resource scarcity and chaos' (Hordhaus and Shellenberger 2009: 18). Yet what today seems self-evident was rarely thought of in the past. Those who wrote about Somalia in the 1960s never imagined that 50 years later a presumably homogeneous culture and society would fragment its nationality and destroy its state, as large areas in southern Somalia degenerated into a fratricidal savagery whose end is nowhere in sight. In the wake of failed external interventions to revive a unified state paradigm of governance in Somalia, there is little reason to believe any country (aside from Ethiopia) will expend significant resources to settle or mediate a conflict situation that does not directly threaten its vital interests. Somalis still wage war over Mogadishu because they perceive major stakes are involved for whoever controls the capital, should a maximal state ever be resurrected there.

During its lifetime as a nation-state, Somalia became an international supplicant, dependent on a global dripline of aid, loans and credit. When the dripline device was yanked in 1991, the country expired. No amount of orderly analysis can escape the fact that fifteen conferences convened outside Somalia since 1991 have made no progress in restoring public security to its capital or resurrecting a single nation-state inside Somalia. Amidst speculation about the political future of Somalia, few admit there may never again be a unitary state with a Somali national composition. Explanations for this predicament require careful attention to historical forces traceable to the early 20th century. For a realistic assessment of how this happened, in a framework that emphasises the links between the manipulation of domestic clan politics and quixotic state engagements with external superpowers, no one has done it better than Ioan Lewis.

The differences between social anthropology and history. The characteristics of the historian include a willingness to hold up evidence from the past to a variety of angles, making connections between apparently disconnected events, recognising the inevitability of unforeseen events, and being prepared to modify deeply held views. The historian seeks to identify the points when significant lines of history converge. Logical coherence, relatedness to experience, openness to debate, and an acceptance of controversy are essential for advancing historical knowledge. An interpretive framework and rendering no final verdict are other hallmarks of the modern historian. Each historian views the past from a distinct perspective. Facts cannot be invented and statements about history must rest on verifiable evidence. Historians constantly ask themselves: is the evidence on my side? Is it good enough to support my conclusion? What questions can I answer with it? The common assumption that 'historians efface themselves in front of the facts "out there" is an illusion,' warns John Tosh (2000: 113). 'The facts are not given, they are selected. Despite appearances they never speak for themselves' (ibid.). The past consists of the facts that happened, while history involves the way we interpret or explain those facts. The historian's assumptions and point of view must be based on his own experiences (Henige 2005: 13).

Historians synthesise large quantities of facts and, as generalisers, look for patterns and tendencies when describing the flux of disorderly experiences. They provide the clarity of hindsight in contrast to the uncertainties and imprecision of one's own times. The central theme of the historical discipline, notes Felipe Fernández-Armesto, is 'to describe and understand how cultures change' (Paine 2008: 17).

Historians construct studies of people over time while anthropologists do so in terms of space. Whereas historical research is based on finding data, 'research in anthropology is based on creating data' (Chakrabarty 2004: 36). The central fact of anthropology is that 'all people lead meaningful lives, and that those meanings can only be discovered within the context of those lives [not] imputed to them on the basis of some previously established ideas about the biological or psychological makeup of people' (ibid.: 22). Another difference concerns the 'starting point' of any endeavour to understand societies and cultures. The anthropologist's fieldwork is 'essentially a process of observing details and mentally constructing an abstraction under which he can subsume the particular observed phenomena' (ibid.: 6). The anthropologist starts with a problem, whereas the historian begins with a gap in our knowledge of a particular period. Yet, despite these basic differences, 'cross-fertilisation' is possible. The foremost scholar of pre-colonial Africa, Jan Vansina, considered that a substantial period of fieldwork 'marks for life the person who undertakes it', adding that it was an essential experience if a historian expected to produce more than 'a shallow and half-spurious tale' (Vansina 1996: 134).[1]

A goal of contemporary Somali historiography is to make sense of a country that no longer exists as a single state, yet survives as multiple constituent peoples. Anthropology organises its data in relation to material expressions of social life and history examines its foundations; Lewis is an exemplar of links between them. He interpreted the interrelatedness of events to show that while Somali life changed dramatically, key cultural institutions endured. As an anthropologist, Lewis untwisted the threads of lineage, clan, sub-clan and social contracts. He relied on historical data like archival documents, photographs, poetry, oral traditions and personal accounts to describe a variety of Somali activities with regard to changes and continuities over five decades. On the basis of deep insights into Somali society generated in this way, he insisted that that society worked rationally if non-Somalis made the intellectual effort to understand its complexities.

Of course, there are always historical lacunae that historians and social anthropologists, as any other scholars, overlook. No one foresaw Somalia as a Cold War battleground. In the 1960s, Lewis was more concerned with Somalia's animus towards Ethiopia than with its strategic allure to military planners in Moscow and Washington. He shared with American political scientist A.A. Castagno the belief that Somalia's biggest problem was its persistent antagonism with Ethiopia, not whether the Somali state would remain sustainable or if its structural weaknesses were terminal. Castagno simply hoped some day the Ethiopian and Somali mutual kinship would 'override secular nationalist considerations and lead the two groups to dissolve their lingering antagonism' (Castagno 1960: 7).

Lewis as a historian of Somalia and the Somalis. Since his first book in 1955, Lewis has written on a diverse array of Somali topics. Beginning with an anthropological focus on nomadic political institutions, his vivid field evidence was summarised in the book *A Pastoral Democracy*, which grew out of his thesis. Lewis later turned his attention to the southern cultivators, produced accessible histories of the Somali people, researched the nature and practice of Somali Islam, harshly criticised Somali state leadership, laboured tirelessly to attract international aid to assist drought victims and refugees, offered a range of governance options to resolve the plight of Somalia after its collapse in 1991, and showed why certain kinds of international intervention were counter-productive to restoring order to Somalia.

When turning to history, Lewis' field expertise enabled him to grasp the strategic workings of lineage and clan politics at the micro- and macro-levels over time. Lewis (2002: viii–ix) candidly summarised modern Somali history:

> As the Somalis have so abundantly demonstrated [...] apart from the problematic area of centralized political organization, the clan system is remarkably flexible and compatible with most aspects of modern life and thus is in no sense an atavistic force [...] clan ties remain profoundly divisive, and combined with a bellicose uncentralized political culture, create formidable obstacles to

> the formation of stable, hierarchically organized political units [...] these aspects of Somali political culture pose bitterly intractable problems for those seeking to fashion a viable future state (or states). Somali cultural nationalism, contrary to the earlier idealistic hopes of many Somalis as well as my own, does not alone suffice. If Somali history has any lessons to teach, this is one of them.

The aspect of Somali society that Lewis deemed crucial for understanding political conflicts was what is called an 'obsession with genealogy' (Drysdale 2000: 143). According to Lewis, pervasive structures of reciprocity form the basis for Somali identity amidst the constant reconfigurations of competing groups as markers of belonging. This was because paternally traced genealogies

> act like passports, mapping out vital spheres of belonging, and of loyalty and obligation. Arrangements for decision-making are extremely decentralized and democratic, requiring family heads to meet in council (*shir*) at every level of grouping. The genealogically defined groups involved are mobilized according to the political context. This fluid segmentary lineage organization is of great interest to professional social anthropologists, but constitutes an administrative nightmare, especially for the ethnocentric European mind, which assumes centralized political authority as the norm (Lewis 2001: 2).

Lewis examined the ways Somalis use kinship (*tol*), lineage identity, and social contracts (*xeer*) to resolve political or legal disputes as well as establish and sustain appropriate behaviour among its members. Social units based on contracts had no fixed membership, but were constantly made and remade according to contingent relations to assure solidarity even without kin ties. Somali patrilineal kinship was ascribed by birth, was justified as a biological idiom, included raising children, and entailed various relationships and alliances through social conventions.

Clearly, this social basis of complex allegiances and identities did not lend itself smoothly to the creation of a modern and centralised nation state. Cultural nationalism seemingly aided the endeavours of the emerging Somali political elites in the 1940s and 1950s, who recognised that for Somalis to be taken seriously in the world, they needed a central state. The post-colonial governments sought to produce a discrete state whose population was almost exclusively Somali. Yet, riven with lineage divisions and clan distinctions that were fluid and hybrid, Somalia was never internally homogeneous. National institutions hastily created during the late colonial period remained precariously in place until the late 1980s. Modern state structures threatened lineal values that were the system of obligation and trust that buttressed every aspect of the economy. Yet 'despite superficial cultural differences in lifestyle, town and countryside remained closely linked by clan ties and mutual economic interests in livestock and land' (Lewis 2004: 503). These arrangements held true within Somalia and in the fragmented, fledgling states that emerged from the former republic (1960–91) and among many (not all) of the one million Somalis now displaced around the world (Luling 2006: 483).

The collapse of the Somali state was manifest in the steady degeneration of daily life in its former capital which, by the late 1980s, was a sprawling place with Westerners everywhere and a building boom underway as the discredited and profoundly hated regime of Maxamed Siyad Barre clung desperately to tyrannical, clan-based power, waging war against its own people.

When the Cold War ended, Somalia lost its strategic value. After a short period of neglect followed by intense international attention and intervention from 1992 to 1995, it reverted to a place that outsiders avoided. There was no functioning central government, an absence of human rights, few schools, and no liberal democratic state seemed likely to take root. By the late 1990s, Mogadishu was rife with militias, criminals and bandits who terrorised the civilian population through an 'overlapping network of mafia-style neighbourhoods, each under the protection of a particular big man and his militia [and] despite its continuing symbolic political salience, such limited sense of the city as a public space and common resource as may have existed in the past had disappeared completely' (Lewis 2002: 297). The south-central regions of the country (Hiraan, Bakool, Bay and Shabeelle Hoose) became especially vulnerable to freelance banditry and clan-based warlords.

Lewis and many others sought answers to the question: what internal and external factors lay behind the Somali calamity as an apparently homogeneous people degenerated into Africa's seemingly most fractious and irreconcilable one? The genius, wit and spirit of Somali culture are the driving forces of its politics, commercial energy and religious networks. Lewis used plain language laced with subtlety and irony to describe the kinds of behaviour that produced those consequences. He argued fervently for the policy implications of his work. His twin concerns about the enduring strength and flexibility of kinship and the ways in which the modern hierarchical state undermined those relations convinced him they were the motivating forces behind both the progress towards modernity and the increasingly dysfunctional aspects of Somali life. When a recent study of local Somali politics noted that 'social intercourse—the politics of everyday life [...] is the key to Somali kinship' (Jama Mohamed 2007: 245), it reiterated a point that Lewis long recognised.

Even with the absence of security, poor public health provisions and little schooling available in Mogadishu, Lewis (2002: 298) reported a 'flourishing commerce in qat, other drugs, bananas, livestock and building materials, as well as imported goods such as tea, rice, sugar, cloth furniture and technical equipment [...] for all the physical destruction and haphazard violence, the city was a hive of business activity and thriving public markets in arms and other hardware.' Telecommunications prospered through radio and television stations, mobile telephone networks, and internet banking systems which led Lewis to repeat that 'Somalia is hardly a backward country. Material culture is well advanced.' (ibid.) Combining historical scholarship with anthropological research, Lewis showed the enduring power of patrilineal descent and wider kinship ties that was inseparable from modern statecraft and the history of the Somali nation. On a more general level, Gladwell (2008: 167–73) recently argued that cultural legacies remain powerful forces with deep roots and long lives. Even as the economic, social and demographic conditions that spawned them have vanished, they may still influence attitudes and behaviour.

By the 1980s, a variety of external forces that previously promoted national Somali solidarity waned and clan and sub-clan rivalries, stimulated and sustained by the ruthless and tyrannical Siyad Barre regime, took over. A culturally uniform, socially linked people began to splinter. To acknowledge that Somali life in a harsh habitat was imbued with lineage connections and to emphasise the fluid nature of other alliances in this society is neither environmental determinism nor clan determinism—it is a historical fact. Somalis had a long tradition of leaving their environment, living abroad and prospering in frigid climates from Cardiff to Hamburg to Toronto, where lineage and family linkages are crucial for the survival of most Somalis. What today seems like a 'toolkit' to help Somalis find their way as a 'globalised nation' spread across various countries (see Healy in this volume) proved a decisive weakness in the face of colonial expansion in the Horn of Africa. Lacking in self-defence, Somalis succumbed to external partition. As an independent state, Ethiopia could 'speak for herself and was listened to [whereas] the Somalis in contrast had no direct voice in the councils of Europe' (Lewis 1965: 203–4). Lewis drew a moral lesson that in such conflicts 'the weak must eventually yield to the strong,' an assessment that he knew would 'ill accord with the exalted sense of independence and intense self-esteem which are prominent features of the Somali character' (ibid.).

In the second edition (1980) entitled *A Modern History of Somalia: Nation and State in the Horn of Africa* Lewis, in an additional chapter on the Somali revolution (1969–76), considered the juxtaposition of two mutually opposed irredentist states (one multinational and other ethnically homogeneous) to be the cause of the 'persistent institutional instability, which is entrenched in the Horn of Africa' (Lewis 1980: 247). As he surveyed the 20th century politicisation of Somali culture that grew into an aggressive nationalism, he acknowledged that nationalism and ethnicity were 'notoriously reactive and infectious' and warned it would be a mistake to 'regard the present geo-political map of the continent as fixed for all eternity' (ibid.: 251–2).

Its fourth edition (2002), entitled *A Modern History of the Somali*, was again expanded in order to trace how Somalia had 'fallen apart into the traditional clan and lineage divisions which, in the absence of other forms of law and order, alone offered some degree of security' (Lewis 2002: 263). Constantly evaluating how the 20th century ended for Somalia, Lewis bitterly condemned the political career and unsavoury character of Siyad Barre whose 'two-dimensional political structure, with clandestine clan politics at the core and surface social nationalism for everyone else' produced a 'disastrous legacy [that] cast a long and deadly shadow over the politics of southern Somalia' as the region was 'left to stew in its own juices' after 1991 when the collapse of national solidarity ignited an unparalleled growth of inter-clan strife (Lewis 2004: 502). The southern Somali land tenure system had been torn apart by 'pastoralist entrepreneurs and government cronies, who had no knowledge of, or interest in agriculture' (Lewis 2001: 3). The remainder of the *History of the Somali* updates local efforts at political revival underway in Somaliland and Puntland where 'the absence of formal modern institutions of government [...] led to enhancement of the duties and power of local lineage elders' that would surprise only those 'without a well-informed understanding of such uncentralized segmentary societies' (ibid.: 288).

Lewis ends his history with a retrospective about 'clinging to the wreckage in the wider political context,' in which he reports 'little evidence of any widely based will to restore government—in the broadest sense—to Mogadishu and southern Somalia.' As a historical reminder, Lewis suggests, 'part of the problem, as must be obvious by now, is that conflict and war are normal conditions in Somali experience down the ages. Thus there is a high tolerance of disorder and violence, especially amongst the recent nomadic invaders of Mogadishu' (ibid.: 308).[2]

Yet Lewis, historian *and* social anthropologist, turns his eyes again to the dynamics of everyday life. The thriving informal business sector and the flow of remittances from Somalis overseas rely on clan ties that 'reinforce the traditionally uncentralized character and self-help ethos of Somali society' (ibid.: 300).[3] In different parts of the country, the situation has both worsened and improved since 2002, leaving Somalia little more than a 'geographical expression'. In his latest book, *Understanding Somalia and Somaliland*, Lewis emphasises 'the pervasive influence in the contemporary Somali world of the traditional nomadic background and its extremely de-centralized character' (Lewis 2008: xii). The slim volume highlights salient aspects of Somali history and culture for the non-specialist. It compresses his earlier histories to span the end of colonialism, the emergence of an independent unified Somali state, its ensnarement in the web of superpower rivalries, the meltdown of state institutions coinciding with the end of the Cold War, and the futility of top-down attempts to resurrect a central state by international institutions, human rights activists and relief agencies. Lewis insists that Somalia is a graphic exception to assumptions about the African state and that trying to reconstruct it in any formulaic fashion tends only to compound the problems.

As a historian trying to understand the realities of the Somali lands in 2009, I do not foresee the re-establishment of a central Somali state in our lifetime. A series of smaller, fragmented entities may be created and sustained, for which ample evidence already exists as Lewis lucidly describes when he addresses developments in the Somali political region since the collapse of the Republic in 1991, including accounts of the functioning and democratic state of Somaliland, which still awaits international recognition, of the various autonomous regions, such as Puntland, and of the Islamist movement that under the banner of the Islamic Courts Union brought a brief period of stability to southern Somalia in late 2006.

While we should avoid ultimate claims about Somalia, in my view the modern state of Somalia cannot be resurrected (Geshekter 1997). The Somali people, their culture(s) and memories will remain. Historian Said S. Samatar is less sanguine as he laments that his 'nation of poets' has become a wistful, supine 'nation of victims and criminals' whose quality of political poetry has grown desiccated and impotent (Samatar 2009, and also in this volume). There may never again be a single Somalia, at best maybe three, four or five Somalias. As the 21st century began, the reality of clan rivalries turned the old dream of a 'Greater Somalia' into an amorphous version of 'Lesser Somalias'. On the other hand, Hagmann shrewdly observed an important new phenomenon, 'the achievement of a "greater Somalia" on the basis of trade, transport and finance networks.' Although the Somali government 'failed to reunite the Somali–inhabited territories politically, its collapse promoted the economic integration of the Horn of Africa's Somali residents through the free flow of goods, services and information' (Hagmann 2005: 533–4).

Accounting for criticism. Lewis was sometimes criticised for underestimating the 'transformative impact [of British colonialism] on the very Somali pastoral customs he describes as authentically and essentially true,' and not recognising that by 'depending on a variety of Somali political entrepreneurs who specialized in making the colonial administration a tool of internal rivalries, British administrators sifted, "cleaned up," codified, froze and thus fundamentally changed what had always been highly contextualized and customized applications of Somali constitutional principles (the *xeer*)' (Kapteijns and Mursal 2001: 720). In more general terms, Lewis was also accused of being a reductionist and presenting a 'cartoon-like' image of Somalia (Besteman 1998; Lewis 1998). Both points of criticism are flawed. Those stressing the transformations under British colonialism overestimate the actual impact of British colonial rule and underestimate the effects of the modern Somali–run post-colonial state (Geshekter 1985). The colonial state in Somaliland lacked a monopoly of legal authority and political identity and the characteristic imperial dominance sought in European settlement colonies was never manifest in the chronically under-funded and meagrely staffed Protectorate administration.

Those who accuse Lewis of an over-determined focus on clan and kinship ignore that Somalis were often masters of their own fate who brought on changes themselves (Samatar 1994). Somalis classify and symbolise their world in ways that constantly shape and change their lives because any culture can be continually modified without being totally transformed. Many factors influence the way people think and act. Somali clans, insists Lewis, are not a thing but a relationship between several generations. Somali conventions dictated that most people behaved in ways like everyone else as kinship became for Somalis a 'natural' vehicle for all forms of joint interest, economic as well as political, in a diversity of ways (Lewis 1994). Lewis explained the complex relationships between political organisation, kinship structure, social contracts and the physical environment. As an anthropologist, he gathered extensive fieldwork data, reported his observations, explained his ideas, amplified his thinking and sought patterns over half a century that reflected the changing fortunes of Somali life. He valued Somali forms of knowledge and used them throughout his national histories. Lewis never limited his explanations by some functionalist or reductive approach that tried to account for Somali changes in terms of the needs or dynamics of a global economic system. His narratives of pre- and post-colonial Somali history synthesised key events and personalities.

In this perspective, some patterns or structures in the historical sense emerged.[4] Somalis were shrewd and calculating because their basic survival demanded it. Throughout nomadic dispersion and competition for scarce pasturage and water, 'the irregularity of genealogical expansion and differentiation' precluded any 'simple hierarchy of balanced descent groups' and, in turn, necessitated contractual political alliances 'to adjust the balance of power without normally disturbing existing genealogical relationships' (Lewis 1983: 149, 151 & 192). Somali pastoralists relied on political contracts to establish supplemental but explicit bonds that remained diffuse and elastic. While contracts would only regularise genealogical discrepancies, Somalis viewed kinship 'like iron and like the testicles it could not be severed or cut off voluntarily.' (ibid.: 137, 299) Lewis considered the continuing power of clanship from the 1950s into the 21st century as an 'ongoing basic component of social cohesion' that is even obvious 'at that shrine of modernity, the internet' (Lewis 2004: 505).

The acute experiences many Somalis had with the precariousness of life as pastoral nomads were a reason why 'political commitments and loyalties seesawed with dramatic variability,' and why personal security required cooperation with others (Lewis 2008: 107). Somali kinship reflected the need to reproduce society and maintain strength in times of duress. Lewis took the sub-clan entity to be the locus of Somali beliefs and practices but knew that Somalis were always part of larger relationships beyond kinship or clan lines and geographically beyond the Horn. He also accounted for social change. In the late 1950s, Lewis observed how status differences that 'referred to wealth, inherited prestige, skill in public oratory and poetry, political acumen, age, wisdom and other personal characteristics' were becoming a basis for increased economic inequities (Lewis, 1983, 196). Under Siyad Barre's regime (1969–91) these distinctions were heightened by clan-based access to privilege, wealth and influence in the Somali state.

Even those scholars who drew further attention to a new intermediary class of livestock merchants, traders, entrepreneurs and real estate magnates that gained economic power in the 1970s and 1980s argued that the latter maintained kinship links to rural producers and with rulers of the Somali state. Moreover, David Laitin and Said S. Samatar conceded that 'the political history of independent Somalia makes the relevance of Lewis and [Enrico] Cerulli's argument painfully clear [...] to understand Somali politics, it is necessary to understand Somali clanship and kinship ties' (Laitin and Samatar 1987: 155). They could not 'think of a significant domestic or foreign development in Somali politics since independence that was *not* influenced to a large degree by an underlying clan consideration,' confirming something which Lewis and fellow social anthropologists had tirelessly pointed out, that a 'fundamental characteristic of the segmentary system is structural instability' (ibid.: 158, emphases added). Recently, Jama Mohamed reached the same conclusion as much of Lewis' analysis by attributing the collapse of the central government to the modern Somali political elite that 'had no interest in such a democratic system. They wanted the kinship relation but not the burden of the rules and ethics of kinship. And so they waged a fierce ideological campaign against the rules that governed kinship even as they ruthlessly used it for political ends. The logical end of such politics was the total collapse of the state in 1990 because Somali politics became a politics without rules, which in reality is not politics at all.' (Jama Mohamed 2007: 245)

Somali Studies 2010: we are all Lewisites

Drawing on vast primary and secondary literature and his own empirical research, Lewis became the central, pivotal scholar in shaping Somali Studies. Anyone who writes about Somalia must take account of his work, starting with *A Pastoral Democracy*, the single most influential interpretation of Somali customary politics. Like most masterpieces it bears the stamp of the time in which it was written, which Lewis admits (Lewis 1999a; Geshekter 2001). His revised histories provide a framework of ethnographic details that explain what happened to Somali political life. Much of the literature produced by others on Somalia and Somali affairs in one way or the other pays tribute to the continued relevance of his findings.

Innovative proposals have recently appeared that reflect Somali uniqueness—that is, that no state has 'remained in a state of complete collapse for such an extended period of time' (Menkhaus 2008: 33). In assessing Somalia's 'governance without government' Menkhaus envisions the country remaining 'a mosaic of localized polities that collectively add up to something less than a conventional state' (Menkhaus 1998: 224). Making a distinction between the local promotion of public order and the revival of a central government, he considers that 'the single greatest source of household and community security in Somalia,' despite its fragility and instability, 'is deterrence—the threat of retaliation by entire sub-clans in response to an attack on a member of the lineage' (Menkhaus 2008: 36–7). Like Lewis, he applauds customary, community-driven governance and conflict management efforts that draw on traditional sources with contemporary political tools in hybrid, pragmatic ways.

In the fledgling Republic of Somaliland, Walls shows how the civilian government is committed to dialogue among antagonists and a consensus-building process whereby family and clan members assume responsibility for people's behaviour in their own area on the basis of norms and customs rooted in a 'conservative but flexible system of clan and religious belief' (Walls 2009: 383).

Hoehne (2009: 274) meticulously explains the 'construction and mobilization of mutually intelligible but opposed political identities in Somaliland and Puntland' as a kind of 'identity game' played between adversaries who define each other genealogically but recognise the mutual need to avoid protracted conflicts. The recent histories of

Somaliland and Puntland are signs of newly emerging clan/regional identities in the wake of the collapse of the central Somali state, another validation of observations made by Lewis. The dominant clan in each state (Isaaq in Somaliland, Majeerteen in Puntland) must still resolve internal sub-clan disputes and is challenged to integrate borderland sub-clans (Warsangeeli and Dhulbahante). Hoehne deftly shows how genealogical markers, clan distinctions and sub-clan splits are addressed in these two fragmentary states whose moderate nature and non-Mogadishu orientation are producing novel markers of distinction (Hoehne 2006, 2007, and 2009).

Powerful and prolific scholars generate respect and admiration even from their academic adversaries. For example, in the United States, Frederick Jackson Turner (1861–1932) was the foremost historian of how Western settlement patterns decisively transformed Europeans into Americans. Although she refuted his core claims about how Western frontier history shaped the American character, Patricia Limerick praised Turner's advocacy of the value of historical understanding that 'embodied the idea of historians as public servants, as scholars whose inquiries into the past could contribute directly and concretely to human well-being in the present' (Limerick 1995: 715).

As a founding father of modern Somali Studies scholarship, Ioan Lewis is also an anthropologist who is a public servant. Posing questions about the enduring power of clan and lineage and the value of collective behaviour over time is preferable to rushing to recreate a state or trying to resuscitate the vanished structure that makes Somalia the longest-running instance of complete state collapse in the post-colonial era. Sometimes explanations for the collapse of the central state make that process seem (retrospectively) inevitable, another example of how 'the present turns out to be even more complicated, more muddled and more maddening than the past' (ibid.: 709).

Lewis understood that debates about the Somali past were also debates about the present and that a careful study of Somali history might contain the seeds of a solution to its contemporary problems. The latest reports from Somaliland and Puntland confirm the functional importance of customary law and order ensured by clan elders or Islamic courts. As Somali Studies researchers, like it or not, aren't we all now Lewisites?

Notes

1. Lewis had already embraced those insights when he remarked, over thirty years ago, 'In making me what I am as an anthropologist, the Somalis have much to answer for' (Lewis 1973: 26).
2. One reviewer, who seemed to overlook the evidence, scolded Lewis for making a 'simplistic and primordial causality between fragmented kinship structure and violence' (Hagmann 2005: 532).
3. A 2009 investigation estimated that the annual transfer flows to Somalia are $1.6 billion and to Somaliland $700 million. This makes Somalia (in its currently rather fictitious pre-civil war boundaries) 'the fourth most remittance dependent country in the world' (Sheikh and Healy 2009: 18).
4. Basil Davidson warned that the essential task is 'to spot the difference between what parts of the evidence are to be seen as ephemeral and contingent, and what parts must be accepted as decisive and structural' (Davidson 1978: 23).

References

Besteman, Catherine 1998. 'Primordialist Blinders: A Reply to I.M. Lewis.' *Cultural Anthropology*, 13 (1), 109–20.

Castagno, Alphonso A. 1960. 'Dilemmas on the Horn of Africa.' *Africa Today*, 7 (4), 5–7.

Chakrabarty, Dipesh *et al.* (eds) 2004. *The Bernard Cohn Omnibus*. New Delhi: Oxford University Press.

Davidson, Basil 1978. *Let Freedom Come: Africa in Modern History*. Boston: Little, Brown and Company.

Diggins, John P. 1999. 'The National History Standards.' In E. Fox–Genovese and E. Lasch-Quinn (eds) *Reconstructing History*. New York: Routledge, pp. 253–75.

Drysdale, John 2000. *Stoics Without Pillows*. London: Haan.

Evans-Pritchard, Edward E. 1962. 'Anthropology and History.' In E.E. Evans-Pritchard, *Social Anthropology and Other Essays*. New York: Free Press.

Geshekter, Charles 1985. 'Anti–Colonialism and Class Formation: The Eastern Horn of Africa Before 1950.' *International Journal of African Historical Studies*, 18 (1), 1–32.

——— 1997. 'The Death of Somalia in Historical Perspective.' In H.M. Adam and R. Ford (eds) *Mending Rips in the Sky: Options for Somali Communities in the 21st Century*. Lawrenceville, NJ: The Red Sea Press, pp. 65–98.

——— 2001. 'Interview with Professor Ioan M. Lewis at his Home in London.' *Bildhaan: An International Journal of Somali Studies*, 1 (1), 53–86.

Gladwell, Malcolm 2008. *Outliers: The Story of Success*. New York: Little, Brown and Company.

Hagmann, Tobias 2005. 'From State Collapse to Duty-Free Shop: Somalia's Path to Modernity. '*African Affairs*, 104, 525–35.

Henige, David 2005. *Historical Evidence and Argument*. Madison: University of Wisconsin Press.

Hoehne, Markus V. 2006. 'Political Identity, Emerging State Structures and Conflict in Northern Somalia.' *Journal of Modern African Studies*, 44 (3), 397–414.

——— 2007. 'Puntland and Somaliland Clashing in Northern Somalia: Who Cuts the Gordian Knot?' *Social Science Research Council*, 7 November 2007. Online at: http://hornofafrica.ssrc.org/Hoehn/printable.html [accessed May 2008].

——— 2009. 'Mimesis and Mimicry in Dynamics of State and Identity Formation in Northern Somalia.' *Africa*, 79 (2), 252–81.

Hordhaus, Ted and Michael Shellenberger 2009. 'The Green Bubble: Why Environmentalism Keeps Imploding.' *The New Republic*, 20 May 2009, 16–19.

Kapteijns, Lidwien and Mursal Farah 2001. 'Review of I.M. Lewis, *A Pastoral Democracy*.' *Africa*, 71 (4), 719–21.

Laitin, David D. and Said Sheikh Samatar 1987. *Somalia: Nation in Search of a State*. Boulder: Westview.

Lewis, Ioan M. 1965. *The Modern History of Somaliland*, New York: Praeger Publishers.

——— 1973. *The Anthropologist's Muse*. London: Broadwater Press.

——— 1980. *A Modern History of Somalia*. London: Longman, 2nd edition.

——— 1983. *A Pastoral Democracy*. London: Africana Publishing Company.

——— 1994. *Blood and Bone: The Call of Kinship in Somali Society*. Trenton, NJ: The Red Sea Press.

——— 1998. 'Doing Violence to Ethnography: Some Comments on Catherine Besteman's Distorted Reporting on Somalia.' *Current Anthropology*, 13 (1), 100–8.

——— 1999a. 'Afterword: Some Reflections on a Long Engagement in Somali Anthropology.' In I.M. Lewis, *A Pastoral Democracy*. Oxford: James Currey, 3rd edition, i–xxvi.

——— 1999b. *Arguments With Ethnography*. London: The Athlone Press.

——— 2001. 'Why the warlords won.' *Times Literary Supplement*, #5123, 8 June 2001, 1–3.

——— 2002. *A Modern History of the Somali*. Oxford: James Currey.

——— 2004. 'Visible and Invisible Differences: The Somali Paradox.' *Africa*, 74 (4), 489–515.

——— 2008. *Understanding Somalia and Somaliland: Culture, History, Society*, New York: Columbia University Press.

Limerick, Patricia N. 1995. 'Turnerians All: The Dream of a Helpful History in an Intelligible World.' *American Historical Review*, 100 (3), 697–716.

Luling, Virginia 2006. 'Genealogy as Theory, Genealogy as Tool: Aspects of Somali "Clanship".' *Social Identities*, 12 (4), 471–85.

Maitland, Frederick 1936. *The Body Politic. Selected Essays*. Cambridge University Press.

Matson, R.J. 2009. Cartoon. *St. Louis Post-Dispatch*, 18 April 2009.

Menkhaus, Ken 1998. 'Somalia: Political Order in a Stateless Society.' *Current History*, 97 (619), 220–4.

——— 2008. 'Understanding State Failure in Somalia: Internal and External Dimensions.' In A. Harneit-Sievers and D. Spilker (eds) *Publication Series on Democracy*. Vol. 6, Berlin: Heinrich Boll Foundation, pp. 30–49.

Mohamed, Jama 2007. 'Kinship and Politics in Somali Politics.' *Africa*, 77 (2), 226–48.

Paine, Lincoln 2008. 'World History and Other Marginal and Perverse Pursuits: An Interview with Felix Fernández-Armesto.' *Itinerario*, 32 (3), 6–22.

Samatar, Ahmed I. 1989. 'Somali Studies: Towards an Alternative Epistemology.' *Northeast African Studies*, 11 (1), 3–17.

——— (ed.) 1994. *The Somali Challenge: From Catastrophe to Renewal*. Boulder: Lynne Rienner Publishers.

——— 2007. 'The Porcupine Dilemma: Governance and Transition in Somalia.' *Bildhaan: An International Journal of Somali Studies*, 7, 39–90.

Samatar, Said S. 2009. 'Somalia: A Nation's Literary Death Tops Its Political Demise.' *WardeerNews.com*, May 17.

Sheikh, Hassan and Sally Healy 2009. *Somalia's Missing Million: The Somali Diaspora and its Role in Development*. Nairobi: UNDP.

Schumpeter, Joseph A. 1939. *Business Cycles*. New York: McGraw-Hill, Vol. 2.

Tosh, John 2000. *The Pursuit of History* (3rd ed.). New York: Longman.

Vansina, Jan 1996. 'Epilogue: Fieldwork in History.' In C. Keyes Adenaike and J. Vansina (eds) *In Pursuit of History: Fieldwork in Africa*. Oxford: James Currey, pp. 127–40.

Walls, Michael 2009. 'The Emergence of a Somali State: Building Peace from Civil War in Somaliland.' *African Affairs*, 108 (432), 371–89.

PUBLISHED WORKS BY I.M. LEWIS

Monographs

1955. *Peoples of the Horn of Africa. Somali, Afar and Saho. (Ethnographic Survey of Africa. North Eastern Africa, Part I.)* London: International Institute. (First Edition)

1957. *The Somali Lineage System and the Total Genealogy. A General Introduction to Basic Principles of Somali Political Institutions.* Hargeisa: Somaliland Government.

1961. *A Pastoral Democracy. A Study of Pastoralism and Politics among the Northern Somali of the Horn of Africa.* London: Oxford University Press. (First Edition)

1962. *Marriage and the Family in Northern Somaliland.* Kampala: East African Institute.

1965. *The Modern History of Somaliland. From Nation to State.* London: Weidenfeld & Nicholson. (First edition)

1969. *Peoples of the Horn of Africa. Somali, Afar and Saho. (Ethnographic Survey of Africa. North Eastern Africa, Part I.)* Reprint with supplementary bibliography. London: International Institute.

1971. *Ecstatic Religion. An Anthropological Study of Spirit Possession and Shamanism.* Harmondsworth: Penguin.

1976. *Social Anthropology in Perspective.* Harmondsworth: Penguin. (First edition).

1980. *A Modern History of Somalia. Nation & State in the Horn of Africa.* London: Longman. (Second edition).

1981. *Somali Culture, History, and Social Institutions. An Introductory Guide to the Somali.* London: London School of Economics and Political Science.

1982. *A Pastoral Democracy. A Study of Pastoralism and Politics among the Northern Somali of the Horn of Africa.* New York: Africana Publishing Company (Second Edition).

1984. *Una democrazia pastorale. Modo di produzione pastorale e relazioni politiche tra i somali settentrionali.* Milan: Franco Angeli.

1985. *Social Anthropology in Perspective.* Cambridge: Cambridge University Press. (Second edition)

1986. *Religion in Context. Cults and Charisma.* Cambridge: Cambridge University Press.

1987. *Prospettive de Antropologia.* Rome: Bulzoni.

1988. *A Modern History of Somalia. Nation and State in the Horn of Africa.* London: Boulder: Westview (Third Edition).

1988. *A Modern History of Somalia. Nation & State in the Horn of Africa.* Boulder: Westview. (Third edition).

1989. *Ecstatic Religion. An Anthropological Study of Spirit Possession and Shamanism.* London: Routledge (Second Edition).

1989. *Schamanen, Hexer, Kannibalen. Die Realität des Religiösen.* Frankfurt a. M.: Athenaeum.

1993. *Understanding Somalia. A Guide to Culture, History and Social Institutions.* London: Haan.

1993. *Possessione, Stregoneria, Sciamanismo.* Naples: Liguori.

1994. *Blood and Bone. The Call of Kinship in Somali Society.* Lawrenceville, NJ: The Red Sea Press.

1994. *Peoples of the Horn of Africa. Somali, Afar and Saho.* New Edition with supplementary appendices London: Haan.

1996. *Religion in Context. Cults and Charisma.* Cambridge: Cambridge University Press. (Second edition).

1998. *Saints and Somalis. Popular Islam in a Clan-based Society.* Lawrenceville, NJ: The Red Sea Press.

1999. *A Pastoral Democracy. A Study of Pastoralism and Politics among the Northern Somali of the Horn of Africa.* Oxford: James Currey, Berlin: Lit Verlag.(Third Edition)

1999. *Arguments with Ethnography. Comparative Approaches to History, Politics & Religion.* London and New Brunswick NJ: The Athlone Press.

2002. *A Modern History of the Somali. Revised, Updated & Expanded.* Oxford: James Currey. (Fourth edition).

2003. *Social and Cultural Anthropology in Perspective.* New Brunswick NJ: Transaction. (Third edition).

2008. *Understanding Somalia and Somaliland.* London: Hurst.

Forthcoming. *The Making and Breaking of States in the Horn of Africa.* Lawrenceville, NJ: African World Press.

Co-authored volumes

1964. With Andrzejewski, Bogumil W. *Somali Poetry. An Introduction*. Oxford: Clarendon Press.

1993. With Farah, Ahmed Y. *Somalia. The Roots of Reconciliation*. London: Action Aid.

Edited and co-edited volumes

1966. (ed.) *Islam in Tropical Africa*. London: Oxford University Press.

1968. (ed.) *History and Social Anthropology*. London: Tavistock.

1975. (ed.) *Abaar. The Somali Drought*. London: International African Institute.

1977. (ed.) *Symbols and Sentiments*. London: Academic Press.

1982. With v. Fürer-Haimendorf, Christoph and Eggan, Fred (eds) *The Atlas of Mankind*. London: Mitchell Beazley.

1983. (ed.) *Nationalism and Self-Determination in the Horn of Africa*. London: Ithaca.

1986. (ed.) *Blueprint for a Socio-demographic Survey and Re-enumeration of the Refugee Camp Population in the Somali Democratic Republic*. Geneva: UNHCR.

1986. (ed.) *O Islamismo ao sur do Saara*. Lisbon: Centro de Estudos dos Povos e Culturas de Expressao Portuguesa.

1988. With Jahuda, Gustav (eds) *Acquiring Culture. Cross-cultural Studies in Child Development*. Kent: Croom Helm.

1991. With Hurreiz, Sayyid H. and As-Safi, Ahmed (eds) *Women's Medicine. The Zar-Bori Cult in Africa and Beyond*. Edinburgh University Press.

1995. With Mayall, James (eds), *A Study of Decentralised Structures for Somalia*. Report presented to the European Union (Somali Unit).

1996. With Hayward, Richard J. (eds) *Voice and Power. The Culture of Language in North-East Africa. Essays in Honour of B.W. Andrzejewski*. London: School of Oriental and African Studies.

Journal articles

1951. With Barlow, R.B. and Ing, H.R. FRS. 'The structure of the product formed from alloxan and o-phenylenediamine in the absence of acid', *Journal of the Chemical Society*, 25, 3242–3245.

1955. 'Sufism in Somaliland I. A Study in Tribal Islam.' *Bulletin of the School of Oriental and African Studies*, 17 (3), 581–602.

1956. 'Sufism in Somaliland II. A Study in Tribal Islam.' *Bulletin of the School of Oriental and African Studies*, 18 (1), 146–60.

1957. 'La Comunita ('Giamia') di Bardera sulle rive del Giuba.' *Somalia d'Oggi*, 2 (1), 36–7.

1958. 'The Gadabuursi Somali Script.'*Bulletin of the School of Oriental and African Studies*, 21 (1), 134–56.

1958. 'Modern Political Movements in Somaliland. (Parts 1 and 2).'*Africa*, 28 (3), 244–61 and (4), 344–64.

1958. 'The Godhardunneh Cave Decoration of North-Eastern Somaliland.' *Man*, 58, 178–9.

1958. With Goldsmith, K.L.G. 'A Preliminary Investigation of the Blood Groups of the Sab Bondsmen of Northern Somaliland.' *Man*, 58, 188–90.

1959. 'The Classification of African Political Systems.' *Rhodes-Livingstone Institute Journal*. Vol. 25, 59–69.

1959. 'Clanship and Contract in Northern Africa.' *Africa*, 31, 274–93.

1959. 'The Names of God in Northern Somali.' *Bulletin of the School of Oriental and African Studies*, 22 (1), 134–40.

1959. 'The Galla in Northern Somaliland.' *Rassegna di Studi Etiopici*, 15, 21–38.

1959. Appendix I. *Bulletin of the School of Oriental and African Studies*, 22.

1960. 'Problems in the Development of Modern Leadership and Loyalities in the British Somaliland Protectorate and U.N. Trusteeship Territory of Somalia.' *Civilizations*, 10, 49–62.

1960. 'The New East African Republic of Somalia.' *World Today*, 16, 287–95.

1960. 'The Somali Conquest of the Horn of Africa.' *Journal of African History*, 1 (2), 213–30.

1961. 'Force and Fission in Northern Somali Lineage Structure.' *American Anthropologist*, 63 (1), 94–112.

1961. 'The So-called "Galla-Graves" in Northern Somaliland.' *Man*, 61, 103–6.

1961. 'Notes on the Social Organization of the Ise Somali.' *Rassegna di Studi Etiopici*, 17, 69–84.

1962. 'Historical Aspects of Genealogies in Northern Somali Social Structure.' *Journal of African History*, 3 (1), 35–48.

1963. 'Dualism in Somali Notions of Power.' *Journal of the Royal Anthropological Institute*, 93 (1), 109–16.

1963. 'The Somali Republic since Independence.' *World Today*, April, 163–73.

1963. 'Pan-Africanism and Pan-Somalism.' *The Journal of Modern African Studies*, 1 (2), 147–62.

1963. 'The Problem of the Northern Frontier District of Kenya.' *Race*, 5, 48–60.

1966. 'Spirit Possession and Deprivation Cults.' *Man*, 1 (3), 307–29.

1967. 'Recent Developments in the Somali Dispute.' *African Affairs*, 66 (263), 104–12.

1967. 'Seminar on Social Research in the North-East African Region.' *Journal of Modern African Studies*, 5 (2), 279.

1967. With Wilson, Peter J. 'Spirits and the Sex War.' (Correspondence) *Man*, New Series, 2 (4), 626–9.

1967. 'Prospects in the Horn: After the Referendum.' *Africa Report*, 12, 4, 37–45.

1967. 'The Referendum in French Somaliland: Aftermath and Prospects in the Somali Dispute.' *The World Today*, July, 308–14.

1968. With Werbner, Richard P. 'Spirits and the Sex War.' (Correspondence) *Man*, 3 (1), 129–31.

1969. 'Some Strategies of Non-physical Aggression in Other Cultures.' *Journal of Psychosomatic Research*, 13, 221–7.

1971. 'On the Philosophy of Witchcraft.' *Encounter*, 37, 66–9.

1971. With Kilton, Steward. "Dream Power'–dreams, ecstasy, shamanism and the Malayan Sonoi.' *OZ*, 36, July.

1972. 'The Politics of the 1969 Somali Coup.' *Journal of Modern African Studies*, 10 (3), 383–408.

1972. 'Somalia's Leaders go forward with Confidence.' *New Middle East*, 51, December, 9.

1976. With Jewell, P.A. 'The Peoples and Cultures of Ethiopia' *Proceedings of the Royal Society of London*, 194 (1114), 7–16.

1977. 'Confessions of a "Government" Anthropologist.' *Anthropological Forum*, 4 (2), 226–38.

1977. 'Culture and Conflict in Africa.' *Millenium: Journal of International Studies*, 6 (2), 175–81.

1978. 'The Ogaden: Ethiopia's Desert Empire.' *New Internationalist*, 62.

1978. 'The Cushitic-speaking Peoples: A Jigsaw Puzzle for Social Anthropologists.' *L'Uomo*, 2 (2), 131–42.
1978. 'Er Ogaden en del af Etiopien eller Somalia? De Skiftender alliancer padet Afrikanske Horn.' *Kontakt*, 7, 36–7.
1979. 'Os Cubanos na Etiopa: Combatentes da liberdade ou agentes do imperialismo?' *Broteria*, 109 (6).
1980. 'The Somali Refugee Crisis.' *RAIN*, 39, 2–3.
1981. 'Acute Crisis in Somalia.' *RAIN*, 43, 10–13.
1981. 'Prophets and their Publics.' *Semeia*, 21, 113–20.
1981. 'What is a Shaman?' *FOLK*, 23, 25–36.
1982. 'Che Cos'e uno Sciamano.' *Conoscenza Religiosa*, 3–44.
1982. 'Somalia: Nationalism Turned inside out.' *MERIP Reports*, 106, 16–21.
1983. 'The Cannibal's Cauldron.' *Research: Contributions to Interdisciplinary Anthropology*, 2, 39–49.
1983. 'The Past and the Present in Islam. The case of African "Survivals".' *Temenos*, 19, 55–67.
1985. 'Die Zukunft der Vergangenheit in der Britischen Sozialanthropologie.' *Wiener Beiträge zur Ethnologie und Anthropologie*, 2, 225–265.
1985. 'International African Institute: Report of Honorary Director for 1984. '*Africa*, 55 (2), 207–211.
1985. 'La legittimita' dell'antropologia applicata.' *Laboratorio di Scienze dell'Uomo*, 1, Politica dello sviluppo, 2 (7).
1986. 'Identity and the Political Economy of Islamic Conversion in Africa.' *Bayreuth African Studies Series*, 4, 75–90.
1986. 'Report of the Honorary Director of the International African Institute for 1985.' *Africa*, 56 (1), 85–88.
1986. 'Forme di organizzazione politica pre- e post-Coloniale in Africa.' *Laboratorio di Scienze Dell'Uomo*, 1 (2).
1986. 'Grande Somalie: un reve impossible.' *Vivant Univers*, 364.
1986. 'Decolonisation and the Ethiopianisation of Africa.' *Povos e Culturas*, 1.
1987. 'Report of the Honorary Director for 1986.' *Africa*, 57 (1), 103–7.
1988. 'Report of the Honorary Director for 1987.' *Africa*, 58 (1), 101–4.
1989. 'South of North: Shamanism in Africa.' *Paideuma*, 35, 181–8.
1989. 'The Ogaden and the Fragility of Somali Segmentary Nationalism.' *African Affairs*, 88 (353), 573–9.

1989. 'Report of the Honorary Director for 1988. Access, Control and Use of Resources in African Agriculture.' *Africa*, 59 (1), 119–21.

1990. 'Parental Terms of Reference. A Patrilineal Kinship Puzzle.' In W. Shapiro (ed.) 'On the Generation and Maintenance of Person—Essays in Honour of John Barnes.' *Australian Journal of Anthropology*, 1 (2–3), 83–96.

1990. 'Shamanism, Ethnopsychiatry.' *Self and Society*, 18, 10–21.

1990. 'Exorcism and Male Control of Religious Experience.' *Ethnos*, 55 (1), 26–49.

1991. 'The Spider and the Pangolin.' *Man*, 26 (3), 513–25.

1991. With Hutchinson, Sharon. 'Rights in Women and the Incidence of Divorce in Patrilineal Societies.' *Man*, 26 (2), 349–50.

1992. 'Il Nazionalismo frammentato della Somalia.' *Politica Internazionale*, (4) 35–52.

1992. 'Il patto sociale dei moderni stati africani.' *Democrazia Diretta*, 7 (2/3), 119–123.

1993. 'Misunderstanding the Somali Crisis.' *Anthropology Today*, 9 (4), 1–3.

1993. With de Heusch, Luc and Douglas, Mary. 'Hunting the Pangolin.' *Man*, 28 (1), 159–66.

1993. 'Spiders, Pangolins and Zoo Visitors.' *Man*, 28 (2), 363.

1993. 'Malay Bomohs and Shamans.' *Man*, 28 (2), 361.

1993. 'Wrong People, the Wrong Place.' *Parliamentary Brief*, October/ November, 71–2.

1994. Appendix II. *Sudanic Africa*, 5.

1994. With B.W. Andrzejewski, 'New Arabic Documents from Somalia.' *Sudanic Africa*, 5, 39–56.

1997. 'The Shaman's Quest in Africa.' *Cahiers d'Études Africaines*, 37 (145), 119–35.

1997. With Farah, Ahmed Y. 'Making Peace in Somaliland.' *Cahiers d'Études Africaines*, 37 (146), 349–77.

1998. 'Doing Violence to Ethnography. Some Comments on Catherine Besteman's Distorted Reporting in Somalia.' *Cultural Anthropology*, 13 (1), 100–8.

1998. With Nabokov, Isabelle. 'Male Control of Women's Spirit.' *Journal of the Royal Anthropological Institute*, 4 (3), 551–2.

1998. 'On Fieldwork and Reciprocity.' *Anthropology Today*, 14 (5), 22.

1999. 'Ekstase.' *Religion in Geschichte und Gegenwart*, 3 (8), 43–5.
2000. With van Bremen, Jan. 'Germaine Dieterlen; Obituary'. *Anthropology Today*, 16 (2), 25–6.
2002. 'Mohamad Siyad Barre's Ghost.' *Journal of the Anglo-Somali Society*, 32, 21–6.
2003. 'Adventures in Social Anthropology.' *Les Annales d'Ethiopie*, 19, 307–321.
2003. 'Recycling Somalia from the Scrap Merchants of Mogadishu.' *Northeast African Studies*, 10 (3), 213–24.
2003. 'Trance, Possession, Shamanism and Sex.' *Anthropology of Consciousness*, 14 (1), 20–39.
2004. 'Visible and Invisible Differences. The Somali Paradox.' *Africa*, 74 (4), 489–515.

Chapters in books

1962. 'Lineage Continuity and Modern Commerce in Northern Somaliland.' In P. Bohannan and G. Dalton (eds) *Markets in Africa*. Evanston: Northwestern University Press, pp. 365–85.
1965. 'Problems in the Comparative Study of Unilineal Descent.' In M. Banton (ed.) *The Relevance of Models in Social Anthropology*. London: Tavistock, pp. 87–112.
1965. 'Shaiks and Warriors in Somaliland.' In G. Dieterlen and M. Fortes (eds) *African Systems of Thought*. London: Oxford University Press, pp. 204–23.
1965. 'The Northern Pastoral Somali of the African Horn.' In J. Gibbs (ed.) *Peoples of Africa*. New York: Holt, Rinehart and Winston, pp. 204–23.
1966. 'Conformity and Contrast in Somali Islam.' In I.M. Lewis (ed.) *Islam in Tropical Africa*. London: Oxford University Press, pp. 253–67.
1967. 'National Integration in the Somali Republic.' In A. Hazlewood (ed.) *African Integration and Disintegration*. London: Oxford University Press, pp. 251–84.
1968. 'Nationalism and Tribalism in Contemporary Africa.' In R.C. Olembo (ed.), *Human Adaptation in Tropical Africa*. Nairobi: East Africa Publishing.
1968. 'Some Aspects of the Literate Tradition in Somalia.' In J. Goody (ed.) *The Development of Literacy*. Cambridge: Cambridge University Press, pp. 266–76.

1969. 'Spirit Possession in Northern Somaliland.' In J. Beattie and J. Middleton (eds) *Spirit Mediumship and Society in Africa*. London: Routledge & Kegan Paul, pp. 188–219.

1969. 'From Nomadism to Cultivation. The Expansion of Political Solidarity in Southern Somalia.' In M. Douglas and P. Kaberry (eds) *Man in Africa*. London: Tavistock, pp. 59–78.

1969. 'Nationalism and Particularism in Somalia.' In P.H. Gulliver (ed.) *Tradition and Transition in East Africa: Studies of the Tribal Element in the Modern Era*. Berkeley: University of California Press, pp. 339–62.

1969. 'Shaikh Aw Barkhadle. The Blessed Saint of Northern Somaliland.' *Proceedings of the Third International Conference of Ethiopian Studies*. Addis Ababa: Haile Selassie I University, Institute of Ethiopian Studies, pp. 75–82.

1970. 'A Structural Approach to Witchcraft and Spirit Possession.' In M. Douglas (ed.) *Witchcraft Confessions and Accusations*. London: Routledge, pp. 293–311.

1970. 'The Tribal Factor in Contemporary Africa.' In C. Legum and J. Drysdale (eds) *Africa Contemporary Record 1969–1970*. London: Africa Research, 12–17.

1972. 'Spirit Possession and Psychotherapy in North East Africa.' In Y.F. Hasan (ed.) *Sudan in Africa*. Khartoum: Khartoum University Press.

1974. 'Pattern of Protest among Non-western Women.' In D. Barrier and R. Prince (eds) *Sex, Marriage and the Family*. Lanham: Lexington Books, pp. 93–103.

1974. 'The Anthropologist's Encounter with the Supernatural.' In A. Angoff and D. Barth (eds) *Parapsychology and Anthropology*. New York: Parapsychology Foundation, pp. 22–35.

1975. 'The Dynamics of Nomadism. Prospects for Sedentarization and Social Change.' In T. Monod (ed.) *Pastoralism in Tropical Africa*. London: Oxford University Press, pp. 426–42.

1975. 'A Structural Approach to Witchcraft and Spirit Possession.' In P. B. Hammond (ed.) *Cultural and Social Anthropology*. New York: Macmillan, pp. 308–15.

1976. 'The Nation, State and Politics in Somalia.' In D.R. Smock and K. Bentsi–Enchill (eds), *The Search for National Integration in Africa*. New York: Free Press, pp. 285–306.

1979. 'L'Islam nell 'Africa subsaharania'.' In A. Triulzi (ed.) *Storia dell'Africa e del Vicino Oriente*. Florence: La Nuova Italia, pp. 66–81.

1979. 'Somalia: Socialism eller stamsamhalle.' and: 'Nationalism och grandfetischism vid Afrikas Horn.' In H. Wiberg (ed.) *Dragkampen pa Afrikas Horn*. Uppsala: Nordiska Afrikainstitutet.

1979. 'Kim Il-Sung in Somalia. The End of Tribalism.' In W.A. Shack and P.S. Cohen (eds) *Politics in Leadership*. Oxford: Claredon Press, pp. 13–44.

1980. 'The Western Somali Liberation Front (WSLF) and the Legacy of Sheikh Hussein of Bale.' In J. Tubiana (ed.) *Modern Ethiopia*. Rotterdam: A.A. Balkema, pp. 409–15.

1980. 'Speaking in Tongues and Possession Syndrome.' In M.A. Simpson (ed.), *Psycholinguistics in Clinical Practice*. New York: Irvington Publishers, pp. 56–66.

1980. 'Pre- and Post-colonial Political Units in Africa.' In H.M. Adam (ed.) *Somalia and the World (Proceedingsof the International Symposium held in Mogadishu on the Tenth Anniversary of the Somali Revolution)*, Vol. 2. Mogadishu: Halgan Publications, pp. 352–8.

1981. 'Exotische Glaubensvorstellungen und die Produktionsweise der Foldforschung in der Anthropologie.' In H. P. Duerr (ed.) *Der Wissenschaftler und das Irrationale*. Erster Band. Beitraege aus Ethnologie und Anthropologie. Frankfurt am Main: Syndikat, pp. 184–212.

1981. 'Somali Democratic Republic.' In B. Szajkowski (ed.) *Marxist Governments: A World Survey*. London: Macmillan, pp. 640–60.

1983. 'Die Berufung des Schamanen.' In H.P. Duerr (ed.) *Sehnsucht nach dem Ursprung: zu Mircea Eliade*. Frankfurt: Syndikat, pp. 174–91.

1983. 'Syncretism and Survival in African Islam.' *Convegno internazionale sul tema Aspetti dell'Islam "marginale", Roma, 24–25 novembre 1981*. Rome: Accademia nazionale dei Lincei, Fondazione Leone Caetani, pp. 59–80.

1983. 'Whither Scientific Socialism in Somalia.' *Horn of Africa: from 'Scramble for Africa' to East-West Conflict*. Bonn: Friedrich Ebert Stiftung, 49–59.

1984. 'What is a Shaman?' In M. Hoppal (ed.) *Shamanism in Eurasia*, 2 Volumes, Göttingen: Edition Herodot, pp. 3–12.

1984. 'Sufism in Somaliland: a Study in Tribal Islam.' In A.S. Ahmed and D.M. Hart (eds) *Islam in Tribal Societies*. London: Routledge, pp. 127–68.

1986. 'Literacy and Cultural Identity in the Horn of Africa. The Somali Case.' In G. Baumann (ed.) *The Written Word. Literacy in Transition: Wolfson College Lectures, 1985*. Oxford: Clarendon Press, pp. 133–49.

1986. 'Islam in Somalia.' In K.S. and J.L. Loughran, J.W. Johnson and S.S. Samatar (eds) *Somalia in Word and Image*. Bloomington: Indiana University Press, pp. 139–142.

1988. 'Keeping the Birds at Bay in the Bay Area.' In A. Puglielli (ed.), *Proceedings of the Third International Congress of Somali Studies*. Rome: Il Pensiero Scientifico Editore, pp. 325–9.

1988. 'Shamanism.' In S. Sutherland, L Heneden, P. Clarke and F. Hardy (eds) *The World's Religions*.

1988. With Jahuda, Gustav. 'Introduction. Child Development in Psychology and Anthropology.' In G. Jahuda and I.M. Lewis, *Acquiring Culture. Cross-cultural Studies in Child Development*. Kent: Croom Helm, pp. 1–34.

1989. 'The Myth of Social Anthropology.' In A. Marazi (ed.) *Antropologia, Tendenze Contemporane*. Milan: Hoepli, pp. 147–78.

1990. 'Gender and Religious Pluralism. Exorcism and Inspiration in the Family.' In I. Hamnett (ed.) *Religious Pluralism and Unbelief*. London: Routledge, pp. 43–51.

1990. 'Foreword.' In Wazir Jahan Karim. *Emotions of Culture. A Malay Perspective*. Singapore: Oxford University Press, v–vi.

1991. 'The Recent Political History of Somalia.' In *Somalia. A Historical Cultural and Political Analysis*. Uppsala: Life & Peace Institute, pp. 5–15.

1992. 'La storia politica recente della Somalia.' In F. Branca and R. D'Arca (eds) *Saluti per tutti?* Milan: Franco Angeli, pp. 77–90.

1992. 'Social Subjectivity and Development. The Social Anthropology of Voluntary Associations.' In A. Cancedda (ed.) *Cittadini, Società e Stati*. Rome, pp. 135–43.

1992. 'Continuing Problems in Somali Historiography.' In H.A. Adam and C.L. Geshekter (eds) *Proceedings of the First International Congress of Somali studies*. New York: Scholar Press, pp. 185–9.

1993. 'Literacy and Cultural Identity in the Horn of Africa.' In B.V. Street (ed.), *Cross Cultural Approaches to Literacy*. Cambridge: Cambridge University Press, pp. 143–56.

1995. 'Introduction. The Uncentralised Somali Legacy.' In I.M. Lewis and J. Mayall (eds) *A Study of Decentralised Political Structures for Somalia*. London: London School of Economics for the European Union, pp. xv–xxxiii.

1995. 'Anthropologists for Sale.' In A. Ahmed and C. Shore (eds) *The Future of Anthropology*. London: Athlone Press, pp. 94–109.

1995. 'Salient Features of the Somali Political Scene.' (Keynote Speech) In J.M. Haakonsen and H.A. Keynan (eds) *Somalia after UNOSOM*. Oslo: Norwegian Red Cross, pp. 14–25.

1996. With Hayward, R.J. 'Introduction.' In R.J. Hayward and I.M. Lewis (eds.) *Voice and Power: The Culture of Language in North-East Africa*. Essays in Honour of B.W. Andrzejewski. London: School of Oriental and African Studies, pp. ix–xv.

1996. With Mukhtar, Mohamed H. 'Songs from the South.' In *African Languages and Cultures, Supplement No. 3*, Voice and Power: The Culture of Language in North-East Africa. Essays in Honour of B.W. Andrzejewski, pp. 205–12.

1996. With J. Mayall, 'Somalia.' In J. Mayall (ed.), *The New Internationalism*. Cambridge University Press, pp. 94–124.

1997. 'Shamans & Sex. A Comparative Perspective.' In *Fourth Conference of the International Society for Shamanic Research*, Chantilly.

1997. 'Clan, Conflict and Ethnicity in Somalia. Humanitarian Intervention in a Stateless Society.' In D. Turton (ed.) *War and Ethnicity. Global Connections and Local Violence*. Rochester: Rochester University Press, pp. 179–202.

1997. 'Comprendere il mistero delle credenze degli "altri".' In C. Gallini and M. Massenzio (eds) *Ernesto de Martino nella Cultura Europea*. Naples: Liguori Editore, pp. 11–22.

1999. 'A Controversial Conference. Mengistu's Friends in Europe.' In A. Rouaud (ed.) *Les Orientalistes sont des Aventuriers*. Paris: Sepia, pp. 199–202.

2001. 'Saints in North East African Islam.' In B.S. Amoretti (ed.) *Islam in East Africa: New Sources*. Rome: Herder, pp. 227–40.

2002. 'Foreword.' In V. Luling, *The Somali Sultanate. The Geledi city-state over 150 years*, London: Haan, pp. xi–xii.

2003. 'Possession and Public Morality: II Other Cosmological Systems.' In G. Harvey (ed.) *Shamanism: a Reader*. London: Routledge, pp. 69–91.

2003. 'Foreword.' In B. Helander, *The Slaughtered Camel*. Uppsala: Acta Universitatis Upsaliensis, pp. ix–xv.

2009. 'The Social Roots and Meaning of Trance and Possession.' In P.B. Clarke (ed.), *The Oxford Handbook of the Sociology of Religion*. Oxford: Oxford University Press, pp. 375–88.

Encyclopaedia articles

1968. 'Tribal Society'. In David L. Sills (ed), *International Encyclopaedia of the Social Sciences* (New Edition) Vol. 16.

1972. 'The Somali Republic.' In *Encyclopaedia Britannica*.

1972. 'French Somaliland.' In *Encyclopaedia Britannica*.

1972. 'Northeastern Africa and the Horn.' In *Encyclopaedia Britannica*.

1972. 'Ethnography.' In *Encyclopaedia Britannica*.

1972. 'Cushitic Peoples.' In *Encyclopaedia Britannica*.

1973. 'Ethiopian and Somalian Cultures.' In *Encyclopaedia Britannica*.

1992. 'Cosmologia.' In *Italian Encyclopaedia of Social Science*, Vol. 21.

1996. 'Descent.' In A. Barnard and J. Spencer (eds), *Encyclopaedia of Social and Cultural Anthropology*. London: Routledge.

1997. 'Somalia. Peoples and Cultures.' In J. Middleton (ed.), *Encyclopedia of Africa*. New York: Charles Scribners Sons.

2003. 'Muhammad ibn Abd Allah Hassan.' In *Encyclopedia of Islam*, 2 (8).

2004. E.E. Evans-Pritchard. *Biographical Dictionary of Anthropology*. London: Routledge.

2005. 'Zaar Cult.' *Encyclopedia of New Religious Movements*. London: Routledge.

Forthcoming. 'Witchcraft: Africa and the World.' In *Encyclopaedia Britannica*.

Reviews

1955. Review of Laurence, M. *A Tree for Poverty: Somali Poetry and Prose*. In *Africa*, 25 (3), 305–6.

1955. Review of Paul, A. *A History of the Beja Tribes of the Sudan*. In *Africa*, 25 (2), 203–4.

1956. Review of Huntingford, G.W.B. *The Galla of Ethiopia: The Kingdoms of Kafa and Janjero*. In *Bulletin of the School of Oriental and African Studies, University of London*, 18 (2), 398–9.

1956. Review of Grottanelli, V.L. *Pescatori dell'Oceano Indiano: Saggio Etnologico Preliminare sui Bagiuni Bantu Costieri dell'Oltregiuba*. In *Africa*, 26 (3), 309–12.

1957. Review of Andrzejewski, B.W. and Muuse Haaji Ismaa'iil Galaal. *Hikmad Soomaali*. In *Africa*, 27 (4), 418–20.

1958. Review of Cerulli, E. *Somalia: Scritti vari editi ed inediti. I. Storia della Somalia. L'Islaam in Somalia. Il Libro degli Zengi*. In *Africa*, 28 (3), 280–2.

1960. Review of Castagno, A.A. *Somalia*. In *Africa*, 30 (1), 93.

1960. Review of Maino, C. *La Somalia e l'Opera del Duca degli Abruzzi*. In *Africa*, 30 (2), 201–2.

1960. Review of Cerulli, E. *Somalia. Scritti vari editi ed inediti. II. Diritto. Etnografia. Linguistica. Come viveva una tribù Hawiyya*. In *Africa*, 30 (1), 92–3.

1960. Review of Leiris, M. *La Possession et ses aspects théatraux chez les Ethiopiens de Gondar*. In *Man*, 60, 28–9.

1961. Review of Karp, M. *The Economics of Trusteeship in Somalia*. In *International Affairs*, 37 (3), 395.

1961. Review of Middleton, J. *Lugbara Religion: Ritual and Authority among an East African People*. In *Africa*, 31 (3), 290.

1962. Review of The Information Service of the Somali Government: *The Somali Peninsula. A New Light on Imperial Motives*. In *International Affairs*, 38 (4), 515–16.

1964. Review of Haberland, E. *Galla Süd-Äthiopiens*. In *Man*, 64, 189–90.

1964. Review of Touval, S. *Somali Nationalism: International Politics and the Drive for Unity in the Horn of Africa*. In *International Affairs*, 40 (1), 153.

1964. Review of Mair, L. *New Nations*. In *International Affairs*, 40 (3), 511–12.

1964. Review of Laurence, M. *The Prophet's Camel Bell*. In *Journal of Modern African Studies*, 2 (2), 320–1.

1964. Review of Jesman, C. *The Ethiopian Paradox*. In *Man*, 64, 68.

1964. Review of Touval, S. *Somali Nationalism: International Politics and the Drive for Unity in the Horn of Africa*. In *Annals of the*

American Academy of Political and Social Science, 352, 213–14.

1964. Review of Buxton, J.C. *Chiefs and Strangers: A Study of Political Assimilation among the Mandari*. In *Bulletin of the School of Oriental and African Studies*, 27 (3), 675–6.

1965. Review of Barclay, H.B. *Buurri al Lamaab: A Suburban Village in the Sudan*. In *Bulletin of the School of Oriental and African Studies, University of London*, 28 (2), 439–40.

1965. Review of Von den Berghe, P.L. Caneville. *The Social Structure of a South African Town*. In *Annals of the American Academy of Political and Social Science*, 357, 187.

1965. Review of Bohannan, P. *Social Anthropology*. In *Man*, 65, 56–7.

1965. Review of Ullendorff, E. *The Ethiopians: An Introduction to Country and People*. In *Man*, 65, 167.

1965. Review of Beattie, J. *Other Cultures: Aims, Methods and Achievements in Social Anthropology*. In *Man*, 65, 202.

1965. Review of Lienhardt, G. *Social Anthropology*. In *Man*, 65, 158.

1965. Review of Cerulli, E. *Somalia: scritti vari editi ed inediti, III*. In *Africa*, 35 (4), 452.

1965. Review of Trimingham, J.S. *Islam in East Africa*. In *Africa*, 35 (4), 445–6.

1965. Review of Chailley, M. *Notes et Études sur l'Islam en Afrique Noire*. In *Africa*, 35 (4), 444–5.

1965. Review of Fallers, L.A. *The King's Men: Leadership and Status in Buganda on the Eve of Independence*. In *Bulletin of the School of Oriental and African Studies*, 28 (2), 438–9.

1965. Review of Friedland, W.H. and Rosberg, C.G. Jr. In *African Socialism. Annals of the American Academy of Political and Social Science*, 361, 160–1.

1966. Review of Scherer, A. *Histoire de la Reúnion*. In *International Affairs*, 42 (4), 747.

1966. Review of Cohen, A. *Arab Border-Villages in Israel: A Study of Continuity and Change in Social Organization*. In *Bulletin of the School of Oriental and African Studies*, 29 (1), 155–6.

1966. Review of Hungtingford, G.W.B. *The Glorious Victories of 'Amda Seyon, King of Ethiopia*. In *Man*, 1 (3), 417.

1966. Review of Gray, R.F. and Gulliver, P.H. *The Family Estate in Africa: Studies in the Role of Property in Family Structure and*

Lineage Continuity. In *Bulletin of the School of Oriental and African Studies, University of London*, 29 (2), 443–4.

1966. Review of Grottanelli, V.L. *L'etnologia e le 'leggi' della condotta umana*. In *Man*, 1 (2), 261.

1966. Review of Shack, W.A. *The Gurage: A People of the Ensete Culture*. In *Man*, 1 (4), 574–5.

1967. Review of Mauss, M. *Sociologie et anthropologie*. In *Man*, 2 (1), 141.

1967. Review of Gluckman, M. *Politics, Law, and Ritual in Tribal Society*. In *Africa*, 37 (1), 98–9.

1967. Review of Hess, R.L. *Italian Colonialism in Somalia*. In *Journal of African History*, 8 (3), 553–4.

1967. Review of Abu-Nasr, J.M. *The Tijaniyya: A Sufi Order in the Modern World*. In *Africa*, 37 (3), 356–7.

1967. Review of Burton, R. and Waterfield, G. *First Footsteps in East Africa*. In *Africa: Journal of the International African Institute*, 37 (4), 495–6.

1967. Review of Edsman, C.M. and Renggren, H. *Studies in Shamanism. Fatalistic Beliefs in Religion, Folklore and Literature*. In *Man*, 2 (4), 640–1.

1968. Review of Cazeneuve, J. *L'ethnologie*. In *Man*, 3 (1), 145–6.

1968. Review of Malinowski, B. and Guterman, N. *A Diary in the Strict Sense of the Term*. In *Man*, 3 (2), 348–9.

1968. Review of Knutsson, K.E. *Authority and Change: A Study of the Kallu Institution among the Macha Galla of Ethiopia*. In *Africa*, 38 (3), 352–3.

1969. Review of De Waal Malefijt, A. *Religion and Culture: An Introduction to the Anthropology of Religion*. In *Man*, 4 (2), 302–3.

1969. Review of Werner, A. *Myths and Legends of the Bantu*. In *Man*, 4 (1), 151–2.

1969. Review of MacMichael, H.A. *The Tribes of Northern and Central Kordofán*. In *Man*, 4 (3), 473.

1969. Review of Geertz, C. *Islam Observed: Religious Development in Morocco and Indonesia*. In *Man*, 4 (3), 472–3.

1969. Review of Thompson, V. and Adloff, R. *Djibouti and the Horn of Africa*. In *Bulletin of the School of Oriental and African Studies, University of London*, 32 (3), 660–1.

1969. Reviews of Nicolas, J. *'Les Juments des dieux': rites de possession et condition féminine en pays hausa*. Zaretsky, I.I. *Bibliog-*

raphy on Spirit Possession and Spirit Mediumship. In *Africa*, 39 (2), 189–90.

1971. Review of Retel-Laurentin, A. *Oracles et ordalies chez les Nzakara*. In *Bulletin of the School of Oriental and African Studies*, 34 (1), 194–5.

1971. Review of Turner, V. *The Ritual Process: Structure and Anti–structure*. In *Man*, 6 (2), 306–7.

1971. Review of Doob, L.W. *Resolving Conflict in Africa: the Fermeda Workshop*. In *Man*, 6 (3), 507.

1972. Reviews of Hoskyns, C. *Case Studies in African Diplomacy: 2. The Ethiopia-Somali–Kenya Dispute 1960–67*. Ganzglass, M.R. *The Penal Code of the Somali Democratic Republic*. OberleÅL, P. *Afars et Somalis: le dossier de Djibouti*. In *Africa*, 42 (4), 343–5.

1977. Review of Bourguignon, E. *Possession*. In *RAIN*, 18, 11–12.

1977. Review of Fry, P. *Spirits of Protest: Spirit Mediums and the Articulation of Consensus Amongst the Zezuru of Southern Rhodesia*. In *Man*, 12 (1), 191–2.

1977. Review of Blacker, C. *The Catalpa Bow: A Study of Shamanistic Practices in Japan*. In *Religious Studies*, 13 (3), 374–5.

1978. Review of Wallis, R. *The Road to Total Freedom: A Sociological Analysis of Scientology*. In *Religious Studies*, 14 (3), 403–5.

1979. Review of Almagor, U. *Pastoral Partners: Affinity and Bond Partnership Among the Dassanetch of Southwest Ethiopia*. In *Man*, 14 (1), 171.

1981. Why me? Review of J. Favret-Saada *Deadly Words. Witchcraft in the Bocage*. In *London Review of Books*, 1. July, 11–12.

1981. Review of Peter, R. *Islam and Colonialism: the Doctrine of Jihad in Modern History*. In *International Journal of Middle East Studies*, 13 (3), 383–4.

1985. Review of Bjerke, S. *Religion and Misfortune: The Bacwezi Complex and Other Spirit Cults of the Zinza of Northwestern Tanzania*. In *Man*, 20 (2), 359–60.

1985. Reviews of Smith, A.D. *African Nationalism. State and Nation in the Third World: the Western State and African Nationalism*. Mazrui, A.A. and Tidy, M. *Nationalism and New States in Africa*. In *Third World Quarterly*, 7 (1), 157–9.

1985. Review of Bjerke, S. *Religion and Misfortune: The Bacwezi Complex and other Spirit Cults of the Zinza of Northwestern Tanzania*. In *Man*, 20 (2), 359–60.

1988. Review of Markakis, J. *National and Class Conflict in the Horn of Africa*. In *Third World Quarterly*, 10 (3), 1391–3.

1990. 'Spirits at the House of Childbirth.' Review of J. Boddy. *Wombs and Alien Spirits*. In *Times Literary Supplement*, 1–7 June, 590.

1990. Review of Stoller, P. *Fusion of the Worlds: An Ethnography of Possession among the Songhay of Niger*. In *Bulletin of the School of Oriental and African Studies*, 53 (2), 396–7.

1990. Review of Samatar, A.I. *The State and Rural Transformation in Northern Somalia, 1884–1986*. In *Africa*, 60 (3), 458–9.

1991. Review of Balzer, M.M. *Shamanism: Soviet Studies of Traditional Central Asian and Siberian Religion*. In *The Slavonic and East European Review*, 69 (3), 548–9.

1992. Review of Schraeder, P.J. *Djibouti*. In *Africa*, 62 (2), 303.

1992. Review of Wafer, J. *The Taste of Blood: Spirit Possession in Brazilian Candomble*. In *Man*, 27 (3), 689.

1993. Review of Sanjek, R. *Fieldnotes: the Making of Anthropology*. In *The British Journal of Sociology*, 44 (2), 355–6.

1994. Review of Flaherty, G. *Shamanism and the Eighteenth Century*. In *Man*, 29 (4), 996–7.

1995. Review of Parkin, D. *Sacred Void: Spatial Images of Work and Ritual among the Giriama of Kenya*. In *Africa*, 65 (3), 482.

1995. Review of Burton, J.W. *An Introduction to Evans-Pritchard*. In *Africa*, 65 (1), 155–7.

1995. Review of Fox, R. *The Challenge of Anthropology: Old Encounters and new Excursions*. In *The British Journal of Sociology*, 46 (4), 744–5.

1996. Review of Perrin, M. *Le Chamanisme*. In *The Journal of the Royal Anthropological Institute*, 2 (3), 562–3.

1996. Review of Thomas, N. & Humphrey, C. *Shamanism, History and the State*. In *The British Journal of Sociology*, 47 (4), 739–40.

1997. Review of Stoller, P. *Embodying Colonial Memories*. In *Journal of the Royal Anthropological Institute*, 3 (2), 387.

1997. Review of Rasmussen, S.J. *Spirit Possession and Personhood among the Kel Ewey Tuareg*. In *Zeitschrift für Ethnologie*, 122, 299–300.

1995. Review of Parkin, D. *Sacred Void: Spatial Images of Work and Ritual among the Giriama of Kenya*. In *Africa*, 65 (3), 482.

1998. Review of MacClancy, J. and McDonaugh, C. *Popularising Anthropology*. In *The Journal of the Royal Anthropological Institute*, 4 (2), 372–3.

1999. Review of Pocock, D. *Understanding Social Anthropology*. In *The Journal of the Royal Anthropological Institute*, 5 (4), 682–3.

2000. Review of Pankhurst, R. *The Ethiopian Borderlands: Essays in Regional History, from Ancient Times to the End of the Eighteenth Century*. In *Africa*, 70 (1), 167–8.

2000. Review of Besteman, C. *Unraveling Somalia: Race, Violence and the Legacy of Slavery*. In *Journal of African History*, 41 (3), 522–4.

2000. Review of Hayamon, R.N. *Taiga. Terre de Chamans*. In *The Journal of the Royal Anthropological Institute*, 6 (1), 138–9.

2000. Review of Pennacini, C. *Kubandwa: La possessione spiritice nell'Africa dei Grandi Laghi*. In *The Journal of the Royal Anthropological Institute*, 6 (3), 529–30.

2001. Review of Kapteijns, L. and Ali, M.O. *Women's Voices in a Man's World: Women and the Pastoral Tradition in Northern Somali Orature, c. 1899–1980*. In *Journal of African History*, 42 (1), 152–4.

2001. Review of Behrend, H. and Luig, U. *Spirit Possession: Modernity and Power in Africa*. In *The Journal of the Royal Anthropological Institute*, 7 (2), 363–4.

2001. Review of Harvey, G. *Indigenous Religions: A Companion*. In *The Journal of the Royal Anthropological Institute*, 7 (4), 771.

2001. Review of Massenzio, M. *Sacré et identité ethnique: Frontières et ordre du monde*. In *The Journal of the Royal Anthropological Institute*, 7 (4), 774.

2003. Review of Salamon, H. *The Hyena People: Ethiopian Jews in Christian Ethiopia*. In *The Journal of the Royal Anthropological Institute*, 9 (2), 384–5.

Newspaper articles

1977. 'Has the Dergue had its day?' *The Guardian*, 15 August.

1992. 'Pacifying the Warlords.' *The Times*, 12 December.

1992. 'In the land of the living dead: Somalia briefing.' *Sunday Times*, 30 August, pp. 8–9.

1993. 'Humanitarian intervention in Somalia. Operation Restore Hope.' *Cooperazione*, January.

1993. 'Out from the shadow of Somalia's warlords.' *The Guardian*, letters, 16 January.

1993. 'Ambush in Somalia.' *Guardian*, 7 October.

2001. 'Writing on Somalis.' *Times Literary Supplement*, June.

2001. 'Why the warlords won.' *Times Literary Supplement*, 8 June.

Miscellaneous

1957. *Population Movements in Somaliland: Current and Projected Research*. Communication to the Second Conference on African History and Archaeology, School of Oriental and African Studies (2), London.

1965. *Tribalism and Nationalism*. Paper presented to UNESCO Conference on the Role of the Human Factor in Development. Paris: UNESCO.

1969. *Nationalism, Tribalism and Urbanisation in Contemporary Africa*. Proceedings of the 4th Annual Symposium. Kampala: East African Academy.

1983. *Decolonisation and the 'Ethiopianisation' of Africa*. Lisbon: Catholic University.

1993. 'Making History in Somalia: Humanitarian Intervention in a Stateless Society'. Centre for Global Governance Discussion Paper, 6. London: London School of Economics.

2002. *M. Siyad Barre's Ghost in Somalia*. Online at: http://www.somaliawatch.org/archivemar02/020429201.htm [accessed 30.11.2009].

NOTES ON THE CONTRIBUTORS

Abdurahman M. Abdullahi (Baadiyow) is a PhD candidate at McGill University, Canada. His specialisation is modern Islamic history. He is the Chairman of the Board of Trustees, Mogadishu University. He writes on the challenges of clan system, Islamism and the state in Somalia. He was involved in Somali reconciliations since 1994 and civil society activism. He promotes moderate Islamism, women's education and democracy. Recently published papers include 'Penetrating Cultural Frontiers in Somalia: History of Women's Political Participation during Four Decades (1959–2000)', 'Recovering the Somali State: The Islamic Factor' and 'Perspectives on the State Collapse in Somalia'.

Anita Suleiman Adam holds an MEd from Harvard University. She worked as teacher and publisher, and as the Principal of the American International School in Mogadishu before the outbreak of the civil war. She is the founder and Director of Haan Associates, a specialist publisher on Somalia. Currently she is completing her PhD research at SOAS on Banaadiri–Reer Xamar culture and society. Her writings include development project analysis reports for UN specialised agencies, including UNESCO, UNSCDHA and ILO, as well as conference papers and seminar presentation on Somalia.

Axmed Cabdullahi Du'aale holds a BA in accounting from Hargeysa University (2007). Subsequently, he worked as research assistant at the Academy for Peace and Development in Hargeysa. In July 2009 he began an MA programme at Kampala International University, Uganda. He has contributed several opinion pieces to daily and weekly newspapers in Hargeysa, Somaliland.

Boobe Yusuf Duale is Programme Coordinator at the Academy for Peace and Development in Hargeysa, Somaliland. He studied geology and political science in Perugia (Italy) and Moscow. Between 1981 and 1991 he participated in the struggle of the Somali National Movement (SNM) and was Secretary of Information of the SNM in 1983–84 and 1990–91, Secretary of the SNM Central Committee and Standing Committee in 1987–90, and then Somaliland's Minister of State for Foreign Affairs in 1992–93. He conducted research on Somali traditions, culture, poetry and politics, and is the author of several books, including *Timocadde's Poetry* (in Somali) (Mogadishu, 1983), 'The Role of the Media in the Political Rebuilding of Somaliland' in *Rebuilding Somaliland* (Red Sea Press, 2005), and *Dhaxal-reeb: Horaad* [Leaving a Heritage] (Flamingo Printing Press, 2008).

Lee Cassanelli (PhD, University of Wisconsin) is Director of the African Studies Center and Professor of History at the University of Pennsylvania. He is author of *The Shaping of Somali Society* (1982), *Victims and Vulnerable Groups in Southern Somalia* (1995), and co-editor with Catherine Besteman of *The Struggle for Land in Southern Somalia: The War Behind the War* (1996, 2003), along with numerous articles on Somali history and the Somali diaspora. He is Editor of *Northeast African Studies* and a contributing editor to *Bildhaan. An International Journal of Somali Studies*.

Luca Ciabarri (PhD, Anthropology) is Research Fellow at the Max Planck Institute for Social Anthropology in Halle/Saale, Germany, where he is completing a research project on 'Post-conflict Somaliland: the Commercial Factor in State Building Practices and Territorial Integration. An Ethnography of Commercial Routes.' His recent publications include 'Productivity of Refugee Camps: Social and Political Dynamics from the Somaliland-Ethiopia Border (1988–2001)' in the journal *Africa Spektrum* (2008), and 'No Representation without Redistribution: Somaliland Plural Authorities, the Search for a State and the 2005 Parliamentary Elections' in A. Bellagamba and G. Klute G. (eds) *Beside the State. Emergent Powers in Contemporary Africa* (Köppe 2008).

Marcel Djama is a senior research fellow at the International Research Centre on Agriculture and Development (France). He holds a PhD in Social Anthropology from the Ecole des Hautes Etudes en Sciences Sociales (Paris). He wrote his dissertation thesis on social change in northwestern Somalia (1995), published several academic papers and a TV documentary on Somali issues. He is also engaged in research activities on the linkages of development and security in the politics of international aid, and is currently preparing a book on the role of non-state actors in global governance.

John Drysdale MBE was educated at Oxford University. He was commissioned in the British Regular Army during World War II and served with Somali troops in the Burma campaign. Later on he held various administrative positions. In 1959, for instance, he was posted to Mogadishu as First Secretary to the British Embassy. In 2007 he founded Somaliland Cadastral Surveys, an NGO which surveys land with theodolites in order to map with coordinates farms and other landed property. Drysdale has published twelve books, including standard references in Somali studies such as *The Somali Peninsula* (1962, commissioned by the Somali government), *The Somali Dispute* (1964), and *Stoics without Pillows* (2002), as well as a history of Singapore.

Charles Geshekter is Professor Emeritus of History at California State University, Chico. He completed his PhD in African history at the University of California, Los Angeles. He co-edited with Hussein Adam *The Proceedings of the 1st International Congress of Somali Studies* (Atlanta, 1992), has written on many aspects of modern Somali history, has produced a documentary film, *The Parching Winds of Somalia* for the US Public Broadcasting System (1984), and recently published 'Myths and Misconceptions of the Orthodox View of AIDS in Africa,' *Ethics and Politics*, IX, 2, 2007, 330–70.

Sally Healy is an Associate Fellow of the Africa Programme at the Royal Institute for International Affairs, Chatham House. She has a BSc in Politics and Sociology from Bristol University and an MSc in International Relations from the London School of Economics. She worked for the Foreign and Commonwealth Office as a specialist on the Horn of Africa. She recently wrote *Lost Opportunities in the Horn of Africa: How Conflicts Connect and Peace Agreements Unravel* (Chatham House, June 2008) and co-authored, with Martin Plaut, *Ethiopia and Eritrea: Allergic to Persuasion* (Chatham House Briefing Paper, January 2007).

Markus V. Hoehne is a PhD candidate at the Max Planck Institute for Social Anthropology in Halle/Saale, Germany. His research focuses on identity and conflict in northern Somalia (Somaliland and Puntland) where he conducted 22 months of field research in 2002, 2003–4, and

2008–9. He is also part of a research project funded by the European Union on 'Diasporas for Peace' (DIASPEACE). His publications include a book entitled *Somalia zwischen Krieg und Frieden. Strategien der friedlichen Konfliktaustragung auf internationaler und lokaler Ebene* (Hamburg, 2002), a co-edited volume on *Borders and Borderlands as Resources in the Horn of Africa* (with James Currey, 2010), and several peer reviewed journal articles and book chapters.

Hussein M. Adam studied at Princeton University, Makerere University College and Harvard University. He has taught at Brandeis University, and at the Somali National University. Currently he is an Associate Professor in Political Science at the College of the Holy Cross. He has published 31 articles and chapters in books. He has also co-edited and published five volumes in Somali Studies: *From Tyranny to Anarchy, Mending Rips in the Sky, War Destroys: Peace Nurtures, Removing Barricades from Somalia*, and *The Proceedings of the First Congress of Somali Studies*. He is the founding President of the Somali Studies International Association (SSIA), which hosted its 10th Congress and 30th Anniversary in 2007/8. During 1985–86, he served as one of two UN Consultants who prepared the Organisation Structure and the Plan of Action for the newly established sub-regional organisation: the Inter-Governmental Authority on Development (IGAD).

Ken Menkhaus is Professor of Political Science at Davidson College. His principal areas of interests are conflict, peace-building, state-building, and local governance systems. He is author of over 50 articles and chapters on Somalia and the Horn of Africa.

Marcel Djama is a senior research fellow at the International Research Centre on Agriculture and Development (France). He holds a PhD in Social Anthropology from the Ecole des Hautes Etudes en Sciences Sociales (Paris). He wrote his dissertation thesis on social change in northwestern Somalia (1995), published several academic papers and a TV documentary on Somali issues. He is also engaged in research activities on the linkages of development and security in the politics of international aid, and is currently preparing a book on the role of non-state actors in global governance.

Mohamed Haji Mukhtar is Interim Chair, Department of Social and Behavioral Sciences, Savannah State University. He is professor of African and Middle Eastern History and a two-time Fulbright scholar. He has written widely on the history of Somalia including *Historical Dictionary of Somalia* (New Edition 2003) and, co-authored with Omar Moalim Ahmed, *English-Maay Dictionary* (2007). His articles appeared in such journals as *History in Africa, Journal of Method, Ufahamu Journal of the African Activist Association, African Renaissance, and Review of African Political Economy*. He was a contributing editor to *Islamiyyat Journal* of the Universiti Kebangsaan Malaysia and the editor of *Demenedung*, Newsletter of the Inter-Riverine Studies Association.

Muuse Cali Faruur is a Somali cultural specialist and poet. He grew up in the north, between Hargeysa and the Haud region. In the 1970s he expressed his opposition to the regime of Siyad Barre in poems, which lead to several brief perods of imprisonment. Currently he works for Radio Hargeysa where he has his own programme on Somali culture. He also appears on Somaliland TV and lectures at the local universities. Occasionally, he works as consultant for the Guurti, the 'House of Elders' in Somaliland, and international organisations.

Mohamed Hashi Dhama 'Gaarriye' (BA) works as Professor of Somali Literature at the Universities of Hargeysa and Cammuud and is very well known as a poet. He is the author of the first articles to be written on the metrical system of Somali poetry (*Xiddigta Oktoobar*, 1976), and his poems have been published in *Hagarlaawe* (Aftahan Publications, 2007) and some in English translation in *Maansooyin* (Enitharmon, 2008).

John Wm. Johnson was born in Texas and is a member of the Cherokee Nation. He holds a PhD from Indiana University (1978). He served in the US Peace Corps in the Somali Republic from 1966 to 1969, and has conducted fieldwork in Mali and Somalia. He taught on the faculty at Indiana University, where he served 28 years in the Folklore Department before retiring in 2006. He published widely on music, poetry, language in Somalia and Africa. His publications include *Heellooy Heelleellooy: The Development of the Genre Heello in Modern Somali Poetry* (Bloomington 1974, second edition 1996), and *Oral Epics from Africa: Vibrant Voices from a Vast Continent* (Bloomington 1997, with Tom Hale and Steven Belcher).

Virginia Luling studied at Oxford and London and took her PhD in Social Anthropology under the supervision of I.M. Lewis in 1972. Her field research was done in Afgooye, Somalia. Her publications include *Somali Sultanate; the Geledi City State over 150 years* (2002) and articles including 'Some Possession Cults in Southern Somalia' (1991), 'Come Back Somalia? Questioning a Collapsed State' (1997), '"The Law then was not this Law": Past and Present in Improvised Verse at a South Somali Festival' (1996), and 'Genealogy as Theory, Genealogy as Tool: Aspects of Somali "Clanship"' (2006). From 1983 to 2004 she worked for the human rights organisation Survival International. She is Secretary of the Anglo-Somali Society and is working on a history of the Begedi clan.

Martin Orwin (BA, PhD, London) is Senior Lecturer in Somali and Amharic at the School of Oriental and African Studies. He is author of *Colloquial Somali* (Routledge, 1995) and various articles on language use in Somali poetry including 'On Consonants in Somali Metrics' (*Afrikanistische Arbeitspapiere*, 65, 103–27).

Gérard Prunier holds a PhD in African History from the University of Paris in 1981. He joined the Centre National de la Recherche Scientifique (CNRS) in Paris in 1984. He served as Director of the French Centre for Ethiopian Studies in Addis-Ababa between September 2001 and August 2006. Currently, he works as an international consultant on Eastern and Central African affairs. His most recent books are *Darfur: An Ambiguous Genocide* (Hurst 2005; revised edition in 2008 under the title *Darfur: a 21st Century Genocide*) and *From Genocide to Continental War: the 'Congolese' Conflict and the Crisis of Contemporary Africa* (Hurst 2009, co-published by Oxford University Press America under the title *Africa's First World War: Congo, the Rwanda Genocide and the Making of a Continental Catastrophe*).

Annarita Puglielli (PhD in Linguistics, Cornell University) is full Professor of General Linguistics at the Università degli Studi Roma Tre, her research interests relate to linguistic theory and typology. Head of the Somali Studies Research Project since 1978, she has produced—in collaboration with others—the *Dizionario Somalo Italiano* (1985), the *Dizionario Italiano Somalo* (1998), and is working at the *Qaamuuska Af Soomaliga* (in preparation). Editor of *Studi Somali* (13th volume: *Lessons in Survival: the Language and Culture of Somalia*, 2009), she has described many aspects of the syntactic and morphological structure of Somali, and written with Abdalla O.Mansur a Somali Grammar for high schools (*Barashada Naxwaha Af Soomaaliga*, London, 1999).

Said S. Samatar (PhD at Northwestern University in 1979) is Professor of African History at Rutgers University, New Jersey. He is the editor of the journal *Horn of Africa* and the author of numerous books and articles on Somali history and culture, including *Oral Poetry and Somali Nationalism: the Case of Sayyid Mahammad 'Abdille Hasan* (Cambridge University Press, 1982) and (with David Laitin) *Somalia: a Nation in Search of a State* (Westview Press, 1987).

Marja Tiilikainen (PhD University of Helsinki, 2003) is a Postdoctoral Researcher at the Department of Sociology, University of Helsinki, Finland. Her PhD research *Arjen islam: Somalinaisten elämää Suomessa* [Everyday Islam: The Life of Somali Women in Finland] was an ethnographic study belonging to fields of comparative religion and medical anthropology and it was published by Vastapaino. Her current research project (2008–10) entitled 'Suffering, Healing and Health-care: The Transnational Lives of Somalis in Exile' is funded by the Academy of Finland.

INDEX